Reading the Legal Case

This volume examines the nature, function, development and epistemological assumptions of the legal case in an interdisciplinary context. Using the question of 'reading' as a guiding principle, it opens up new ways of understanding case law and the doctrine of precedent by bringing the law into dialogue with the humanities. What happens when a legal case is read not only by lawyers, but by literary critics, linguists, philosophers, and historians? How do film makers and writers adapt and transform legal cases in their work? How might one interpret fiction in the context of the historical development of the common law? The essays in this volume test the boundaries of the legal case as a genre by inviting perspectives from other disciplines, and in doing so also raise more fundamental questions of what constitutes law and legal thinking. This book will be of interest to anyone seeking a better understanding of the common law, the humanities, and the intersection between them.

Marco Wan is Assistant Professor of Law and Honorary Assistant Professor of English at the University of Hong Kong. He has published on literary trials in England and France, and on law and visuality in Hong Kong.

Reading the Legal Case

Reading the Legal Case

Cross-Currents between Law and the Humanities

Edited by
Marco Wan

LONDON AND NEW YORK

First published 2012
by Routledge
2 Park Square, Milton Park, Abingdon, Oxon OX14 4RN

Simultaneously published in the USA and Canada
by Routledge
711 Third Avenue, New York, NY 10017

A GlassHouse Book

Routledge is an imprint of the Taylor & Francis Group, an informa business

First issued in paperback 2013

© 2012 Marco Wan

The right of Marco Wan to be identified as author of the editorial material, and of the authors for their individual chapters, has been asserted by them in accordance with sections 77 and 78 of the Copyright, Designs and Patents Act 1988.

All rights reserved. No part of this book may be reprinted or reproduced or utilised in any form or by any electronic, mechanical, or other means, now known or hereafter invented, including photocopying and recording, or in any information storage or retrieval system, without permission in writing from the publishers.

Trademark notice: Product or corporate names may be trademarks or registered trademarks, and are used only for identification and explanation without intent to infringe.

British Library Cataloguing in Publication Data

A catalogue record for this book is available from the British Library

Library of Congress Cataloging in Publication Data
Reading the legal case : cross currents between law and the humanities / edited by Marco Wan.
  p. cm.
  ISBN 978-0-415-67354-9 (hbk)—ISBN 978-0-203-12169-6 (ebk)
  1. Law—Study and teaching—Methodology. 2. Case method.
  I. Wan, Marco.
  K100.R43 2012
  340.071'1—dc23   2011042455

ISBN 978-0-415-67354-9 (hbk)
ISBN 978-0-415-73728-9 (pbk)
ISBN 978-0-203-12169-6 (ebk)

Typeset in Baskerville
by RefineCatch Limited, Bungay, Suffolk

Contents

Acknowledgements vii
Contributors viii
Foreword x
THE HONOURABLE MR. JUSTICE BOKHARY, Permanent Judge of the Court of Final Appeal, Hong Kong

Introduction 1
MARCO WAN

PART I
Rereading the legal case 9

1 **Reading cases in interdisciplinary studies of law and literature** 11
ALAN DURANT

2 **'I crave the law':** *Salomon v Salomon*, **uncanny personhood and the Jews** 29
CHRISTOPHER HUTTON

3 **Three close-ups in search of truth: law, cinema, psychoanalysis** 47
MARIA ARISTODEMOU

4 **Everyday law in the court writing of Sybille Bedford** 61
ELAINE HO

5 **Sir William Jones and the translation of law in India** 80
ROBERT YOUNG

6 The illegality of Empire: moral evasion and confusion of historians and literary critics in their reflections on the impeachment trial of Warren Hastings   90
ANTHONY CARTY

PART II
Perspectives on precedent   107

7 The making of legal cases and the idea of precedent in the common law   109
THANOS ZARTALOUDIS

8 On the edge of reason: law at the borderline   128
JANNY LEUNG

9 *Stare decisis* in China? The newly enacted Guiding Case System   142
PING YU AND SETH GURGEL

10 Judging judgment in Chinua Achebe's *No Longer at Ease*   159
KATHERINE ISOBEL BAXTER

PART III
Reading literature in a legal frame   173

11 The dramatic imagination and the dream of law   175
PAUL RAFFIELD

12 The intellectual – *Hamlet*   190
KENJI YOSHINO

13 *Stare decisis*, binding precedent, and Anthony Trollope's *The Eustace Diamonds*   205
MARCO WAN

14 Binding precedent: Robert Louis Stevenson's *Strange Case of Dr Jekyll and Mr Hyde*   217
SCOTT VEITCH

Index   231

Acknowledgements

First and foremost, I would like to thank the contributors for sharing their work, and for their participation in the colloquium on the legal case at the University of Hong Kong which forms the origin of this collection of essays. Elaine Ho, my partner-in-crime in organising the colloquium, has been a wonderful friend and interlocutor since my first day at HKU. I would also like to thank Johannes Chan, SC and Kam Louie, the Dean of Law and the Dean of Arts respectively, for their support for the colloquium. In particular, I would like to thank Professor Chan for encouraging the development of law and literature and law and humanities in Asia. Alan Durant, Scott Veitch and Tony Carty gave very helpful comments on the introduction to this volume. I would also like to thank Cora Chan, Sarah Cheng, Douglas Kerr, Gina Marchetti and Sun Haochen for agreeing to act as Chairs for the panels in the colloquium, and Priscilla Chan for her administrative support. Colin Perrin has been wonderfully helpful and patient throughout the entire project. Finally, I would like to thank the Master and the Fellows of Sidney Sussex College, University of Cambridge; much of the editing work for the book was done during my time as a visiting scholar there.

Contributors

Maria Aristodemou is Senior Lecturer in Law at Birkbeck College, University of London. She is the author of *Law & Literature: Journeys from Her to Eternity* (Oxford University Press, 2000).

Katherine Isobel Baxter is Senior Lecturer in English Literature at Northumbria University. She is the author of *Joseph Conrad and the Swan Song of Romance* (Ashgate, 2010) and is working on a monograph provisionally entitled *Imagined States: Law and Literature During Nigeria's Decolonization*. She received the Bruce Harkness Young Conrad Scholar Award from the Joseph Conrad Society of America in 2004.

Anthony Carty is the Sir Y.K. Pao Chair Professor in Public Law at the University of Hong Kong. His most recent book, *Philosophy of International Law* (Edinburgh University Press, 2007), has been the subject of close attention in recent review articles in the *American Journal of International Law*, the *Journal of the History of International Law* and the *Modern Law Review*.

Alan Durant is Professor of Communications at Middlesex University. He has published extensively in areas ranging from English literature and music through to linguistics and communication law.

Seth Gurgel is the Shanghai Research Fellow for the U.S.-Asia Law Institute at the New York University School of Law.

Elaine Ho is Professor of English at the University of Hong Kong. She is the author of *Timothy Mo* (Manchester University Press, 2000) and *Anita Desai* (Northcote, 2006) and has published extensively on Anglophone Hong Kong literature.

Christopher Hutton is Chair Professor of English at the University of Hong Kong. His most recent book is *Language, Meaning and the Law* (Edinburgh University Press, 2009).

Janny Leung is Assistant Professor of English at the University of Hong Kong. She has published articles on second language acquisition, law and language, and law and psychology.

Paul Raffield is Professor of Law at the University of Warwick. He is the author of *Images and Cultures of Law in Modern England: Justice and Political Power, 1558–1660* (Cambridge University Press, 2004) and *Shakespeare's Imaginary Constitution: Late Elizabethan Politics and the Theatre of Law* (Hart, 2010). He is the founding co-editor of the journal *Law and Humanities*. In 2009 Raffield became a Fellow of the Higher Education Academy.

Scott Veitch is the Paul K.C. Chung Chair Professor of Jurisprudence at the University of Hong Kong. His first monograph, *Moral Conflict and Legal Reasoning* (Hart, 1999), was the winner of the European Award for Legal Theory. His most recent monograph is *Law and Irresponsibility: On the Legitimation of Human Suffering* (Routledge-Cavendish, 2007).

Marco Wan is Assistant Professor of Law and Honorary Assistant Professor of English at the University of Hong Kong. He has published articles on nineteenth-century literary trials in England and France and on law and visuality in Hong Kong.

Kenji Yoshino is the Chief Justice Earl Warren Professor of Constitutional Law at the New York University School of Law. His first book, *Covering: The Hidden Assault on our Civil Rights* (Random House, 2006), received the Randy Shilts Award for Gay Non-Fiction from the Publishing Triangle (2007), a Stonewall Honor Book Award from the American Library Association (2007), and a Myers Outstanding Book Award from the Gustavus Myers Center for the Study of Bigotry and Human Rights (2006). His latest book is *A Thousand Times More Fair: What Shakespeare's Plays Teach Us About Justice* (Ecco Press, 2011).

Robert Young is the Silver Professor of English and Comparative Literature at New York University. He has published widely on colonial discourse and on Post-colonialism. His most recent book is *The Idea of English Ethnicity* (Blackwell, 2008).

Ping Yu is a Senior Research Fellow at the U.S.-Asia Law Institute at the New York University School of Law and an adjunct professor at Shanghai Jiaotong University School of Law in Shanghai.

Thanos Zartaloudis is a Lecturer in Law at Birkbeck College, University of London. He is the author of *Giorgio Agamben: Power, Law and the Uses of Criticism* (Routledge-Cavendish, 2010).

Foreword

The Honourable Mr. Justice Bokhary, Permanent Judge of the Court of Final Appeal, Hong Kong

(Originally the Opening Address delivered at 'The Legal Case: Interdisciplinary Perspectives' at the University of Hong Kong)

A colloquium on law and literary studies is a worthwhile thing at any time. It is especially worthwhile when it comes as the forerunner of a double degree programme on law and literary studies. Such a programme will soon be introduced at this university. It will join – and will undoubtedly take an honourable place among – a number of other studies which combine law and other disciplines. This promises to be a most valuable colloquium: a credit to its organisers and participants. I esteem it a great honour to take part in opening it.

Let me begin by observing that you cannot learn the law merely by learning propositions of law. A wider outlook is necessary. We can say that on the authority of Lord Radcliffe, a judge high in the list of modern legal thinkers. So studies by which the law and other disciplines are combined will serve lawyers well. But will they also benefit others in their own areas of endeavour? I think that they will. Take history as one example. Professor F W Maitland, of great and deserved renown as a legal historian, considered it possible to be a lawyer without knowing history. But he did not consider it possible to be a historian without knowing some law.

It is a fact that lawyers must have – and often do have – a working familiarity with other disciplines. You only have to listen to a criminal lawyer cross-examining a scientific witness, or a commercial lawyer cross-examining an accountant, to appreciate that. And these things are at least as true of legal advisers as they are of advocates. They are certainly true of judges, both at trial, on appeal and on final appeal.

Now let us consider the arts, starting with the performing arts. Many people think – with some justification perhaps – that there is a comparison to be made between the trial advocate and the actor – or the actress of course. That most dramatic of advocates, Sir Edward Marshall Hall KC, once made such a comparison, but put a limit on it. No lines, he said, were written for him to speak. There was, he said, no backdrop to heighten the illusion. Out of the living drama of the lives of men and women, he had to create an atmosphere. For that, he said, is advocacy.

At least it is advocacy of a certain type. Not a type to which I was ever suited. Well do I remember my English teacher telling me, in deep sorrow, that I recited

Shakespeare like someone reading out the label on a tin of soup. Although that somewhat dismayed me at the time, it has not turned out to be so great a disadvantage after all. For the truth of the matter is that *all* commercial documents, *all* statutes and *most* judgments far more resemble the label on a tin of soup than they resemble Shakespeare. And in that dusty environment I survived and even managed eventually to make some progress. Today, amidst the magnificent generalities of the constitution, I am striving to reclaim some part of my lost lawyer's soul.

So much then for the performing arts. What about the creative arts? A youth of 14 once wrote to Mr Justice Frankfurter, saying that he intended eventually to study law, and asking for a list of law books to read by way of preliminary preparation. The learned judge advised him not to read any law books at all. Time enough for that later on. Meanwhile, the advice ran, he should enjoy great works of literature, listen to wonderful music and look at splendid paintings. For these things would stimulate the imaginative faculties so essential to anyone who would be a great lawyer. Therein lies the fundamental truth from which a combined course on law and literature derives its essential merit. There you will find the abiding benefit to all of its participants, whether as teachers or as students.

At a different level, such a course can enhance the way in which lawyers express themselves. I do not mean by adorning their utterances with literary allusions – although that is not necessarily a bad thing, in moderation of course. What I have in mind is the discovery of a mode of expression that better captures attention and generates interest. Acceptance must depend on underlying merit, but attention and interest pave the way to acceptance. The judgment in every leading case should tell people as plainly as possible where the case leads.

Of course there is much that matters apart from mode of expression. Both the law and literature must find acceptance in the real world: with its splendours and also its grim realities. At their best, the law and literature alike operate to expose injustice and bring about progress. And progress includes laying aside things which, even if once acceptable, are no longer in harmony with the state into which the aspirations of society have evolved and ripened.

It is difficult to imagine a plea in mitigation to surpass Emily Brontë's *The Prisoner*. Any judge would be proud to have a judgment of his or hers on free speech compared with Milton's *Areopagitica*. No judicial activist would be ashamed to have half of Charles Dickens' zeal for social reform or talent for making out a case in its favour. Yet let the non-lawyer reflect upon how much less effective Dickens would have been if he did not know the law as well as he did. Mr Bumble would have been silent. And we would not have cases like *Bardell* v. *Pickwick* and *Jarndyce* v. *Jarndyce* so graphically to portray the injustice that can be done by oppressive advocacy or undue delay in the law's process.

At the same time, non-lawyers have something to learn from the way in which lawyers express themselves. Persuasion does not lie in passion alone. Vitally important, too, are detachment and due acknowledgement of the arguments on the other side of the question. And these are elements prominent in the best legal writings, the best submissions of counsel and the best judgments. They go to the very heart of the common law system by which law is fashioned from the fabric of real life and a desire to do practical justice.

Some literary works – the *Winslow Boy* based on the *Archer-Shee* case is a good example – owe a great deal to actual cases. Chaucer's Serjeant-at-Law may have been drawn from Serjeant Thomas Pynchbec. And no academic lawyer would ever dream of objecting to being seen as the inspiration for Professor Charles Kingsfield of *Paper Chase* fame. But very often it is the law that makes use of art. Sir John Mortimer QC admitted that he had often spoken through Horace Rumpole, knowing that many people who would not accept ideas from him would accept them from Rumpole. Anthony Trollope did much the same sort of thing. He acknowledged in his autobiography that he had frequently expressed his political and social views through the characters in his Palliser novels.

James Joyce is credited (or debited) with the boast that if Dublin were destroyed in a conflagration, it could be rebuilt on the description found in *Ulysees*. No lawyer could possibly make any comparable boast about his or her own works, even though some lawyers might be brought within the phrase 'Self-school'd, self-scann'd, self-honour'd, self-secure' by which Matthew Arnold famously paid tribute to a literary figure greater even than Joyce. But if the whole of the common law were lost, the common law method would enable the legal community working together to restore it in time – and with the improvements that the organic nature of the common law always permits if not demands.

Whether we are interpreting legislation, developing the common law or expounding the constitution, we do so in the context of – and for the purpose of – how people live their lives. To my understanding at least, that is also the context from which literature draws its raw material, into which it sends forth its finished products and within which it exercises its influence.

Introduction
Marco Wan

To a common law lawyer, the question of what constitutes a legal case seems self-evident. However, when one pauses to reflect upon what a case is, it quickly becomes obvious that the word defies attempts to fix its meaning. The entry on 'Case' in the *Oxford Companion to Law* begins by defining it as 'an individual legal dispute, particularly one involving litigation' (Walker 1980: 189). A case therefore seems to be conceived of as an event or a process. However, the entry further states that the word is 'also used of the body of pleadings, arguments, and submissions for one of the parties'. On this view, a case is not so much an event but a corpus of written and oral texts presented in court. The entry concludes by giving a third definition: in legal literature a case is 'the report of an action'. Here, the word is given a generic definition, that of the law report. The 'case' hovers between different registers, each representing a prevalent way of speaking about it in legal practice, but none of which manages to fully address the multiple dimensions in which it exists.

How, then, might one broach the question of what a case is, how it creates meaning, and what is at stake in regarding a situation as a noteworthy case rather than a trivial or isolated occurrence? Lauren Berlant provides one point of entry into these questions when she notes that the case 'represents a problem-event that has animated some kind of judgment. [...] What matters is the *idiom* of the judgment' (Berlant 2007: 663; my italics). One way of defining a 'case' is therefore through the specific *language* which constitutes it: the terminology which defines the domain to which it belongs (law, medicine, psychiatry, etc.), the tone which supposedly reflects the rationality and knowledge of the person making the case, the metaphors and analogies inherent in its reasoning, and the structural underpinnings along which its argument proceeds. In other words, one could offer a substantially adequate definition of a case by examining the way in which it is written.

This volume shares Berlant's view that language is crucial for understanding what a case is and how it works, but it approaches the issue from a different vantage point: instead of asking how cases are written, it focuses on how they are *read*. The process of reading is especially important in the context of the legal case in the common law: to train someone to be a common law lawyer is to a great extent to train that person to read cases 'properly'. This point becomes evident when one examines the dynamic of any law school classroom in common law jurisdictions: law students are taught how to delineate, refine and extract the *ratio decidendi* of a case, to separate the *ratio* from the *obiter dictum*, to apply the legal principles of a precedent case to the situation at hand, and to distinguish unhelpful cases based on points of law or fact. These legal techniques are in fact the building blocks of becoming a competent *reader* of case law, even though they are not usually presented to students as techniques of interpretation (in contrast to, for example, specifically interpretative rules such as the literal rule or the mischief rule in statutory interpretation). The legal case, then, is as much defined by the way in which it is read as it is by its genre, its structure and its narrative conventions. Indeed, given that the distinctive feature of the common law is the centrality and authority of case law, it is possible to argue that interpretative practices are pivotal not only to the understanding of case law, but also to what it means to be a common law lawyer more broadly. Moreover, commentators have highlighted that the case hovers between the singular and the universal, between the individual and the general. In the specific context of the legal case, this tension is arguably premised on the way common law lawyers are taught to read cases in order to extract universal legal principles applicable across space and time from factual situations marked by singular or unique circumstances.

Given that much of legal education and practice emphasize understanding the *content* of a case, it is perhaps easy to forget how much the understanding of content is premised on the reading process. In fact, the reading process can even be said, to a significant extent, to create the 'content' in the first place, insofar as one learns how to read in a way that leads to the recognition of a specific content that is deemed desirable or useful. In *The Law-Making Process*, one of the most widely used reference texts in introductory law courses, Michael Zander introduces students to the concept of *ratio decidendi* by stating that 'the *ratio* [. . .] of a case is its central core of meaning, its sharpest cutting edge' (Zander 2004: 268). This seemingly simple, even incontestable, definition of *ratio decidendi* is in fact already part of an interpretative pedagogy: to state that the search for the *ratio* is the *raison d'être* of reading a case is to initiate a reading practice which designates certain facts in the case as important and discards other facts (which may be significant in other interpretative contexts) as trivial, which bypasses questions of style or tone in favour of issues of doctrine, which sidelines description as a means of creating meaning and highlights legal categories or concepts as the key to understanding a case.

Just as one could question the necessity of asking what a legal case is in the first place, so one could question the point of underscoring the conventions and methods of reading cases. It is possible to argue that even if one accepts that the legal case can be defined by the way in which it is read by lawyers, judges and legal academics, one could say that the insight is largely irrelevant given that law students are taught to read legal cases in a certain way simply because of the demands of the profession; one cannot be a lawyer without being able to perform basic tasks such as identifying the legal issues at hand, extracting the relevant principles, and pinpointing potentially useful *obiter dicta* in court. That much is certainly true, but the necessity of a particular reading process in face of the demands of legal practice should not obscure from us the problems associated with it. Legal reading is not an innocent activity, and has profound implications for the reader's conception of the relationship between the law and reality, for the view of law's role in society, and for the understanding of the reader's own place in a social community. Writing about the now well-rehearsed story of the establishment of the case method of teaching at Harvard law school, Peter Goodrich points out that when 'the case became the pure unit of law', the law became 'separated from its history, excised from its context and with all links to the patterns of precedent severed' (Goodrich 2007: 699). To read a legal case by regarding the *ratio* as its 'central core of meaning' – to read it as a common law lawyer – is to a great extent to sever the case specifically, and the law more broadly, from its cultural, historical and social contexts, to the intellectual impoverishment of both the case and its reader. As a result, the seemingly unquestionable process of legal reading means that 'the pedagogy of *rigor iuris* comes to look a lot like *rigor mortis*'. Peter Brooks pinpoints a further problem with the way legal cases are conventionally read, which is that it pays insufficient attention to cases as a form of narrative. Brooks notes that the law suffers from an unhealthy disciplinary hermeticism and is in need of 'a greater awareness of its own narrative logic', an awareness which he argues literary analysis can offer (Brooks 2003: 100). Reading cases with a heightened awareness of their narrative dimension – the way beginnings and endings are related, the way discrete events are linked together, the role of rhetoric in the creation of meaning – is crucial to a better understanding of the way legal logic operates, and hence ultimately to the achievement of more well-reasoned legal judgments.

The aim of this volume is to destabilize, to interrupt, to rethink those reading methods and conventions that are so central to the disciplinary understanding of the legal case, and to the formation of the common law lawyer. Of course, the intention is not to create a manifesto for the replacement of current reading practices in the common law with another: one cannot conceive of a lawyer who cannot, say, differentiate between *ratio* and *obiter*. However, the problems associated with the conventional mode of reading legal cases need to be addressed and a change of perspective could provide insight into how cases can be taken out of their disciplinary confinement. What happens, the essays in this volume collectively ask, when legal cases are not read as lawyers are traditionally taught to read them? Would we see something different about legal cases by placing them within a new interpretative context? What can be gained from the experience of reading them differently? These questions lead to another: if the project is to read legal cases differently, then from exactly which perspective should we read them? *How* should we read them differently? This volume proposes that we turn to the humanities, where questions of reading have received the most intense scrutiny in areas such as literary criticism, historical interpretation, philosophy of language, film studies, to name but a few. In turn, the encounter with the legal case can also reveal new or hitherto overlooked aspects of the humanities. Alan Durant's essay, which opens this volume, also epitomizes its spirit: Durant points out that the law report is a genre of its own, and as such comes with its own reading conventions. He notes that shifting a text to a different interpretative environment could create new meanings in it, and that such new meanings can be of interest and value both to lawyers and interdisciplinary scholars. What is proposed in this volume is a re-contextualisation of the legal case within the frame of the humanities, so that cases are read through the techniques of interpretation developed in other disciplines, or read in conjunction with cultural products with which the law is not commonly associated, or read in a historical milieu which is usually ignored in the process of courtroom citation. In the process, new dimensions of both the legal case and the humanities are opened up. The 'cross currents' between law and the humanities in the title are conceived of as a criss-crossing of contexts; the legal case is read in the context of the humanities, and texts from the humanities are read in the context of law.

The volume is divided into three parts. The essays in the first section, 'Rereading the Legal Case', perform the task of reading legal cases in new interpretative domains outlined above, and in their different ways the essays all show that when we move legal cases away from strictly disciplinary reading practices their boundaries start to fade and they are revealed to be continuous with wider historical, social and cultural worlds. The chapter by Durant outlines the argument for a shift in the 'community of practice' when reading cases, specifically in 'law and literature' studies but with implications for the study of law and the humanities more broadly, and sets the tone for both this section and for the volume as a whole.

Christopher Hutton's ' "I crave the law": *Salomon v Salomon*, uncanny personhood and the Jews' shifts the terrain of interpretation by placing this landmark company law case within the narrative of the history of Jewish people in England. A solely doctrinal understanding of *Salomon* as a case about corporate personality erases the historical context in which it was decided; Hutton's essay restores this forgotten historical dimension and brings to the forefront the case's multiple imbrications with the social and cultural prejudices of its time.

In 'Three Close-Ups in Search of Truth: Law, Cinema, Psychoanalysis', Maria Aristodemou examines a specific moment in which the legal case was recontextualised, in the form of director Abbas Kiarostami's transformation of an actual Iranian court case into the medium of film in *Close-Up*. Adopting a Lacanian mode of analysis, Aristodemou argues that film, as an art form, brings us closer to the 'truth' of the case than the law, and also reveals truth as itself a vexed notion.

Elaine Ho's 'Everyday Law in the Court Writing of Sybille Bedford' examines the engagement with the law of a figure whose work crosses the boundaries of fiction, autobiography, travel writing and journalism. Ho's piece examines the ways in which Bedford creates a link between the legal domain and the world beyond the law by interrogating the status of 'the literary' in her work, and in doing so Ho also underscores the role which non-lawyers play in the creation of legal meaning.

The shift of interpretative context enacted by Robert Young's essay is more literal, in that he presents us not only with a disciplinary shift but also with a geographical shift. 'Sir William Jones and the Translation of Law in India' argues that linguistic translation also represents a form of cultural translation; what changes in the process is not simply the language in which the law is written or spoken but the very conception of law itself. The form of the written case as it was transplanted into British India was in this context part and parcel of a larger process of cultural imperialism.

Tony Carty's 'The Illegality of Empire: Moral Evasion and Confusion of Historians and Literary Critics in their Reflections on The Impeachment Trial of Warren Hastings' might be interpreted as a contrapuntal reading of the readings performed by the other essays in this section. Carty examines the primary material from the Warren Hastings trial of the late eighteenth century and expresses his reservations with the interpretation of the trial posited by a number of literary critics. Carty agrees that the law and literature movement can make a positive contribution, but he also reminds us of the moral and intellectual responsibility involved in the pursuit of interdisciplinarity, and sounds a note of caution against overly hasty or easy movements from one domain into another.

'Perspectives on Precedent', the second section of the volume, continues the interrogation of what it means to read legal cases in different contexts. But this section expands the frame of analysis: while most of the essays in the first section concentrate on a single case or figure, the essays in this section concentrate on the way in which cases are read in relation to one another. The doctrine of precedent is at its core a set of inter-textual relations between cases: to say that one case ought to be considered as a precedent of another, or that the decision in one case binds another, is to begin to construct a lineage between cases often widely separated in time and space. The doctrine is at once firmly entrenched and also highly precarious. One classic study stresses that 'the peculiar feature of the English doctrine of precedent is its strongly coercive nature. English judges are sometimes obliged to follow a previous case although they have what would otherwise be good reasons for not doing so' (Cross and Harris 1991: 3). The most oft-cited benefit of coercive precedent is the certainty of judicial outcomes: judges cannot decide a case based on their own personal preferences or beliefs, and the doctrine is thus a safeguard against unpredictable or arbitrary decisions. However, writing in the American context, Judge Benjamin N. Cardozo notes that a high degree of discretion can exist even within the confines of precedent. He notes that the law 'is more plastic' and 'more malleable' than commonly believed, and that the restraint of precedent is less strong than normally understood (Cardozo 1921: 161). Judge Cardozo recalls how, in his first years on the bench, he was 'much troubled in spirit [. . .] to find how trackless was the ocean' in which he sailed. He 'sought for certainty', only to realize that 'the quest for it was futile' (Cardozo 1921: 166). Of course, he is not advocating a nihilistic view of the law, nor is he calling for the abolition of precedent, but his comments reveal that the notions of precedent which underpin the common law are marked by a fundamental contradiction: they are supposed to be coercive and inflexible but they simultaneously allow for a high degree of creativity.

The essays in the second section ponder over the stakes involved in the task of reading cases inter-textually. Thanos Zartaloudis's 'The Making of Legal Cases and the Idea of Precedent in the Common Law' places the notion of precedent in dialogue with continental philosophy. It examines how the very designation of something as a legal case creates distinctions between what is and is not part of the law, and also forges a particular legal reality.

Janny Leung's 'On the Edge of Reason: Law at the Borderline' examines the idea of restraint through legal precedent from the perspective of a linguist. She challenges the belief that the use of precedent could give a solution to the problem of linguistic ambiguity in legal discourse, and argues that indeterminacy of meaning remains a fundamental feature of the law and of language.

Ping Yu and Seth Gurgel's '*Stare Decisis* in China? The Newly Enacted Guiding Case System' provides a historical framework for understanding the operation of precedent in a non-common law jurisdiction. Through an examination of the Guiding Case System in China, the essay explores the possibility of analyzing aspects of China's civil law system through the seemingly incongruous common law notion of *stare decisis*.

Finally in this section, Katherine Baxter's 'Judging Judgment in Chinua Achebe's *No Longer at Ease*' develops from the acknowledgement that precedent is not a feature specific to the law. She discusses the different kinds of precedent in Achebe's novel and provides a useful comparison of the functions of precedent in literature and law.

The third section of the book, entitled 'Reading Literature in a Legal Frame', reverses the paradigm of the first section. Rather than reading legal cases in the context of the humanities, it reads literary texts in the context of the law, and more specifically in the context of the philosophy and history of the legal case. Re-contextualisation is a two-way process: the legal case can be read in the context of the humanities, which means that texts from the humanities can also be read in the context of the law. Recent interdisciplinary work often focuses on the ways in which law can learn from literature or the humanities more broadly, but what intellectual gain can be made from a legal reading of literature or other texts from the humanities? This question often becomes elided perhaps because the act of contextualising literary, philosophical or film texts in legal history is itself not new. However, further theorisation could shed light on the exact nature of the relationship between the two domains. This section focuses on the way in which literature is read in a legal frame. Does legal history function as a means of enhancing our understanding of literature, or is it the other way around, with literature functioning as a tool for a better understanding of legal history? Or perhaps re-contextualisation could shed light on the wider question of the methods and practice of interdisciplinarity, so that the focus is not on a re-evaluation of literature or law *per se*, but on achieving a new understanding of what it means to stage an encounter between them? Would the encounter problematise the difference between literary 'text' and legal 'context'? The essays here explore the range of new meanings that is created by the shift in interpretative terrain. Paul Raffield's 'The Dramatic Imagination and the Dream of Law' examines a number of legal and literary texts in the early modern period and argues that they are intertwined: legal terms and concepts form an integral part of literature, and literary metaphors are an inextricable part of the legal texts. The intertwining of law and literature in early modern times makes the hermeticism of legal discourse in our own century seem all the more curious.

Kenji Yoshino's 'The Intellectual – *Hamlet*' focuses on a single literary text – William Shakespeare's *Hamlet* – to ask what it might mean for a reader to approach a literary text as a lawyer. Would a legal reading of this famous play tell us something new about it? By placing *Hamlet* in a legal hermeneutic framework, Yoshino posits an answer to the famous conundrum about Hamlet's delay in killing his uncle Claudius: he argues that the delay is part of an active pursuit of poetic justice. Just as the reading of the legal case in the context of the humanities can lead to new understandings of the case, so the reading of the literary text in a legal framework can give fresh insight into old questions about literature.

Marco Wan's '*Stare Decisis*, Binding Precedent, and Anthony Trollope's *The Eustace Diamonds*' sets the novel in the context of the development of the doctrine of precedent in the second half of the nineteenth century, and argues that the novel can be read as a response to these developments in legal history. Law and literature are shown to be in constant dialogue; literature responds to the legal debates of its time and can reveal problems or blind spots in the law.

In 'Binding Precedent: Robert Louis Stevenson's *Strange Case of Dr Jekyll and Mr. Hyde*', Scott Veitch uncovers an unexpected legal dimension in the famous novella. He argues that there is evidence to show that Stevenson was familiar with aspects of the Roman law of obligations, and he places *Jekyll and Hyde* in dialogue with the concept of binding and being bound in Roman law to tease out the jurisprudential significance of Stevenson's tale.

The multiple re-contextualisations of legal cases by the contributors in this volume aim to take them outside of their usual interpretative confines. When we stop reading cases solely for their legal rules and principles, when we read them within the frame of the humanities, we start to recover facets of the legal case which the conventional modes of reading have sidelined, hidden, or even erased: a case can be, amongst many other things, a linguistic construct, a literary event, a moment in history, a tool of imperialism, a philosophical meditation, and an integral part of the human cultural heritage. Given the centrality of the case to the common law, it is hoped that this volume will contribute towards a fuller, more complex, and more nuanced understanding of what a case is and how it operates. In turn, the task of reading literature and film in a legal context can foster new ways of thinking about familiar narratives from the humanities.

In closing, I should note that this volume began as a conference entitled 'The Legal Case: Interdisciplinary Perspectives' at the University of Hong Kong. The conference marked the inauguration of a new double degree programme in Law and Literary Studies designed for undergraduates, the first of its kind in Asia. Mr. Justice Bokhary's elegant foreword gives a sense of the philosophy and scope of the programme. Perhaps because of the location of the conference, a number of the essays focus on the interaction of law and the humanities in areas outside Europe and North America, including India, Nigeria and China. As the discussion moved across texts from different temporal and geographical contexts, the political, cultural, and epistemological stakes involved in reading a legal case gradually emerged as a unifying theme. The question of what it means to read well – a vast question which encompasses issues such as the relationship between text and context, the creation or discovery of meaning, the politics of interpretation, and the understanding of the legal case as a distinct genre – is of concern both to legal and literary scholars. By shifting the terrains of reading, the essays in this volume explore the multiple ramifications of this question and open up new possibilities of dialogue between law and the humanities.

Bibliography

Berlant, L. (2007) 'On the Case', *Critical Inquiry*, 33: 663–73.
Brooks, P. (2003) ' "Inevitable Discovery" – Law, Narrative, Retrospectivity', *Yale Journal of Law and the Humanities*, 15: 71–103.
Cardozo, B.N. (1921) *The Nature of the Judicial Process*, New Haven: Yale University Press.
Cross, R. and Harris, J.W. (1961; 4th edn 1991) *Precedent in English Law*, Oxford: Clarendon Press.
Goodrich, P. (2007) 'The New Casuistry', *Critical Inquiry*, 33: 673–710.
Walker, D. (1980) *The Oxford Companion to Law*, Oxford: Clarendon Press, 1980.
Zander, M. (1980; 6th edn 2004) *The Law-Making Process*, London: Butterworths.

Part I

Rereading the legal case

Chapter 1

Reading cases in interdisciplinary studies of law and literature

Alan Durant

The concept of a 'case' differs between law and other fields in which the term is used, including literature. So establishing what a case *is*, in interdisciplinary studies of law and literature, is an important step in identifying what is distinctive about such work. It is also important to establish what is involved in 'interpreting' a case, since each of the fields contributing to this interdisciplinary endeavour follows its own, distinctive approaches. Historically, the study of law and literature has been shaped by a series of approaches to interpretation which serves to define the field's purposes and significance.

An influential example of interaction between interpretive approach and the value associated with studying law and literature provides my starting point for this chapter. As far back as his Preface to the second edition of *Law and Literature*, Richard Posner observed that 'literary' approaches to interpretation of legal discourse had 'diminished in the face of a growing sense that interpretation is relative to purpose and therefore unlikely to raise the same issues for different interpretanda (dreams, operas, labels, constitutions, sonnets' (Posner, 1998: viii). Later in the same volume, Posner observed that the decline of interest in 'literary' approaches to interpretation he was reporting also reflected considerations of method. Specifically, he argued, interpretation is 'not much, and maybe not at all, improved by being made self-conscious, just as one doesn't become a better reader by studying linguistics' (1998: 211). In this chapter, I ask how far Posner's scepticism about the value of 'literary' styles of interpretation applied to legal discourse (as well as his reservation about the usefulness of linguistic self-consciousness in reading) holds for cases in common law traditions, which differ in important respects from the statutes and constitutions on which Posner based his original argument.

My discussion[1] has two stages. To begin, I look at the general concept of a 'case', questioning how far the notion is coherent if extended beyond legal cases to literary topics and to literary works with legal themes. I suggest that invoking an undifferentiated sense of 'case' in interdisciplinary enquiry opens up interpretive possibilities but risks vagueness and ambiguity. In the second half of the chapter, I focus on 'case reports' in law: the genre of publication usually known as 'law reports'. Such reports offer the most precisely defined legal representation of cases; they also often attract expansive comment as well as legal exegesis, including along lines influenced by literary studies. I explore how far genre considerations associated with law reports constrain the interpretive approaches that can be usefully brought to bear on them, as Posner argued was the case for statutes and constitutions. In partial agreement with Posner, I conclude that close links between the formal characteristics and purposes of law reports do place obstacles in the way of alternative readings. But I suggest that those obstacles need not undermine an extended sense of interpretation which can result in illuminating critical readings. My agreement with Posner's argument is only partial, however. Against his further claim that reflexiveness in interpretation is generally unhelpful, I argue that even highly insightful literary readings of particular legal cases are less important than increased self-consciousness as regards *how* meanings are created by interpretive practices that differ in important ways, as well as overlap, between the two fields.

Different kinds of 'case'

There is little risk of someone who is following an academic course in law and literature becoming confused by what is meant by a 'case' in different edited collections they are directed to read. If you open a literary-critical 'casebook' (such as *Thomas Hardy: the Tragic Novels (Casebook)* (Draper, 1991) or the 'new casebook' *Tess of the D'Urbervilles* (Widdowson, 1993)), you will find a selection of essays introducing the reader to critical approaches to the text or texts in question. The general purpose of such volumes is clear. In the General Editor's Preface to the Casebook series, launched in 1968, A.E. Dyson explained that each 'single author' casebook would present critical readings of a well-known work, or cluster of closely related works, along with contemporaneous reviews and comment. In the General Editors' Preface to the 'New Casebook' series, John Peck and Martin Coyle widened that aim to reflect a shift in literary studies: the new volumes, they wrote, would also reveal how contemporary criticism has 'changed our understanding of commonly studied texts and writers, as well as of the nature of criticism itself' (Widdowson, 1993: ii).

In striking contrast, in a legal textbook of cases and materials (such as *Cases and Materials in Intellectual Property* (Cornish, 2006) or *Media Law: Cases and Materials* (Barendt and Hitchens, 2000)), the reader is presented not only with a very different selection but with sources that serve a contrasting purpose. Such case collections in law are designed to bring together 'legislative texts and extracts from cases which form the basis of United Kingdom law' (Cornish, 2006: vii). In Barendt and Hitchens, focus is on 'the range of topics comprising media law' (2000: xi); and in Cornish on the 'various aspects of intellectual property rights proper and those topics, such as liability for breach of confidence and passing off, which form adjuncts' (2006: vii). Such texts provide either a combination of 'key materials with critical commentary' (Barendt and Hitchens, 2000: xi), or are 'intended to be used together with texts that give an account of the law as a corpus ... [the book] does not therefore have its own commentary' (Cornish, 2006: vii).

Both kinds of volume – legal and literary – offer useful collections of 'case' material. But they deploy the idea of a 'case' differently. The contrast I have drawn between them is significant because the same word 'case' can be used of either type of publication. It is therefore worth examining what the word 'case' denotes, then relating the word's varying meanings to wider understandings of 'case' at work in law and literature scholarship.

Even confining ourselves to common dictionary definitions, we find a range of senses. We may immediately rule out, as not relevant, the idea of case as grammatical category, formally marked by inflection. We might also take the view that the meaning 'container, receptacle or box' (which gives rise to upper-case and lower-case keyboard characters) is simply figurative in marking edges or boundaries, and again irrelevant. But there are other meanings which complicate what a 'case' is for the purpose of interdisciplinary work in law and literature.

We may pause, for example, over 'a particular situation or instance, especially one that you are using as an example of something more general'. Based on evidence from the Cobuild dictionary project,[2] this is the most common contemporary sense of 'case'. When we talk about 'the case of literature', we mean matters pertaining to literature as an instance of some more general phenomenon, in contrast with other cases (such as 'the case of physics'). Those other cases are viewed as being different while also being members of the same larger class (in this case, that of objects of study).

This combined sense of particulars treated in terms of their membership of a superordinate class has ramifications both in law and in literature. A legal 'case', for example, is a highly detailed social and discursive event: it encapsulates an episode of what might loosely be called real-life drama; and its events are important lived experiences for the parties, sometimes deeply damaging or even tragic, which are selectively framed as a distinct entity for legal analysis and judgment.[3] At the same time, each legal case is an instance of a more abstract, general category: a copyright case, negligence case, murder case, fraud case, etc. In relation to this superordinate classification, the facts of the particular case are exactly *subordinate*: the case is remembered in legal circles, if at all, as dealing with a legal crux of some kind, and the question at law has the effect of displacing the persons and their actions, despite the case being permanently labelled with their names as the parties.[4] When juxtaposed with the first idea of 'case', this second, abstract notion suggests a different act of framing: a 'case' is less a specific situation that needs to be settled than a springboard offered by a set of particulars into generalisations which set out a legal principle.[5]

The 'instance and category' meaning is also applied beyond law. A *literary* 'case' depends similarly on a combination of particulars and overarching, discipline-specific categories. The particulars include details of production, such as a writer's source materials, chosen themes, and habits of composition. There are also the different kinds of agency involved in the preparation, publication and circulation of a literary work, including the work of editors who amend passages and guide publication, reviewers and critics who advance alternative views, and literature teachers and students who argue over techniques and significance. In addition there are institutional settings: publishing houses, college seminar rooms, and reading groups. There are also equivalent abstract, disciplinary categories that a literary 'case' may exemplify. These include works by the particular author, work in a given genre, and work treating some recognised critical or historical theme or problem. Something similar also occurs beyond literature. Cases are treated as both specific instances and exemplars of a general category in professional fields variously concerned with disease, injury and hardship. The word 'case' is used of people attended by a doctor, for example, or who are in treatment with a psychoanalyst, or who become clients of a solicitor or financial advisor. In each of these professional fields of cases, casework, caseloads and case workers, the combination of 'particulars plus treatment on the basis of membership of a disciplinary category' is the clearly active meaning of 'case'. What can nevertheless complicate the *interdisciplinary* study of 'cases' is that the general formula may be applied in ways that impose too strong a likeness on distinguishable instances of particulars and categories. Insufficient attention to differences may blur the distinction between principles of selection of an instance, and mix models of what will qualify any given instance as a member of the relevant category.

A further shading in the meaning of 'case' highlights special complexity when the 'instance and category' model is applied to verbal discussion. In such circumstances, 'case' can mean not only a topic of discussion, as with 'the case *of* electoral reform' (contrast: 'the case of education reform'), but rather some argument or evidence supporting a particular position within such discussion (cf. 'the case *for* electoral reform'). This meaning has considerable scope. It extends to the view of a literary work as an object of competing literary critical appreciations (e.g. 'the case for seeing Tess as heroine rather than victim'). A literary case, then, may be not just a case study or test case, but a 'topic' case about which 'argument' cases are put forward from different critical positions.

What is significant about such polysemy (which if over-emphasised can begin to feel like a semantic game) is mostly not the prospect of local misunderstanding. Rather, it is that, when a notion such as 'case' is used in a new field or in interdisciplinary work between established fields, it is uncertain, without clarification, how a given 'case' should be investigated or exactly why a particular case deserves attention.

What sense or senses of 'case', we should therefore ask, are in play in interdisciplinary work on law and literature? Clearly the 'court proceedings' sense occurs frequently (used either of actual legal cases or applied to depictions of trials in fiction or drama, such as the scarcely narrated murder case in which the character Tess is the defendant). The 'argument' sense is also relevant (e.g. the defence case implicit in Tess's circumstances at the moment she kills Alex, the formulation or rebuttal of which oddly features hardly at all in the novel). The 'instance and category' sense will also be found (e.g. 'in the case of Tess but not of Hardy's other protagonists in his "Novels of Character and Environment"'); and there will be the broad 'framed narrative' sense (as in 'the case of Tess seems unique in nineteenth-century fiction'). This last meaning is challengingly wide, however. It evokes an only vaguely indicated category: possibly something related to actual events which took place during the controversy surrounding the novel's publication, or alternatively some unspecified, more general social phenomenon, or alternatively again some compound of fictional characteristics of the character Tess with an unspecified mix of social and historical conditions in nineteenth-century England and Hardy's known imaginative interests.[6]

We should take stock at this point. I am suggesting that contrasts between different kinds of 'case' collection reveal potentially important differences between legal and literary uses of the idea of a 'case'. Each contrast problematises the issue of what should be studied in this field, and how any given 'case', as an object of study, should be treated.

There is a contrast of subject matter and treatment

Even where a selected literary 'case' (a novel, play, author's work) directly represents a legal situation or trial, the treatment of legal material is different. This difference points to a deeper contrast: that between something *being* a court case or part of a court case (a rule-governed discursive event), and something being a *representation* of a court case in a different discursive form (whether drama, novel, or law report).

In literary analysis there is typically one 'case': a selected novel, play, collection of poems, or author

A literary 'casebook' anthology is a collection of commentaries on a work or author, published because its, his or her significance is considered worthy of commentary and further investigation. The selected excerpts are interpretations converging on that single case, which is set apart from the commentaries on it not least by the fact that the work is in a conventionally literary genre while the essays commenting on it take a literary critical form. The legal analogy is less that of a volume of case materials than an extended treatment of a single set of proceedings consisting of further documentary evidence and submissions.

While both law report and literary work deploy exposition and narrative in their representation of a case, there are differences as regards the claims being made

The literary 'case' consists of narrated events that are mostly imagined or fictional (and which have their own complex origins in the author's experience or subjective formation). Where material draws on an actual legal case, it does so by means of imaginative condensation, projection or exaggeration. In legal cases, on the other hand, a great deal of effort is made by judges to set out the facts to which they then apply the law. Reports of legal cases abbreviate the statement of such facts and the evidence that led to particular findings of fact. But this type of condensation serves to limit reports to legally relevant material; it does not alter the truth-claims made with respect to factual material.

Interpretation differs as regards how moves are made from evidence to significance

The facts which guide interpretation of a *literary* case include patterns observed in a text's language; external circumstances of authorship and creative intentions; and details of publication and reception. Interpretation of the text would almost certainly differ if techniques of legal construction rather than ordinary language comprehension were followed in reading its language. Doctrines of legal construction offer normative guidance in the interpretation of *legal* language (e.g. by interpreting ambiguity in favour of the defendant or against the meaning claimed by the party drafting a contract). Literary interpretation, by contrast, combines general intuitions regarding discourse meaning with awareness of specialised stylistic techniques adopted in literary works.[7]

The underlying 'problem' being addressed differs between the two fields, with no shared standard of what constitutes satisfactory resolution of the problem that a case is thought to illustrate

In law, concern is mainly with how the law stands in a particular area, and how the law in that area (as it stands) applies to particular findings of fact. Settlement of a dispute in a civil action, or the outcome of a criminal trial, is sought through legal reasoning applied to findings of fact, drawing on authorities that take the form of decisions made in relevant, earlier cases. There is therefore directionality in any sequence of cited cases which is more than chronological: a directionality that explains why the facts of any given case, once that action is concluded, are less important than the legal reasoning applied to them (since it is the reasoning which can establish a legal rule that is then carried forward).[8] Literary cases also present a cumulative record of argument and insight. But 'rules' governing moves in a literary critical debate are less constrained as regards direction. Often, the more 'well read' or 'cultivated' a literary discussion, the more references will be triggered outwards, into an array of literary works and critical stances that the topic engages.

Cases differ between the two fields as regards how they are read

Literature students typically read only one case per 'casebook', albeit against a background of extensive reading and with a view to analysing alternative cases (in the argument sense of 'case') submitted in relation to it. Their law counterparts read many cases in *their* collection. For the law student, the greater number of prescribed cases follows from the principle that each case illustrates legal submissions which informed the decision arrived at by the court. In this way, each case both presents a legal problem and sets out a legally reasoned solution to that problem in the form of judgment and verdict. Each case also refers to earlier cases which may themselves be read (in extract form) in the same edited volume. Together, the various cases form the series of steps carrying forward a developing legal argument which builds towards a statement of what the law now is.

While in each kind of case accumulated interpretations and judgments form traditions, the nature and significance of those traditions differ

Literary-critical opinions form a tradition in the sense of a succession of arguments. They combine individual inventiveness and communal critical belief in a variable mix, and respond to changing artistic and social conditions. In literary critical history (as more visibly in the history of modern art), such traditions show uneven development, and follow unpredictable patterns of influence, adaptation, subversion, critique and rejection of schools and positions. This is so both in creative work and in commentary on such work. It requires general artistic conservatism (e.g. some form of Classicism), or a more specific, idealist construct of the sort put forward by T.S. Eliot in his essay 'Tradition and the Individual Talent' (Eliot [1919], 1922), to see literary tradition as development of cultural wisdom leading to a normative standard. The legal volume, by contrast, presents its series of cases not because they constitute a tradition in a loose sense of influence, but because, together, cases represent 'case law': an accumulating body of adjudications which fill in and clarify statute law, and as we see below may become precedents that bind later judgments within an overall common law system.

'Reporting' cases

The contrasts I have listed highlight (some would say unfairly accentuate) a number of differences within the broad class of 'cases' that are of interest in law and literature. In setting out the distinctions, I have nevertheless stayed away from a persistent, underlying issue: that of the *mode of representation* of such 'cases'. When we read a case, what exactly is it we are reading? Different ways that 'case material' is presented in published form are not mere stylistic alternatives; they stand in different relation to a fundamental problem in all representation, the problem of claims to truth (or to some other standard of meaningfulness).

What, for example, distinguishes 'reporting' a case from 'depicting', 'narrating', or 'representing' one? And how important is the difference between those alternatives? In (and surrounding) any trial, there is a cascade of different kinds of 'legal discourse': from statutes, indictments, pleadings and oaths; through courtroom cross-examination, witness statements, and sometimes confession; into various kinds of news story, feature, dramatic and fictional account, and more definitive (but still varying) forms of published law report. Each of these 'case' genres may exhibit – indeed is likely to exhibit – a different epistemological commitment. It is therefore important to engage with questions of storytelling and authority in the representation of cases, and to consider what constitutes a 'report'. Within the general concept of reporting identified, it is then important to clarify how the most authoritative vehicle of legal narrative and exposition, the law report, guides case interpretation.

Consider the general notion of a 'report' first. The varying kinds of meaning potential outlined above in relation to 'case' are echoed, if not amplified, when we take into account the written forms in which cases circulate.

The word 'report', as either noun or verb, has a cluster of meanings. We may immediately filter out 'statement of progress at school' ('school report'); and we are also likely to exclude 'job reference'. More relevantly, though, there is the meaning of a 'statement widely made or known', or alternatively a statement 'communicated privately to a particular addressee'. More significant again is the meaning of an 'account prepared for the benefit of others', especially an account that provides information obtained through investigation, such as the 'deliberations of a committee or other body'. 'Report' across these senses has as a core meaning not only that such accounts serve an information-giving purpose but that they aspire to being definitive: a report offers some kind of update, synthesis, or indication of outcome.

Scope for variation in the reporting of legal cases is nevertheless considerable, at least in principle. Representations of a case tell a story of that case: they record it, depict it, describe it or narrate it. In doing so, they frame an open-ended human or social experience that could be seen from more than one point of view. The legal case is given its particular shape not only by imposition of a beginning and an ending, but by the structuring of the intervening narrative in such a way that special attention is given to sequence of events, causation, and responsibility or liability. Point of view is provided by a secondary level of framing, imposed by a shift that takes place from specific actions and events to generic classes of action and event, and from particulars to abstract legal categories and rules.[9] In these respects, law reporting is unlike other kinds of storytelling about law. It makes a stronger claim than that of merely collecting and telling good stories about real people (like a documentary), or narrating the facts of a case and recording the decision made on those facts by the court. A further claim is implied: that the reported decision emerges from and illustrates due process. Law reports are in this respect a canonical instance of the factivity and closure that underpin notions of reporting. In a manner that parallels scientific reporting, they follow procedures aimed at controlling the truth-status of information they present: the evidence they record was tested in court; and statements of points of law are accompanied by doctrines of construction promulgated to guide legal interpretation.[10] Law reporting extends the rigour of the court by carrying over the court's social and epistemological authority into the structure and style of the report on the page.[11] Collectively, these features are what make a law report a report.

It sounds odd, by comparison, to ask the question 'Is this a "report"?' of most literary works. Daniel Defoe's *Journal of the Plague Year* (1722) might be felt to be a report in a sense related to journalistic reporting, or reportage. A 'state of the nation' novel, or political satire, might be viewed as at least figuratively a 'report' on the events or social climate of a given society. But most literary works, including those with legal themes, seem unsuited to the term. Nor is description of literary critical writing as 'reporting' any more intuitive. Terms with less epistemological loading seem preferable, such as review, response, appreciation, or assessment ('analysis' may be closest in meaning to 'report' in a literary context).

Law reports

How do these considerations affect interdisciplinary work in law and literature? The ways in which law reports of cases are interpreted, and how they might be interpreted differently, highlight the interpretive complications that Posner identified as potentially undermining work between the two fields. How far Posner's concerns may be warranted can be illuminated by considering the law report's history, structure and functions.[12]

History

In Britain, the earliest court decisions were stored in the minds of judges and court officials. But there have been what are recognisably law reports from the thirteenth century onwards, growing out of early mediaeval Plea Rolls which recorded basic details of litigation and were kept to establish the rights of the parties as well as to assist enforcement of decisions. During the period between the late thirteenth and mid-sixteenth century, reports take the form of what are now known as the *Year Books*, hand-written first in 'law French' and Latin, then later in English (Harding, 1973: 194–215). The *Year Books* were initially private documents, but were gradually addressed beyond the court and the parties involved to a wider public consisting largely of law students who were less interested in the details of any particular case than in understanding the reasoning applied in it, since this would offer a general picture of the system of law and might also be useful in arguing later cases. Law reports from the mid-sixteenth century are now described, especially after 1578 (the date of Edmund Plowden's *Commentaries*), as 'nominate' reports: commercially published, of variable accuracy, and so-called because they were known by the names of their authors (Plowden himself, Sir Edward Coke, later James Burrow, and others). The nominate reports adopted a more expansive commentary form, elaborating on and interpreting the stages of litigation and decisions handed down. Although these reports circulated widely in a rapidly expanding law profession, there was still nothing resembling a public *system* of law reporting. Over time, however, reports shifted in emphasis from simply recording judicial decisions to reporting arguments as illustration of legal reasoning, inevitably blurring the distinction between a record of particular decisions and a statement of what the law as decreed by judges was. Such reports also became more closely linked to another field of publication: that of collections of reports for several years at a time, condensed and arranged by subject-matter, and known as 'abridgements'.[13] It is only later, during the second half of the eighteenth century, that more precise conventions in reporting were actively sought, for instance as regards practical arrangements for authorised reporters, agreement on which cases to report, and in order to minimise delays in publication.

From the 1860s, the *Law Reports* series conferred greater authority on published reports and incorporated counsels' arguments as well as opinions revised by judges. The second half of the nineteenth century also brought other kinds of standardisation: the *Incorporated Council of Law Reporting for England and Wales* dates from this period, followed by *Weekly Law Reports*, *Times* reports (with antecedents in the earlier *Universal Register*), then later the *All-England Reports*. While in principle any report of a judicial decision could be cited in court, law reporting gradually became a more specialised profession within the Bar; and a procedure of 'exclusive citation', under which preference was given to authorised reports, was adopted and periodically restated.

Following this nineteenth-century period of reforms, English law reports have largely resembled modern reports. Even now, however, in a period of online access to most decisions of courts of record (e.g. via *BAILII*), less than 5 per cent of English cases are reported in an authoritative, published form, with the selection of those cases (out of a vast number that inevitably go unreported) based on commercial as well as legal criteria. Even *Law Reports*, the most official reporting channel and so mouthpiece of legal authority, covers only about 10 per cent of that 'less than 5 per cent' reported overall.

Structure

One important thread in the history of law reporting has been a concern with standardising the conventions that govern the structure of reports as documents. The internal organisation of reports has been gradually adapted to the conditions in which they are used, as well as to the purposes for which they were used in successive periods. During the 20th century, reports were increasingly presented in layouts which facilitate searching, skimming and citation: clearer sign-posting of the sequence of topics; adoption of more restrictive conventions of vocabulary and sentence structure; and more explicit signalling of shifts of speech act (for example from narration of facts, through exposition of legal arguments, to the handing down of a verdict).

Allowing for some variation in different types of publication, the following list indicates how a modern law report sets out its material.

- Names of the parties, court where the case was heard, names of the judges, date
- Catchwords: compiled by the law reporter
- Headnote: summary of the facts of the case, questions of law, decision (in US, known as 'syllabus')
- List of cases cited in judgment
- List of other cases cited in argument
- Details of the proceedings: short history of the case

- Résumé of counsels' arguments
- Judgment: the facts, legal issues, and outcome (in the highest courts this may consist of several opinions, including dissenting opinions)
- Formal order (i.e. outcome, such as 'appeal dismissed').

These largely standardised stages are now effectively conventions of the law reporting genre. Each involves a formulaic mode of expression; and collectively the sections impose a distinct, overall structure (Biber and Conrad, 2009). The reader's attention is managed both synoptically, as he or she takes an overview of the document by flicking (now scrolling) through, and also temporally, as the reader progresses from exposition to opinion to judgment and formal order. With such conventions settled, a normative instructional literature has developed *around* the genre: for law reporters, on how to compose a report; for students, on how to locate cases and efficiently skim, scan and absorb material that conforms to the standardised structure; even for judges' clerks, on how to draft an opinion suitable for reporting.

Function / use

The structure of modern law reports emerged, then, from an iterative historical process of innovation, use and review by producers and users. Specific features evolved through ergonomic adaptation, in order to facilitate a particular approach to reading based on professional requirements.

The guidance that genre features give to reading, however, must be re-activated on each occasion of use. Some practical assistance is given with this by design features: citation conventions, to signal how to find the right report; layout, to assist with consulting an appropriate section in a report while talking at the same time. Other requirements for use are less tied to textual features than to aspects of professional behaviour. Core legal arguments are extracted from the report by means of a process of inference, for example. Two common law procedures that are closely interwoven with the form of the law report, but which are problematic in relation to any idea of the report genre consisting purely of textual features, stand out as in need of comment in this context: the role of the *ratio decidendi* in a legal argument; and the claim of a particular case to constitute a precedent in relation to a subsequent case.[14]

The *ratio* of a case is the point or rule taken to be of legal significance when abstracted from the facts of that case. It is the *ratio* which enables a case to contribute to the series of steps which carry forward legal principles from case to case on the basis of the common law principle of *stare decisis*, or 'decision in accordance with precedent'. The *ratio* cannot, however, be itemised in a list of the sections contained in a report, because it is never directly stated: the *ratio* is not a quotable episode but an inferred construct. It is discovered – or more accurately, worked out – through a specialised practice of reading. Apart from having to be constructed, the *ratio* must also be distinguished from points made by a judge as *obiter dicta* (things said 'in passing'). Such *obiter dicta* comments, which may resemble the *ratio* in making general points but differ from it in status and effect, have only 'persuasive authority'; they do not bind later courts in the way that the *ratio* can. It is the *ratio*, once determined, that serves as the motor of common law precedent. A case submitted as a precedent may be deemed either to be 'in point' (and so apply), or not to apply because the case under consideration is 'distinguished' from it (in that what is presented as the *ratio* of the earlier case does not fit sufficiently when transposed to the facts of the case to which the precedent is claimed to apply). The inferred *ratio* and the legal purpose of observing precedent combine with the textual form of a law report to create an overall common law system of legal proceedings: a system which requires both a hierarchy of courts in which a senior court binds lower courts and, completing the reciprocal influence between textual form and professional practice, a system of accurate law reporting to ensure that citation of any claimed precedent is reliable.

Reading cases: the role of genre

The brief outline I have given of the history, structure and use of law reports will have offered nothing new to the 'ordinary reader' of such reports (i.e. a legal practitioner wishing to cite them in advancing a case, or a law student seeking to understand how cases function alongside statute to clarify the law, and in some circumstances extend it). In interdisciplinary work combining law with expectations of a different field, on the other hand (in this case the field of literary study), such reading conventions may appear specialised, even slightly alien. In law reporting it may be taken for granted that genre conventions 'beyond the page' will be activated when a report is consulted. In a law and literature forum, on the other hand, established strategies for interpreting cases appear less certain, even up for grabs. Instead of being adhered to, 'norm-based' interpretive procedures associated with law reports may be open to interrogation and challenge – or simply ignored.

How far, in such circumstances, are meaningful reading strategies limited to those which take account of procedural expectations associated with the conventions of a document 'on the page'? Exploring this question calls for clarification of how the genre of a document serves as a guide to meaning.

Mostly, genre (of any kind, not only law reports) is described in terms of formal features, especially the conventional structures which are used to construct a complete text within the given genre. Such structures are typically manifest in one-off features that direct the text along a given path so that it achieves its intended purpose through a series of steps or moves. The headings, layout of sections, and progression through different topics culminating in a verdict or decision are genre features of a law report in this sense. Genre features of this structural kind co-occur with other markers, of linguistic register, which show continuous selection between alternative forms that have different connotations but might in other respects communicate the same meaning (Biber and Conrad, 2009: 1–49). In addition, this combination of structural and register features links with genre characteristics at another level, that of audience expectations brought to bear on a text which exhibits such formal features: what the text is likely to be about, how seriously it should be taken, in many cases what kind of pleasure or insight it will offer. There appear, therefore, to be genre-defining features at two levels: a level of linguistic expression; and a level of what might be called inferential modelling, or 'ways of reading'.

In conjunction with these two levels, however, a third, strategic level of interpretation is also important: that of the action-orientation of the interpreter, or practice in which the interpreter is engaged (arguably a different way of describing Posner's wider concept of 'purpose'). At this level, to extend the term 'interpretive community' used by Fish (1981) to indicate social groups of interpreters who follow common interpretive strategies, readers are members of groupings or 'communities' not only in terms of overlapping meanings they are likely to assign but also in sharing a disposition to behave, on reading and interpreting a text, in a particular way (often by performing a text-oriented professional task or duty). Meaning for a lawyer, viewed in this way, is not only unlikely to be the same as for a literary critic; it is also likely to have a different significance in its connection with social action.

A 'community of practice' of this kind (that is, a community organised around common priorities of a profession, such as lawyers or literary critics) is something more than an interpretive community in a purely 'meaning attributing' sense.[15] What makes it something more is the shift of perspective, signified by the term 'practice', from entertaining meanings as cognitive or affective representations to using meanings as a basis for some specialised social or professional conduct.

Interpretive practice, however, like other kinds of social practice, varies and changes. When a new or different interpretive community brings to bear interpretive strategies in attributing meaning to a text that differ from those anticipated in the text's composition, a range of new, 'unprecedented' meanings and kinds of significance are likely to be ascribed.

The interest and value of such new meanings is properly subject to query and contestation. Posner's response to the question of how far license should extend in interpreting legal discourse in alternative ways has been that 'literary' approaches neglect crucial considerations of legal purpose. His test case for this view was that of statutes and constitutions, which, read in a different way, no longer function 'legally', as defining, normative documents. With law reports, following the same reasoning, if a report is removed from its legal moorings then a re-reading of it will similarly fail to recognise the relevant sense of legal purpose. This analogy may be imperfect, however. If a text such as a law report is reinterpreted beyond its customary discourse setting it takes on an interpretive purpose associated with its new setting as well as losing the settled meanings of the interpretive context from which it was taken. What is significant then is not so much what is lost but whether something of value is gained. In Fish's celebrated classroom anecdote of his students who thought the names of 1970s stylisticians on a blackboard were a religious poem, for example, the second class of students were not just 'not stylistics' students but something else: they were would-be interpreters learning how meanings are created from linguistic cues in religious poetry (Fish, 1980).

Law reports, we have seen, follow genre conventions that are normative, embedded in the institutional functioning of law as well as in textual features. To this extent, law reports resemble Posner's statutes and constitutions. But legal cases serve purposes that directive statements do not. They narrate events in a world beyond the courts, in ways that resemble historical narrative and literary writing, especially realist fiction. There are characters, actions and motives drawn from life, overlaid with a fabric of themes, moral contrasts and kinds of significance. Composition of law reports mediates between the referential world of lived experience that can be seen from multiple points of view and a set of imposed categories of legal reasoning, in ways that differ fundamentally from the re-reading of statutes or constitutions. So while it may not be easy to see the purpose of literary re-interpretation of the performative language of a statute or constitution, there may still be value in re-interpreting 'cases', whose narration creates legal and moral contrasts that lead towards judgments based on discourse in court but also have potentially life-changing implications in the extra-discursive world beyond the court.

What makes re-interpretations of cases significant is still a question of purpose, as Posner suggests. What can give value to such new readings, however, is how they revisit facts and circumstances with additional, contextual depth or insight (drawing attention to 'silent' or 'neglected' facts), or how they adopt a fresh perspective (opening up some previously unexplored line of reasoning or teasing out a subtext or hidden meaning). Apparent priorities in the original treatment of a case may be juxtaposed with competing values possibly only touched on in the margins of the proceedings themselves. Such reading is not the stuff of a legal hypothetical, asking whether the case would have been decided differently in a different set of circumstances or at a different date. Subjected to suitable literary re-reading, legal issues may instead be connected to wider questions of ethics, social attitude, or change during the period in which the proceedings took place. Readings along such lines also have scope to reinstate material left out-of-frame when the complex texture of a given social experience was funnelled into a cause of legal action and the proceedings that followed.

Understanding inference and rhetoric

Many of the interpretive techniques deployed in such re-readings have affinities with, and in some cases are directly derived from, specialised kinds of interpretive work developed for reading novels, plays and films (as well as other kinds of textual analysis, including in religious scholarship). Such strategies and methods have been examined in great detail by, among others, the film scholar David Bordwell in his analysis of an 'industry' of interpretation in the humanities (Bordwell, 1989). Bordwell shows how interpreting involves not only problem-solving but also rhetorical expertise, features notably shared with law. At the same time interpretation is also, Bordwell shows, a conventional and to some extent formulaic social activity. To illustrate this conventional aspect, Bordwell identifies and illustrates a series of typical stages in interpreting or re-interpreting a text: explicating what is directly said; selectively assigning general semantic fields, by picking out details and elevating them into contrasts from which more general themes are derived; forming interpretive hypotheses (for instance by assuming that the text will show unity, or will leave its core message unsaid, or will be ironic or exaggerated), then mapping the chosen semantic fields onto the selected hypothesis by means of schemata (which supply evidence, possibly using metaphors and puns to strengthen relevant links); finally, presenting the interpretation in a chosen rhetorical genre, as some form of proof, exemplification of a theory, or moral parable.

The techniques of analysis and persuasion examined in Bordwell's study are recognisable across a range of interpretive fields. What is most striking about them in this context is how they cut across the conventional division between literary criticism and the legal discourse of reported 'cases'. There is no need to illustrate here the many kinds of insightful work that can result. Other chapters in this book amply illustrate the richness of comment and critique that can be achieved. Unfolding in the course of such readings, however, is also a further level of insight: into *how* textual interpretation is made possible by processes of attributing significance to complex kinds of narrative and expository linguistic evidence, from different points of view and for different purposes.

Conclusion

Both 'case' and 'report', I have suggested, are ordinary words whose polysemy complicates interdisciplinary study, while passing largely unnoticed. Exploiting such polysemy, in order to produce insightful, interdisciplinary readings of legal cases, opens up new and potentially important responses to legal topics and themes. But what quickly becomes evident in such work is that 'reading' and 'interpretation' are similarly complex words and concepts.[16] Whereas 'case' and 'report' are words whose polysemy might be viewed as somehow incidental, however, 'reading' and 'interpretation' are foundational terms of art in both literature and law. As with other terms of art, these words call for analysis of the different meanings they can reasonably bear in different contexts, as well as analysis of why other meanings for them appear strained or extraneous. To strengthen understanding of how such terms function in law and literature, and to what effect, reflexiveness and critical interrogation is required of a kind that Posner considered – perhaps oddly, given the centrality of skills of construction in law – merely unlikely to contribute to legal understanding.

Endnotes

1 I am grateful for comments on an earlier draft of this chapter from colleagues at Middlesex University Business School, London, especially Maureen Spencer, Ifan Shepherd, and John Weldon.

2 'Cobuild' is the name of a lexicographical project which results in a range of dictionary and language products, in this context notably the *Collins Unabridged English Dictionary*, based on a 2.5 billion-word database. For a historical account of interaction between various senses of 'case', see the *Oxford English Dictionary* (in which meanings and examples are grouped on historical principles).
3 The personal and social impact of cases is explored by, among others, Brian Simpson in *Leading Cases in the Common Law* (Simpson, 1995). Explaining his choice to excavate the background of cases in the manner of an archaeologist, rather than confining attention to points of legal significance, Simpson describes how most 'case studies' analyse cases 'without anyone knowing or indeed caring who the litigants were, why they litigated, what they were trying to achieve, what they did achieve', and so on (1995: 10). A recent collection in a similar spirit to Simpson, looking at a range of well-known cases across different areas of law, is McDougall (2010).
4 One oddity of cases being known by the names of the parties is that, in Victorian law reporting (if less markedly since), reference to the parties by name *within* a report was minimal. Instead, parties were referred to as 'plaintiff' and 'defendant', commonly without articles, as effectively ciphers in a legally-constituted universe of discourse rather than people whose lives had been disrupted by involvement in a social dispute that had escalated into a legal action. See Ayelet Ben-Yishai, 'Victorian Precedents: narrative form, law reports and *stare decisis*' (Ben-Yishai, 2008: 385, 394).
5 Hence the contrast Simpson draws in his advocacy of a more contextual approach: 'Litigation entails a process of filtering – sometimes pushing and shoving – the messy and untidy business of life into artificial legal categories' (1995: 11). The distinction between two levels (social and legal) has been explored more theoretically in Ronald Dworkin's *Law's Empire* (Dworkin, 1986). Dworkin's first chapter ('What is Law?') reviews established distinctions between facts, legal problems and legal reasoning; the book then develops (as much of Dworkin's more recent work also does) by investigating difficult questions that surface at the legal level, including what makes some cases 'hard cases' that require additional principles of legal reasoning if they are to be settled by something more than judicial discretion.
6 Any number of different novels could be chosen to illustrate different senses of 'case' in literature. Franz Kafka's *The Trial* (*Der Process*, 1925) makes the issue of what constitutes a case peculiarly prominent, but has the complication for English readers of potentially different polysemy (in addition to Kafka's extensive use of metaphor) in the original German. Hardy's *Tess of the D'Urbervilles* was chosen here because the issues were practical ones for the present author in preparing the Penguin student edition of the novel (Durant, 2002).
7 The 'facts' underlying literary interpretation are no less contested than facts in legal cases, either in their detail or even as regards whether they exist at all. Vigorous criticism of the independent existence of 'patterns' in a text as facts can be found in, for example, Stanley Fish's arguments against stylistics in, 'What is stylistics and why are they saying such terrible things about it?' (Fish, 1981).
8 Note, however, that the facts of a case continue to be relevant in assessment of whether an earlier case can properly serve as an analogue to a later case in which it is cited as a possible authority (see discussion below).
9 Ben-Yishai (2008) shows how a range of techniques were employed in law reports of the period to address the challenge of mediating between reference to a world beyond the report itself (as in historical writing, or in realist fiction) and more self-contained reference *within* the legal world of argument. Such techniques (which include widespread use of gerunds – selling, beating, attacking – to denote general classes of event and action in preference to specific actions such as 'A sold to B', 'A attacked B', etc.) are argued to have resulted in an 'anti-narrative' style in Victorian law reporting.

10 See Manchester, Salter, and Moodie (2000). Construction of legal terms is itself monitored and reported as a section in *The Consolidated Index to Leading Law Reports* (published by the Incorporated Council of Law Reporting for England and Wales), also known as the Red Book, and in supplements to it (the Pink books); these indices cite cases during a given year that include judicial comment on the term in question.

11 Ben-Yishai (2008) traces a further feature of law reports during the Victorian period: their adoption of a style with an absent narrator, in contrast with earlier 'nominate' reports of writers such as Coke and Plowden, in which the presence of a learned author was acknowledged, even accentuated.

12 The outline which follows is bare summary. Modern law reporting is dealt with in most guides to legal research; see for example Clinch (2010), Knowles (2009). An accessible history of common law procedures is Harding (1973). Early cases collected as the *English Reports* (with over 100,000 cases reported between 1220 and 1873) have been reprinted by the Selden Society and in the Rolls series, and are also available online through providers such as Heinonline and Justis. Examples of contemporary reporting can be accessed by means of services including Westlaw, Lexis Library and BAILII (British and Irish Legal Information Institute), as well as, for relevant cases, on the website of The Supreme Court (from 2009) and for HL decisions pre-2009 on the House of Lords website. For context and background to law reporting, see the ICLR website.

13 On abridgements, including especially the influence of Sir Anthony Fitzherbert's *Grand Abridgement* (1516), see Harding (1973: 198–9).

14 More detailed discussion of the *ratio decidendi* in a case and the operation of precedent in UK law, linked to analysis of a series of illustrative cases, can be found in Manchester, Salter and Moodie (2000). For an introduction to the relevant history, see Harding (1973). More theoretical discussion of the interaction between *ratio* and precedent can be found in legal-philosophical essays collected in Goldstein (1987). The first two chapters of this volume (by Gerald Postema and by Jim Evans) provide detailed historical background, both about the origins of common law precedent and about arguments over its operation and status during the nineteenth century.

15 The term 'community of practice' is used here without the emphasis on 'group learning' stressed in Wenger (1998).

16 A recent analysis of meaning and interpretation in relation to legal language is Hutton (2009); my own recent investigation of issues raised by 'interpretation', with particular reference to media law and regulation, is Durant (2010).

Bibliography

Barendt, E. and Hitchens, L. (2000) *Media Law: Cases and Materials*, London: Pearson.

Ben-Yishai, A. (2008) 'Victorian Precedents: narrative form, law reports and *stare decisis*', *Law, Culture, and the Humanities*, 4: 382–402.

Biber, D. and Conrad, S. (2009) *Register, Genre, and Style*, Cambridge: Cambridge University Press.

Bordwell, D. (1989) *Making Meaning: Inference and Rhetoric in the Interpretation of Cinema*, Cambridge, MA: Harvard University Press.

Clinch, P. (2010) *Legal Research: a Practitioner's Handbook*, London: Wildy, Simmonds and Hill Publishing.

Cornish, W. (2006) *Cases and Materials on Intellectual Property*, 5th edition, London: Sweet and Maxwell.

Draper, R.P. (ed.) (1991) *Thomas Hardy: the Tragic Novels (Casebook)*, Basingstoke: Palgrave.

Durant, A. (ed.) (2002) *Thomas Hardy's Tess of the D'Urbervilles*, Penguin Student Edition, Harmondsworth: Penguin.

Durant, A. (2010) *Meaning in the Media: Discourse, Controversy and Debate*, Cambridge: Cambridge University Press.
Dworkin, R. (1986) *Law's Empire*, London: Fontana.
Eliot, T.S. (1922) [1919] 'Tradition and the Individual Talent', in *The Sacred Wood: Essays on Poetry and Criticism*, London: Faber.
Fish, S. (1980) *Is There a Text in this Class: the Authority of Interpretive Communities*, Cambridge. MA: Harvard University Press.
Fish, S. (1981) [1973] 'What is stylistics and why are they saying such terrible things about it?' in Freeman, D. (ed.), *Essays in Modern Stylistics*, London: Methuen.
Goldstein, L. (ed.) (1987), *Precedent in Law*, Oxford: Clarendon Press.
Harding, A. (1973) *A Social History of English Law*, Gloucester, MA: Peter Smith.
Hutton, C. (2009) *Language, Meaning and the Law*, Edinburgh: Edinburgh University Press.
Incorporated Council of Law Reporting for England and Wales, *Consolidated Index to Leading Law Reports* ('the Red Book').
Knowles, J. (2009) *Effective Legal Research*, London: Sweet and Maxwell.
McDougall, I. (ed.) (2010) *Cases that Changed our Lives*, London: Butterworths Law.
Manchester, C., Salter, D. and Moodie, P. (2000) *Exploring the Law: the Dynamics of Precedent and Statutory Interpretation*, 2nd edition, London: Sweet and Maxwell.
Posner, R. (1998) *Law and Literature*, 2nd edition, Cambridge, MA: Harvard University Press.
Simpson, A.W.B. (1995) *Leading Cases in the Common Law*, Oxford: Clarendon Press.
Wenger, E. (1998) *Communities of Practice: Learning, Meaning, and Identity*, Cambridge: Cambridge University Press.
Widdowson, P. (ed.) (1993), *Tess of the D'Urbervilles (New Casebook)*, Basingstoke: Palgrave.

Chapter 2

'I crave the law'
Salomon v Salomon, uncanny personhood and the Jews[1]

Christopher Hutton

The House of Lords judgment in *Salomon v A. Salomon & Co Ltd* (1897) is one of the most famous decisions in English law. 'Great cases' of the stature of *Salomon* have a special kind of authority, which has led them to be dubbed 'superprecedents'.[2] A superprecedent demonstrates extraordinary generative power, and can be read as a microcosm of compressed meanings, compacted conflicts, and historical and social values. Under the flag of *Salomon*, modern company law has created beings of immense power and scope, potentially immortal, holding perpetual symbols in the form of trademarks, yet enjoying many of the rights and privileges of natural persons. But the canonical status of a superprecedent, its role as an unmovable anchor to an entire tradition of legal decisions and their associated social practices, requires that it be left undisturbed, and as a consequence that it be systematically 'underread'. *Salomon* is seldom analyzed by economic or social historians, nor is it discussed in works of jurisprudence and legal theory. Company law scarcely figures in the writings of Marxist and other left-critical theorists of law,[3] and the case has the kind of paradoxical invisibility that true celebrity can endow.

In their study of the reception of *Lawrence v Fox* (1859), an American case about the third-party privity in relation to a debt, Hoeflich and Perelmutter show how it was not until the 1960s and 1970s that it became a leading case 'in the full sense of that phrase' (1988: 734). In its time, *Salomon* was seen as a significant decision, understood primarily as clarifying the law in relation to so-called 'one-man companies'. Yet *Salomon* has become a cornerstone in the development of the global capitalist system (McQueen 2009: 318).[4] Talk in the 1970s and 1980s of the 'gradual decline' in the importance of this case and of the rise of the social and 'soulful' corporation run as part of a benevolently managerial and technocratic social order (Stanley 1988: 100) proved premature[5] as deregulation, neo-liberalism and increasingly abstract forms of value took hold in the world's largest economies (Ireland 1999: 54).

The *Salomon* decision represented a crucial step in the creation of an autonomous company law, independent of partnership law (Ireland 1999). It affirmed that the company form would be available to businesses of very different kinds and scales, leading to the tension between legal and economic form, which persists to this day in company law. *Salomon* was a formalistic judgment, since it recognized no restraint on the application of a registration procedure beyond conformity with the requirements of that procedure itself as laid down by Parliament: 'the motives of those who took part in the promotion of the company are absolutely irrelevant in discussing what those rights and liabilities are' (per Lord Halsbury, at p. 30). Indeed, the early reception of this case was often in terms of statutory interpretation.[6]

This chapter seeks to 'overread' the *Salomon* case, in order to contextualize it in nineteenth century debates about the company form and representations of the uncanny personhood of both companies and Jews. It argues that *Salomon* is in important senses a 'Jewish case', and that it reflects profound ambivalence within Western culture, as part of its Christian heritage, about the line between business morality and 'excess' and the tangled 'jurisprudence of greed' (Posner 2003).[7]

Salomon as the 'one-man company' case

The rule in *Salomon* is today understood in fundamental, one might say, ontological terms. In Lord Macnaghten's famous words (*Salomon v A. Salomon & Co Ltd* 1897, at 51):

> The company is at law a different person from subscribers to the Memorandum; and, though it may be that after incorporation the business is precisely the same as it was before, and the same persons managers, and the same hands received the profits, the company is not in law the agent of the subscribers or trustee for them. Nor are the subscribers, as members, liable in any shape or form, except to the extent and in the manner provided by the Act.

For its contemporaries, however, the case was not about legal personality *per se*. It was the 'one-man company' case, in that it concerned the limited liability status of a business owned and managed by a single individual prior to incorporation (see [Comment] 1896, 1897). As Lindley LJ noted in the Court of Appeal (*Salomon v A. Salomon & Co Ltd* 1895, at 336): 'Such companies were unheard of until a comparatively recent period, but have been very common of late years'. At the time of the *Salomon* case, it was not fully evident that the legal form of the company was open to a business effectively run by one individual, given that in such enterprises there was no real 'separation of ownership and control', to use a phrase made famous by Berle and Means ([1932] 1967).

Prior to the Joint Stock Companies Act of 1844, a parliamentary charter was required to set up a company. The limited liability of these companies was only recognized by the Limited Liability Act of 1855, then affirmed by the Joint Stock Companies Act of 1856. The first Companies Act, a consolidating measure, was passed in 1862. The 'great monomania' (Spearman and Farries 1865: 5) for the company in the mid-nineteenth century raised considerable public disquiet. Hostility to the company form can be traced back much further: the joint-stock company was a 'Society of Artificers, who blow the Stock up and down, as best suits their design of enriching themselves by the ruin of others' (White 1691: 5; Poovey 2008: 82). Adam Smith's famous remarks in the *Wealth of Nations* ([1776] 2009: 439) on Joint Stock Companies still resonate:

> The directors of such companies, [. . .] being the managers rather of other people's money than of their own, it cannot well be expected that they should watch over it with the same anxious vigilance with which the partners in a private copartnery [partnership] frequently watch over their own. [. . .] Negligence and profusion, therefore, must always prevail, more or less, in the management of the affairs of such a company.

One moral principle that has underlain opposition to limited liability and corporate personality is that those who stand to profit individually should also bear their individual share of the potential liability.[8] The *New York Times* noted that the lower courts had delivered 'actual and substantial justice [. . .] without regard to any narrow technicalities', but the House of Lords threatened to turn limited liability under English law into 'unlimited authority to cheat'.[9] However, the liberal-utilitarian view was that limited liability was a means of unleashing economic creativity and entrepreneurial energy (Rajak 2008: 5), a way to turn what was referred to as 'the magic key of limited liability' (Manson 1895: 188).

The case itself

Mr Salomon incorporated his business in 1892 as a limited liability company under the Companies Act of 1862, and in the process issued a secured debt or debenture to himself of £10,000. Though it has been argued that the price paid by Salomon & Co Ltd to Aron Salomon for the company was high (£39,000), a price of course determined by its managing director, Mr Aron Salomon, Salomon paid off all the creditors of the sole trader business prior to incorporation (Dignam and Lowry 2009: 18). The trustee for the new company was Adolph Anholt, Salomon's wife's nephew (Johnson 2010: 153). In a recent work Salomon is called an 'unsavoury leather merchant' (Micklethwait and Wooldridge 2003: 52), but there is no evidence that he engaged in any dishonest practice. The previously profitable company had been hit by labour unrest and strikes in the boot trade (Johnson 2010: 155). Even though the valuation of the company was inflated, 'the creditors at the time of liquidation had only ever dealt with the business as company', and Salomon transferred the debenture to a Mr Broderip in exchange for £5,000 to be injected into the ailing business (Dignam and Lowry 2009: 22).[10] The question to be determined was whether, on dissolution, the debt owed by the company to Mr Salomon could be given precedence over debts owed to other creditors. The company, A. Salomon & Co Ltd, and the person, Mr Aron Salomon, were distinct entities in law, yet the company was his creation and, it was argued, entirely subject to his control. The other shareholders were family members who held only one share each, with the balance of the 20,007 shares being held by Mr Salomon himself. Although A. Salomon & Co Ltd was registered and formed entirely in accordance with the required formalities, with its seven members or shareholders, it was felt by many observers to be an abuse of the company form.

In the Divisional Court, Vaughan Williams J. found that Mr Salomon was personally liable for the debts of the company, on the basis that the company was his agent or 'mere nominee' (at 229).[11] The fact that the agent in this case was a company and not a person made no difference to the nature of the relationship between the agent (the company, A. Salomon & Co Ltd) and the principal (Mr Aron Salomon). Just as an individual agent or servant would have called on the principal to meet business obligations that had arisen under the principal's direct control, so the company could also call on the person running it to make good its debts. The relationship of agency between the company and its managing director made Mr Salomon personally liable. Though there was no question of fraud, the price which had been paid for the company was 'exorbitant' and there must have been 'an implied agreement by him to indemnify the company' (at 331).

In *Salomon v A. Salomon & Co Ltd* (1895), the Court of Appeal went further both legally and rhetorically, concluding that Mr Salomon's wife and children held their shares on trust for him, and that the company was a trustee for Mr Salomon. The underlying ('beneficial' or 'equitable') ownership remained with Mr Salomon. Since Mr Salomon was in this sense the real owner, he, rather than the company or its shareholders as a whole, stood to benefit as an individual from its operations. By the same reasoning he was also personally liable to indemnify the company for its debts. In the judgment, a whole semantic field of epithets and allegations, including that the company was a 'fraud on the creditors' (at 328), were directed at Mr Salomon. For Lindley LJ, the company, was a corporation 'created for an illegitimate purpose' (at 337), it was 'a trustee improperly brought into existence' which Salomon used 'to screen himself from liability' (at 338). Companies formed in this manner were 'mere devices'; Salomon had laid a 'trap' for the creditors; he and his advisors were 'evidently very shrewd people'; such schemes did 'infinite mischief', bringing the statute into 'disrepute', by 'perverting its legitimate use'. The sale of the business was a 'mere sham'. The 'scheme' was 'a device to defraud creditors' (at 339). The shareholders merely assisted in the 'scheme' or 'mere scheme', which was 'contrary to the true intent' of the statute (at 340). In the judgment of Lopes LJ, the company's incorporation was described as 'in every respect perfect' but it was a 'mere *nominis umbra*', a 'cover' for the sole-trader business. To allow this 'scheme' to succeed would be 'lamentable'; it would be to authorize a 'perversion' of the Joint Stock Companies Act (at 341). In so doing the court would be 'giving vitality to that which is myth and a fiction' (at 341); this 'ingenious device' meant that the company would 'consist of one substantial person and six mere dummies' who had no 'real interest in the company' (at 341); the Act contemplated seven independent members with 'a mind and a will of their own', rather than being the 'puppets' of one individual (at 341). It would be a 'scandal' if this state of affairs were legalized (at 341). The sale was a 'fiction' and therefore 'invalid'; the arrangements were 'merely devices to enable him to carry on business in the name of the company with limited liability' (at 341). Lopes LJ even expressed the view that the certificate of incorporation might be repealed. In concurring, Kay LJ noted that Salomon 'must have had careful advice' (at 342); this was a 'pretended association' (at 345); the sale of the company was an 'utter fiction' (at 345); the wife and children 'were mere trustees' (at 347). The fact that Salomon had sent up his company in a 'perfect' and 'faultless' manner so as to comply with the law was repeatedly held up as proof of a devious and scheming plot.[12]

Following the Court of Appeal's tongue-lashing of his client, Salomon's solicitor, Ralph Raphael, wrote to the *Financial Times* expressing dismay at the allegations of dishonest dealing by his client:

> The mere perusal of the liquidator's evidence shows clearly that instead of Mr Salomon having gained anything by the transaction, he has been deprived of what was admitted to be a valuable business, and £5,000 which he borrowed from Mr Broderip and lent to the company; also £2,000 which he and his own family advanced to the company. The result of all this has been the utter ruin of Mr Salomon, and he is now left penniless.[13]

The *Financial Times* itself had been following the case closely. In an initial report it had spoken of a 'Chinese puzzle in the boot trade', implying that the network of 'complicated' family and business interests involved raised questions which the creditors would want answering.[14] However, subsequent pieces affirmed Mr Salomon's sound trade reputation. The paper cast doubt on the reasoning which had led the lower courts to conclude that the board was merely the passive instrument of Salomon's will:

> We must confess to extreme difficulty in following this line of argument. To the lay mind it appears much more probable that a member of the family would object to anything he thought wrong in the conduct of the business than an employee who had been made a present of shares – and was liable to dismissal.[15]

The widely held assumption that A. Salomon & Co Ltd was in fact, if not in law, a 'one-man company' rests on a particular reading of the family's internal relations, in particular Salomon's presumed status as unchallenged patriarch. The family has been presumed to be transparently the creature of Salomon's will, and this has warranted a parallel reading of the company. However, Salomon gave pressure from his sons as one of his reasons for incorporation: 'They troubled me all the while' (Rubin 1983). This alternative reading makes Salomon more Lear than Shylock, a father who wished 'To shake all cares and business from our age;

conferring them on younger strengths, while we unburthen'd crawl toward death' (*King Lear*, Act I: I). Taking this further, one scholar has sought to write Salomon's wife, Mrs Schoontje Salomon, and her fragile legal subjecthood, back into the story (Spender 1999: 240):

> The case of *Salomon v Salomon & Co Ltd* was the first significant recognition by the law of a company owned by a family. Yet the participation of the family was ignored. Aron Salomon was identified as the only human legal subject and the issue for consideration by the Court of Appeal, House of Lords and one hundred years of legal scholars was whether legal personality could be conferred upon the 'one person company'.

The House of Lords unanimously reversed, on the simple basis that the company had been created according to the formal legal requirements. In fact, both lower court judgments logically rested on the principle of legal personality, since the company was in the one case determined to be the agent of Salomon, and, in the second, his trustee (Rajak 2008: 10). There was nothing in the Act that prohibited the kind of arrangement set up by Mr Salomon, and there was no fraud. Either the company existed in law or it did not. If it did exist as a legal entity – and there were no principled grounds for denying that it did – then the Act applied in a straightforward manner. The alternative was to leave the law in a state of confusion, with no clear criteria for distinguishing between a properly formed company and a fraudulent sham. The decision was welcomed by *The Times* for removing 'obscurity' from the legal rules:

> Whether the plaintiff – who it will be noted, sued in the House of Lords in *forma pauperis* – will be entirely satisfied with the net result is open to doubt. He may feel a little like a patient who, submitting under high surgical advice to an amputation of both legs, is then told on still higher authority that he ought to have lost only one, and at last is informed on the highest authority of all that he need never have lost either.[16]

Its massive historical reputation notwithstanding, one could define the *ratio* of *Salomon* in extremely narrow terms, as a decision in relation to an incorporated 'one-man' company, where the 'one-man' had caused himself to be issued a debenture in the form of a floating charge, thereby securing a place at the head of the queue of creditors – 'however objectionable this may be' (Lindley and Lindley 1902: 305).[17] The *New York Times* was particularly exercised about the lack of a public register for debentures of the kind Salomon was holding.[18] As Lord Macnaghten had noted in his judgment: 'Everybody knows that when there is a winding-up debenture-holders generally step in and sweep off everything; and a great scandal it is' (at 53). Following the *Salomon* decision 'the virtual owner of the business cannot be made liable for debts contracted after its formation' (Lindley and Lindley 1902: 160).[19]

Aron Salomon as Shylock

One intriguing aspect of the *Salomon* case is its place in the social and economic history of Jews in Britain. Aron Salomon had been born in Prussia around 1837, migrating to England in the late 1850s (Spender 1999: 219). He was represented by the well-known Jewish solicitor Ralph Raphael. Other parties in the case with Jewish background or heritage were the Liberal politician and barrister Arthur Cohen (1830–1914), born in Frankfurt-am-Main, who appeared for Salomon in the first appeal; Henry Charles Lopes (1828–1899), Lopes LJ of the Court of Appeal, whose family were Sephardic Jews by origin, though now converted to Christianity; Lord Herschell of the House of Lords (Farrer Herschell, 1st Baron Herschell, 1837–1899), whose father, born in Prussian Poland, had likewise converted from Judaism to Christianity. At the time of the *Salomon* case the Dreyfus affair was in full swing in France; George Du Maurier's novel, *Trilby* (1894), featuring an evil Jewish hypnotist Svengali, was a bestseller in Britain.

Aron Salomon, the Jewish immigrant, the outsider, came before the law in relation to a debt. He sought his literal, legal rights, that is, recognition of the simple fact that he had formed his company in strict accord with the law, and affirmation that the debt he was owed by the company, the corporate entity, was indeed owed to him as a private person. In the end, reduced to the status of a pauper and the target of vituperation from the Court of Appeal, Salomon won in the House of Lords. Lord Macnaghten commented: 'I cannot help thinking that the appellant, Aron Salomon, has been dealt with somewhat hardly in this case' (at 47). Salomon died of a stroke six months after the judgment, in May 1897, though the company that bore his name survived until 1907 (Rubin 1983: 120).

When Shylock declares: 'My deeds upon my head! I crave the law, the penalty and forfeit of my bond' (*Merchant of Venice*, Act IV: I), his craving is for an impersonal law, one with the authority to override the networks of interpersonal relations, insider norms, and hostility to Jews that dominate Venetian life. The law that he seeks is not a law of mercy and compassion. For outsiders, a legal system built on such emotions must inevitably be dominated by discretion and favour. Shylock craves the law and his rights under the contract much more than he craves money itself; he denies that he is answerable to logic, reason or even self-interest in his pursuit of justice. But in the end the law takes his literalism and legalism, and destroys him with it.

Literalism and legalism, long associated with Jews and Judaism,[20] have often been set against a Christian morality which defines itself 'the quality of mercy' or in the avowal that 'the letter killeth, but the spirit giveth life' (2 Corinthians 3:6). The trial scene in the *Merchant of Venice*, rather than being concerned with the clash of law and equity,[21] might be better understood as a confrontation between Christian and Jewish conceptions of law, justice and mercy, though of course both conceptions are defined from the Christian point of view.

Shylock asserts the bodily naturalness of the Jew, against an understanding of Jews as 'uncanny' beings, as strangers to the natural-cosmological order.

Personhood is very much at issue in one of the play's iconic speeches: 'I am a Jew. Hath not a Jew eyes? Hath not a Jew hands?' (Act III: I). In the context of the play, the insistence on revenge places Shylock outside a moral order which emphasizes norms of mercy and forgiveness. The drama that plays out pits a Christian evocation of the morality of mercy against a monstrous, artificial Other consumed by desire for law. The Otherness of the Jew is identified with literalism, legalism and unnatural, uncanny personhood.

In modernity, Jews are profoundly identified with both law and capitalism.[22] The idea that modern capitalism was founded on forms of exchange that ultimately reduced everything to monetary relationships was shared by a range of nineteenth-century social critics, from the radical to the conservative. Carlyle spoke of 'Cash Payment the sole nexus; and there are so many things which cash will not pay! Cash is a great miracle; yet it has not all power in Heaven, nor even on Earth' (Carlyle 1858: 41). This nexus, and the alienation which it represented, was repeatedly associated with Jews in philosophy, literature and popular culture. One powerful and controversial commentary on this process was the famous essay by Karl Marx, 'On the Jewish Question' ([1844] 1967), a polemic against Bruno Bauer (1809–1882). Rejecting Bauer's notion that the emancipation of the Jews must require the renunciation of their religious faith, Marx argues that a more profound liberation is at stake. He depicts the Jews and Judaism as the creation of civil society: 'Out of its own entrails, civil society continually produces the Jew' (Marx 1967: 245), though 'Christianity arose out of Judaism' but it has 'again dissolved itself into Judaism' (Marx 1967: 247). But it is the Jewish spirit that underlies modern capitalist society. The 'practical need' and 'egoism' that underlies Judaism now becomes the norm of modern civil society, and 'externalized man and nature' have been converted into 'alienable and saleable objects subservient to egoistic need' (Marx 1967: 247). The essay elevates Jews to a centrally symbolic point in modern capitalism (Marx 1967: 245–6):

> Money is the jealous god of Israel before whom no other god may exist. Money degrades all the gods of mankind – and converts them into commodities. Money is the general, self-sufficient *value* of everything. Hence it has robbed the whole world, the human world as well as nature, of its proper worth. Money is the alienated essence of man's labor and life, and this alien essence dominates him as he worships it. The god of the Jews has become secularized and has become the god of the world.

At the heart of the essay was the notion that the political and social emancipation of the Jews involved an inversion: Christians become Judaized in a mercantile modernity. The essay ends with the paradox that '[t]he social emancipation of the Jew is the emancipation of society from Judaism' (1967: 248).

For the philosopher Georg Simmel (1858–1918), while his analysis differs from Marx in important respects, the rise of money as a universal, mobile measure of value also characterizes modernity: 'money symbolizes the fluctuating relationship of all values by being its one indifferent exception' (Morris-Reich 2003: 131; Simmel 1900). Jews, previously distinguished by their role as traders and mobile strangers, become typical for the universal alienation of modern money-based societies in which in a sense everyone is a stranger, and relationships are primarily mediated by 'objective' money values (Morris-Reich 2003: 135). Werner Sombart (1863–1941), the theorist of capitalism, understood Jews as being originally a people of the desert, a nomadic, Oriental people, for whom exile and wandering became a form of selection (*Auslese*) (Sombart 1911: 415). Nomadism ultimately gave rise to capitalism and, given that the modern city was 'the direct continuation of the desert' (Sombart 1911: 415), it was a natural environment for the adaptable and mobile Jews (Sombart 1911: 240):

> Money is just as lacking in concreteness as the land from which the Jews came; money is only mass, only amount, like the flock; it is fleeting like the wanderer; it is nowhere rooted in fruitful soil like flowers or trees. Their continual preoccupation with money drove the Jews away continually from a qualitative, natural view of the world and inclined all their senses towards quantitative and abstract conceptions and judgments.

Jews and the modern company

Through the nineteenth century, public debate reflected rising concern about what has been termed 'rising middle class criminality' in relation to the corporate form (Sindall 1990: 281; McQueen 2009: 233) and the various speculative panics and manias associated with it (Anon 1865b: 166). There was a sense that society was being driven by increasingly abstract forms of economic value, by what was termed 'the spiritual or ethereal nature of stock or capital' ([TCC] 1867: 133), and that it was becoming dominated by powerful corporate beings: 'Is it an evil or a good thing that individuality seems to be dying out among us?' (Anon 1865b: 166). For some theorists, by contrast, the rise of the company represented an opportunity for greater social and economic justice, in that the joint-stock company offered a model for corporate socialism. Society would undergo a 'joint-stock modification', and become 'one great joint-stock company, composed of an indefinite number of smaller companies, all laboring, producing, and exchanging with each other on terms of the most perfect equality' (Bray 1839: 168, 170; Gray 1946: 283–8).

Yet popular culture was sceptical of the morality of the corporate form, and of the legal personality which accompanied it. Texts like *The Bubbles of Finance* were intended as warnings for the unwary (Anon 1865a). The uncannily impersonal personality of the company form lent itself to satirical literary treatment, as in Edward P. Rowsell's *The Autobiography of a Joint-Stock Company* (1861). There the narrator's father sets up a joint-stock company with the help of a lawyer, Mr Sparkle (arguably a name suggestive of Jewish origins), and with the obligatory baronet, Sir Willoughby Wiggs, as its proposed chairman. The company is tied in spirit to the newly born son, and the father believes 'a mysterious connection or sympathy' existed between them (Rowsell 1861: 79). Rather than 'a harmless but singular hallucination', this connection turns out to be real (Rowsell 1861: 79):

> The company throve and I throve. I sickened and the company sickened. I am dying and the company is winding up. My father was right, I repeat. The company had a spirit. I was that spirit.

The scheme involves setting up 'The Saving Laundresses' Mutual Benefit and General Elevation and Enlightenment Society'. Once the company is set up as 'the inhabitant of a splendid suite of offices', the narrative voice becomes a fusion of that of the child and the company (1861: 128):

> The reader will observe that I am now speaking, as I have a right to speak, in view of that mysterious connection which my father, from the first, believed in, and which time has proved to exist, between me and the institution, the idea which entered my parent's brain as I entered the world.

Both baby and company acquire 'an appearance of vitality' (1861: 129), even though the scheme is a fraud, like many a 'pigmy imposter' before and after, whose 'beauty and vitality' hides a lack of true 'value'. The child dies at the moment the fraudulent enterprise is wound up (1861: 183).

Samuel Warren's economic novel, *Ten Thousand A-Year*, depicts enthusiasm for the joint-stock company as 'mercantile madness' and a 'monstrous passion' (1841, III: 106).[23] There are a number of anti-Semitic asides in this work, including a reference to 'the validity of the bond held by the infuriate and inexorable Jew' who arrests the character Mr Tag-rag (1841, III: 336–7), and a description of 'a little Jew Attorney in Chancery Lane' of Swindle Shark 'into whose office (with a due understanding of the division of profits) the dirtier work of Quirk, Gammon and Snap was swept' (1841, II: 227). In Laurence Oliphant's short fiction, also with the title 'The Autobiography of a Joint Stock Company, Limited' ([1876] 1882), the company similarly acquired a confessional voice. It is a gloomy observer of the follies and frauds that are perpetuated in its name.[24] The text is a didactic warning about the dangers of investing in the joint-stock company, though the company does not paint an entirely bleak picture of the legal form and of human nature in general (1882: 107):

> I may yet hope that a process of natural selection is in progress, and that joint-stock companies, like the human race, are to rise into new and better conditions through the 'survival of the fittest'.

The financing for the company is provided by a German Jew named 'Mire', who with Mr Sarmist (who has 'a seedy-looking clerk with a hooked nose', 1882: 136–7), ends up profiting from its demise. The text lays out how the fraud works, with the overcapitalization of the company, and the attendant financial jargon: 'In the particular instance you are investigating, the Jew and the Christian each stole half of this amount, which rightfully belonged to my shareholders' (1882: 140).

In Gilbert and Sullivan's *Gondoliers* (which premiered in 1889), the Duke of Plaza-Toro seeks a solution to his financial woes by turning himself into a limited company, echoing the way in which aristocratic titles were traded for positions in the new speculative economy (Act I, p. 8):

> CASILDA (their daughter) I, the Queen of Barataria! But I've nothing to wear! We are practically penniless!
> DUKE That point has not escaped me. Although I am unhappily in straitened circumstances at present, my social influence is something enormous; and a Company, to be called the Duke of Plaza-Toro, Limited, is in course of formation to work me. An influential directorate has been secured, and I shall myself join the Board after allotment.
> CASILDA Am I to understand that the Queen of Barataria may be called upon at any time to witness her honoured sire in process of liquidation?
> DUCHESS The speculation is not exempt from that drawback. If your father should stop, it will, of course, be necessary to wind him up.[25]

On April 3, 1899, the *Daily Mail and Empire* reported that an aristocratic couple had formed themselves into a Stock Company: 'The Warwicks "float" themselves on London Exchange: Shares Eagerly Taken Up. [. . .] Thus Gilbert's fantastic joke of the Duke of Plaza Toro, Ltd, in his opera the "Gondoliers", has been realised by this remarkable couple.'

A further Gilbert and Sullivan text, *Utopia Ltd or The Flowers of Progress* (first performed in 1893), dealt with the company form in the context of the British Empire. The monarch of the South Sea island of Utopia, King Paramount, is seeking to emulate British forms and manners: 'His Majesty, in his despotic acquiescence with the emphatic wish of his people, has ordered that the Utopian language shall be banished from his court, and that all communications shall henceforward be made in the English language [. . .]' (Act 1, p. 2).[26] At the opening of the play his daughter has just returned from Girton College Cambridge, bringing with her six British wise men, known as the 'flowers of progress', to assist in the civilizing mission. Among the six advisors is a company promoter with the name of Goldbury, who is describing as providing speculators 'with financial leaven' (Act I, p. 35). The new managerial slogan for the colony is 'companification' (Act I, p. 36).[27] Seeking radical reform, the King accepts Goldbury's proposal to turn the entire colony of Utopia itself into a limited company for which as Goldbury explains (Act 1, p. 38): 'Some seven men form an Association, (If possible, all Peers and Baronets)', and he explains how they can manipulate the value of the company to yield maximum profit for themselves. The name 'Goldbury' clearly is intended to suggest a Jewish identity.

Contemporary novels such as Anthony Trollope's *The Way We Live Now* (1875) and George Eliot's *Daniel Deronda* (1876) highlighted the tensions and ambivalences surrounding the increasing presence of Jews in the fabric of British life. In *The Way We Live Now*, one sub-plot concerns the increasingly dismal marriage prospects of Georgiana Longstaffe. Eventually she announces her intention to marry the Jewish banker Ezekiel Brehgert, who is described by both the narrator and various characters in unflattering physical terms, as 'fat and greasy'. Reflecting on the possible match, with all its drawbacks and prospect of a social fall from grace, Georgiana ruminates on the identity of her proposed husband, and the marriages of her acquaintance Julia and others which increasingly involve 'decent people' marrying Jews (1875: 490–1):[28]

> The man was absolutely a Jew, – not a Jew that had been, as to whom there might possibly be a doubt whether he or his father or his grandfather had been the last Jew of the family, but a Jew that was. So was Goldsheiner a Jew, whom Lady Julia Stuart had married [. . .] Though she hardly knew how to explain the matter even to herself, she was sure that there was at present a general heaving-up of society on this matter, and a change in progress which would soon make it a matter of indifference whether anybody was Jew or Christian.

Georgiana's parents are furious at the plan, her mother describing Jews as an 'accursed race', '[s]cattered all over the world, so that nobody knows who anybody is'. Georgiana retorts: 'One of the greatest judges in the land is a Jew' (1875: 635). Following a subtly depicted exchange of letters the marriage plans come to nothing, but Brehgert emerges as honest and straightforward.

Trollope's Britain is one of markets: intersecting exchange systems of political, financial, literary, and sexual-matrimonial value in which the declining stability of landed income is juxtaposed to mobility of speculative capital. At the centre of this new symbolic order, this new 'way we live now', are Jews. Their very access to these markets is a sign of new forms of social mobility, the economic importance of migrants, and the decline of a land-based economy with its wealth passed on through family lineages. The ethnicity of the financier at the heart of the novel, Augustus Melmotte, is never directly specified, though the strong implication is that he is Jewish. Trollope directs his cynical eye at the manipulation involved in Melmotte's Joint Stock Company, the Great South Central Pacific and Mexican Railway. For the object of the company is 'not to make a railway' but 'to float a company', so that vast fortunes were to be made out of the enterprise 'before a spadeful of earth had been moved' (1875: 70).

In an important sense Melmotte's identity is arguably 'post-ethnicity', in that Trollope's target is not the association of Jews and capitalism – greed is fairly evenly distributed among the characters of the novel – but rather the assimilation of both Jews and non-Jews into a financial system based on speculation, corruption and alienation from true value, a process reflecting the inability of the land economy and the landed classes to sustain themselves. Jews by their mobility, both in geographical and class terms, are at the heart of the 'way we live now', as economic values are alienated from cultural traditions and abstracted from their rootedness in the practical economy of need and use. Value is now determined in a mobile social market where symbolic currencies of different kinds are interchangeable and therefore available for exchange.

Conclusion

Under the flag of *Salomon*, modern company law has institutionalized a very strong presumption against 'lifting the veil of incorporation' in order to search for the corporate conscience within the company machinery. Formalism has also implied acceptance of the amoral struggle for survival in the so-called 'free market' or corporate ecosystem. The modern company has neither a soul nor a body, 'No soul to damn: no body to kick',[29] yet it has generative power, the traditional rule in corporations law that 'one corporation cannot make another' notwithstanding (Shepheard 1659: 112).[30] *Salomon*, the 'one-man company' case, has been transformed into a nearly all-powerful trump-card, a warrant for the exploitation of holding, shell and other multiply-layered national and transnational company structures (*Adams v Cape Industries plc* 1990). In legal discourse, a dehistoricized *Salomon* is evoked as a general answer to questions about the corporate self, and this effectively obstructs more profound discussion of the nexus of issues that constitute this case.

The company is the creature of law, but not controlled fully by law; it is created by human agency, but it takes on a life and drive of its own. For that reason, it is frequently compared to Frankenstein's monster (Laski 1916: 407; Foster 2006: 300). The massive literature on the nature of the company and legal personality focuses on the metaphysics of corporate personality, with its mix of solipsism and sociality. Yet the individual self of the 'natural person', the standard against which the corporate person is viewed as artificial, no less evades our understanding. Taylor (1989: 177) points out that the idea of the autonomous individual self is temporally and culturally local:

> So we come to think that we 'have' selves as we have heads. But the very idea that we have or are 'a self', that human agency is essentially defined as 'the self', is a linguistic reflection of our modern understanding and the radical reflexivity it involves. Being deeply embedded in this understanding, we cannot but reach for this language, but it was not always so.

The idea of the autonomous individual, associated with western economic and political liberalism, was being deconstructed at the moment of its apparent triumph in the late nineteenth century. Modernism rejected the idea of a unitary self which generates meaning from a conscious centre, and organicist theories of ethnic and racial collectivities were common currency among European intellectuals. System theoretical models, grounded in autopoiesis, were developing in biology, sociology, economics, linguistics, anthropology and psychoanalysis. The Freudian model evoked the self as situated at the intersection of different forces or drives, viewed as in conflict, yet motivating and shaping the behaviour of the individual. For Freud, there is no single centre with agency over the whole self, possessing a transparent rational self-insight (Freud 1915). Our difficulties in understanding the company form and legal personality are inseparable from fundamental questions about the human self.

The fact that *Salomon* is a 'Jewish case' is not incidental, since the decision affirmed that the basic capitalist form of the company was open even to a small 'Jewish' firm. The Court of Appeal treated Salomon as a Shylock figure, in that his abstract legalism, respect for form, and 'craving for law' were viewed as a sign of his rejection of generally accepted standards of morality and compassion. In *Salomon*, the House of Lords had to recognize that the 'scheme', the 'sham', the 'mere device', the 'perversion', 'utter fiction', 'myth', put together in such a 'shrewd' and 'ingenious' fashion by Aron Salomon under the 'alias' of the company, was no more than a reflection of mainstream capitalist practice. The company was affirmed by the House of Lords to be a universal form open to all within the boundaries laid down by the law, rather than subject to local morality, prejudice, or presumptions about motive. Yet in so doing the House of Lords had to incorporate (what the Court of Appeal in effect identified as) 'Jewish legalism' into the universal company form. *Salomon* enacts the process described by Marx, Trollope and Simmel.

There exists a fatal parallelism in the western imaginary between the Jew and the key institution of modern capitalism, the company, both of which become highly visible in the form of uncanny or unsettled personhood. This parallelism reflects not only their symbolic abstractness, unnaturalness and artificiality, but also their imbrications with law. Jews enter modernity marked with the stigma of formalism, nomocratic legalism, mobility, uncanny personhood, nomadic rootlessness, materialism and abstractness, therefore as representative citizens of the new open space of mercantile capitalism: 'The chimerical nationality of the Jew is the nationality of the merchant, particularly of the monied man' (Marx [1844] 1967: 246). The personhood, histories and personalities of actual Jews are obliterated from view by the symbolic role which modernity coercively allocates to the Jew as type. Win or lose in the games of law and capitalism (and *Salomon* showed how the difference could be very slight), Jews ultimately could not be forgiven for their assigned role of representing the age in which they lived.

Cases cited

Adams v Cape Industries plc [1990] Ch 433.
Berkey v Third Avenue Railway Co 244 N.Y. 602 (1927).
Broderip v Salomon [1893] B 4793.
Clough v Leahy (1904) 2 CLR 139.

Grace v Smith (1775) 96 ER 587.
Grand Trunk Railway v Ontario (Department of Agriculture) (1910) CarswellNat 24.
Lawrence v Fox 20 N.Y. 268 (1859).
R. v. Gartshore 1919 Carswell BC 124.
Salomon v A. Salomon & Co Ltd [1895] 2 Ch. 323.
Salomon v A. Salomon & Co Ltd [1897] AC 22.
Waugh v Carver (1793) 126 ER 525.

Endnotes

1 An earlier version of this chapter was presented at 'The Legal Case: Interdisciplinary Perspectives' held at the University of Hong Kong, June 23–26, 2010. My gratitude goes to the colloquium organizers Elaine Ho and Marco Wan, to Marco Wan as editor of this volume, and to Katherine Baxter for helpful suggestions.
2 See discussion in Sinclair (2007), Gerhardt (2008).
3 An exception is Stanley (1988: 97): 'it is surprising that little attention has been paid to company law [in Critical Legal Studies] since the corporate entity exists as the dominant locus of those relations'.
4 A full historical discussion would of course require extensive analysis of other jurisdictions, and cases such as *Berkey v Third Avenue Railway Co* (1927).
5 In Hong Kong for example there are no citations listed for this case between 1976 and 1985, but the case has been regularly cited since then (see the Consolidated Index to All Reported Hong Kong Decisions, Butterworths: Hong Kong, 2000 and supplements).
6 See *Grand Trunk Railway v Ontario* 1910, at 43, *R. v Gartshore* 1919, at 30, *Clough v Leahy* (1904), at 4.
7 Christianity, in particular Protestantism, has a profound investment in the desire to 'drive the economics out of belief' (Stallybrass 2002: 280).
8 *Grace v Smith* (1775); *Waugh v Carver* (1793), see Rajak (2008: 4–5). This argument from moral disapproval underlies the oft-cited attack on the decision by Kahn-Freud (1944).
9 *The New York Times*, 'The English "One Man" company', 1/12/1896, p. 4.
10 'In February 1893 these original debentures were returned to the company and cancelled, and fresh debentures to the same amount were issued to Broderip to secure repayment of his loan, with Aron Salomon named as the beneficial owner' (Johnson 2010: 155).
11 Cited here from the Court of Appeal judgment, *Salomon v A. Salomon & Co Ltd* [1895] 2 Ch. 323.
12 See Pickering (1968: 17–18) for a list of the epithets that have been directed at corporations.
13 *Financial Times*, Mercantile Memos, 23/8/1895, p. 3.
14 *Financial Times*, Mercantile Memos, 9/10/1893, p. 3.
15 *Financial Times*, Mercantile Memos, 16/10/1893, p. 2.
16 *The Times*, 18/11/1896, p. 9.
17 See Armour (2006: 5ff).
18 The Companies Act 1900 s. 14 introduced the requirement of public register for floating and other charges. The Companies Act 1907 s. 13 allowed for the setting aside of certain floating charges introduced shortly before winding-up proceedings (Armour 2006: 6).
19 Lord Lindley had been one of the judges in the Court of Appeal decision: 'In the opinion of the author such a proceeding was never contemplated by the Legislature' (Lord Lindley 1902: 160).

20 Barabas in *The Jew of Malta* (Marlowe 1633) responds to accusations of murder with the cry 'let me have law' (Act V: i).
21 'Shylock is actually undone by excess of law, rather than by any exception to it' (Watt 2007: 6).
22 This is a huge and complex topic. See for example Poliakov (1966: 87), Muller (2010).
23 In *The Ladder of Gold*, the mania for railway shares is referred to as a 'national delusion' (Bell 1850, II: 88).
24 On this text, see Poovey (2008: 269–75).
25 Full text at: http://diamond.boisestate.edu/gas/gondoliers/gn_lib.pdf.
26 Full text at: http://math.boisestate.edu/gas/utopia/utopia.pdf.
27 This theme is given much bleaker treatment in Conrad's *Victory* (1915). The novel is set on an island, Samburan, which had been controlled by the Tropical Belt Coal Company.
28 Citations are from the on-line Gutenberg edition, http://www.gutenberg.org/ebooks/5231, revised 2005.
29 Remark attributed to Edward, First Baron Thurlow, 1731–1806 (Coffee 1981).
30 There is a parallel here between the idea of usury as the unnatural generation of money by money (Parker 1982), and the unnatural generation of one corporation by another.

References

Anon (1865a) *The Bubbles of Finance: Joint-Stock Companies, Promoting of Companies, Modern Commerce, Money Lending, and Life Insuring, by A City Man*, London: Sampson.
Anon (1865b) 'The dressmaking company', *The London Review of Politics, Society, Literature, Art and Science* (Saturday, February 11) 10 (241): 166–7.
Armour, J. (2006) 'Should we redistribute in insolvency?', Centre for Business Research, University of Cambridge, Working Paper No. 319.
Bell, R. (1850) *The Ladder of Gold: an English Story*, 3 vols, London: Bentley.
Berle, A. and Means, G. (1967) *The Modern Corporation and Private Property*, 2nd edn, New York: Harcourt, Brace and World. First edition, 1932.
Bray, J. F. (1839) *Labour's Wrongs and Labour's Remedy; or, the Age of Might and the Age of Right*, Leeds: David Green.
Carlyle, T. (1858) *Past and Present*, London: Chapman and Hall.
Coffee, J. (1981) " 'No soul to damn: no body to kick": an unscandalized inquiry into the problem of corporate punishment', *Michigan Law Review*, 79: 386–459.
[Comment] (1896) 'One-Man Corporations. *Broderip v. Salomon* Reversed', *Harvard Law Review*, 10 (5): 304–305.
[Comment] (1897) 'Comment', *Yale Law Journal*, 6: 108–109.
Conrad, J. (1915) *Victory: An Island Tale*, New York: Doubleday Page.
Dignam, A. and Lowry, J. (2009) *Company Law*, Oxford: Oxford University Press.
Du Maurier, G. (1894) *Trilby*, London: Osgood, McIlvaine.
Eliot, G. (1876) *Daniel Deronda*, London: William Blackwood.
Foster, N. (2006) 'Perception, language and "reality" in the corporate law theory', *Kings College Law Journal*, 17: 299–324.
Freud, S. (1915) Triebe und Triebschicksale, *Internationale Zeitschrift für (ärztliche) Psychoanalyse*, 3: 84–100.
Gerhardt, M. J. (2008) *The Power of Precedent*, New York: Oxford University Press.
Gray, Alexander (1946) *The Socialism Tradition: Moses to Lenin*, London: Longmans, Green and Co.

Hoeflich, M. and Perelmutter, E. (1988) 'The Anatomy of a Leading Case: *Lawrence v. Fox* in the Courts, the Casebooks, and the Commentaries', *University of Michigan Journal of Law Reform*, 21: 721–44.
Ireland, P. (1999) 'Company law and the myth of shareholder ownership', *The Modern Law Review*, 62 (1): 32–57.
Johnson, P. (2010) *Making the Market: Victorian Origins of Corporate Capitalism*, Cambridge, Cambridge University Press.
Kahn-Freud, O. (1944) 'Some Reflections On Company Law Reform', *Modern Law Review*, 7: 54–66.
Laski, H. (1916) 'Personality of Associations', *Harvard Law Review*, 29: 404–26.
Lindley, N. (Lord) and Lindley, W. (1902) *A Treatise on the Law of Companies considered as a Branch of the Law of Partnership*, sixth edition. London: Sweet and Maxwell.
Manson, E. (1895) 'One-man companies', *Law Quarterly Review*, 42: 185–8.
Marlowe, C. (1633) *The Jew of Malta*. London: Printed by I. B. for Nicholas Vavasour.
Marx, K. (1967) *Writings of the Young Marx on Philosophy and Society*, L. Easton and Kurt H. Guddat (eds), Garden City, N.Y.: Doubleday.
McQueen, R. (2009) *A Social History of Company Law: Great Britain and the Australian Colonies 1854–1920*, London: Ashgate.
Micklethwait, J. and Wooldridge, A. (2003) *The Company: A Short History of a Revolutionary Idea*, New York: The Modern Library.
Morris-Reich, A. (2003) 'The beautiful Jew is a money-lender: money and individuality in Simmel's rehabilitation of the "Jew" ', *Theory, Culture and Society*, 20: 127–42.
Muller, J. (2010) *Capitalism and the Jews*, Princeton, NJ: Princeton University Press.
Oliphant, L. (1882) *Traits and Travesties Social and Political*, Edinburgh and London: William Blackwood & Sons. First published, Blackwood's Magazine, 1876.
Parker, A. (1982) 'Ezra Pound and the "economy" of anti-Semitism', *boundary 2*, 11: 103–108.
Pickering, M. (1968) 'The company as a separate legal entity', *The Modern Law Review*, 31: 481–511.
Poliakov, L. (1966) *The History of Antisemitism: From the Time of Christ to the Court Jews*, trans. R. Howard, London: Elek Books. First published, 1955.
Poovey, M. (2008) *Genres of the Credit Economy: Mediating Value in Eighteenth- and Nineteenth-Century Britain*, Chicago: The University of Chicago Press.
Posner, R. (2003) 'The jurisprudence of greed', *University of Pennsylvania Law Review*, 151 (3): 1097–133.
Rajak, H. (2008) 'Director and officer liability in a zone of insolvency', *Potchefstroom Electronic Law Journal*, 1: 1–36.
Rowsell, E. (1861) *The Autobiography of a Joint-Stock Company*, London: Ward and Lock.
Rubin, G. (1983) 'Aron Salomon and his circle', in J. Adams (ed.), *Essays for Clive Schmitthoff*, Abingdon: Professional Books Ltd.
Shepheard, W. (1659) *Of Corporations, Fraternities, and Guilds*, London.
Simmel, G. (1900) *Die Philosophie des Geldes*, Leipzig: Duncker & Humbolt.
Sinclair, M. (2007) 'Precedent, super-precedent', *George Mason Law Review*, 14: 363–412.
Sindall, R (1990) Middle class crime in nineteenth century England, in L. A. Knafla (ed.), *Crime, Police and the Courts in British History*, Westport, CT and London: Meckler.
Smith, A. (2009) *An Inquiry into the Nature and Causes of the Wealth of Nations*, Massachusetts: Digireads. First published 1776, London.
Sombart, W. (1911) *Die Juden und das Wirtschaftsleben*, Leipzig: Duncker.

Spearman, R. and Farries, E. (1865) *Joint Stock Companies; being a Practical Treatise on their Formation, Management and Winding-Up*, London: Farries.

Spender, P. (1999) 'Resurrecting Mrs Salomon', *Federal Law Review*, 77: 217–41.

Stallybrass, P. (2002) 'The value of culture and the disavowal of things', in H. Turner (ed.), *The Culture of Capital: Property, Cities, and Knowledge in early Modern England*, New York: Routledge.

Stanley, C. (1988) 'Corporate personality and capitalist relations: a critical analysis of the artifice of company law', *Cambrian Law Review*, 19: 97–109.

Taylor, C. (1989) *Sources of the Self: The Making of the Modern Identity*, Cambridge: Cambridge University Press.

[TCC] (1867) *The Comic Cocker, or Figures for the Million*, London: Ward & Lock.

Trollope, A. (1875) *The Way We Live Now: A Novel*, London: Chapman and Hall, available at http://www.gutenberg.org/ebooks/5231.

Warren, S. (1841) *Ten Thousand A-Year*, 3 vols, Edinburgh: Blackwood.

Watt, G. (2007) *Todd and Watt's Cases and Materials on Equity and Trusts*, Oxford: Oxford University Press.

White, G. (1691) *An Account of the Trade to the East-Indies*, London.

Chapter 3

Three close-ups in search of truth

Law, cinema, psychoanalysis

Maria Aristodemou

The cases of Hossein Sazbian

Tehran 1990. A young man is reading a book on the bus. The lady next to him shows interest in the book and asks him where he got it. In a bookshop, he says, and offers it to her. When he says he is the author of the book and maker of the film, none other than the film director Mohsen Makhmalbaf, her interest widens to admiration and we can see she is rather star-struck. She keeps chatting to him and suggests that her sons, who are big fans of his, would like to meet him. They exchange numbers and the rest belongs to journalistic, legal, cinematic, as well, as now, academic history – in that order. Except of course that order is not ready-made, waiting for us to consume, but has to be made: in each case by the writer. It belongs also more poignantly to the characters' personal history and it is for the purpose of recording those case histories that I turn to psychoanalysis.

The media appears on the scene to tell its version of the story at the same time as the law. Indeed they seem to precede and facilitate the law's involvement, as the journalist is much more interested in the case than the police are. The film starts with Mr Farazmand unable to contain himself with excitement as he rides in a taxi with two policemen on their way to arrest the defendant. Throughout the film, the journalist appears more in charge of the circumstances leading to and including the defendant's arrest and conviction than the young, shy, and taciturn policemen sitting with their guns at the back of the taxi. It is no coincidence, therefore, that the taxi driver mistakes Mr Farazmand for a policeman.

Following the newspaper report, another film director, Abbas Kiarostami, just as intrigued by the defendant playing himself as the lady on the bus was intrigued by the defendant playing Mohsen Makhmalbaf, visits him in prison and asks and obtains permission to film the subsequent court proceedings. The result is a semi-documentary, semi-fictionalized depiction of the accusation and trial for deception of Sazbian, a poor unemployed cinema fan, who impersonates the famous film director and misleads the rather embarrassed and annoyed middle-class Ahankhah family who initially believed him. As the narrative unfolds, we learn that the Ahankhah family had welcomed Sazbian to their home where he became a regular visitor. Soon he suggested to them that their house would be perfect for a new film he had in mind, and that their young sons would be the perfect lead actors. Initially at least, the Ahankhah family hung on Sazbian's every word; as Sazbian puts it, while, as Sazbian he could never get anyone to listen to him, as Mohsen Makhmalbaf, everyone did whatever he told them: 'If I told them to cut a tree in their garden, or rearrange the furniture in their house, they would do it.'

Kiarostami's film combines characters who play themselves with characters who simply play, court proceedings and questioning by the judge with questioning by the director, contemporaneous filming of the court proceedings with reconstructions of events leading to and including the defendant's arrest. At first watching at least, the spectator is not certain which scene is constructed, and what reconstructed, what belongs to the director's imaginative retelling of the story and what takes place contemporaneously (if not spontaneously). The borders between fact and fiction, art and reality are therefore opened to investigation and, thereby to contestation. It is impossible to say, legislate, or judge which is the more real, the more true, representation of the case. Art and law dissolve into each other through the medium of the film which creates its own history, which in turn rewrites the legal case and the characters depicted in it. Not surprisingly, following the release of *Close-Up* the 'real life' case, its journalistic as well as legal report, were eclipsed by its cinematic retelling, a development that further confused the inter-penetration between fact, law, and film.

There is nothing new about competing discourses trying to relate the same case and fighting for the right to have the last word. *Close-up* self-consciously blurs the genres of film, law, and journalism and therefore transgresses the law that 'Genres are not to be mixed. I will not mix genres. I repeat: genres are not to be mixed. I will not mix them'. (Derrida 1992: 223). It also illustrates Derrida's point that the law which tries to institutionalize and preserve the purity of genres always fails because genres inevitably exceed their boundaries and are open to contamination by other genres. In the process it problematises the nature of truth, of truth-searching, and of truth-telling, as imagined, if not dictated, by the different discourses and their representatives: from the defendant and his victims, to the director and his project, and from the ambitious journalist looking for a sensational media story, to the court judge seeking to reach some kind of 'right' answer. The lingering question is whether the truth can ever be fully unveiled, let alone represented, by any of the competing discourses.

It would be easy here to rehearse the postmodern debate about the end of the grand narratives of modernity and in particular the claims made by science on behalf of knowledge as truth, even as the only truth. Knowledge as truth in science takes one of three famous forms, the debate raging between (a) the correspondence theory, according to which something is true if it 'corresponds' to the way things are, (b) the coherence theory, according to which something is true if it forms a harmonious part within a system and (c) the confirmation model, according to which something is true if it falls within the class of what we count as evidence for that class. All three forms, however, have more in common than they have apart: they all share the assumption that there is a reality out there that we can access, represent, and measure our statements as well as judgments against. Or as

Thomas Aquinas put it 'A judgment is said to be true when it conforms to the external reality'.[1]

Modernism further insisted on the possibility, as well as desirability, of 'scientizing' this external reality, preferably through the accumulation of facts. Proceeding on the assumption that oral testimony is both valuable and reliable, the journalist, film maker and judge (in that order), set out to interview the defendant. They therefore follow the tradition, or prejudice, that the presence of the speaking subject will confer origin, unity and authority to their utterances, whether the latter concern their past actions or future purposes. The judicial process in this story, as with every story the law attempts to tell, also aims to be the author, origin, and source of meaning, with the trial narrative trying to give an appearance of causality, order and closure. The fact that different characters give different accounts and different interpretations of the same events, however, quickly disabuse us of the illusion that the speaker's presence will deliver the 'truth'.

From a law and literature perspective, one that I argued for passionately in the past, we can point out that modernism's fetishism of facts has led us to lose sight of law's kinship (if not origins) in the literary imagination. To extend Hayden White's protest, whether one is a historian, lawyer, journalist or film-maker, "our attempt to accord diverse sources with meaning cannot take place without selecting, hierarchizing, supplementing, suppressing and subordinating some facts to others. This process cannot be other than literary" (White 1978: 99). The filmmaker's tools, like the lawyer's or journalist's, are the same as those of the writer: that is, the techniques of figurative language.

Kiarostami's film therefore, just like the trial narrative and the journalist's report, is a construction, not a reflection of the past, dictated not by the events themselves which are now irretrievably lost, but by his interpretation and retelling of those events. So rather than one right answer, the truth of Sazbian's case is again deferred: in Kiarostami's depiction of the events, while the accumulation of facts may aim at an empirical explanation of the events, the Apollonian impulse towards rationality is continually subverted by asides that hint at a different truth inspired less by Apollo than by Dionysus, less by reason than by imagination and less by fact than by literature. Participants in this minor drama for example, continually appeal to metaphors to make sense of the story only to find that metaphors also defer rather than confer meaning. Despite the resulting accumulation of facts, characters, statements, images, and metaphors, simultaneous and retrospective, the 'truth' remains elusive.

It would be easy, in other words, and not at all insupportable, to suggest that there is no such thing as one truth here, that the case, and the truth, depend on the lenses we wear with which to see, as there is not one overarching, Platonic perspective which would enable us to see it all. However, this is not the argument I will make. In contrast to so-called postmodern hermeneutics of suspicion, and endless language games, I will venture the suggestion that there is such a thing as truth that we can try to reach, and that, as Edgar Allen Poe put it, it is not necessarily at the bottom of a well but quite often superficial: 'there is such a thing as being too profound. Truth is not always in a well. In fact, as regards the most important knowledge, I do believe she is invariably superficial' (Poe 1967: 204). Superficial but not, as we will find out, simple.

Truth and her sisters

In common with Poe, Lacan suggests that truth is not in a well, but manifest and indeed on the surface. That surface is none other than the surface of the signifier: speech. Not just any speech, however, but speech that implicates the subject's desire. Truth in psychoanalysis has nothing to do with correspondence to reality, or coherence within a system, or with facts, or with knowledge, but with enjoyment. Since every subject has her own idiosyncratic, and invariably embarrassing (if not perverse) way of enjoying herself, that 'truth' is not a universal truth but a particular truth, unique to each subject: The truth of the subject, as Lacan puts it, is not a superior law but 'a truth that we will look for in a hiding place in our subject. It is a particular truth' (1992: 24). And it will come as no surprise that for Lacan that place is not far from the place where the subject's enjoyment resides: truth, he says, is 'the sister of that forbidden jouissance' (Lacan 2007: 61).

How do we access this truth? Since for Lacan truth is not an epistemological or ontological entity but a place, indeed a 'hiding place', the only chance we have of accessing it is if we speak topologically. That is, we need to explore and inhabit more than one universe since, for psychoanalysis, all human beings inhabit, to a greater or lesser extent, and with various degrees of success, the distinct yet intertwined registers we refer to as real, symbolic and imaginary universes. Topologically speaking, truth lies at the intersection between the three registers and the task of analysis is to find out how they are knotted together in the case of each subject.

Do the combined forces of three discourses, that is, of law, film, and psychoanalysis enable us to get closer to the subject's truth? This chapter will chart the attempts made by the different discourses to make sense of Sazbian's tale, pointing out the problems and pitfalls they encounter along the way. We look first at the imaginary register, that is the tale as 'reflected' by the participants in the drama, Sazbian in particular but also his alleged victims, the Ahankhah family. Psychoanalysis, as we'll see, is quick to cast doubt on the truth afforded by the participants' imaginary reflections: for Lacan what the subject sees, of herself or of others, does not guarantee knowledge, at least not knowledge of the 'truth', because there is always one point from which we can never see, that is, the point from which we are looked at. This is the point Lacan famously refers to as the gaze or blind spot: as he explains, 'I see only from one point but in my existence I am looked at from all sides.' (Lacan 1977: 72). There is, in other words, always a 'missing bit' in our field of vision, just as there is always a 'missing' bit in our attempts at representation.[2]

The tale as told by the media and the law in our case, represents the intrusion of the symbolic dimension into the imaginary register Sazbian and his victims have been inhabiting. Do the law or the media succeed in understanding the complex web of Sazbian's and his victim's motivations? Psychoanalysis is not so sure: that is, if psychoanalysis is suspicious of the truth to be had from the image, it is no less suspicious of the truth to be had from language and representation. For psychoanalysis the symbolic register focuses on 'reality', on what we can know and represent, at the expense of what Lacan called the Real, that which is contingent and unknowable (Lacan 2006: 296). The distinction here is between 'reality', which dwells in the realm of the symbolic, that is, in the register of language, and the Real, which exceeds our capacities for representation. The significance of this distinction is to point out the limits of our capacities of knowing: Lacan's intervention confuses our confidence in seeing and in knowing it all and alerts us to that which is beyond representation and beyond knowledge.[3]

Does Kiarostami's film succeed where the media and the law fail? Significantly Kiarostami chooses to call his film "Close-Up", after the special lens he uses to hone in on Sazbian during the court hearing. Does this lens get closer to the subject's hiding place? My argument in this chapter is that Kiarostami's cinematic lens, and indeed metaphor generally, does have a greater potential to approximate the truth than the participants' imaginary reflections, or the symbolic interventions of the law and the media. Cinematic lenses and metaphors, however, even great ones, also come to an end, even, as the film suggests, a dead end. At that point Kiarostami resorts to a trump card and draws the film to a winning, if not necessarily true, conclusion.

Imaginary: journey of misrecognitions

What is the unconscious truth that we remain in ignorance of? For Lacan it has a name and it is called the *objet petit a*: the irreducible particularity of each subject, that is, their hidden essence. For psychoanalysis the knotting of the three registers is unique for each subject; the only thing that is universal is that the knotting is more or less a failure for each and every one of us. This is because the birth of our subjectivity involves losing an object that we are thereafter and forever in search of. Lacan's formulation of the subject is that of an incomplete, lacking, pathetic organism that is always looking for its missing bit: that missing bit, that gap, is the subject itself.[4]

If we are so messed up, how do we possibly manage? The short answer is because we live in a world of delusions: we delude each other but more than anyone we delude ourselves. So we find our unity and completeness, not in our self, which is lacking, but by borrowing bits of other people. And not just any people, but usually those we emulate but also, sadly, those whom we courted and who rejected us: identity is the waste bin of all our abandoned or lost object choices. So, not surprisingly, identification is always ambivalent: it can imply idealisation of the other that the subject is identifying with, but also competition with and destruction of the other (Freud 2001, XVIII: 105).[5]

If the ego is essentially a misrecognition we are afflicted with from childhood, things do not get easier as we grow up. The ego seeks to construct the centre-less absence that is the self by propping it up on the one hand with ideal images of what it hopes to be, and falsely assumes it already is, and on the other hand with persons for whom it wants to be that ideal. This is the oscillation that Lacan elucidates as the distinction between ideal ego and ego ideal. The ideal ego, as Lacan elaborates, is the image we emulate, while the ego ideal is the point from which we emulate: so if the ideal ego is the person we strive to be, the ego ideal is the person for whom we want to be that ideal (Lacan 1977: 268).[6] In short, rather than acknowledging the essential mis-recognition we encounter in the mirror or in another's gaze, we not only adopt and revel in it, but also keep looking for others who will ratify and endorse that mis-recognition. Needless to say, the story we create and endlessly tell to ourselves (and to anyone who cares or is paid to listen) to account for our history is riddled with fictions and false connections that Lacan calls 'meconnaissances'.

How does this apply to Sazbian? Sazbian's precious identity, like all of our identity, so dear and protected by us, is actually not inside him but outside; with the other (Lacan 1991: 44).[7] In Sazbian's case it resides in fragments of characters he has encountered in cinema. Cinema provides him with images with which he can identify and teaches him what and how to desire. He watches the suffering depicted in films, identifies with the characters, and imagines their suffering to mirror and express his own; more, he longs for that suffering to be his own. Like Flaubert, he watches Makhmalbaf's films and proclaims, 'Yes, that character, c'est moi': the cyclist who embarks on a marathon cycling race to make money to pay his sick wife's hospital bill is him; the boy who sleeps through the football match he has been desperate to watch is also him. After meeting Abbas Kiarostami the characters in Kiarostami's films are also him. When Kiarostami asks Sazbian about filming the trial, he readily agrees because, he says, 'you are my audience'. He also asks Kiarostami to pass a message to his hero and alter ego Makhmalbaf: 'tell him the cyclist is part of me'.

Throughout the film Sazbian's trail of mis-recognitions continues and grows. Further, he collapses his ideal ego (the glamorous sufferer whose toils and deprivations are worthy of cinematic depiction) with his ego ideal (Mohsen Makhmalbaf, the person in whose eyes these sufferings are worthy of depiction). Ironically, the son Ahankhah picks up Sazbian's sickness: 'He is still playing a part', he tells the Court. 'Before he was playing the part of Mohsen Makhmalbaf, now he plays the part of a sentimental man'. There seems to be no end to the identifications Sazbian will appropriate in the vain hope that they will make up for the absence that is him. Sazbian, that is, like all of us, refuses to acknowledge the lack at the core of his subjectivity, but goes further than many of us in the measures he will take to fill that lack with replacement objects.

Symbolic: law and media

So the imaginary, plagued, as I have just described by a string of mis-recognitions, for the defendant as much as his victims, does not help us discover the truth about the subject. Does the symbolic register get closer? The first people to get hold of the story, in Tehran as anywhere else, are of course the media. Mr Farazmand is thrilled with his scoop: 'It's an Oriana Falacci story' he claims, one that sniffs out the painful reality of being a lacking human being. He wants to be the first to record and report Sazbian's arrest, in the hope of deciphering the defendant's illicit motives: 'no one knows what his intentions were', he enthuses. However, we are quickly disabused of any hope that this rather shady character will sniff out the complexities, let alone the truth, of the case. In the course of the film we witness Mr Farazmand behaving like a bigger crook than Sazbian and his motives are even less laudable, as well as less interesting. First he hires a taxi without having enough money to pay for it and borrows the fare from Mr Ahankhah. He then scours the street in search of a tape recorder from people he has never met, his parting words 'You'll get it back' inspiring anything but confidence in the listener or us the audience.

What about the lawyers? Do they get closer to the truth? The law is not too impressed with the case; in contrast to the journalist and to Kiarostami, the officers of the law find the case quite tedious and neither the prison officers nor the court officials can recall the details of Sazbian's offence: 'It's just a small fraud case', they say, 'there is nothing about it worth filming'.[8] More importantly, the law is not interested in finding out Sazbian's motives and it is left to Kiarostami to ask Sazbian the probing questions in Court. From Sazbian's point of view the law is so simple that he promptly admits his guilt to attempted fraud: 'I confessed', he explains, 'because, though I am not a crook, what I did looks like fraud on the outside'. Conversely when one of the brothers implies that he was planning to burgle them, the law doesn't give Sazbian a chance to protest: 'You are not accused of that', the judge tells him, interrupting his protests.

At the same time, law's 'simplicity' comes as a welcome relief to Sazbian amongst the confusing identifications he has been engaged in: accepting legal guilt and submitting to law's punishment is easier for Sazbian than finding his way round his wily desires and lack of identity. As he finds out, assuming someone else's identity is no easy matter: it's hard enough being one person, let alone two. Law therefore functions as a defence to his impossible desire which explains his readiness to be arrested and his welcoming of the legal punishment.[9] Law for Sazbian is a convenient smokescreen, making his impossible desire legally reprehensible: now he can claim that the reason he cannot be Mohsen Makhmalbaf is because the law will not allow it, rather than because he is not a talented film director.

From the family's point of view, the simplicity of the law also does not help: they bring the complaint to regain a bit of dignity after being hoodwinked by Sazbian's story. The law would be useful if Sazbian were shown to be a crook because then responsibility for their blunder would have shifted to the perpetrator. Unfortunately the law doesn't help them save face as it doesn't unambiguously declare Sazbian a crook. As one of the sons complains: 'The report doesn't tell the whole story. It portrays us as simple people'. So the law is simple. So simple, that it doesn't satisfy anyone. From the journalist, to the victims, or us the spectators whose desires Kiarostami has excited, including, more flamboyantly, the Italian film director Nanni Moretti in his opening tribute.

Why the lack of conviction in legal language even when it *convicts* and indeed punishes? What causes our unease and suspicion that something has been left out? For psychoanalysis the answer is simple: despite legal injunctions, we can never know the 'truth, the whole truth and nothing but the truth' because only the unconscious doesn't deceive. So despite the fact that we insist, on oath and on more, 'to tell the truth, the whole truth and nothing but the truth', for Lacan that is precisely what we will not say.[10] That is because symbolic language, whether in a newspaper or in a court of law, is all too often no more than 'empty speech', which does not implicate the subject's desire. Such speech, in contrast to 'full speech', is in the service not of truth, but of deception and not of understanding but of mis-communication. The castration wrought by language is so central, that our ability to lie is in fact what constitutes us as subjects. Indeed for Lacan the human being becomes a subject not when she starts to speak but when she starts to lie: beginning to lie means the subject has worked out how to manipulate language, in other words, she has entered the linguistic community. Since 'the word is the murder of the thing', the minute we use language we alienate not only ourselves but others from the truth of both their being and of ours. If we communicate with each other at all, then, it is not because we touch each other's truth but because we successfully mis-understand each other (Lacan 1993: 184).

For psychoanalysis, the kernel of our being is not the bits we know and speak, but precisely the bits we do not know and therefore cannot speak (Lacan 1977: 270). Indeed for Lacan it is when we stop thinking, when we utter stupidities, that we may find out something about desire. The wager of psychoanalysis is that free association can bridge the gap between knowledge and truth but only half-so as free association, even dreams, domesticate the unconscious: that is why 'the whole truth is what cannot be told' (Lacan 1998: 92). Which brings us to the royal road to the truth: not dreams, or not only dreams, but speech: full speech.

The royal road to the Real: speech

Close-up refers to the zoom lens Kiarostami uses to hone in on Sazbian during the court proceedings. What can a close-up camera record that the court itself cannot? And, more importantly, what is there that even a close-up camera cannot see? Can the camera penetrate the subject's hiding place? The subject of course already knows that truth, even if they don't know that they know it: we can be sure, however, that the subject will do everything possible to prevent us from finding it. What is the royal road to this place then? For psychoanalysis the answer is simple: the royal road to this place is speech. Truth, we can say, speaks. Indeed, as Lacan says, repeatedly, truth is only a meaningful concept in the context of language:

'the dimension of truth emerges with the appearance of language'. (2006: 436) And, 'There is neither true nor false prior to speech' (1988: 228); truth is a property of the 'said': 'the dit-mension', the dimention or mention of what is said (1998: 107).

So truth can be found on the surface of the signifier and is contained in the patient's speech; it appears not in facts, or thoughts, or feelings, but in words. Signifiers, we can say, have all the luck. At the same time, not just any speech but what Lacan calls 'full' speech; speech whose utterances are ethically engaged, in other words speech that engages the subject's desire rather than the Other's desire. Why is speech in a court of law not likely to be 'full speech'? Like law: 'In the first resort, psychoanalysis is an art of interpretation' (Freud 2001, XVIII, 239). Unlike law however, in analysis the only right answers lie with the analysand, not with the judge: the interpretation of the dream lies with the dreamer, not with the analyst (Freud 2001, XVIII, 240–41). Needless to say, proof is also irrelevant in analysis; not only because you can't prove you had a dream or what it was but because truth goes beyond proof. Truth transcends what can be known or proven because truth sets its own conditions beyond coherence, correspondence or confirmation: 'provability is a weaker notion than truth' (Hallward 2003: 155).[11] In contrast also to legal decisions, there is no *stare decisis* in analysis: truth is not ready-made for the analyst or analysand to uncover or recover from a mass of precedent, but is constructed during the treatment itself. Each interpretation, therefore, cannot be foreseen but is unique to each case.

If the subject is already in unconscious possession of the truth, what is the role of the analyst? The analyst is not there to judge, or to understand, or to explain, or to produce right answers, or to exert power, or even to sympathise or empathise with the patient. What the analyst must do, and it is not an easy task, is to install herself at the place which causes the analysand's desire. In other words, she has to take the place of the enigmatic object a. To that end, interpretation aims not to produce right answers but more associations: not to fix meaning (which would put the analyst in the position of the master) but, by being equivocal and allusive, to enable the patient's desire to emerge (Lacan 1977: 212).[12]

So analysis is not about judging or sentencing or punishing. It is about something much worse: ultimately it aims at the destitution of the subject. Sazbian, like all of us, is bound to his social position, a position that he wants, not to abolish, but to replace with that of someone else's. A true subject, on the other hand, is one free of relations of support, obligation or justification (Badiou 2001: 56). Has Sazbian risen to the status of such a true subject? Usually a trauma would lead to the transformation of the subject but as we have seen Sazbian's experience with the law was not traumatic enough; if anything he invited his own arrest and welcomed the prison sentence. The less shocking but nevertheless still traumatic experience of analysis is another route to de-subjectification. Is there a third way? In the next section I suggest that, failing analysis, a work of art can enable us to approximate, albeit of course not reach, the truth that cannot be seen, and the truth that cannot be spoken.

Art and the Real

As literature has never taken (too) seriously modern philosophy's restrictions on what counts as truth and knowledge, the hope is that art can approximate truth and help us lift the veil separating us from the Real. Why is that? What does art have in common with the Real? One suggestion is that, since the Real rebels against representation, the only way we weave it into reality is through fiction. Fiction sustains the structure of reality, and it does so through language: language, as Jeremy Bentham explored in his *Theory of Fictions*, performs the power of fiction by *pretending* that something exists and that pretension works.[13] Following Bentham, Lacan uses the term fiction to suggest, not a lie, but an imaginary construct which supports the symbolic order so that 'every truth has the structure of fiction' (1992: 12). Without fiction, in other words, we would not be able to approximate truth or represent reality, indeed without fiction we would have no language.

In addition to the inextricability between truth and fiction, the process of analysis has always, from its outset, taken advantage of the fact that truth often expresses itself in lies and that lies can reveal the truth about the subject's desire more eloquently than so-called honest statements. As Freud showed in *The Psychopathology of Everyday Life*, the subject's desire can be revealed by mistakes, slips, jokes or parapraxes. So deception and lies are not the opposite of truth but reveal the subject's desires: people impersonating someone they are not reveal the truth about their desire more eloquently than if they had repressed those desires. For psychoanalysis those subjects are not only 'not guilty' but truly ethical because they haven't given up on their desire. Sazbian has not only not given up on his desire, but played his role to its deadly end: even when he realizes his deceit has been uncovered, he returns to the Ahankhah house one last time knowing that he is about to be arrested.[14]

Literary language, and metaphor in particular, takes language's power to produce working fictions to a higher level; poets appreciate that the Big Other of the symbolic order who has castrated us with language, has also left enough gaps in that language for us to derive enjoyment and be able to speak fragments of the truth that eludes us. Lacan agrees that poetry can have a transformative effect on the subject by taking advantage of the fact that the relationship between signifier and signified is 'always fluid, always ready to come undone' (Lacan 1993: 261). Metaphor uses and abuses that shaky relationship by transferring attributes from one object to another; that process can have the transformative effect of unchaining the signifier that is stuck to the subject. As Catherine Millott explains, since the essence of an object is the desire it conceals, metaphor, by transferring attributes from one object to another, can reveal the desire which is hidden in an object (1991: 133–4).

Kiarostami is not alone in according art in general and metaphor in particular the privilege of accessing the truth. Other characters in the drama share the view that art has access to a higher truth than discourses such as science. The Ahankhah sons, having studied respectively civil and mechanical engineering, harbour ambitions to engage in the arts: 'I had a choice between art and bread', says one of the brothers, 'and I chose art'. This statement is not only literal (at the time the son is working in a bread factory) but obviously also metaphorical: it is the family's enamour of the arts that led them to welcome Sazbian in their home and show their willingness to sacrifice their 'bread', their money, home and possessions, for the sake of art.

We can now see the affinity between art and analysis: as Plato discusses in the *Symposium*, what is distinctive about poetry is that it brings something new into being in the sense of *poesis*. Analysis similarly aims to enable the subject to cause herself anew, to become her own, rather than the Other's cause; it is only such a subject, Badiou insists, that is a true subject.[15] The artistic process, therefore, in contrast to the legal process, and in close alliance with the psychoanalytic process, suggests that truth can only be reached, slowly and in pieces, through the medium of metaphor, poetry and fiction: in other words, through lies.

The subject of truth

'Strange this sensational story should come from a dead end' says Mr Farazmand at the start of the film, appealing, again, to metaphor to try to understand this strange story. Metaphors, however, just like the street where the family live, and just like free association, also come to an end. However far one goes with free associations, explains Freud in *The Interpretation of Dreams*, ultimately we will reach a dead end: what he called the navel of the dream, 'the spot where it reaches down into the unknown' (2001, IV: 525). If interpretations have run out, if metaphors reach a dead end, if a close-up camera cannot penetrate the subject's hiding place, then Kiarostami has a trump card and he uses it. As Sazbian leaves prison having served his sentence for fraud, Kiarostami arranges for him to come face to face with his ideal ego, the man he was impersonating.

The experience of the double is one of the experiences Freud discusses under the term 'uncanny'; that part of ourselves that is so extremely intimate that we have hidden even from ourselves. Lacan's term for this is the extimate, something so intimate and yet so well hidden that it is unfamiliar to us and thus blurs the boundaries between inside and outside. 'What is involved', Lacan says, 'is that excluded interior which . . . is excluded in the interior' (1992: 101). What is most extimate to the subject is the small object a, that which is most unique to the subject and is precisely what is lost in order for the subject to become a subject. What the experience of the double brings us face to face with is an encounter with what we don't normally see, that is, the small object a, because between the subject and her double only one of us possesses the small object a. The encounter with our double provokes anxiety because we are dealing with the truth of our being: we are forced to confront our own idiosyncratic mode of enjoying ourselves, something which is invariably both stupid and embarrassing.

As guides to this hiding place, Lacan warns, 'feelings are deceptive' (1992: 30). But the only affect that doesn't lie is anxiety. The anxiety caused by the uncanny, in Sazbian's case the encounter with his double, is one of the ways we can approach the small object a. For Lacan such an encounter has the potential to be an ethical experience; for ethics in psychoanalysis is not, or not just, about one's relation to the other but about one's relation to herself (Lacan 1992: 22). The ethical advantage of the uncanny experience is to enable us to see the Other, the stranger, in ourselves and thus to confront what is most intimate to us and yet unknown to us.

As I discussed earlier, there is no camera that is sufficiently 'close-up' to enable us to penetrate this hiding place. Encountering our double, however, is one way of achieving what is normally impossible, that is enable us to see ourselves from outside. The moment of encountering our double, is also, ideally, the moment of analysis and the possibility of ethics. Like a subject at the end of analysis, the subject is forced to shed her imaginary identifications and is left with her own irreducible particularity, that is, the small object a. This knowledge however cannot be attained in isolation: we need the intervention of the third party of the analyst to distinguish between the self and its image. Kiarostami's camera in this case functions as the silent witness to the uncanny encounter that ideally should help Sazbian distinguish between his real and imaginary ego.

Of course finite beings that we are, we do everything we can to resist encountering ourselves, forever blaming the other for our failings and frustrations, forgetting the part we play in our own suffering. For Sazbian to go to the other side of the looking glass and encounter himself from the outside, would mean acknowledging the lack not only in himself but also the lack in the other, in this case in Mohsen Makhmalbaf and Abbas Kiarostami. It would mean acknowledging the fundamental uncertainty, unknowability and incompleteness of the other rather than continuing to treat Makhmalbaf as the sublime other that would fill his lack.

'I am tired of being myself' says the real Mohsen Makhmalbaf on meeting his double. Ideally this admission should alert Sazbian to the fact that as Lacan put it, 'there is no other of the other', that is, there is no higher authority which can ratify or disqualify Sazbian's identifications, that there is 'no-one' before whom he has to be 'someone'. Unfortunately Sazbian is not ready to let go of his ego ideal. His reaction to the encounter is to start crying, with the directors (in the plural now), as well as us the spectators, functioning as his ego ideal: the point from which he wants to be looked at as lovable, worthy, filmable, and above all, as suffering.

Endnotes

1 According to the correspondence theory, the truth or falsity of a representation is determined by whether it accurately describes 'things'. For example for Thomas Aquinas *Veritas est adaequatio rei et intellectus* ('Truth is the equation [or adequacy] of things and intellect'). For a lucid introduction see Hallward 2003, pp. 153–80.
2 I develop this theme in my "Democracy Or Your Life! Knowledge, Ignorance, and the Politics of Atheism in Saramago's *Blindness* and *Seeing*", *Law, Culture, and the Humanities*, 1743872111400680, first published on April 20, 2011.
3 Ibid.

4 See Lacan 1992 at 52, and 118: 'It is in its nature that the object as such is lost. It will never be found again . . . It is to be found at most as something missed'; and 'The object is by nature a refound object'. I discuss this further in my 'Does the Letter of the Law Always Arrive at Its Destination? A Study in Feminine Psychology', *Law & Literature*, Vol. 22, Issue 3, pp. 394–417.
5 'Identification, in fact, is ambivalent from the very first; it can turn into an expression of tenderness as easily as into a wish for someone's removal. It behaves like a derivative of the first, oral phase of the organization of the libido, in which the object that we long for and prize is assimilated by eating and is in that way annihilated as such.'
6 'The point of the ego ideal is that from which the subject will see himself, as one says, *as others see him*, – which will enable him to support himself in a dual situation that is satisfactory for him from the point of view of love'.
7 'The core of our being does not coincide with the ego. . . There's no doubt that the real *I* is not the ego.'
8 The case concerns the fraud of 1,900 tomans, about £10, which Sazbian borrowed from one of the sons in the family.
9 Sazbian spends several weeks in prison, both awaiting his trial and subsequent to the trial.
10 Quoted in Bruce Fink, *Fundamentals of Psychoanalytic Technique: A Lacanian Approach for Practitioners*, New York: Norton 2007, p. 32.
11 Quoting Douglas Hofstadter.
12 'Interpretation is directed not so much at the meaning as towards reducing the non-meaning of the signifiers, so that we may rediscover the determinants of the subject's entire behaviour.'
13 'To language then, to language alone, it is that fictitious entities owe their existence – their impossible yet indispensable existence': quoted in C.K. Ogden, *Bentham's Theory of Fictions*, New York: Kegan Paul, 1932, p. xxxii. See also in *Essays on Language*, Vol, VIII, at 325 'A fictitious entity is an object, the existence of which is feigned by the imagination, feigned for the purpose of discourse, and which, when so formed, is spoken of as a real one.'
14 Lacan 1992: 189: 'jouissance implies precisely the acceptance of death'.
15 *Infinite Thought*, pp. 44–5: 'A truth is, first of all, something new. What transmits, what repeats, we shall call knowledge. A language that is related, not to things already presented, but to things which have not yet arrived . . . such a language can be found in the poem.'

Bibliography

Badiou, Alain (2001) *Ethics: An Essay on The Understanding of Evil*, London: Verso
Badiou, Alain (2005) *Infinite Thought*, London: Continuum
Bentham, Jeremy (1843) *The Works of Jeremy Bentham*, ed John Bowring, XI volumes, Edinburgh: William Tait
Derrida, Jacques (1992) 'The Law of Genre' in *Acts of Literature* ed. Derek Attridge, New York and London: Routledge
Freud, Sigmund (2001) *The Standard Edition of the Complete Psychological Works of Sigmund Freud*, 24 volumes, trans. James Strachey, London: Vintage
Hallward, Peter (2003) *Badiou; A Subject to Truth*, Minneapolis: University of Minnesota Press
Lacan, Jacques (1977) *Four Fundamental Concepts of Psychoanalysis* trans. Alan Sheridan, ed. Jacques-Alain Miller, Harmondsworth: Penguin

Lacan, Jacques (1988) *The Seminar. Book I. Freud's Papers on Technique, 1953–54.* ed. Jacques-Alain Miller, trans. John Forrester, New York: Norton

Lacan, Jacques (1991) *The Ego in Freud's Theory and in the Technique of Psychoanalysis Book II 1954–55*, ed. Jacques-Alain Miller, trans. Sylvana Tomaselli, New York: Norton

Lacan, Jacques (1992) *The Ethics of Psychoanalysis, Book VII, 1959–60*, trans. Dennis Porter, London: Routledge

Lacan, Jacques (1993) *The Psychoses Book III, 1955–56*, ed. Jacques-Alain Miller, trans. Russell Grigg, London: Routledge

Lacan, Jacques (1998) *Encore, The Seminar of Jacques Lacan Book XX; On Feminine Sexuality, The Limits of Love and Knowledge*, ed. Jacques-Alain Miller, trans. Bruce Fink, New York: Norton

Lacan, Jacques (2006) *Ecrits*, trans. Bruce Fink, New York: Norton

Lacan, Jacques (2007) *The Other Side of Psychoanalysis, Book XVII*, ed. Jacques-Alain Miller, trans. Russell Grigg, New York: Norton

Millott, Catherine (1991) 'The Real Presence', *October* Vol. 58, Autumn, pp. 109–37

Poe, Edgar Allan (1967) *The Murders in the Rue Morgue* in *Selected Writings*, London: Penguin

White, Hayden (1978) *Tropics of Discourse: Essays in Cultural Criticism*, Baltimore: Johns Hopkins University Press

Chapter 4

Everyday law in the court writing of Sybille Bedford

Elaine Ho

Part I

In the most recent edition of *Law and Literature* (2009), Richard Posner praises Sybille Bedford as one of the few novelists who "have done brilliant nonfiction writing about law" (4). Posner does not elaborate what he means by "brilliant" except to say briefly elsewhere in his work that readers comparing American and French criminal procedure can do better studying Bedford's "record of actual trials" than reading "novelistic descriptions." (63)[1] These comments are made within the general context of Posner's well-known reservations about law and literature studies which had already attracted vigorous rejoinders (see, for example, Weisberg 1989, West 1993), and it is not my intention here to revisit the arguments. In not elaborating his praise, however, Posner makes of Bedford an unargued case within his sceptic's discourse about law and literature. Posner's remarks about Bedford appear, on the one hand, to acknowledge that authorial talent can straddle fictional writing and legal writing, such as the trial report, with its truth and factual claims, and on the other, to insist that they are strictly separated generic categories. In disputing fiction's likely contribution to the law, one of Posner's complaints may help to explain his positive appraisal of Bedford. He writes: "only rarely can we learn much about the day-to-day operations of a legal system from works of imaginative literature even when they depict trials or other legal processes." (21)[2]

The opening of "The Worst We Can Do," one of Bedford's essays in the collection *The Faces of Justice* (1961), appears to meet Posner's criterion of quotidian knowledge:

> Not the worst. Not about the great wrongs. Not about bad laws. Not about Adolph Beck or Chessman or judicial errors; not about hanging or flogging or the Labouchere Amendment. About the small things men do to each other every day if they have the power and the lack of imagination, or if their convictions happen to run that way. It goes unrecorded, it is hardly noticed, but it lives on in the memories of those concerned.
>
> (63)[3]

In this brief but resonant example, Bedford addresses the reader in personal, almost intimate, tones. Actual persons and laws are named – Beck, Chessman, Labouchere Amendment – but the reader is invited to put them aside in favor of that which is "unrecorded", and even more nebulously, of memory, individual and collective. Contrary to Posner, what strikes any reader who knows the trial report as genre is how Bedford's writing *departs* from it – from its factual tenor, its registers of objectivity, its sequenced narrative. The "literary" in Bedford's writing signifies these departures and how they mobilize her "record of actual trials" toward the interconnection of the legal and extra-legal.

Bedford's choice not to report on "the worst" or "the great wrongs" is deliberate for as a court reporter in post-Second World War England, she covered a number of "famous trials" for English and American broadsheets and magazines – the cases of Henry Bodkin Adams, the doctor suspected of murdering his aged patients in 1957, Stephen Ward, the society doctor at the center of the Profumo scandal (1963), the trial of *Lady Chatterley's Lover* (1960), of Jack Ruby, in Dallas (1964), the proceedings against twenty-two members of the Auschwitz staff (1963–5).[4] From the perspective of this chapter, it is her narratives of the British and European continental magistrates' courts and trials, collected in *The Faces of Justice* and *As It Was* (1990), that deliver the challenge of literature's capacity to represent imaginatively, in Posner's words, "the day-to-day operations of a legal system." In these narratives of the quotidian court from the 1950s and 1960s, it is not just the case on trial or routinized legal proceedings or the incarnation of legal subjects that come under scrutiny, but the movement of affect and the entire life-world of the court itself.

Reading Bedford's writing about everyday law raises questions of whether the strict categories of fiction and fact that Posner imposes on her writing are sustainable, and whether her "brilliant" writing really does support Posner's case against literary representations of the law. These are questions this chapter wishes to address as it explores Bedford's achievements. At the same time, to make a case for the "brilliance" of Sybille Bedford as law writer in terms other than those laid down by Posner will involve engaging the wider issue of how a study of her work contributes to the ongoing academic inquiry and conversation we call "law and literature." In this chapter, I will argue that Bedford's texts, read alongside examples of generic writing on relations between the law and the general public, offer singular insights on such relations in the everyday courtroom. The courtroom takes alternative shape in her narratives in at least three important ways: as an ensemble of legal voices that can be heard as extra-legal polyphony; as the space of the interhuman encounter; as the space of law's elaboration beyond itself that responds to the demand of the observer-narrator as public witness. From the point of view of this chapter, these are the major contributions of her court writing to our understanding of law as quotidian practice and as culture, and may argue against her neglect in law and literature scholarship.

It is the case that Bedford as a writer about the law has not really been studied in any detail; in this respect, Posner's laconic mention is not untypical. Celebrating her recent centenary in 2011, Caroline Moorehead writes, with notable understatement, that Bedford's "coverage of trials" is "sometimes overlooked." (15)[5] Critical attention before and after Bedford's death in 2006 has been mainly focused on her Mexican travelogue (1953), and her semi-autobiographical novels and memoir for what they reveal of her family and peripatetic life between the two World Wars.[6] In contrast, *The Best We Can Do*, the record of the Adams trial, and the essays about magistrates' courts in *The Faces of Justice* and *As It Was*, have been critically neglected despite earlier reviewers' positive reception and praise for their *literary* qualities. For example, a reviewer of her account of the Adams trial writes:

> It is restrained and faithful reporting at its best, journalism without the double-spread headlines or any other contrived hint of sensationalism. It is good journalism plus – and the plus factor is more than sufficient to make the book literature. A trained lawyer might have done it differently, with greater emphasis on the trial techniques displayed by respective counsel, and the procedural and substantive points of law involved. But it is doubted that he would have done as well. He would probably have wound up with something like the ordinary law review article, a product which seldom merits the literary accolade.
>
> (Boyd 1959: 1066)[7]

The reviewer, a legal professional, attributes to Bedford's writing "literary" qualities beyond factual reporting that has the capacity to extend legal discourse toward a wider reading public. Here, the "literary" is stylistic medium and verbal accomplishment that mark the movement across the discursive space between the law and society at large. And quoting the specific account in *The Faces of Justice* of a trial for car theft in a Parisian court, another early reviewer comments:

> The . . . passage appears to be merely a bit of casual reporting. In fact it is a piece of masterly selection, obviously reduced to its shocking essentials. In a few lines, and without comment of her own, Miss Bedford has managed to say as much as Victor Hugo about French justice. The indictment is devastating and without appeal . . .
>
> (Bewley 1963)

Both reviews show that as a narrative of the many dimensions of the law, *The Faces of Justice* is itself multifaceted: both "factual" and "imaginative", it attends to how the day-to-day operations of the most ordinary courtroom can be made to yield up a referentiality beyond itself – both in the judicial and legal system in which it is situated, and in the domains of literature and culture.

The quotation from *The Faces of Justice* and the reviews direct attention to the generic ambivalence of Bedford's writing. Neither strictly trial report nor memoir of her court reporting experiences, it has observable literary qualities – in an instance when the "literary" and the "fictional" are not synonymous terms. Equally noticeable is how this "literary" space connecting what is inside and outside the law is also generically marked. To Robert Ferguson, this space is the "continuum of publication" that issues from "a courtroom trial – from indictment, to transcript, to judicial decision and on from there to newspaper report, journal article, historical account, and fictional projection." It is in this space, Ferguson opines, that "the cultural work of interpretation in courtroom analysis lies" and where "the hidden and neglected connections . . . *between* legal and nonlegal narratives" are forged and brought to light. (84, emphasis in original) But the exact location of Bedford's law writing in this space is elusive for it traverses all the generic categories that make up Ferguson's "continuum". Important for his insight on the necessary connections between the legal and nonlegal, Ferguson's positioning of the "courtroom trial" in the etiology of generic narratives continues to privilege the trial as the nexus of meaning production. In Bedford's writing, however, "courtroom" and "trial" are coeval terms and coterminous spaces: direct speech in evidentiary discourse, cross-examination and judicial pronouncements intermingle with free indirect observation, analytic interpellations, and reflexive comments, all framed by a narratological consciousness that, beyond the formal structure of the trial, confers shape and temporality.

Among the pressures acting upon the generic indeterminacy of Bedford's writing are the contrary demands of factuality and theatricality. In her memoir, *Quicksands*, Bedford admits to an "early fascination with the Law" (357) dating from her first visit to a London law court when she was captivated by the "blend of gravity and theatre of it all" (238), and would rather "watch trials" instead of "going to films and matinées." (Guppy 2006) During the Adams trial, she found herself daily amidst a media circus at once fanning and inflamed by popular views of the doctor's guilt.[8] Her decision, after the trial, to write "a comprehensive, unsensational account" of its "facts and atmosphere" (*Quicksands* 357), however, shows a desire to keep her fascination under control, and to restrict her literary skills to the trial's "atmosphere", the indeterminate but vital complement to the factual report.

In her description of the opening of a trial, for instance – "The gradual filling of the place with men and papers; the Judge's coming on with the flurry of sudden rising and subsiding which is the stroke of transsubstantiation into Court" (*FJ* 16) – Bedford's rhetoric arbitrates between law as auratic and as rehearsed and ritualized performance. Referencing Foucault's advocacy of *I, Paul Rivière*, Paul Rabinow observes, "Good journalism required a passion for stalking the elusive singularity of the present. More challenging yet was the task of observing oneself, with a certain distance, in the process of practising this *métier* . . ." (xviii). Bedford's self-reflexiveness as law writer is transcribed in the concise economy of her writing recognized by the reviewers as "restrained and faithful reporting at its best", "a piece of masterly selection". In his study of the semiotics of the common law, Peter Goodrich describes how, in the courtroom, "an architecture of place" (222) is ordered perspectivally by and towards the bench, and legal actors perform their roles with rehearsed and richly symbolic gestures that create the aura of the law's presence. Goodrich's insight on the court's theatricality is part of his critique of "the forms of appearance and representation of law in the public sphere" that make its legitimacy and sovereign authority visible to the public. (209–10) In the light of this critique, Bedford's accuracy and restraint may offer a spectating witness's sober mediation of the inherent theatricality of the courtroom, its mystification of the law and legal process and exploitation by a sensationalist media.

Paradoxically, concise economy also works as deliberate imprecision in alluding to the vast areas subterranean to the law's pomp and ceremony. Bedford's "guesswork, silences, evasions" open up, for a fellow writer, "gaps in which the imagination could breathe – truths might emerge, though seldom final truth" and offer insight into "the real drama flickering in hidden arbours and shadows." (Vansittart 2006) Both concise and allusive, Bedford's writing orchestrates the space "between" the legal and non-legal so that new perspectives on the everyday courtroom can emerge. In the "real drama" she visualizes, individuals in the performance of legal roles become the point of departure toward encounters in which the law both asserts itself and invokes the demands of the other. The courtroom is both the place of law and the space of affective life – always under the watchful gaze of an attentive member of the public.

We can catch a glimpse of her intricate maneuvers in the opening lines of "An Ordinary Trial", the first chapter of *The Faces of Justice* about a minor theft:

> Above the dais, the ornate chair, the robe, the still head of the Judge rises above the court as if suspended.
>
> "Thirty-two cheeses, my Lord, valued three hundred pounds four shillings and nine pence."
>
> The first moments inside a Court of Law are like the first moments at a play – the eye notes the scene, sound begins to reach the ear, then words. Sense converges later.
>
> (13)

Bedford breathes life into a courtroom so that as an "architecture of place" principally ordered, as Goodrich avers, from the perspective of the bench, it becomes the space of voices and other bodies. A reader familiar with modernist poetry may be reminded of the lines from T. S. Eliot's "East Coker":

> . . . As, in a theatre,
> The lights are extinguished, for the scene to be changed
> With a hollow rumble of wings, with a movement of darkness on darkness,
> And we know that the hills and the trees, the distant panorama
> And the bold imposing façade are all being rolled away—
> (Eliot 1963: 200)

Both passages refer pointedly to spectating subjects; it is their perspective on the scene, their "eye", and above all, their expectation that the narrative registers. But while Eliot's spectators – in the controlling intelligence of "we know" – maintain their distance from what is spectated on, Bedford is both watcher and the watched. As her senses become engaged, the courtroom comes to life; in her very physicality, the spectating subject becomes part of the action on the courtroom stage. As we shall see in greater detail later, in "An Ordinary Trial" and other essays, the everyday business of the court – or Posner's "day-to-day operations" – emerges in ways that redefines what is ordinary. This redefinition is generic as it selects *and* departs from established strategies of the trial report; it is also thematic for it pertains to the renascence of life in the courtroom suppressed by the court report's dominant legal focus.

Part 2

To consider the court report as genre, Ravit Reichman observes, is to study the relationship between "storyteller and audience" as both aesthetic and ethical. (146) In moving away from the court report, Bedford also mobilizes this relationship to aesthetic and ethical effect. "Storyteller" and "audience", rather than designating separate legal and lay categories or fixing positions inside and outside the courtroom, become narrative perspectives that overlap and disjoin. In Bedford's own time, there were notable efforts to explain the law to the public – or generic writing adjacent to hers where the law can speak with a more personal voice, and it is in this context that her originality can be more sharply perceived.

The end of the Second World War saw a revival of debates about reforming the magistrates' courts in England, in which the central issue was whether unpaid lay Justices of the Peace should be replaced by stipendary legal professionals working full-time. The law profession itself was by no means unanimous in its view on this issue. While Henry Slesser KC, a former Solicitor General and retired senior judge, asked "how impossible is it to expect that the benevolent untrained will continue to be able to discharge ... onerous duties" thrust upon them by "innumerable statutes" (5), E.V. Mills, a lawyer and JP, believed that lay magistrates who only needed to attend court once or twice a week came "to the work with a fresh mind ... the intervals of their time being occupied by other and brighter things." (5)[9] Mills' argument points to a world "other" than the law, a regular engagement with which makes for improved judicial acumen. In their majority Report (July, 1948, Cmd. 7463), the Royal Commission on Justices of the Peace reaffirmed the foundational importance of public intelligibility to the Common Law as the principal justification for commending the system of lay magistrates:

> because, like that of trial by jury, it gives the citizen a part to play in the administration of the law. It emphasises the fact that the principles of the common law, and even the language of statutes, ought to be ... comprehensible by any intelligent person without specialised training. Its continuance prevents the growth of suspicion in the ordinary man's mind that the law is a

> mystery which must be left to a professional caste and has little in common with justice as the layman understands it.
>
> (qtd in Whiteside 1949: 83)

In upholding the established system, the Report also recommended various measures for reforming the lay magistracy. "The ideal", the report states, "is that they shall learn what is expressed in the term 'acting judicially'." (Whiteside 1949: 76)

These recommendations became law with the passage of the Justices of the Peace Act (1949) but the debate on the "Common Law" and "common law", as they relate specifically to the magistrates' courts, continued to draw different principled views.[10] The legal scholar, Glanville Williams QC, acknowledges that lay or "amateur justice" may be less susceptible to "staleness and cynicism... from the never ending series of sordid cases" in the lower courts. (1955: 274–5) Against this, however, he cites as evidence the public esteem in which several stipendary magistrates were held as proof that they "may show all the qualities of freshness and humanity to be expected of a layman." (275)

Some of the justices whom Williams held up as positive *exempla* have written about their lives in law and experiences on the bench. In such memoirs, the impulse of self-explication is often imbricated with the aim of explaining the law to the public at large. The titles of Claud Mullins' *Fifteen Years Hard Labour* (1949), J.B. Sandbach's *This Old Wig* (1950), and James Avery Joyce's *Justice at Work: The Human Side of the Law* (1952) give a general idea of how they attempt the task of bridging the inside and outside of the law. Of the three, Sandbach's most closely approaches the personal memoir. After describing sequentially his early education and legal career, he then ranges over individuals and groups he encountered as Circuit Court judge in a narrative that is episodic and anecdotal. There are no accounts of actual trials, and much of the narrative is given over to summary descriptions of "loyalty, cheerfulness, gratitude and generosity in criminals." (93) These seem to invoke a colorful and diverse social world but as the word "criminals" indicate, no one is brought into the text who is not already a legal subject. On Sandbach's retirement, the London Street Traders Association presented him with "a truly magnificent silver snuff-box" (123), an incident he remembers with obvious satisfaction: "I imagine the barrow boys are as good judges as anybody, and if they have weighted me in the balance and not found me wanting, then I say I have had my triumph." (124)[11] Here, late in the narrative, the ordinary citizen's quick appearance is immediately incorporated into a legalistic order of value and social relations. At the same time, the anomalous conjunction of the barrow-boys and the snuffbox may reopen the distance between law and people which Sandbach is attempting to close.

The subtitle of Joyce's work, "the Human Side of the Law", and his declared aim – to write "for that important class of citizen, the 'general reader' " who would like "to look at the picture of 'the Law' *as a whole*" (8, emphasis in original) – speak of worthy intentions. "Wholeness", as it turns out, means comprehensive coverage: in four separate parts, Joyce summarily describes the current roles and functions of legal institutions (e.g. The Temple) and legal agents and subjects (judges, witnesses, prisoners, the Lord Chancellor, Attorney-General etc.), the meanings of legal terms (treason, murder and manslaughter etc.), and legislation on different aspects of social life (domestic and community). These descriptions take into account historical development and case precedents, and Joyce's mastery over the vast amount of materials he had to choose from is impressive. The result is an informative if necessarily selective manual enlivened, like Sandbach's, by vignettes of idiosyncratic individuals and witty exchanges between the bar and bench. In Joyce, as in Sandbach, the "human" is interpreted exclusively from a legal vantage, and often specifically from the vantage of the judge as legal agent. For instance, a chapter entitled "Prisoners" turns out not to be about prisoners but sentencing; its subtitle, "The *Art* of Sentencing" (my emphasis), points to the imaginative possibilities of how to act judicially and the law's "human side". The "human" as an everyday reference or narrative interest is absent from the text.

My intention here is not to accuse Sandbach or Joyce of failing in their narrative tasks. The point at issue is that as memoir or manual, their works represent the most common generic attempts to bring the law and general reader closer to each other, but that they do so on the premise that the world the reader inhabits has few other dimensions besides the legal. Chapter IX of Joyce's book, "Summing Up. How a Judge Thinks" begins with an epigraph, a verbal precedent by a famous predecessor on the bench: " 'Commonsense, as we all know, is the foundation of common law'." (93) "Commonsense", "we", "common law" – the voice of the "we", in Sandbach and Joyce, is the collective voice of bench and bar, the exclusive interpreters and agents of "common law" and legislator of "commonsense". There is no other "we".

Claud Mullins' *Fifteen Years Hard Labour* can be read as an attempt to question this univocal legalized "we". An account of Mullins' experiences as a stipendary magistrate and legal reformer, the book is part memoir and part explanation of the law with case references. It was written, Mullins declares, in the hope that it "will do something towards promoting much-needed changes in the administration of our criminal law." (9) The title speaks of an uphill struggle because, as Mullins avers, "in the world of the law new ideas are far from welcome" (9); this also helps explain the allusion to criminal penalty in the title which situates Mullins in the dock rather than on the side of his judicial peers. Instead of the seamless incorporation of the social world into the law we have earlier seen, Mullins speaks of disjunction. The law, in its failure to take into account social changes, is defective: ". . . I had realised", Mullins writes, "how neglectful Parliament had been in providing up-to-date law to govern the relationships between man and man [*sic*]. Now I realised that there was equal neglect in regard to the law of magisterial procedure." (43)

The perception of a disordered sociality – or "relationship between man and man" – that requires the law's governance is the source of much of Mullins' ambivalence about lay involvement in the law. Though he supports the system of lay magistrates, he is openly sceptical about trial by jury: juries, he opines, are "gullible" (49), "inherently sentimental." (52) He finds the general public wanting in the valuable quality of "commonsense": "Despite decades of universal schooling, magistrates have to deal with plenty of men and women whose intelligence is of the poorest." (54)[12] Looking at the everyday court, Mullins argues "that sentiment, sympathy, or a fellow feeling should have no place in magistrates' work" only to contradict himself almost immediately by saying "[w]ith some defendants he [the magistrate] can be sympathetic, helpful and occasionally cheerful." (59) Again, on the point of language, while Mullins objects to the theatricality of some barristers' oratory that "reduces a criminal trial to a game" (51), he himself is not averse to the occasional rhetorical flourish:

> The fixed seats for counsel and solicitors, divided by barriers about three feet high, the little boxes in which sat the higher police officers, and sometimes the probation officers, all gave the impression that everybody working on the floor of the court was placed in his seat by a helicopter.
>
> (61)

Reading this passage alongside Bedford's quoted earlier on shows that a common interest in the "human" in the courtroom produces very different kinds of spatial narratives. Mullins criticizes the legal ordering of the court by pointing to the absence of human, voluntaristic agency, while Bedford, as we have seen, narrates space by intimations of human presence. To be sure, in being ambivalent and self-contradictory, Mullins reveals himself as "human". A gap remains, however, between his legal self which dominates the narrative and the legal and lay subjects he attacks for their inadequacies. In contrast, the perspective of the ordinary or lay person, is one that Bedford herself adopts and also ascribes to many unknown others collectivized as "one" or "we" in the text; their shifting perspectives inscribe spectating as intersubjective practice and performance.

As narrator, spectator, and the spectated, the "I" in Bedford's text articulates subjective reflection, first-person witnessing of the legal process, and different modes of addressing a larger audience, drawing the latter into the public gallery or invoking their presence beyond the law in everyday life. The "public" in Bedford is positioned both inside and outside the law, an aesthetic function that inscribes Bedford's pursuit of the extra-legal sanctions of law's authority in culture and society. Admitting to her own "unprofessional limitations", Bedford justifies her writing about law by declaring that "Justice is supposed to be seen being done [*sic*], and this must surely mean seen also by the likes of us." (*FJ* 84) The slippage from her individual shortcoming to the plural "the likes of us" argues that her concern with the quotidian courtroom is part of a larger project to show how the lay person becomes involved as witness to law's performance of social justice.

Long before notions about the law as reflecting "the customs, values, and ideas associated with particular places" (Sarat *et al.* 2003: 1), or how law needs to be considered as part of " 'the cultural processes that actively contribute in the composition of social relations'" (Sarat and Kearns 1993: 7, quoting Silbey) are widely accepted, Bedford proposes law as cultural paradigm, and culture as law's alibi:

> The law, the working of the law, the daily application of the law to people and situations is an essential element in a country's life. It runs through everything . . . It shapes a country's modes of thought, its political concepts and realities, its conduct.
>
> (*FJ* 83)

From the everyday courtroom, Bedford argues that the lay observer can form judgments not only about a particular judicial system but the country to which it belongs. *The Faces of Justice* is her eye-witness record of the connection between law's everyday practice and culture in England and a number of European jurisdictions including Germany, her birthplace from which, as a Jew, she was exiled, first to France and then to the United States in 1940.

Speaking of *The Faces of Justice*, the novelist Rebecca West, also a court reporter, marvels: "So good is the theme of *The Faces of Justice* that one finds oneself asking . . . and wondering why nobody has done it before." (7) Though the idea for the book may be original to Bedford, as West observes, the notion that culture is constituted *in* and *of* everyday life has a far wider contemporary resonance. Two years before *The Faces of Justice*, Raymond Williams had announced that "Culture is Ordinary" (1958), in a moving tribute to the working class family and community of his origins, and to retrieve from them a possible structure that could co-ordinate emerging relations between popular education, the media, and mass communication. "A culture has two aspects", Williams states:

> the known meanings and directions, which its members are trained to; the new observations and meanings, which are offered and tested . . . [T]he nature of culture . . . is both the most ordinary common meanings and the finest individual meanings. We use the word culture in these two senses: to mean a whole way of life – the common meanings; to mean the arts and learning – the special processes of discovery and creative effort.
>
> (4)

The "common" is a notion to which, as we have seen, Williams' legal contemporaries make recurrent appeal. In the 1958 essay, Williams did not mention the law, but the gulf between his cultural understanding of the "common" and the legal understanding is very visible during his appearance as defence witness in the Chatterley trial. That Williams was called because as Workers Education Association (W.E.A.) lecturer, he was teaching students from a particular social class, was made very obvious in the question put to him by the defence counsel, Jeremy Hutchinson QC. Referring to a passage in *Lady Chatterley's Lover* that the prosecution held up as example of salaciousness, Hutchinson asked, " 'Mr Williams, in your classes which you take, and having regard to the kind of people who attend them, would you think it right to discuss it and for those people to read it?' " Williams' reply: "I should be very glad to discuss it. It has not, of course, been commonly available." (Rolph 1961: 135)

Williams' use of the word "commonly" shrewdly translates "the kind of people" that Hutchinson's question separates off as a particular social class into subjects of a generally shared discursive space. Though she does not appear to share Williams' political imperative, Bedford's writing reveals similar concerns about the "common" that for Williams is grounded on the lived experiences of a particular institution – the working class family. If for Williams, culture is or ought to be ordinary, Bedford had a similar conviction about the law: it is in law's most ordinary everyday practice that she searches for and seeks to bear witness to a culture's attention to otherness as measure of its capacity for justice. Aligned with Williams' advocacy of culture as collective and individual meaning-making in everyday life, Bedford invents a metonymic narrative of legal culture *as* culture.[13] The cultural analyses of law are supplemented in Bedford's writing by moments when culture calls law to account or appears beyond legal capture.[14]

Part 3

A reading of Bedford reveals the courtroom as the place of law and not-law, where law's imposition on society and its restraint, and society's legal subjection and elusiveness circulate. In a characteristic narrative movement, Bedford marshals two contrary orientations: individuation and aggregation. Staging the court, she introduces the legal *dramatis personae*; as spectator, she registers the human subjects materializing as they perform their legal roles:

> The Judge's head does not stir. It is the head of a man aged first into a face only, the face of a very old woman, aged now into a fine dry shell, the almost transparent covering of precise slow workings – an ear, a brain, a hand . . . An usher moves about softly, careful not to trip. A handful of extraneous and upset looking people sit neatly . . . A tall Silk, splendid as Pompey, strolls into court, bends over a colleague who turns up a dimpled Boswellian face . . . At the far end of the court . . . sits the prisoner in the dock . . . His small, smooth face is all profile; smarmed palish hair, pale stretched baby-skin, showing the bones, showing the skull, showing the thoughts move: swimming slowly, carefully, showing the nerves stretch: showing fear . . . In the dock with him like an idle umpire in the ring, sits a warder in uniform, bulky, relaxed, unconcerned.
>
> The charge is fraudulent conversion to his own use and benefit of certain property. He is, in fact, accused of having stolen some apples and some cheeses from his employer.
>
> (*FJ* 13–15)

Individuating legal actors as human subjects through vivid aural and visual detail, the passage also rearranges the court's normative hierarchy as a more communal ensemble. Each of these subjects is linked by an invisible sightline to a spectating – and watchful – public eye. Initially represented by the narrator, the public is also elaborated as the "other" to whom the more knowing narrator owes the responsibility of translating legal into everyday language.

Elsewhere in the essay, "An Ordinary Trial", Bedford comments on her practice of her *métier* by drawing attention to the narrative as palimpsestic: as notes of a trial taken down in court that shape or are excluded from her court report, supplemented by the *post-hoc* workings of memory and reflection. It is a text driven by a desire to establish "a kind of yard-stick" (16) for comparative measurement of different jurisdictions – a "yard-stick" that is less a doctrinal standard than an assessment of the performance of forms of English and European justice as seen in the experience of the quotidian court. "The standard of proof in the criminal law is proof beyond reasonable doubt", states Lord Devlin who, as Judge Devlin, presided at the Henry Bodkin Adams trial. (29) Bedford's "yard-stick", while it would certainly include the "standard of proof" principle, is also more elastic, and suggests other kinds of standards, some of which, such as the good manners or otherwise of a judge addressing a prisoner, would not even be registered in an ordinary court report.

To Bedford, the trial is structured by predetermined codes that legal subjects reinscribe through compliance, and rituals they reenact in performance. Judge Devlin described the formula drily: "Most trials are no more than the acting out of the prosecution's opening speech diversified by the struggle of the defence to infect the mass of material with reasonable doubt." (8) From this perspective, what Bedford offers is less *and* more than the record of a trial. While it is true that the judgment on each case and point of law is not really her central concern, her narrative is not designed to exalt randomness and plurality *per se*. The interest in individuation, for instance, is consistent with her declared aim of showing how the judicial treatment of individuals can throw light on a society's values. It is not meaning in law that her narrative pluralizes but the process by which meaning can be produced, informed by the concern that meaning-making, while evident in the everyday work of legal actors, is a culturally inclusive and instructive activity.

Meaning-making embraces but also goes beyond "yard-stick" or level-setting. In a typical instance, she observes, "The law that must seem to hound, also protects the silent prisoner in the dock: the formidable wheel stays its course, standing still almost before it may crush this exceedingly small fly." (*FJ* 19) The law as equitable and exacting, protective and punitive, the spectator, both vigilant and morbidly fascinated – the relations between the law and its witnessing are collaborative, mobile, and changeable in a single instantiating moment. From time to time, the "apples and cheeses" case is colored by shades of fantasy so that in its quotidian ordinariness, it acquires the kind of archetypal cultural resonance normally reserved for fairy-tales. The jury, listening to the cross-examination of witness and prisoner, seem to be in a "collective day-dream" (22); the defence counsel portrays a floating world in which "memory is fallible, behaviour unaccountable, actions not always what they appear to be." (24) Watching the judge deliver his concluding speech, the narrator realizes that "every fact and word" that have already been spoken in the cross-examination and the two counsels' speeches "are here again in a new order." This iterative process appears well-rehearsed to the point of being mechanized, and yet she admits to being captivated by it, in an extended metaphor that accentuates the fantasy character of the trial:

> . . .one is gripped by a sense of watching the perfect automaton at work, the computer inside the old-fashioned illusionist contraption in the cabinet of wonders . . . deliver a creaking train of marshalled fact and datum, now from this angle, now from that . . .
>
> (25)

The courtroom trial as fantasy narrative situates the audience as captivated spectators, but it also raises the critical question: what are they "gripped by"? The law in performance? Or rather, the metaphorical and allusive narrative that, in exploiting the law's dramaticality, estranges it?

Instead of the extended account of a single trial, the essay, "Summary Justice", narrates an ordinary day at the magistrates' courts where "instantaneous justice" is dispensed, and where "[s]ummary" can mean "dispatch from charge to sentence in one breath." (27) Bedford's description of the court's fixtures focuses on their spartan difference from those in the higher courts, and pays special attention to how space provision shapes perspective on the other:

> A single man or woman in the dock, however down-at-heel, however pugnacious, miserable or slick, is a human being alone, an individual isolated, in trouble. Two, crammed into that contraption, are at once reduced to an exhibit.
>
> (31)

Between these two perspectives on the other as human and dehumanized, the narrative appears to put the law itself on trial, challenging it to demonstrate that even at its most mechanized, its capacity to deliver justice remains unfaltering.

In the first seven cases, all to do with drunkenness in public places, each of the defendants is named and the narrative attention to their individual appearance graduates from minimal description of the first to unravelling the personal predicament of the last. The narrative's exponential sequencing alludes to a quotidian trial schedule that arranges for the case with the least possible complication to be heard first. Its observable focus, as it moves from one case to another, is the magistrate in different interlocutory modes *vis-à-vis* the defendants. "Quick as small-arms fire" at the beginning, the magistrate "very slightly alters his voice" in questioning the second defendant (28), then alternates between scrutinizing the defendant with his spectacles off and burying his "nose in [a] ledger" (29), to the careful probing of the seaman as to why he had no fixed abode and didn't know how to plead (30). He is kindly to an elderly first-time shoplifter, his tone "not unfriendly, rational" (33) to a man charged with receiving, requires a "listless" (33) young man to seek help from his probation officer, does a "lightning calculation" to set a bail that is "large enough and not prohibitive" (34), hesitates over another bail, "flays" another defendant for a "senseless action" (35), ensures that foreign defendants have had access to interpretation, gives a final chance to a shoplifter with previous convictions, and presides in a full trial where the plea is not guilty. The narrative appears to corroborate, and to collaborate with, the judge in staging the unexceptional cases as so many discrete encounters with otherness. Its descriptive diction recurrently attends to an affective connection between judge and accused so that in interlocutions between the two, the formal interpellations – "Your Honour", "prisoner" – are shown to carry responsibility beyond the legal.

Disrupting the seamless extension of positive affect from court to public, the narrative calls the spectating audience once again to attention: "The emotional climate of a trial is strange," Bedford observes,

> it breeds a compound of scepticism and faith ... an ultimate turning to the man in the chair. And afterwards, it is a shock to find that one had looked to him to provide a miracle. The third shock is that of course he must be right.
> (40)

The passage's content appears to confirm the judge's authority and prestige, but from another perspective, it alerts the spectator-witness to the profoundly destabilizing process by which trust in the law is arrived at – a process that has less to do with the law's innate worth than with subliminal desires for security and belief. The issue of law's mystery is shifted away from its auratic presence to the non-rational, unfathomable process by which such presence takes public hold.

In another essay, "The Worst We Can Do", Bedford further elaborates law's ambivalent relation to non-rational processes through several cases where lay justices, rejecting police and expert advice and counsel's mitigation pleas, insist on a punitive sentence. Here, in the "small things men do to each other every day" (63), she discloses the court's habitual aversion to "psychiatric opinion" (66), or its tendency to reify emotional and psychological distress as crime, or its fetishization of property loss as the only social harm. As a signifier of the collective, "we" in the chapter's title has broadened beyond legal professionals to lay members acting in the name of the law; it is individuals in the aggregate but also refers to a social collective acting against itself, in its own "worst" interest. In this internally contradicted "we", the law's systemic defects become symptomatic of a much wider communal failure to engage the otherness within itself.

As a Jewish exile from National Socialist Germany, Bedford was no stranger to the catastrophic failure of this engagement. One of her famous-trial essays, "The Worst that Ever Happened", is on the trial of twenty-two former staff of Auschwitz concentration camp. (*AIW* 218–60). But it is in her essays on the post-war German court that we can follow her continued pursuit of the meaning of everyday law as both cultural metonym and collective cultural endeavor. Out of the plethora of trials she observed, two are selected for detailed narrative, the first in Karlsruhe, West Germany's law capital, where it seems all signs of "the recent bad old days" (*FJ* 88) have been removed – "no eagles, no emblem of any kind." (85) The trial, in which a medical doctor is accused of shooting a man in a park who has indecently exposed himself to his (the doctor's) daughter, had become a *cause célèbre* dividing German opinion into two factions, one of which hails the doctor as hero while the other sees his behavior as a too obvious reminder of the recent past. Using the common law adversarial trial as "yard-stick", Bedford details the differences of the German inquisitorial system. Speaking of the judge, specifically in his cross-examination of the doctor's young daughter, she is full of praise: "It was well done . . . I should perhaps say that it was a performance of high human quality and that a German court of law was the last place where I should have dreamt to encounter it." (103)

In narrating how the trial opens up from legal to public event, the significant moment is when the entire court, together with members of the press, physically leave the courtroom, and, aided by the police who held up traffic at crossings, make their way to the park for a reconstruction of the shooting; on the way, they are observed, followed and joined by members of the public. The narrative moves between the trial personnel, the park visitors, and the many others who switch between the roles from moment to moment as they spectate, witness and comment on the reconstruction or continue to enjoy the "slanting sun", or watch the "red squirrels chasing acorns". In other words, the move to the park is a literal re-insertion of the trial into the scenery of the everyday. But in another sense, the move has a de-realizing effect, as Bedford, who has been talking to a "psychiatric professor from Heidelberg", notices that people "believed us to be a film company." (106) On another day in the trial, law students debate the case heatedly among themselves; Bedford calls them "the populace . . . because that is what they were, with a fine streak of *tricoteuses* among them." (113) In knitting together the trial as event, Bedford narrates a Germany very different from the one she left behind thirty years before and vowed never to return – a difference so radical that she is struck by a sense of its unreality. Both inside and outside the court, she observes an exemplary otherness toward whom she is drawn as if in a dream: a dream of law that is also a dream of her German self as other *and* herself and Germany as others – alterities reincarnated from the annihilating alienation of death.

The drama of her encounter with post-war Germany continues in Munich; she admits to prejudice against Munich's inhabitants, a prejudice haunted by her memory of the city's reputation as "the breeding-ground and sanctuary of National Socialism." (159) Contending against the specter of the past is her narrative of select trials where humane judges seek to reconcile the legally permissible with an exploration of the humanly possible in the given circumstances. Among these cases is one in which a foreigner, a Czech illegal migrant, is accused of stealing small amounts of food and clothing from an empty weekend shack in the Bavarian woods. His desperate situation after trekking three days and nights from the border did not elicit the owner's sympathy. In court, the judge balanced the owner's demand for punishment with a careful deliberation about "Necessity" that covers in some detail each of the items that was taken, down to eighteen cigarettes over which the court pronounced that for a man used to smoking forty a day, "the taking of one packet must be considered provision for his journey and therefore Appropriation through Necessity rather than Theft." (161) Receiving a sentence of four months deferred, the Czech is discharged. As she leaves the court, Bedford sees the stranger surrounded by people from the public gallery: "They had sent round the hat and were stuffing the proceeds into his pockets and limp hand." (162)

At this point, Bedford the spectator is noticeably reticent: the scene outside the courtroom is represented with no narratorial comment. In this characteristic self-restraint, Bedford draws back from pushing the "yard-stick" of compassion inside the courtoom, and the "yard-stick" of spontaneous neighborliness outside the courtroom to a common conclusion. From one point of view, the representation appears to make visible a possible European future when what happens in law has learnt from a revived culture of responsibility for and to the other, and what happens outside the courtroom shows legal example being transcribed as everyday practice. But as she looks in another direction, the everyday and otherness within it continue to be incarcerated in an alternative temporality of the past-in-the-present: it comes to her that of the "some eleven thousand German judges", "two hundred – at least! – must have been active Nazis," (*FJ* 223) and that of "[a]t least 6,000 men who worked at Auschwitz, . . . there were only . . . 22 defendants." (*AIW* 223). Confronting this much darker horizon, the law appears inadequate, and the everyday shot through with the frisson of a haunted neighborliness. Between law and not-law, in the space of the "literary", what "is" and what "ought to be" attend on each other, and these contrary forces, even as they gain traction through opposition, are also brought into everyday engagement.

That Posner did not elaborate the case for Sybille Bedford's "brilliance" may seem, at first sight, to be a technical omission. Such omission, this chapter argues, can be traced to his exclusive identification of "literature" as fictional texts, and the fact that no one else has taken up Bedford's case suggests that such identification is not limited to Posner but is normative of law and literature studies. In assigning Bedford's court writing to the category of non-fiction, Posner posits for it an epistemological status similar to that of trial and court reports predicated on factuality. This renders as secondary a consideration of their qualities as literature and so undermines the case of their "brilliance" while also casting doubt on the purpose and value of their advocacy as such. Thus, this chapter's inaugural assent to Posner's praise of Bedford also inaugurates a turning away from his categories and categorizing. In attending to select moments from Bedford's court writing, the chapter shows how they broaden the understanding of the "literary" in law and literature studies. This expansion includes new vantages on the court and its everyday administration of the law and importantly, ways of writing about both that depart from conventionalized reports and accounts. Narrating, as opposed to just reporting, the trial, Bedford demonstrates qualities of the "literary" and how they vivify even the most routinized legal processes. Factual reporting and imaginative representation are discursively mixed; the law as formal system and the lived experience of interhuman encounters receive comparable attention and in the process, become co-extensive and co-existent. A discussion of the "literary" also maps the points of connection between law and non-law in Bedford's writing. From the law as an ethical encounter with the other, Bedford moves further to reflect on how a legal system operates as a signifying practice of society in general, and how in small everyday acts, ordinary citizens collaborate in making and unmaking legal meaning. Reporting on the culture of quotidian law, and on legal practice as culture, Bedford also imagines an everyday in which the law's ambivalent presence testifies to a culture's doubled capacity for self-reform and persistence in error.

Endnotes

1 Bedford is not mentioned in the 1st (1988) and 2nd (1998) editions of *Law and Literature*.
2 Again, this statement does not appear in the first two editions of *Law and Literature*. Both the 1988 (p. 71) and 1998 (p. 11) editions read instead: ". . . I shall argue that the frequency of legal subjects in literature is partly a statistical artifact and that law figures in literature more often as metaphor than as an object of interest in itself . . ."
3 Hereinafter known as *FJ*.
4 These are collected in a later work, *As It Was*, hereinafter known as *AIW*, published after Bedford achieved wider public recognition when *Jigsaw* (1989) made the Booker shortlist. *As It Was* collects her court writing from the 1960s that includes the everyday account, "A Look at Judges at Work", and the famous trial reports.
5 Moorehead's lengthy essay captures the revival in the centenary year of interest in Sybille Bedford, and her biography of the writer should be something to look forward to. See also the very informative website <http://www.sybillebedford.com>
6 These are *A Legacy* (1956), *Jigsaw* (1989), and *Quicksands* (2005).
7 In a more recent reference to *The Faces of Justice*, a reviewer comments that it offers "excellent analyses of the law at work" and that "few lawyers have explained the system as well." (Goldfarb 2002)
8 The trial is described as "one of the first murder trials to attract the burgeoning interest of an increasingly vociferous media" in the immediate post-war period. (Cullen 2006: 11)
9 Mills signs himself as "Deputy Chairman, Bromley Magistrates' Court." (5)
10 And indeed, on and off, until recent times. See Jackson, Diamond, Morgan and Russell.
11 This is highlighted in Glanville Williams (1955: 275) as evidence that stipendary magistrates are not out of touch with the "other" public world.
12 It is very ironical that Mullins is himself accused of lacking in "common sense" in his strenuous advocacy of reform in the matrimonial and juvenile courts. (Fulton 1948)
13 What emerges as a result are much more positive images of experiences and expectations of the law in her writing than in Williams'. This contrast becomes even sharper when we look at Williams' 1980s essay, written during the miner's strike, in which he speaks out explicitly against law as a regulatory regime manipulated by a capitalist social order. (See Raymond Williams 1989: 125)

14 Recently, critical work is beginning to address ways in which the legalization of the everyday may be counteracted or evaded by discursive subjectivities. See, for example, Wai Chee Dimock's article on Soviet law and the Russian poet, Osip Mandelstam. (Sarat *et al.* 2003: 21–42)

Bibliography

Barrow, Andrew (2004) 'Sybille Bedford: Secret History', *Independent on Sunday*, 23 May. Online. Available HTTP: <http://www.independent.co.uk/arts- entertainment/books/features/sybille-bedford-secret-history-564205.html> (accessed 26 Sept 2010).

Bedford, Sybille (1953) *The Sudden View: A Mexican Journey*, London: Gollancz. (rpt) (1960) as *A Voyage to Don Otavio: A Traveller's Tale from Mexico*, London: Collins

Bedford, Sybille (1956) *A Legacy: A Novel*, London: Weidenfeld and Nicolson.

Bedford, Sybille (1958; rpt 1961) *The Best We Can Do. An Account of the Trial of John Bodkin Adams*, London: Penguin.

Bedford, Sybille (1961) *The Faces of Justice*, London: Collins.

Bedford, Sybille (1966) "Letter to Hannah Arendt, 15 July." in *The Hannah Arendt Papers*, Library of Congress, USA. Online. Available HTTP: <http://memory.loc.gov/cgi-bin/ampage?collId=mharendt&fileName=02/020150/020150page.db&recNum=0> (accessed 31 January 2011).

Bedford, Sybille (1989) *Jigsaw. An Unsentimental Education*, London: Hamish Hamilton.

Bedford, Sybille (1990; rpt. 1992) *As It Was. Pleasures, Landscapes and Justice*, London: Picador.

Bedford, Sybille (2005; rpt. 2006) *Quicksands. A Memoir*, London: Penguin.

Bewley, Marius (1963) 'An International Episode', *The New York Review of Books*, 1 June. Online. Available HTTP: <http://www.nybooks.com/articles/archives/1963/jun/01/an-international-episode/> (accessed 1 February 2011).

Boyd, T. Munford (1959) 'The Trial of Dr. Adams', *American Bar Association Journal*, 45: 10, p. 1066.

Cullen, Pamela V. Halliday (2006) *A Stranger in Blood. The Case Files on Dr John Bodkin Adams*, London: Elliot & Thompson.

Devlin, Patrick (1985) *Easing the Passing. The Trial of Doctor John Bodkin Adams*, London: Faber and Faber.

Diamond, Shari Seidman (1990) 'Revising Images of Public Punitiveness: Sentencing by Lay and Professional English Magistrates', *Law & Social Inquiry*, 15: 2, pp. 191–221.

Eliot, T.S. (1963) *Collected Poems. 1909–1962*, London: Faber & Faber.

Ferguson, Robert A. (1966) 'Untold Stories in the Law', in Peter Brooks and Paul Gewirtz (eds.) *Law's Stories. Narrative and Rhetoric in the Law*, New Haven, CT: Yale University Press, pp. 84–98.

Foucault, Michel (ed.) (1973, 1975) *I, Pierre Rivière, having slaughtered my mother, my sister and my brother*, New York: Random House.

Fulton, Eustace (1948) 'Letter to the editor', *The Times*, 23 August, p. 5.

Goldfarb, Ronald (2002) 'Review of Anthony Chase's *Movies on Trial: The Legal System on the Silver Screen*', Online. Available HTTP: <http://www.dcbar.org/for_lawyers/resources/publications/washington_lawyer/october_2002/books.cfm (accessed 25 November 2010).

Goodrich, Peter (1990) *Languages of Law: From Logics of Memory to Nomadic Masks*, London: Weidenfeld and Nicolson.

Guppy, Shusha (2006) 'Sybille Bedford', *Independent*. 20 February, Obituary.

Hammelmann, H.A. (1962) '[R]eview of *The Faces of Justice*', *Modern Law Review*, 25: 1, pp. 124–6.
Joyce, James Avery (1952) *Justice at Work: The Human Side of the Law*, London: Chapman and Hall.
Kavanagh, Dennis (1987) *Thatcherism and British Politics: The End of Consensus?* Oxford: Oxford University Press
Mills, E.V. (1948) 'Advantages of Lay Bench: Psychological Factor', *The Times*, letter to the editor, 19 August, p. 5.
Moorehead, Caroline. (2011) 'The Warm South. Sybille Bedford at 100', *Times Literary Supplement*, 15 April pp. 14–15.
Morgan, Rod and Neil Russell (2000) 'The Judiciary in the Magistrates' Courts', Report prepared for the Home Office. (December)
Mullins, Claud (1948; 2nd edn 1949) *Fifteen Years Hard Labour*, London: Victor Gollancz.
Posner, Richard (1997) 'Against Ethical Criticism', *Philosophy and Literature*, 21: 1, pp. 1–27.
Posner, Richard (1988; 3rd edn 1998) *Law and Literature*, Cambridge, MA: Harvard University Press.
Rabinow, Paul (ed) (1997) *Michel Foucault. Ethics. Subjectivity and Truth*, New York: The New Press.
Reichman, Ravit (2009) *The Affective Life of Law. Legal Modernism and the Literary Imagination*, Stanford, CA: Stanford University Press.
Rolph, C.H. (ed.) (1961) *The Trial of Lady Chatterley. Transcript of the Trial*. Privately Printed.
Sandbach, J.B. (1950) *This Old Wig Being Some Recollections of the Life of a Former London Metropolitan Police Magistrate*, London: Hutchinson & Co.
Sarat, Austin and Thomas R. Kearns (eds) (1993) *Law in Everyday Life*, Ann Arbor, MI: University of Michigan Press.
Sarat, Austin, Lawrence Douglas, Martha Merrill Umphrey (eds.) (2003) *The Place of Law*, Ann Arbor, MI: University of Michigan Press.
Slesser, Henry (1948) 'Trained Lawyers as Magistrates', letter to the editor, *The Times*, 17 Aug, p. 5.
Vansittart, Peter (2006) 'Sybille Bedford', *Guardian*, 21 February, Obituary.
Weisberg, Richard H. (1989) 'Entering with a Vengeance: Posner on Law and Literature', *Stanford Law Review*, 41: 1597–626.
West, Rebecca (1961) 'Judged by Their Courts', *Sunday Telegraph*, 21 May, p. 7.
West, Robin (1993) *Narrative, Authority, and Law*, Ann Arbor, MI: University of Michigan Press.
Whiteside, James. (1949) 'Report of the Royal Commission on Justices of the Peace', *The Modern Law Review*, 12: 1, pp. 73–84.
Williams, Glanville (1955) *The Proof of Guilt*, London: Stevens & Sons.
Williams, Raymond (1989) *Resources of Hope. Culture, Democracy, Socialism*, (ed) Robin Gale, London and New York: Verso.

Chapter 5

Sir William Jones and the translation of law in India

Robert Young

What happens when you translate a legal system from the metropolitan imperial centre to a colony? The case of Sir William Jones provides one instructive answer.

Sir William Jones (1746–94) is an unusual figure in that he worked directly within the fields of literature and law: he was both poet and lawyer (he is credited with the invention of the concept of 'the reasonable man' in his *Essay on Bailments* (1781) (Oldham 1995)), translator (notably in his own day of the Persian poet Hafiz), judge and jurist, and a central figure in the development of English law in India. Jones' interdisciplinary talent and professional energies are one reason why his work has remained hard to assess within any of the individual fields in which he worked. Even within the two fields of literature and law individually considered, his work was generally comparative – before the subjects of comparative literature or the historical and comparative school of legal philosophy had been invented. He was also a historian, and of course a linguist, or more properly a philologist – indeed he is customarily credited with the invention of historical or comparative philology as a discipline in Britain, and it is in this context that in the twentieth and twenty-first centuries he has been most regularly cited (Momma 1997). He was not the first to recognize the affinities between Latin, Greek and Sanskrit, but it was Jones who suggested that, together with Gothic, Celtic, and Old Persian, they were related languages genealogically derived from a common root – a language that in 1813 Thomas Young would name Indo-European (albeit in a different and more eccentric genealogical configuration).

Jones' own remarkable talent for languages, and relatively unusually for his time and for ours, non-European languages – meant that by the end of his life he knew English, Latin, Greek, French, Arabic, Hebrew, Turkish, Persian, Sanskrit. His famous writings on the comparative historical relations between those languages notwithstanding, as a good utilitarian, his view of language was always instrumental: as he put it in the Introduction to his translation of *Al Sira-jiyyah: or, the Mohammedan Law of Inheritance* 'practical utility being my ultimate object in this work – it has nothing to do with literary curiosities' (Jones 1792: iv). He did not regard knowledge of languages as learning in its own right; rather it formed the means to learning. And the learning that each language contained he considered always translatable into another language. His work is founded on a deep principle of translatability, of equivalence between languages. While he believed in linguistic translatability, paradoxically the whole rationale of his legal work was at the same time founded on a principle of cultural untranslatability. This, however, did not prevent a profound cultural translation from taking place.

The British began to exercise certain judicial functions in India as early as the seventeenth century, but it was not until the East India Company took on the official Mughal post of Diwani for Bengal, Bihar and Orissa in 1765 that its officers became generally responsible for the administration of justice in those territories. In 1772 Warren Hastings became governor of Bengal (the following year he became the first Governor-General of India) and instituted a series of reforms designed to rationalize the legal system that the East India Company had taken over. Hastings created separate civil and criminal courts, the British presiding over the first, and Mughals the second. Following his belief that good governance in Bengal could be achieved through the continued use of Indian customary law, an arrangement that was both practical as well as ideological, the civil courts were organized to administer Hindu law to Hindus, and Muslim law to Muslims, while the criminal court applied Muslim law only (Benton 2002: 133–4). Throughout these arrangements, the ethical principle of Hastings and his followers (James Forbes, Nathaniel Halhed, William Jones), or even enemies, such as Edmund Burke (though Burke was a friend of Jones), was that British common law should not be forced on a subject Indian population (Haldar 2007: 114). Wishing to found the authority of the East India Company on the ancient laws of Bengal, while at the same time being responsible for their administration, put the British in a position of dependency on the local pundits who had access to the secret sources of the law and its interpretation (Cohn 1996: 25). With the paranoia characteristic of the uncertain colonizer, the British distrusted the pundits, felt that they were manipulated by them and disliked being effectively caught in the power of the native's 'sly civility' (Bhabha 1994: 93). Hastings therefore commissioned translations of local Hindu and Muslim legal writings, as well as compilations of digests of local laws (Cohn 1966). The first product of his initiative was Nathaniel Halhed's *A Code of Gentoo* [i.e. Hindu] *Laws, or, Ordinations of the Pundits*, from a Persian translation, made from the original, written in the Shanscrit language (Halhed 1776). Halhed, who had published the first Bengali grammar, introduced the rudiments of the Sanskrit language at the beginning of the *Code*, but it was a language that he never fully learnt. His code of laws was drawn up by eleven Bengali pundits from twenty different sources in Sanskrit, and then translated via Bengali into Persian. Halhed then translated this into English. Halhed was ridiculed by Jones and many others since for the inaccuracies that this triple translation produced (though in fact Jones himself in his translations first translated the Sanskrit texts into Latin and then from Latin into English). However inaccurate, it was nevertheless a very practical digest and for that reason continued to be used well into the nineteenth century, illustrating the first paradoxical law of translation, that a bad translation does not prevent it from being a good translation, in the sense of one that people choose to continue to use or even prefer to 'good' or accurate translations. Jones, who arrived in India in 1783 to be a judge in the Supreme Court of Calcutta, had ambitions that were altogether greater – he wished to effect a complete Justinian Corpus Juris Civilis ('Body of Civil Law') or collection of fundamental works in Indian jurisprudence. Justinian's corpus had included both complete texts and digests, and this provided Jones with a model whereby he would incorporate both. His two translations, *Al Sira-jiyyah: or, The Mohammedan Law of Inheritance* (Jones 1792) and *The Laws of Menu* (Jones 1796) were published in his lifetime, while *A Digest of Hindu Law* was completed by his successor judge H.T. Colebrooke and published in 1801 (Colebrooke 1801). Following his genealogical linking of Indian and European languages, Jones maintained his preference for local law while at the same time claiming that it formed part of a wider universal law – an affiliation which he achieved by linking *Menu* to Roman law, with the suggestion that like European and Indian languages, they all shared some common primordial revelatory source (Haldar 2007: 118–19).

Jones begins the Preface to *The Laws of Menu* with two sentences that take up a page apiece. In the first, he writes:

> It is a maxim in the science of legislation and government, that Laws are of no avail without manners, or, to explain the sentence more fully, that the best intended legislative provisions would have no beneficial effect even at first, and none at all in a short course of time, unless they were congenial to the disposition and habits, to the religious prejudices, and approved immemorial usages, of the people, for whom they were enacted; especially if that people universally and sincerely believed, that all their ancient usages and established rules of conduct had the sanction of an actual revelation from heaven: the legislature of Britain having shown, in compliance with this maxim, an intention to leave the natives of these Indian provinces in possession of their own Laws, at least on the titles of contracts and inheritances, we may humbly presume, that all future provisions, for the administration of justice and government in India, will be conformable, as far as the natives are affected by them, to the manners and opinions of the natives themselves; an object, which cannot possibly be obtained, until those manners and opinions can be fully and accurately known.

These are the main considerations, Jones writes, which have led him to translate the *Laws of Menu*, 'a system so comprehensive and so minutely exact, that it may be considered as the Institutes of Hindu Law' – a remark that transforms the identity of *Menu* at a stroke into the systematic form of a European legal text (Brine 2010). Even though Jones considers *Menu* to consist of the 'institutes' of Hindu law, he nevertheless expresses the wish for the law to be systematized further, beyond Halhed's *Digest*, it being, he suggests:

introductory perhaps to a Code, which may supply the many natural defects in the old jurisprudence of this country, and, without any deviation from its principles, accommodate it justly to the improvements of a commercial age.

(Jones 1796: 75–6)

A number of things stand out in Jones' opening remarks in the Preface. First of all, by 'manners' Jones means something close to what we would mean today by culture – the typical phrase of the time was 'customs and manners', where custom in this sense has a meaning close to law. The relation of law to manners has always, it could be argued, been central to legal theory – articulating the relation of law which is universal, we might say natural law, to local traditions and practices, or customary law. Laws, Jones says here, are not translatable, but have to relate to the manners, or culture, of the people by and for whom they are prescribed. The transferability or non-transferability of law was a central question for colonial or imperial rule. The traditional position had been that laws could be transferred by right of conquest; this was certainly the case for colonies in the original, Greek sense, such as those of North America, which utilized British law. But for trade and administration colonies, rather than settler colonies, where the country was already, as it were, fully settled, the matter was rather different. Here we come to the central distinction between French and British colonialism with respect to law in colonies such as in India: whereas the former transferred the French civil code, based on Roman law, to the colony oblivious to its indigenous legal systems, the latter utilized the local laws where extant and then tried to adapt them to British practices. In so far as these were often based on tradition, on a form of accumulated wisdom, they were typically subsequently gradually adapted to the structure of English common law, whose principles, particularly of *stare decisis*, were henceforth incorporated into the colonial legal system.

If Jones argues that laws themselves are not translatable, because they must be suited to the manners of the people, the paradox is that the manners of the people cannot be known unless they are translated for the conquerors. So law is at once untranslatable and yet requires and demands translation, for the British can only administer the law if they are familiar with the local manners. The situation which they faced in Bengal was complicated (though scarcely less complicated than obtained in Britain itself at that time) – there were a whole variety of courts and legal codes in practice, most obviously between Muslim and Hindu law. Muslim law, which was the law of the previous generation of Mughal conquerors, was generally both written, and written in a language by now accessible to the British – whether Persian, which remained the official language of the East India Company until 1835, or Arabic. Even this however was not altogether straightforward. Jones' first translation of the *Al Sira-jiyyah: or, the Mohammedan Law of Inheritance* (1792) was of a book written in and translated into verse. Jones, as a lawyer with a profound knowledge of classics, was not uncomfortable with the idea of law being written in verse – or being largely a matter of sententious prescriptions, as was the case with his next and major translation, *The Laws of Menu*. Even English law invokes the

Bible and Shakespeare, and certainly in earlier periods has founded its authority on religious and poetic texts, such as the *Aeneid*.

Why though, we might ask, was Jones so insistent on cultural relativism at this time – at a time when English rule of the catholic Irish, for example, was hardly respectful of local customs or religion? At one level it was entirely pragmatic, the East India Company wanted to disturb the Indian population as little as possible in order to maintain its own power – it was for this reason that it also refused to allow Christian missionaries into India. It was also due to the influence of Burke, himself an Irishman, who in *Reflections on the Revolution in France* (Burke 1790) had at a stroke transformed the organic principles of English common law into the national and constitutional identity of England. Burke's *Reflections* 'defined the main ideas underpinning the tradition of the common law as the ruling political ideology of the time' (Majeed 1992: 2). Common law was 'the collective wisdom of many centuries' as Blackstone put it, both human and quasi-natural organic at once (Haldar 2007: 116). William Jones was thus in a sense being both liberal and conservative at once, but it was the conservatism that was to make him the object of attack in James Mill's *The History of British India* (Mill 1817), a book that was at once a critique of the ideology of the East India Company and of the conservative ruling ideology in Britain itself – for Mill regarded common law as, paradoxically, the instrument of the aristocratic ruling class (Majeed 1992: 27).

Law was foundational to the ideology and practice of colonial rule. For the British, in particular, it became at times the justification for colonial rule – rather than claiming to bring civilization, like the French, they justified themselves by introducing the rule of law. In that, their primary model was that of the Roman Empire, whose history, language and texts made up the bulk of the education of the British colonial administrators. When the Romans conquered new territories, they generally did not interfere with the religion or laws of the local inhabitants, and indeed often incorporated them into their own system.

In the development of Postcolonial Studies, while there has been some interest given to the topic of colonialism and law, given the importance of law to colonial rule, this has been relatively slight. The reason for its relative neglect is probably due to the fact that, in all the long work of cultural and military resistance developed by the various anti-colonial movements around the world to colonial rule, law was rarely questioned. Whereas writers would reject the coloniser's language and write in their own indigenous language, politicians would reject colonial rule and offer nationalist alternatives, very few rejected colonial law as such, with the exception of Gandhi, himself a lawyer, in *Hind Swaraj* (Gandhi 1997). And as a result, when colonies became independent, in almost all cases, the legal system continued unchanged. The new government may have changed individual laws, but, as in the United States, the extant colonial law remained law unless countermanded. In that sense, ironically perhaps, the British justification of colonial rule was *de facto* accepted and never questioned by the post-colonial sovereign state. As products of the period of a globalized imperialism, most countries of the world today follow one of two legal systems (which are themselves interrelated), Roman civil law or British common law. In some countries, such as the United States, we find both – after Louisiana was purchased from the French, the French legal system was not changed, and continues to be practiced there to this day.

When the British took over responsibility for the administration of justice in India in 1772, there was, arguably, nothing like law in the European sense in India at that time. In the first place, the authority of law was religious, and justice was largely dispensed by the rulers, with reference to sharia or Hindu law, as appropriate. Whereas sharia law was largely written and sourced in the Qur'an, together with established commentaries and elaborations, and could be relatively easily dispensed by the British (Strawson 1995), Hindu law was based on custom and tradition, much of it oral, as well as a wide variety of texts in Sanskrit that existed only in manuscript, sacred texts that were available only to the pundits. To that extent Hindu law was an example of customary law, though not focused on the individual defining case, as in the case of common law. Under Hastings' direction, the pundits were encouraged to provide texts for translation, thus implicitly relinquishing their sacerdotal function, although their legal function was not altogether abolished until the major reform of the Indian legal system and the institution of the Indian Penal Code in 1860 (Benton 2002; Derrett 1961).

Jones describes his *Menu* as a companion to Halhed's *Digest*, but in fact it consists of a full translation of one version of one of the many different texts that made up Hindu law. Jones' mistake, as later commentators, particularly James Mill, saw it, was precisely that he did not provide a digest, but translated a complex, aphoristic religious text that contains perhaps only two chapters that are actually concerned with law proper, as we would now say (Doniger 1992). It was for this reason that Mill took Jones as the apogee of the Orientalists whom he attacked in his *History of British India* (1817), ridiculing him for mixing law with literature and religion in a hodge podge that bore no resemblance to rationale law. Jones' attempts to codify Hindu law was dismissed by Mill as

> a disorderly compilation of loose, stupid or unintelligible quotations and maxims; selected arbitrarily from books of law, books of devotion, and books of poetry; attended with a commentary which only adds to the mass of absurdity and darkness; a farrago by which nothing is defined, nothing is established.
>
> (Mill 1817, III: 341)

Mill's position, which in fact caricatures Jones' two published translations of Indian legal texts, was to be enforced in the 1830s, and particularly after 1857, the laws of India were promulgated as Civil and Penal Codes. By that stage, however, the use of common law precedents as a supplement to indigenous law meant that, as Bernard Cohn has pointed out, Indian law had in any case begun to resemble British law, despite the original caution of the Orientalists (Cohn 1996: 75). The main agent in that transformation was Thomas Macaulay, who wrote the original draft of the codes which, ironically given the widespread ridicule of his 1835 'Minute', remain the basis of Indian law today.

Mill, like Lord Macaulay after him, had dismissed the value of local Indian knowledge, and succeeded in precipitating a change from the Orientalist policies of Governor Hastings to the Anglicist policies instituted by William Bentinck who became Governor-General in 1827. The basis of Mill's critique was that the use of indigenous law was flawed because there was too much literature (and religion) in the translation, and that what Jones provided did not conform to the rational, reasoned, clearly stated set of precepts that he and other utilitarians such as Bentham expected and required in modern law freed from the tyranny of custom (in Bentham and Mill's eyes, English law was equally culpable). Their complaint against Jones was that his law was literature rather than law. Macaulay's famous 'Minute on Indian Education' of 1835 dismissed indigenous knowledge:

> What then shall that language be? One-half of the Committee maintain that it should be the English. The other half strongly recommend the Arabic and Sanskrit. The whole question seems to me to be, which language is the best worth knowing?
>
> I have no knowledge of either Sanskrit or Arabic. – But I have done what I could to form a correct estimate of their value. I have read translations of the most celebrated Arabic and Sanskrit works. I have conversed both here and at home with men distinguished by their proficiency in the Eastern tongues. I am quite ready to take the Oriental learning at the valuation of the Orientalists themselves. I have never found one among them who could deny that a single shelf of a good European library was worth the whole native literature of India and Arabia.
>
> (Macaulay 2003: 230)

Macaulay instituted a process by which Indian students were henceforth taught the difference between literature and law by studying them as separate disciplines. Government support of local languages and Sanskrit in education was shifted to the teaching of English, particularly of English Literature in its modern form for the first time anywhere in the British Empire, including Britain itself (Viswanathan 1990). As part of the process of creating a whole new body of 'mimic men', the ideological rationale for teaching of English literature at this early point was to enforce the disciplinary divisions that had developed in Europe between literature, law, and religion – the very mixture of elements so visible in *The Laws of Menu*. Governor Bentinck's decision to switch the language of the courts from Persian to English in 1835 meant that henceforth the colonial power could bypass the problem of translation. In the end, what happened was that law in India evolved neither as the Orientalists nor the Anglicists planned, but on more Burkean principles, as a hybrid form of indigenous law drawn from ancient texts, common law from Indian judges based on *stare decisis*, together with statute and codification by the Government of India after 1857.

Though the Mill/Macaulay critique in a sense precipitated the very 'disorderly compilation' that Mill had decried, it also remains the case that Hastings' attempt to endorse indigenous local law rather than impose an imperial law from the outside was intrinsically flawed to the extent that it was the British themselves who after 1772 administered the law. If law is founded on violence, as Walter Benjamin (1996) and many since have argued, which is certainly the case with respect to a colony, then the East India Company sought legitimacy through taking on the authority and the legal systems of the previous conquerors, the Mughals, in order to establish its own authority and so as to disavow its own originary colonial violence. But they also sought to control it and to administer it, which effectively meant that they took on the function of being both law preservers and law makers. The difficulty for Hastings, Halhed, Jones, Colebrooke *et al.*, therefore, was that despite their determination not to force British common law on India, since the British were responsible for its administration, they could hardly avoid involvement. For Hastings and Jones, the problem was that, particularly with respect to Hindu law, only the court pundits had access to the secret and sacred knowledge of the legal texts. The British magistrate or judge was therefore dependent on the knowledge and advice of the pundits. This would have always been the case for earlier rulers, but the colonial dynamics meant that, as we have seen, the British did not trust the pundits, and were frustrated at being dependent on them. They wanted to use indigenous law, but in a typical colonial perspective, at the same time they did not trust the indigenous interpreters of that law. It was for this reason that they sought to find the authentic source of their knowledge, and began the translation project. However, in doing so, they made a series of assumptions about the nature of Hinduism that were to change its identity for ever (Cohn 1996: 71). In the first place, they assumed that it was a unitary religion like Christianity or Islam, based on sacred texts. They assumed that it was more or less consistent across India, and if they found differences they assumed that this was a result of corrupted texts, or, in the case of Colebrooke, of different sects within Hinduism. The position of the Brahmins as the source of legal and religious knowledge led them to assume that they spoke for both true Hinduism and all Hindus, and that other popular and syncretic forms of Hinduism were not to be taken seriously as part of the religion. In so far as the Brahmins carried out a sacerdotal function, the British assumed Hinduism, and Hindu law, to be based on a group of sacred texts that gave it an unchanging nature: here the principle of religious truth as unchanging came into conflict with the possibility of customary law as changing and developing. Finally, they did not recognize that the presence of pundits in different places, regions, speaking different languages etc., meant that it was a fluid, flexible, and heterogeneous religion based on custom, oral sources, as much as upon a single or more sacred texts. In putting the framework of their own assumptions around Hinduism, therefore, in giving primacy to the information supplied by particular pundits, particularly the conservative pundits of Benares, Brahmins who tended to promote the interests of their own caste, the British interpretation of Hinduism tended to unify it into a single religion, and make it more rigid, unchanging and inflexible, particularly with respect to caste. Meanwhile in stressing the glory of the recovered ancient texts, the British supplied an interpretation of Hinduism that formed the basis both for the Hindu nationalism that developed against British rule as well as for the precepts of Hindutva today. Just as Jones was also flawed in his assumption that Hinduism was a static religion, so too did he assume that its law should be based on the authority of the ancient texts, rather than a developing processual institution that, like British common law, adjusted over time to the changing manners and customs of the people. Moreover, Jones did not realize that by translating the law, he was inevitably changing it from an oral to a written form, and therefore fixing it while putting a new framework of European assumptions around it. The whole process of Jones' translations, as Piyel Haldar puts it, 'required the reduction of ancient systems of thought to translatable and translated versions of an ungraspable and enigmatic original' (Haldar 2007: 13). Meanwhile the various Digests, which selected relevant extracts from texts and took them out of context, invariably manipulated those texts so as to make them conform to British ideas of justice, and to correct the 'natural defects' of the indigenous law, as Jones put it, as well as updating it so as to 'accommodate it justly to the improvements of a commercial age'. In a classic colonialist gesture, the law was appropriated from the Hindus, and then re-presented to them in a refined and 'improved' form.

So Jones' translations of law inveigled law into one of the general laws of translation – which is that there can be no pure translation, and that all translation is a form of cultural translation. Jones sought to translate law because law required *manners*, but translating law into a foreign, that is English idiom, in turn meant that it became culturally translated into the mental framework of the translators. The attempt to institute and practice indigenous law under a colonial regime could never succeed in its object, however liberal its intention. This was not the least because the status of case law itself changed with the transformation of Hindu legal practice from a written and oral form to one in which all authority was exclusively written. While the pundits mediated between a written and oral tradition of historical legal memory that provided a considerable degree of institutional and individual flexibility, often with positive results but generally to the frustration of the East India Company administrators, the setting down in writing of individual cases as a form of legal precedent on the British system, together with the later linguistic transformation from Persian to English, entirely destroyed the mediated and more personalized system that had operated during the time of the Mughals. The institution of written case history, together with statute and codification, meant that Indian law was anglicized beyond recognition. The British project of the colonizer respecting the form of indigenous law was never anything more than a legal fiction and was no match for the power of the legal case.

Bibliography

Benjamin, Walter (1996) 'Critique of Violence' in *Selected Writings*, ed. Marcus Bullock and Michael W. Jennings, Cambridge, MA: Harvard University Press, pp. 236–52.

Benton, Lauren (2002) *Law and Colonial Cultures. Legal Regimes in World History, 1400–1900*, Cambridge: Cambridge University Press.

Brine, Kevin R. (2010) 'Law and Translation', unpublished paper given to CNRS-Transitions, 'Postcolonialism and Enlightenment Seminar', New York University, Feb. 2, 2010.

Bhabha, Homi K. (1994) *The Location of Culture*, London: Routledge.

Burke, Edmund (1790) *Reflections on the Revolution in France, and on the Proceedings in Certain Societies in London Relative to that Event*, London: Dodsley.

Cohn, Bernard S. (1996) *Colonialism and its Forms of Knowledge: The British in India*, Princeton, NJ: Princeton University Press.

Colebrooke, H.T. (1801) *A Digest of Hindu Law, on Contracts and Successions*, translated from the original Sanscrit by H.T. Colebrooke, 3 vols, Calcutta: printed at the Honourable Company's Press.

Derrett, J. Duncan M. (1961) 'The Administration of Hindu Law by the British', *Comparative Studies in Society and History*, 4: 1, 10–52.

Doniger, Wendy (1992) 'Rationalizing the Irrational Other: "Orientalism" and the "Laws of Manu" ', *New Literary History*, 23: 1, 25–43.

Gandhi, M.K. (1997) *Hind Swaraj, and Other Writings*, ed. Anthony J. Parel, Cambridge: Cambridge University Press.

Haldar, Piyel (2007) *Law, Orientalism, and Postcolonialism: The Jurisdiction of the Lotus Eaters*, London and New York: Routledge-Cavendish.

Halhed, N.B. (1776) *A Code of Gentoo Laws, or, Ordinations of the Pundits*, from a Persian translation, made from the original, written in the Shanscrit language, London: n.p.

Jones, William (1792) *Al Sirájiyyah: or, the Mohammedan Law of Inheritance, with a Commentary*, Calcutta: Joseph Cooper.

Jones, William (1796) *Institutes of Hindu law: or, the Ordinances of Menu, according to the Gloss of Cullúca: Comprising the Indian system of Duties, Religious and Civil*. Verbally translated from the original Sanscrit, with a preface, by Sir William Jones, Calcutta: printed by order of the government.

Macaulay, Thomas Babington (2003) 'Minute on Indian Education' (1835), in *Archives of Empire: From the East India Company to the Suez Canal*, ed. Mia Carter, Barbara Harlow, Durham, NC: Duke University Press, pp. 227–38.

Majeed, Javed (1992) *Ungoverned Imaginings: James Mill's The History of British India and Orientalism*, Oxford: Clarendon Press.

Mill, James (1817) *The History of British India*, 3 vols, London: Baldwin, Cradock and Joy.

Momma, Hal (1997) 'A Man on the Cusp: Sir William Jones's "Philology" and "Oriental Studies" ', *Texas Studies in Literature and Language*, 41, 160–79.

Oldham, James (1995) 'The Survival of William Jones in American Jurisprudence' in Garland H. Cannon and Kevin Brine, *Objects of Enquiry: The Life, Contributions and Influence of Sir William Jones*, New York: New York University Press, pp. 92–101.

Strawson, John (1995) 'Islamic Law and English Texts', *Law and Critique*, 6: 1, 21–38.

Viswanathan, Gauri (1990), *Masks of Conquest: Literary Study and British Rule in India*, London: Faber.

Chapter 6

The illegality of Empire
Moral evasion and confusion of historians and literary critics in their reflections on the impeachment trial of Warren Hastings

Anthony Carty

Introduction

In the late 18th century an Impeachment Trial of a former governor of the East India Company took place before the House of Lords in London. Warren Hastings was accused of embezzlement, extortion, and of forcing an Indian ruler, Chait Singh, out of his possessions. The case has aroused a considerable measure of interest from literary critics and historians. However, the purely legal aspect of the Impeachment has aroused less interest. The belief of non-lawyers that the legal complexities of the issues are inaccessible, or the view that there were in fact no legal rules at the time suitable to resolve the issues, are two possible explanations. However, another explanation may be that the implications of legal analysis are usually the attribution of individual and also collective guilt. If legal analysis of the Impeachment Trial points in this direction it can open a "pandora's box" not only in India but in other parts of the former British Empire. A distinctive feature of the British conquest of India is that it began with a trial – the Impeachment of Warren Hastings. Law is about precise allocation of responsibility. It is not easily an accompaniment to the literary and historical nostalgias of Empire.

In any case it may be said, firstly the Trial appears to have attracted primarily the attention of literary critics and historians who consider it to be perhaps the spectacle of late 18th century England, not just Nicholas Dirks (Dirks 2006) himself, but also David Musselwhite in his online article *The Trial of Warren Hastings* (Musselwhite 1982) and Sara Suleri, with her book *The Rhetoric of English India* (Suleri, 1992). Secondly, a trawl of Google alerted me to the really fierce critical reviews of Dirks' *The Scandal of Empire* (2006) and of Dirks himself. For instance, there is William Dalrymple's review article in the *New York Review of Books*, 26 April 2007, called *Plain Tales from British India* (see further below), and, to take just one further example, from the *Oxford History of the British Empire* (volume V, *Historiography*, 1999), Robert Frykenberg's comments, in the chapter on "India to 1858" on Dirks' earlier work, *The Hollow Crown: Ethnohistory of an Indian Kingdom* published with Cambridge University Press in 1987 (Frykenberg, 1999). The treatment of India and this Trial in particular arouses as many passions now in Anglo-centric circles as it did two centuries ago. However, it is probably the case that Frykenberg's concerns about the possible weaknesses of Dirks' scholarship are similar to my own, but applied to historical method generally rather than to missed opportunities of legal history. He criticizes historians listening "to the siren song of antihistorical literary criticism" (Frykenberg, 1999: 211). Fashions such as colonial discourse, deconstruction or whatever avoid engaging with empirical evidence. However, it is likely that Frykenberg is in the same defensive camp as Dalrymple when he goes on to group these categories and methods along with "whatever else such nihilist impulses might be called", intemperately concluding that "fulminations of this sort cannot be accepted as genuine historical understanding, certainly not by historians as such" (ibid).

I think it is necessary to engage with both the literary treatment of the Trial and with the heat of the criticism which Dirks provokes before approaching the Trial itself. The Trial was ostensibly about whether the head of the East India Company had behaved illegally, and also whether the expansion of Britain in India was illegal. Perhaps the treatment of the Trial as theatre, as a literary event, could serve as an evasion of a close examination of legal issues. Secondly, the storms raging in scholarly circles, around Dirks and others appear to me not unrelated to the possibility of evasion of the legal issues.

However, it could simply be that historians and literary critics simply do not care about law. The one extensive legal examination of the case has been by the now deceased Pakistani international lawyer, formerly at Edinburgh University, Kabir-Ur-Rahman Khan (Khan, 1988). This is a very competent and complete analysis of the legal issues from the wider context of international law as it affected European Asian relations from the 17th to the 19th century, besides also going into the full detail of the Trial itself. I hope to come in the subsequent stages of this chapter, to concluding aspects of the Trial itself and ask whether there is any insuperable difficulty – the records themselves of the Trial are very substantial – in treating the Impeachment as a legal case about which one can form a legal view – once one has chased the literati off the stage of the Trial. This did not seem difficult for Kabir Khan.

Literary critics and the Trial

Musselwhite's article is well known, openly accessible online. He begins by saying he refuses to be drawn into debate on the correctness of the verdict or the validity of the evidence, or even, in any general way, on the merits of the protagonists. However, he does claim that the rules of evidence in the Trial were strict, while much of the case against Hastings was circumstantial and characterological. Technically outflanked, the Prosecution:

> threw legal and logical decorum to the winds and argument turned to rhetoric and rhetoric seemed more like bluster. Burke, goaded to frenzy by the massive propaganda campaign of Hastings' supporters, his language lost all constraint and seemed at times to have come direct from Bedlam.
>
> (Musselwhite, 1982: 4)

In contrast to Burke's invective the language of "Hastings is restrained, informed, almost disdainful – it was this tone that infuriated Burke". His careful attention to Islamic systems of land tenure – zeminder, pollah, sunnus and inheritance drains the wind out of Burke and Sheridan.

Musselwhite concludes that Burke's picture of India was mythical, built with a view to public opinion and contributing to Thomas Macaulay's more elaborate 19th century construction. The picture of India before the British intrusion is dismissed as the loveliness of myth. Burke is the first Orientalist in the Edward Said sense. So the Manager's defense of Chait Singh, i.e. Burke's defense of him (in article One of the Indictment, to which I will return), makes him "the hero of romantic pastorals with gothic overtones". Hastings, argues Musselwhite, will have nothing to do with such posterings which "are romantic, theatrical and literary". Hastings is technical, pragmatic, analytical and philological, having the Islamic laws translated so India can speak for itself" (Musselwhite, 1982: 11–12).

But, of course, Musselwhite does not want to argue over the correctness of the verdict or the merits of the protagonists. So let us leave him and move to Sara Suleri. Her book has a chapter "Reading the Trial of Warren Hastings" (Suleri, 1992: 49–74). She claims Burke's larger goal was to inform England of the representational difficulty of colonial India and England's response to his rhetoric was a declaration of awareness that morality was moribund where colonialism was concerned. Burke's narratives of Hastings' violations, in Suleri's view, were designed to obliterate a belief in the graspability of India's narrative. Suleri appears to object to the very idea of a trial. Hastings' transgressions conform to the extortion of the East India Company. Suleri continues to argue that to read the proceedings of the Trial is thus to

> confront less a trial than a documentation of the anxieties of oppression, both where the prisoner and the prosecutors are equally implicated in the inascribability of colonial guilt. For 18th century England, however, the theatricality of the event overshadowed the historical and political questions that it raised, causing the popular imagination to believe that it observed a spectacle with a definite end.
>
> (Suleri, 1992: 53)

Suleri makes the vital point

> that the legal failure to impeach Hastings is illustrative of an essential alegality in colonial discourse in that neither the pre-existing law of Britain nor those of the subcontinent could supply a precedence against which to measure the illegality of both Hastings' and the Company's actions.
>
> (Suleri, 1992: 55)

She wants to say that colonialism should be judged as a system rather than a set of misdeeds. She challenges Burke's employment of the metaphor of rape to describe the treatment of India. Instead one should be aware of the rather homoerotic struggle between Burke and Hastings, so that "rape is a deflection from a contemplation of male embattlement" (Suleri, 1992: 61), where the audience knows that as Burke represents India as the hapless virgin, "a more accurate representation of colonialism would examine the shared responsibility that obtains between Hastings and Burke" (Suleri, 1992: 62). Nonetheless, she does insist that Burke was wrongly aestheticized by Macaulay to leave out his more horrific realizations of what the colonization of the subcontinent would entail (Suleri, 1992: 63). Burke was not an orientalist, but someone who insisted on the prior reality of a place that resisted translation into western images. She credits him in the end with articulating a damning catalogue of the consequences of the failure of colonial law.

Yet ultimately Suleri says that a trial cannot deal with a systematic ill in which she equates Burke and Hastings. At no point does she address any of the charges made against Hastings or deal with any concrete incident involving Hastings' conduct. The trial itself remains unexamined in Suleri's chapter "Reading the Trial of Warren Hastings".

So literature, whether Musselwhite or Suleri, seems to tell us we cannot read a case, that a legal issue cannot be defined, that the protagonists are entrapped in other forces, playing to other galleries. Therefore, a close reading of the case is either impossible or unnecessary. The Law as such is disdained. It has no integrity of its own, no authority or compelling power.

Literary criticism, historians and the Impeachment Trial

William Dalrymple may come to Dirks' book as a historian or as a literary critic given his own record, but here it is as a historian (Dalrymple, 2007). A lengthy review article in the *New York Review of Books* by a figure of Dalrymple's stature of a book by a Columbia University historian such as Dirks can reasonably be taken as indicative of how open contemporary Anglo-American intellectual culture is to revisiting the Impeachment Trial of Hastings. His review of Dirks is complex. Dalrymple describes the ruin of India and especially Bengal, through the extortionist policies of the East India Company. But the impeachment of Hastings meant targeting the wrong man. Burke had never visited India, whereas Hastings was fluent in Hindustani, collected Indian religious manuscripts, and according to Dalrymple, patronized a new Asiatic Society of Benghal, founded in 1784 by the Sanskrit scholar, Sir William Jones. This Society was a case of unique cross-cultural appreciation.

In contrast, in Dalrymple's view, Dirks ignores the interplay of culture (such as also shown in his own *White Mughals*) in favour of a reductionist picture of binary oppositions. Dirks' argument is old fashioned, in the style of Edward Said, i.e. late 1970s etc. and concentrates on the rhetoric and theatre of Hastings' impeachment, second hand, as discussed by others, most notably by Peter Marshall (Marshall, 1965). Dirks' passionate Anglophobia and the parallels he makes with the present war in Iraq are all that is new about his book. He makes no use of Persian, Urdu or Bengali sources, but relies on Burke himself, who was notably ill informed about India and who, like Dirks – and unlike Hastings – had none of the relevant North Indian languages.

Furthermore, Dirks does not place the British incursion in the context of previous events such as the Moghul conquests, US expansion westward, and the fact of life of the Chinese Empire in the 18th century. These events are scandalous from a contemporary perspective but it is questionable whether indignation at Empire would have meant anything at the time. Dirks' writing style is a little preachy and stodgily academic. This language is a vehicle for him to conclude that the British Raj presided over the destruction of Indian political institutions and cultural self-confidence, with economic figures speaking loud for the consequences. In 1600 when the East India Company was founded, Britain generated 1.8% of the world GDP and India 22.5%. By 1870 Britain generated 9.1% and India was a global symbol of famine. Yet now, concludes Dalrymple, the roles are once again being reversed.

Dalrymple continues in a rejoinder to Dirks' attempt to respond to him, that Dirks was wrong to roundly criticize Peter Marshall's painstaking work on Hastings. Dirks falls down by concentrating on the theoretical post-colonial studies of his academic friends, failing to appreciate the degree to which Burke's assault on Warren Hastings was based upon misinformation fed to him by Hastings' rapacious enemy, Philip Thomas, himself out for personal revenge. After all, Burke had never visited India and like Dirks, relied mostly on secondary sources. Dalrymple concludes that Dirks' work is Manichaean, simplistic and replete with major factual errors.

Once again, as with Suleri and Musselwhite, Dalrymple seems to avoid the Impeachment Trial itself, ostensibly the main topic of Dirks' book. Dirks' book is partially about the Trial, but it is in fact primarily, in turn, a historiography of British treatment of the Trial and what he takes to be the sanitization of 18th century scandal in the course of the 19th century. Dirks does not appear to me to concentrate upon Hastings at all, making his primary targets to be subsequent historians of the British Empire, itself a passageway to understanding contemporary British self-images. From this perspective Dalrymple's review is, as they say, "very interesting".

So, the impeachment of Warren Hastings is also very largely absent from Dirks' work. Nor does he make any judgment about the Empire and the East India Company other than to say that at least the Trial itself and the campaigning of Burke, Charles James Fox, Richard Sheridan and Charles Grey showed there was serious concern in the 18th century at scandalous behaviour. The post-colonial theory in Dirks' work is that, somewhat like Suleri, he appears to engage in a type of fatalistic cosmic historicism which sees the outrage of Burke and company as part of a grand historical process whereby the British Establishment recognized the need to sanitize the appearance of its operations, which Lord Cornwallis began to do afterwards by hugely raising the salaries of high East Indian Company officials. The sanitizing process meant Burke was instrumental in repressing scandal and even contributed to the ever so clever British tactic – and this is the main point of Dirks' book – whereby scandal is transferred from the British to the Indians themselves, with the 19th century campaigns against Sati and the thugs. The Civilizing Mission required increasing focus on the scandalous Indians. British historians obliged. That is Dirks' argument. He says they continue to do so.

He takes the example of Peter Marshall, as Dalrymple has complained. It is what Marshall says of the Trial itself. There is just one forty-four-page chapter in Dirks' three hundred and eighty nine-page book devoted to the Trial and, needless to say, the chapter is called "Spectacle". The chapter is about the charges brought against Hastings but it is scarcely based on a reading of the Trial proceedings. Still it does show full awareness of the ambiguity of the Francis–Burke relationship, Dalrymple notwithstanding. Dirks' chapter favours the view that a major issue such as the first charge on the removal of Chait Singh, the ruler of Benares, was essentially not justiciable because the true nature of the legal relationship between Chait Singh and the East Indian Company – where ultimate sovereignty rested between the Mughal, the company and Chait Singh – was totally undefined (Dirks, 2006: 203).

Zaanunders (maybe landlords for Hastings) were, for Dirks, sometimes revenue officers and sometimes local sovereigns. Burke and the Managers accused Hastings of extortion by demanding revenues well beyond the originally agreed Treaty. Dirks agrees with Hastings that this cannot be proved legally. Hastings' practice of collecting revenue and expecting financial support from a subordinate was only a matter of doing what the Company had done before. While not excusing Hastings' excesses, Dirks says

> In larger historical terms the question of excess was irrelevant, given the overwhelming historical evidence that this was the way the Company was able to expand from being a trading company.
>
> (Dirks, 2006: 103)

In other words Dirks is also unwilling to concede that there could be any inherent, human interest in the legal aspects of the "Spectacle". It is rather the historiography of the Trial and its consequent place in British consciousness which worries Dirks. So he comments on Peter Marshall, as typical of contemporary Imperial historians, that their neutrality means that they nowhere suggest that empire itself is a problem (Dirks, 2006: 124). He notes that Marshall regarded the impeachment as a sham. Yet he objects to the neutrality of Marshall which treats both Hastings and Burke as victims.

The strangeness of Marshall's view, for Dirks, is that he, Marshall, like Macaulay and James Mill, all thought the charges brought against Hastings did stand up – were sound – and yet "there can be no doubt of the severity of Hastings' punishment even though he was acquitted" (Marshall, 1965: 189). This is even though Marshall says on the same page that "by most standards of justice Chait Singh was sacrificed to the needs of the Company and the same accusation can be brought against Hastings' treatment of the Begams . . ."

Dirks' main concern is the general one of the quality of British imperial historiography. So Louis, in his chapter on Historiography, in volume 5 of the *Oxford History of the British Empire*, betrays the continued acceptance on the part of most historians that the Empire was a legitimate political and economic form (Dirks, 2006: 329). So Dirks quotes Marshall as saying that now, i.e. since 1947, it is felt that, with the subsidence of anti-colonialism, imperial history can be written today where historians do not have to take sides, as Marshall says in the preface to *The Impeachment of Warren Hastings*. Dirks quotes Marshall:

> Since 1947, however, the incentive to pass judgment on British India by acquitting or condemning Hastings is obviously much reduced, and the historian can concentrate on explanation rather than verdicts . . . Detachment also makes it possible to do justice to the intentions of both Burke and Hastings and to appreciate the suffering inflicted by the impeachment on both of them.
> (Dirks, 2006: 329; Marshall, 1965: xiv)

This is merely to normalize Empire in imperial historiographical literature. What probably aggravates Dalrymple is the following type of remark by Dirks with respect to Louis' canonical introduction to volume V of the *OHBE* (1998–1999) on Historiography:

> Louis betrays the continued acceptance on the part of most imperial historians that empire – whether good or bad for either colonizers or colonized – was a legitimate political and economic form. Empire is written about as if it can be evaluated "neutrally" now that the passions (and promises) of anti-colonial nationalism have subsided. Somehow despotism continues to be more acceptable when exercised in imperial contexts than in European ones, where the same kind of neutrality would be considered unseemly, as we see consistently in the historical evaluation of fascist regimes in Europe. Neither fascism nor slavery could ever be written about in the terms used for empire.
> (Dirks, 2006: 329)

It is difficult to reduce Louis' "canonical introduction" to a single idea, but it does conclude with the phrase that the history of the British Empire will always be of interest "simply because of human curiosity to know more about the domination of one people or nation over others, and the interaction of peoples and cultures" (Louis, 1999: 41). Nonetheless, it is difficult not to agree with Dirks' view that Louis' "neutrality" consistently flips over into complacency. For instance, consider Louis' comment on Seeley, Professor of Modern History at Cambridge from 1869 to 1895. Seeley is the author of the famous phrase that the British conquered and peopled half the world in a fit of absentmindedness. This remark was for Louis a provocative device, good for stimulating class discussion. It reflected "the unconscious acceptance by the English public of the burdens of Empire, particularly in India" (Louis, 1999). This was presumably a problem exacerbated by the fact that Greater Britain, how Seeley describes the Empire, "was an empire of kith and kin in which India formed a perplexing and alien part" (Louis, 1999: 8). Louis continues his descriptive survey of British historiography to say later that it was the dominant mode of study in British universities and wider society that "people generally believed that constitutional solutions could be found to problems of such magnitude as Ireland, India and Palestine" (Louis, 1999: 27).

Yet given Dirks' lack of interest or engagement with the precise legal issues of Empire and the Trial of Warren Hastings, on what standard precisely is he basing his protest at what has been happening? I propose in the final part of this chapter to consider the Impeachment Trial itself, in particular the Benares charge under Article One of the Impeachment, where Hastings was blamed for the revolt of Chait Singh by provoking him, by attempting to arrest him in his palace, and by violating the Company settlement with the Raja by making unauthorized demands beyond this. I will begin with the account of Marshall and then consider the arguments of Burke and Grey. I will follow this with a glance at the final debates in the House of Lords in January to April 1795, and then end with an interpretation of Burke's stance which is given by Uday Singh Mehta in his *Liberalism and Empire*. I am focusing on the legal nature of the ties of Chait Singh to the East India Company.

The Impeachment Trial

Marshall states that the Company installed Chait Singh "with a complete and uncontrolled authority over his Zaminderry" under the sovereignty of the honorary Company. Hastings had a proposal approved with the payment agreed. The Proposal stated that "no more demands shall be made upon him by the Company of any kind, nor under any pretence whatsoever shall any person be allowed to interfere with his authority" (Marshall, 1965: 90–108). The sum agreed was Rs 2,340,249. So the Managers, i.e. Burke *et al.*, could argue that now Chait Singh had a binding agreement, relying upon all of the above terms (90). Hastings' reply was that the consultations and resolutions of the Council of the Company were not legally binding and that the formal *sanad* contained no promise about uncontrolled authority or exemptions from demands beyond the stipulations. Therefore Chait Singh was the same as any other, liable to pay what revenue the sovereign thought fit (91).

Marshall says that Hastings' argument was open to serious objections. The Resident had been instructed to tell Chait Singh there would be no increase in the tribute, so that this would be a breach of a verbal pledge. Chait Singh's tenure of *sanad* was understood in Company circles to be a *zemander* tenure (91). Hastings himself claimed that he understood *zemander* to mean a government official collecting revenue on the part of the government, but others saw it as an owner of land paying the government a fixed, unalterable part of its produce (91–2).

Hastings' counsel agreed at the Trial that the Council Resolution and the Resident's instruction ("we do not mean to increase the tribute") were binding. However, the claim of the Company to sovereignty meant, in the Company's view, an implied residual power to call for further military assistance where there was a case of emergency. This was not an attempt to increase rents (92).

In fact the evidence showed Hastings increased the tribute eventually to what was most likely beyond the absolute amount that Chait Singh could raise. Hastings did this because the Company finances required it. It led to the ruin of Benares, the abandonment of cultivation over a wide area. Furthermore, the written evidence showed Hastings admitted the action was personally motivated by a belief that Chait Singh was opposing him personally and not the Company. In addition through his choice of Resident, Graham, Hastings interfered repeatedly in the choice of the Raja's staff (107–108).

Marshall concludes that Chait Singh had the alternative faced by other Indian rulers confronted with the expanding power of the Company: either see his independence slowly eroded or to try to resist the tide and be swept away (108).

Burke's final speeches from 28 May 1794 cover the same ground as Marshall and correspond with Marshall's analysis of the legal issues (Bond, 1859). It will not be my argument that Burke does not resort to rhetoric but merely that it is also possible to locate some argument about law and facts. On the first day, 28 May 1794, Burke set out two points: when Hastings acted according to a measure of discretion he was still bound to follow the established rules of political morality, humanity and equity; that when he acted under a law – as Burke contended that he did – with regard to all foreign powers – he was obliged to act under the law of nature and under the law of nations. In relation to Great Britain he had to act under its law. Burke explains that Hastings contends (ibid.: 356) that India has no laws, no fixed property and is affected only by punishment. He quotes from Hastings' own written evidence. He says that no UK Parliament granted the Company sovereignty over Benares, but the particular interferences (interventions) of the Company show that it has seized it. Since the Mohammedan conquests, argues Hastings, the Hindoos were kept in order only through power. The whole of Asia is nothing but precedents to prove the invariable exercise of arbitrary power. Zeminders are mean, depraved and always prone to resist allegiance to their sovereignty: So, concludes Burke from Hastings' argument:

> All Asia is by him disenfranchised at a stroke. They have no rights, no laws, no liberties. Their state is mean and depraved; they may be fined for any purpose of court extravagance, exactly as in the case of Chait Singh, not only upon every war but upon every pretence of war.
>
> (ibid.: 358)

So it is Hastings who paints a picture of government misrule in India, productive of no happiness till subverted by the free governance of Britain. Burke claims that the Managers assert the contrary. Where you go into a country where you suppose mankind is degraded, servile (ibid.: 361–2), these ways of thinking will take from you that kind of sympathy which naturally attaches you to men feeling like yourselves. In Burke's words, if you go to India with the idea of the mean, degraded state of the people, we know that those people whom you despise you will never treat well.

Burke describes at length the rule and practice of Genghis Khan and Tamerlane, that their power was derived from heaven and God would punish unwise and unjust rule. Tamerlane's *Institutes* told (ibid.: 369 *et seq.*) that he should rule according to a sacred law and he never claimed an arbitrary power. Burke continues:

> When you name a Mohammedan you name a man governed by law, a prince governed by law, a people entitled to protection by law . . . the imposing of a tribute upon a Mussulman without his previous consent is impracticable. . . . (The Imam) must be elected by the general consent of the Mussulmans. He must be a protector of the person and property of his subjects; and a right of resistance is directly established by law against him, and even a duty of resistance.
> (ibid.: 371, 373)

These propositions Burke extracts from the Institutes of Timur and from a book published by Hastings, called the *Hedaya* and other texts, mostly translated on the orders of Hastings (ibid.: 371).

Burke completes his first day by saying that if any prince has abused his authority in India that is no more a precedent than a robber on Hounslow Heath saying people have robbed before him. The law is the security of every person whether Indian or English. There is but one law, the law of nature and of nations. (ibid.: 377) He elaborates:

> The law is the security of every person that is governed. It is the security of the people of India; it is the security of the people of England. There is but one law in the world, namely that law which governs all law – the law of our Creator, the law of humanity, justice, equity, the law of nature and nations (ibid.: 377).

On 30 May 1794 Burke argues that Hastings is bound in all transactions with foreign powers to act according to the rules of the law of nations, with respect to all powers that are sovereign, whether dependent or independent (ibid.: 381). He is bound also by the laws and customs of the country which he governs. Yet it is Hastings himself who says that whether powers were delegated to him by any Act of Parliament "I confess myself too little of a lawyer to pronounce".

The claims made of Chait Singh, as shown by Charles Grey's speeches (see below), were contrary to fundamental treaties between the East India Company and Chait Singh, and he merely delayed to pay more than in his agreement, while eventually doing so. He is guilty of nothing more. Chait Singh was a sovereign. His agreement stipulated the company should not interfere in his internal government. The military, the civil power, the whole revenue rested in him. He was sovereign within Benares, but is also dependent on another, according to his compact (ibid.: 389). Burke continues, that the law of contracts between sovereign powers is the law of nations, the law of India as well as the law of Europe, because it is the law of reason and the law of nature, drawn from the pure sources of morality, from the pure sources of public good and equity, recognized and digested into order by the labour of learned men, such as Vattel (ibid.: 389–90).

Vattel in Book I, chapter 16, of the *Law of Nations* treats of breaches of agreements, the protector refusing to give protection and refusing to perform his side. Chait Singh was bound to object to the hazarding of the whole benefit of the agreement upon which his subjection was founded. In other words, following Vattel, whom he cites at length, Burke characterizes the agreement between Chait Singh and the Company as a protectorate. Vattel then states that where the protector violates the protection, the protectorate re-enters into the possession of all its rights and recovers its independence (ibid.: 390).

Hastings admits in written evidence, says Burke, that he fines Chait Singh 500,000 l. for his insulting behaviour and also admits that he saw the opportunity to take advantage of this contumacy for the Company's affairs, as it was in financial distress (ibid.: 396–8). Burke notes Hastings' tendency in his evidence to slip in the word "sovereignty" for himself and forgets the word "compact" (ibid.: 408), because it is plain that wherever he uses the word "sovereignty", it is to destroy the authority of all compacts and accordingly Hastings is declaring the invalidity of all compacts entered into in India from the very nature of the place. His evidence is: "From the disorderly form of its government there is an invalidity in all compacts and treaties whatever" (ibid.: 408).

By way of conclusion of this section I will present parallel arguments by Charles Grey which add more weight to the claims Burke makes about the strength of the legal compact that Chait Singh had with the East India Company. He refers to the terms of the agreement with Chait Singh also as being a treaty. Grey noted that there was some controversy as to whether the instruments granted to Chait Singh were in the nature of a common zaamindary or a treaty. The Secretary to the Board thought that while in the first case only the Governor General would sign the instrument in this case it was different and the Secretary informed the Board that the instrument ". . . may be considered more in the light of a treaty . . ." and should be signed by the whole Board (ibid.: 24). Chait Singh owed certain duties to the Company, such as not contracting engagements with their enemies and the payment of a fixed and stipulated tribute, "but that over and above that, he was exempt from any demands of any kind" (ibid.: 24).

As for the supposed emergency – the threat from the French – the manner in which Chait Singh was treated was not permissible. Whatever definition of sovereignty may be accorded to the British Governors

> this trust must be exercised in accordance with some known law or some principle of equity, or else there would be no distinction between an act of

government and an act of tyranny; for, if there is no known law or equitable discretion, sovereignty would be only another name for wrong and violence. If we admit, then, that there is any difference between good and evil or any discrimination between an act of sovereignty and an act of tyranny, the thing that marks the difference is this: that individuals are selected to bear burdens beyond their ability; or are called upon to bear them, when others in similar circumstances are not obliged to contribute . . . Whatever the form of government may be, the object of government is the protection, and not the destruction, of every individual member of the state.

(ibid.: 35–6)

More precisely Hastings himself stated to the Council of the Company that the danger from the French came in the form of an attack by sea against Bombay or Fort George, while Bengal will be their last and most distant object. This argument is taken from the minutes of the Company's meetings (ibid.: 41). Grey goes on to verify, as does Marshall, that the actual taxing of Chait Singh was beyond the whole of his revenue (ibid.: 73). Finally, Grey concludes with the quotation of a long statement under oath from Hastings in which he directly avows to resentment against Chait Singh which led to the demand of taxes beyond the person's revenues and the expulsion from his dominions (ibid.: 103).

The limited purpose of my exposition of the arguments used by Burke and Grey in the Impeachment Trial is to show that it is easily seen how their arguments had a legal character, that they were simply expressed and that a reading of the record will reveal readily in broad outline what the legal issues were. The aim is to throw into question the ethnically reductionist tendency to write off Burke as a flamboyant Anglo-Irish parliamentary politician regularly choking on his own rhetoric. This broad outline has been found to correspond to Marshall's account of the Impeachment Trial, generally regarded as "canonical".

However, Khan's more extensive knowledge of the legal background of these legal issues demonstrates even more so the possibilities of real legal research. He explains the still powerful role of the constitutional law of the Moghul Empire in locating precisely where sovereignty lay in India. He considers also at length the constitutions of the East India Company to show how restrictions were always imposed upon its activities from London. In particular, drawing heavily from a work published in 1841, *The Law Relating to India and the East India Company*, Khan points to an official rejection of a policy of conquest and expansion in India in the 18th century. The East India Company was only authorized to use force defensively (Khan, 1988: 161). The Charter itself of the East India Company envisaged only defensive war (ibid.: 154). Indeed, 33 George, Ch 52, section 42, declared a principle of public policy that the "scheme of conquest and extension of dominions of India are measures repugnant to the wish, the honor and policy of the (English) nation" (ibid.: 153). Besides, in his own close reading of the actual arguments of the case, Khan brings to bear the generally known scholarship which accepted the international law significance of treaties between Asian potentates and European powers throughout the 18th century. Their legally binding nature has been recognized by the International Court of Justice in the 20th century (ibid.: 151–2). Khan confirms, from every angle, how there was every possibility in the 1790s to frame the contest between Hastings and Burke in legal terms, from a British constitutional and international law perspective. One might find support here in the argument of Frykenberg; his disdain for the "siren-song of anti-historical literary criticism". This could usefully be applied also to the "Law and Literature" movement as, on balance, an unhelpful development in the way of understanding so-called "legal cases". It will prefer to obfuscate legal issues for aesthetic reasons, or possibly even for reasons of political bias.

In addition what is still lacking in the treatment of the Hastings Trial is a convincing political analysis of the final process of decision-making in the House of Lords which led to Hastings' acquittal. There were significant voices for conviction, including William Pitt's newly appointed Lord Chancellor. Lord Loughborough replaced Lord Thurlow in 1793 – who had been the driving force behind Hastings' defense – and voted for a conviction, although with several other very prominent peers, including the Duke of Norfolk, the Lord Marshall of England (Debrett, 1797). 1793 was also the year of the Statute 33 George Ch 52, section 42, already mentioned by Khan. Little of the acquittal of Hastings is explained by supposing, as Musselwhite does, that there was a fatal deficiency of legal competence in Burke's team.

British liberal political culture and the history of international law

The whole argument of this chapter is that the facts of the Impeachment Trial are by no means inaccessible in themselves, that there is something immensely strange in the continued unwillingness of any discipline approaching these issues to deal directly with the facts. I intend to conclude with a book length vindication of Burke's stance from Uday Singh Mehta, who shows how the issues of the case continue to challenge the whole spectrum of British intellectual culture, to its very foundations, producing a split it is unable to handle. Burke is so embarrassing to this culture because he offers a frontal critique of what he describes as the liberal justification of Empire (Mehta, 1999: 2). The primary question is taken by Mehta to be in what sense India existed at the time of the British incursion. Was there an India to be conquered? He asserts that there was an Indian sense of collective existence which was not understood by British liberal, imperial culture, but could be grasped from Burke's conservative perspective. The terms of this debate can easily be translated into the international lawyer's concern with whether India had an international legal personality which could and should be recognized and respected by western powers.

Mehta elaborates on the nature of India's identity in terms of territoriality and the people's attachment to place (ibid.: 132). He presents the mosaic of India's states as resembling the diversity of German states at the same period, i.e. the late 18th century (ibid.: 137). The Indian people do have a collective attachment to territory, which has been instrumentalized by an Empire which disturbs its spaces. In other words Indians have the same sense of belonging as Europeans (ibid.: 147). However, Lockean liberals merely saw societies in India which were not based on contractarian consent and drew the inference that these societies lacked political integrity and norms of accountability. In contrast, for Burke, contract is no basis for a political society, as no society has an origin, not even a territorial one. The attachment of people to territory and to homeland is already there. Collective political identity rested in a sense of belonging and nationhood, while by the middle of the 19th century British intellectuals had repudiated any link between a sense of territorial belonging and nationhood (ibid.: 149 *et seq.*). Mehta mentions a number of leading figures. John Seeley was to write in *The Expansion of England* (1881) India had no jealousy of the foreigner because it had no sense of national unity; there was no India. The leading colonial administrator, John Strachey (1911) insisted there is not and never was an India, possessing any unity, no people of India. This view was shared throughout the 19th century by James Mill, Macaulay and John Stuart Mill.

In contrast Burke's whole task was to challenge Empire, whether in Ireland, America or India. He saw through the civilizational hierarchies and assumptions of cultural superiority justifying British expansion (Mehta, 1999: 160). He objected simply to the members of one community unsettling the integrity and coherence of another. India is such a community. We possess and are possessed by places. For Locke, it is only the former that is the case – an extension of individual will. However, society depends on psychological sharing in a common inhabiting over time, place and a common history (ibid.: 161). Political society does not rest exclusively on individual reasoning capacity but upon a shared order on the ground (ibid.: 1622). Mehta accepts that such a perspective remains vague about exact institutional forms. But India and America have the requisite sense of sharing in common, beyond merely contingent sharing of overlapping individual interests.

So Burke parts company with liberals who saw an absence of political community in India. Liberal Empire is then justified as tutelage. From Locke's perspective, "Indians" (whether in India or in America) are born to freedom, but not yet capable of exercising it. Instead, Burke sees British practices in India as fracturing the country for reasons of commercial and political greed and recombining them by wilfully denying all the considerations that gave India a sense of social order. This British dislocation of India must also serve to unsettle Britain's own sense of social order and cohesion (ibid.: 164). What Burke will not countenance is power arrogating to itself the right to meddle in other people's histories. Unlike the antiquarian Sir William Jones, Burke is not drawn to India's civilizational riches, but to the fact that India has implicated British power (ibid.: 165).

To the criticism that he was obsessed with Hastings' trial, Burke wrote to Mary Palmer:

> I have no part in this Business . . . but among a set of people, who have none of your Lilies and Roses in their faces, but who are the images of the great

Pattern as well as you and I. I know what I am doing; whether the white people like it or not.

(ibid.: 167)

To French Lawrence, he wrote shortly before his death:

> Above all make out the cruelty of this pretended acquittal, but in reality this barbarous and inhuman condemnation of whole Tribes and nations, and of all the abuses they contain. If ever Europe recovers its civilization that work will be useful. Remember! Remember! Remember!
>
> (ibid.: 168–9)

Mehta is trying to make clear that what was at issue for Burke was not merely the presence of one corrupt Governor General, who had embezzled, countenanced the humiliation of an Indian, begun and perhaps directed the murder of one local official – all merely a history of one official abusing his office. Some commentators conclude that Burke's huge effort with respect to such small matters must, therefore, be seen as disproportionate and so an obsessional pathology. However, Mehta's comment is that this is to overlook that for Burke,

> these efforts were nothing less than an attempt to "save the nation" and to make possible a redemption of European civilization despite its inhumanity towards whole tribes and other nations. They involved the "Shame and Guilt" of Great Britain . . .
>
> (ibid.: 169)

Rather than engage with the moral seriousness of Burke's charges, his critics accuse him of pathological obsession, a clear abuse of the facts. Instead, for Mehta,

> Burke's writings are a sophisticated and moving elaboration of the idea of sympathy, the means whereby one develops a feeling for another person or collectivity of persons (ibid.: 170).

Conclusion

Mehta brings to his reader's attention a terrible possibility arising from the letters of Edmund Burke written after the acquittal of Hastings. It is that the moral and legal defeat, entailed by the acquittal, was also a defeat for European Civilization so profound that for centuries, maybe forever, Europe will not recover. Burke's death bed message is, so represents Mehta, that Europe's inhumanity towards India can probably never be redeemed. This chapter has intended to show the continuing truth and power of Burke's words. Far from the essentially racist, literary characterization of Burke as a hysterically loquacious Anglo-Irish rhetorician, choking himself with his own melodramatic speeches, it should not have been particularly difficult for the literary critic to perceive that Burke constructed moderately clear legal arguments, which are substantially the same as those reconstructed by the canonical historian of the Impeachment Trial of Hastings, Peter Marshall. The literary criticism of the Trial, even by Suleri, appears to be trapped in an essentializing of individuals as representatives of powers, races and civilizations or the lack thereof. This literary criticism marks also a failure of humanity, which has to start with individual responsibility and accountability.

Added to this general failure of literary criticism, the viciousness of the exchanges between Dalrymple, Dirks and Frykenberg indicate that the whole of contemporary historiography of the Trial, at what should be the most distinguished levels of scholarship, is completely flawed by moral evasion and confusion. Here this chapter endorses Dirks' critique of contemporary historiography, while not accepting his belief that the legal issues in the Trial were not justiciable. Dalrymple's description of Dirks as Anglophobic does nothing more than to show that the *Scandal of Empire* continues. While there is considerable substance in Frykenberg's critique of postmodern or "literary" history, this should not be taken so far as to exclude the historian's engagement with issues of personal and collective responsibility. Traumatic events of the past continue to determine the limits of contemporary collective consciousness.

Law and Literature is a movement for which the author has every sympathy (Carty, 2000). However, the treatment of Law as Literature, i.e. subject to the standards and methods of literary criticism, should not be taken, as it has been seen here, as an alibi for moral evasion in the case of Musselwhite and moral confusion in the case of Suleri. Nor should it have to be that those such as Dirks, who try to locate at least moral responsibility for "the deeds of Empire", be abused as Anglophobic. Instead, there is need for much more serious legal historical scholarship on the actual institutional mechanisms of Empire, such as Khan bravely undertook in his solitary essay. This chapter boasts of nothing more and nothing less than having rooted out the original records of the Trial of Hastings, read through some of the Managers' speeches and found them to be perfectly intelligible in legal terms and corresponding broadly with the clear, if overly brief, account of the Impeachment Trial by the historian around whose reputation at least some consensus hovers, Peter Marshall. Such a discovery, however limited, should be a clarion call for an exhaustive history of the illegalities of Empire.

Bibliography

Asiatic Society of Benghal (1784). Available http://www.archive.org/search.php?query=creator%3A%22Asiatic%20Society%20of%20Bengal%22.

Bond, E,A. (ed) (1859) *Speeches of the managers and counsel in the trial of Warren_Hastings*. Available http://openlibrary.org/books/OL7053670M/. Published by the Authority of the Lords

Commissioners of Her Majesty's Treasury, London, for Longman, Brown and Green. Volume 4.

Carty, A. (2000) 'The Law and Literature Debate in Britain and the United States', *Studia Occidentalis*, 167–75.

Dalrymple, W. (2007) *Plain Tales from British India*. Available http://www.nybooks.com/articles/archives/2007/apr/26/plain-tales-from-british-india/.

Debrett (1797) *Debates of the House of Lords on the Evidence Delivered in the Trial of Warren Hastings*, London.

Dirks, N.B. (2006) *The Scandal of Empire*, Cambridge, MA: Harvard University Press.

Frykenberg, R.E. (1999) 'India to 1858', in R.W. Winks (ed), and A. Law (associate ed), *Historiography*, volume V, *The Oxford History of the British Empire*, New York: Oxford University Press, pp. 194–212.

Khan, K.R. (1988) 'The Impeachment: Certain Issues of International Law', in G. Carnall and C. Nicholson (ed), *The Impeachment of Warren Hastings, Papers from a Bicentenary Commemoration*, Edinburgh: Edinburgh University Press, pp. 145–63.

Louis, W.R. (1999) 'Introduction', in R.W. Winks (ed), and A. Law (associate ed), *Historiography*, volume V, *The Oxford History of the British Empire*, New York: Oxford University Press.

Marshall, P. (1965) *The Impeachment of Warren Hastings*, London: Oxford University Press.

Mehta, U.D. (1999) *Liberalism and Empire*, London and Chicago: University of Chicago Press.

Musselwhite, D. (1982) *The Trial of Warren Hastings*. Available http://privateview.essex.ac.uk/-muss/hastings.htm.

Suleri, S. (1992) *The Rhetoric of English India*, Chicago and London: University of Chicago Press.

Part II

Perspectives on precedent

Chapter 7

The making of legal cases and the idea of precedent in the common law*

Thanos Zartaloudis

Introduction

The point of an inquiry into the philosophical elements of the making of legal cases is not to conceive of a philosopher-king or a philosopher-judge. The point is also not to disregard (legal) practice or pragmatics, for example, in judging or legislating to contrast practice to theory in some naïve antinomianism. As Fish suggests, for instance, judging and giving an account of judging are two independent activities 'even though the successful performance of the first will often involve engaging in the second' (Fish, 1987: 1779). That theoretical questions arise and are often presupposed in the practice of judging and in giving accounts of it is fairly obvious. In judicial interpretation the distinction or relation between the 'real nature of things' to which the words of a statute refer as opposed to legal or ordinary conventions governing the use of such words, entails presuppositions as to the distinction between ordinary reality and legal reality or better about the relationship between ordinary convention and legal convention, and much can be gained by interrogating such presupposed relations (a distinction is always a relation). Furthermore, the long-standing claim of legal practice and legal reason as to consistency or what Dworkin calls 'articulate consistency' (Dworkin, 1977: 88), entails a presupposition of the knot between a particular decision of a case and the reasoned continuity of earlier cases, implying a particular understanding of the legal 'whole' in relation to the legal particular or case. Such a whole has been often called legal history or jurisprudence, the work of which it is presumed takes place in the figment of each particular case before the court.

It remains a question to ask: what kind of history is such a presumed chain enterprise of cases? And, also, what kind of figmentation takes place when it is presupposed that a particular case fits (or does not fit) such a proposed historical evolution? Ultimately the question is one of what kind of historizing takes place or is internalized by the judge in the making (or the seeing; in gr. *idein*, etymologically linked to idea) of a legal case, in deciding, that is, cutting (*decidere*) the past?

It is worth keeping in mind from the outset three elementary notes as to the particular approach here to the making of legal cases. First, the law is a routine, an apparatus, allowing certain arguments to be argued and certain decisions to be presented each time in the pragmatic – though inherently political – manner of presenting one's decision 'in a form most likely to secure its acceptance' within the systemic understanding of law and decision making (Fish, 1987: 1790). Such a legal practice through the politics of its rhetorical persuasion conceals in the guise of juridical metaphysics, the fact that decisions are preceded and followed by the unfolding of their force each time: they are *made*.[1] Yet juridical metaphysics are presupposed 'in the name of the law' as such, which renders judicial decisions and legal pragmatics, more generally, as inherently uncoupled from both an exposition of being merely-made and from their entailed desire.

The making of a legal case or decision is presented as taking place in law and in the name of the law and the desire of the subject making that law or decision is at best discoursed as legislative or judicial intention, once more, in the name of the law. This is not to deny that subjectivity and desire are themselves always subject to interpretive constructions or to deny that any action (including judicial decision-making) requires a 'forgetfulness' as its condition of possibility (Fish, 1987: 1798). But it is to stress the need to not abandon the exposition of such forgetfulness as such. Forgetfulness may be a necessary condition but when exposed as such it turns law-making and case-making to their original contingency and construction as well as to the ever-political agency of their making. Theory, in turn, cannot offer some unforgetful condition of conditions, nor can it escape its own constructions and contingency, yet theory can provide for a means to turn the law towards its making as such, towards the showing, at least, of the existence of other potential *legal* paths amidst the already decided legal *cases* (conceived in the widest sense of 'things' or 'examples'); as well as to point to the existence of other *non-legal* paths.

Second, what prompted here the turn to the question of the making of cases and the setting of precedent as a key element to the understanding and standing of cases in English common law was the rereading of cases whereby when judges attempt to apply a legal principle and discuss the very applicability as such in question they state things like the following: 'This court is a court of law, not of morals, and our task has been to find, and our duty is then to apply, the relevant principles of law to the situation before us – a situation which is quite unique.'[2] The question of interest here is the way the court conceives of its judicial role with regard to what may essentially be seen as a moral question, as well as the way a situation is demarcated as a singular case that falls (*casus*) before the court. Another question of interest is internal to judicial decision-making: how to draw analogical reasoning between different situations? For example, the court, in *Re A (children) (conjoined twins) [2000]* asked: if there are rules concerning the killing of non-conjoined persons, do these rules apply in an identical fashion to conjoined persons?[3] Similarly of interest are questions raised in courts like the following in a more general sense: there may be indeed no right or just decision to be found here, yet we must reason a decision that connects the facts of the situation at hand with the legal principle that is said to govern such situations. How is the particularity or exceptionality of a case in relation to a rule in question be seen to be applied, let alone, in certain cases, be seen to redefine the so-called foundation of that same rule anew? It, thus, remains useful to reopen the questioning of the making of connections in legal cases and decisions. That is, of interrogating the seeking of the so-called true or real basis of (legal) things at the very moment when it is presupposed or, better, made up.

In need of initial reflection is the making of legal things as such through the presupposed distinction between legal things and non-legal things. While this is a philosophical question as to the ontology of the creation of legal categories and entities, it is foundational for the making of law in practice as it forms a presupposition of its logic and discourse. This inquiry triggers the questioning of legal reality as such or what could be called the vantage point claimed by law as its way of looking at the world, or life. As Honoré puts it: 'To attain this point of vantage requires the transformation of the data of ordinary life into those of a special drama with its own personages, costumes, and conventions, not to mention the invention of new personages and relationships not found in the state of nature' (Honoré, 1977: 112). In asking the question, therefore, of the making of cases, the question extends to the very understanding of what renders life and knowledge into legal life and knowledge.

This leads to a third preliminary element to note for the purposes of this inquiry. What does the very word in the title as to the *Idea* of Precedent refer to? Reference to the term idea is made here in a particular etymological and philosophical sense. What is referred to is, in fact, an experience, from the Greek word *Idein* which means to see. Reference to seeing is usually made in the sense of a general capacity or function of human beings, which is more often than not taken for granted – 'we simply see because we see'. It is of interest, though, that from as early on as in Homer 'to see' signified many different things humans do with their eyes. In fact to see meant everything except to see in the sense in which we self-referentially understand the term in late modernity. The eye it can be said, in this sense, then, is not the 'origin' of sight. To see involves an internal growth, what the ancients called the Soul, to which the eye is already a migration or 'a metaphor'.[4] In other words, our ways of seeing are from the start technological or constructed – they are as contingent as fabricated (made as well as fictional or made up); they are contingent experiences. This is so to such an extent that the process of seeing and the things we see, as a result, cannot be separated. In this sense, the term *Idea* refers to the empiricism of what can be called *knowability*, a certain potential capacity of human beings that stands beside (*para*) the actually seen on each occasion. If the condition of (legal) sight is a certain knowability or sight-ability, then how is this *ability* to be thought with and against its instantiated limitation? Does not the law in its *interpretatio verborum* also refer to a parallel *ability* in the sense of finding in the immanent legal *logos* (or discourse) the supposedly unwritten or sigetically declared law which is not yet incarnate in a formal legal declaration or decision? How is this presupposed and much silenced ability, or 'faculty', to be thought?

On making (legal) things

In law as a systemic operation, as well as in thinking law more generally, we are accustomed, explicitly or implicitly, to the making of distinctions. The primary distinction in all legal systems is that between the legal and the non-legal (the distinction between the legal and the illegal is conditioned on this primary distinction). It is worth stressing that this key distinction or differentiation takes place *within* the systemic understanding of law. That is, it is a *legal* distinction that purports to differentiate the legal from the non-legal. The continuing relevance of this internal distinction between what is inside and what is outside the law can be illustrated in many ways for current purposes. For instance, with regard to thinking about precedent this could serve to illustrate the missing question prior to the peculiar presupposition of the distinction between law as *made* and as merely *exposed* or *found*. This also serves to underlie the question as to the difference between thinking of the reasoning of common law via precedent and thinking of the reasoning that one acquires more generally through ordinary experience; as well as through the differentiation between (legal) customary thinking and precedential thinking as formally reasoned. Recurrent debates, finally, as to whether precedential case law is law at all point to the continuing significance of the questioning proposed here.

Central to what can be called the making of legal things with particular reference to the common law, at least in England, is the mechanism known as precedent: as the operation of the making of legally binding or persuasive (or both) case-law. Hence thinking of precedent with regard to the making of case-law remains key to the wider understanding of at least one part of the legal system (case-law), that is, its internal self-understanding; as well as to its self-differentiation with whatever is held to lie outside the legal system. The question of this understanding is reopened here, and more specifically, it is suggested that this self-understanding remains the latest nihilistic form of the old problem of the law's self-understanding and autonomy, its presupposition of self-law-giving, of a legal self-sufficiency. MacCormick defines precedent in the following way: 'The judicial opinion which sets or constitutes a precedent is a judge's opinion considered as stating a justification of a decision' (MacCormick, 1987: 155). This can be reread to stress the making of a precedent as taking place in the statement of a decision, that is, in the act of saying right. What can be stressed at this point is not just the normativity of legal decision-making of and through precedent, but first of all the taking place of a form of normalization in the rendering *intelligible* of legal things (to use Foucault's term: an act of *problematization* – rendering something as a *legal* problem) (see Foucault, 1985). Not just a questioning of the normative justification and logical legitimacy, then, but also of the act of presupposition or application (or both) as such: the saying of right as ever being an act upon another act that must allegedly always conceal a nonetheless exclusive right to say right, to act or decide 'in the name of the law'.

The problem in other words is not with the occasional need to decide on things or to fabricate legal things or fictions, but with deciding 'in the name of law, justice and so forth' to silence the act of doing so as a particular action by an agent. Hence, a secondary act of deciding on legal things presupposes and silences problematically another act: the primary act that decisively renders ordinary things, each time, *as* legal things, as legal names in the first place. That law is a necessary institution is widely accepted, but that life in its totality should be institutionally integrated into legal forms needs to be avoided. To risk a formula of inescapable abstraction, this preliminary questioning serves to interrogate the non-legal being of things *in* the legal being of things; which implies their difference at the very same time of showing their indistinction in institutional practice. Yet it should be stressed from the start that this is not a claim to some neo-natural 'real' or 'pure' state of things that we could 'save', or some pre-legal substance that could be posed as before/outside/against the law. Instead the task remains to expose such presuppositions of reality as adjacent and internal productions to/of legal operations and to question the negative relation posed between non-legal things and legal things in the process of the ever-increasing juridification of ways of life.

As indicated earlier what is presupposed by this primary distinction is in fact, first of all, the very notion of *some* thing being-already or becoming a legal thing (*res*) that the law renders justiciable or determinable in a legal process. How is this becoming of justiciability to be thought? The making of law involves first of all the making of *some* thing into a legal dispute, a legally relevant dispute, that is as something for which the law is capable to say right generally as well as *its* right, to speak of right-*things* as well as of things *of* right. It is with reference to an ability that precedent first is grounded within a legal system and this capacity is a particular understanding of what it means to act and to act legally, in particular to judge. A reference to an ability of the legal agent, be it a judge or else, refers to an act and its potential ability foremost to not only act (or not act) on some thing, but necessarily to refer itself to itself as its normative justification.

Things in becoming legal things must suffer a sigetic (silencing) transmutation, a parabolic metamorphosis, for the law must cut (*decidere*) things into legal things in order to be able to operate. The making of legal cases negates, at the same time, a presupposed metaphysical assumption about things 'as such' (in the fabricated distinction of (non-juridical) things and legal things), their coming to be (their pseudo-emergence, as ever, from some natural state of unreason, a chaos, a *factum brutum*) and their legal actualization 'as' legal things within a legally governed totality, a legal universe. The intelligibility of the making of cases – and of precedential authority as such – as well as the normativity of case-*law* is based on the act of stating a right as a binding or persuasive (or both) exclusionary statement in the name, at least in recent modernity, of reason; a particular episode of reason, a legal reason formed itself on the basis of a presupposed ontology of legal discourse: a *nomology*. A key part of this ontology has come to be known in the *ratio decidendi*: 'the rule or principle of decision for which a given precedent is the authoritative source, whether that rule or principle of decision is then to be treated as binding or only as persuasive in some degree for other later deciders of similar questions' (MacCormick, 1987: 156). Here the silenced act of presupposing the immediate relationship between law and reason (reason itself decides and law is itself reason), is presented through the apparatus of authorial 'imperatives without *imperator*' (reason is not a subject; let alone a responsible or accountable subject) (Schütz, 2009: 233–43).

Questioning precedent

There are many still pertinent questions that can be raised with regard to the making of cases with particular reference to precedential reasoning. As to conceptual questions of precedential thinking we can raise questions in relation to what precedent is held to be, by reference to what precedential thinking is more often said not to be: precedent is not law but the exposition of law; it is almost always a decision but not necessarily so; it is not a hypothetical instance; it is not reasoning from experience; it does not sideline the past but wishes to render it usable in the present; it can set an example but it is not just exemplary; it is neither custom nor a mere necessity; it is not followed simply because it exists; there is a certain element of fiction and not strict legal authority to its binding effect; it is not coercive and it cannot be described as a legal rule and so forth.[5]

Historically speaking these questions multiply further: take for example a comparison as to what legal reason more generally is between Austin, Hobbes and Coke. Hastily sketched, here, it can be said that for Austin a precedent is not law or good law or even a marginally valid law; for Hobbes it can be law but it is not an authoritative law and for Coke it is the perfection of artificial reason, rather than as in Hobbes the application of natural reason (a reason supposedly shared between the sovereign and his subjects) (Duxbury, 2008: 16–25). But the more interesting historical questions become more poignant in relation to the birth of precedential thinking in the common law and what was largely merely customary practice before its late modern formulation. Common law judges in England, as is well known, have not always resorted to earlier judicial decisions as sources of authority, let alone to written sources or reasoned ones (Ibid.: 25–42). Precedent was conceived in a very different manner as merely evidentiary: precedents could be entered on a plea roll as early as the thirteenth century, as the source of a plea, and litigants and advocates would very occasionally search the rolls for precedents which might help their cause (see Pollock and Maitland, 1968/1898: 183–4). But precedent here was nothing more – and nothing less – than evidence of the law and hence a very different notion to the one perceived today (see Duxbury, 2008: 31–7).

In addition common law operated as customary law long before the introduction of even this notion of precedent as mere evidence of the law; and the oral erudition of the legal profession, the common learning and the constant flux of the evolution of the common law in the minds of the common people was far more important (ibid.). A period of transition and eventually of change took place in the sixteenth century when while common learning as a source of law is still evident in case law, the revival of the special verdict, and an increasing inclination on the part of judges to determine the law by decisions on demurrer and motions after trial meant 'that courts were more likely to treat earlier decisions as supportive (though not yet determinative) of a particular result, at least where those decisions were followed by reasons' (Ibid.: 33–4). We also have to note that it is during this period when the emergence of compilations of cases and the increased reliance of lawyers on abridgements led to case law being perceived more and more as a source of some kind of authority (as Coke will say *argument drawn from authority is the strongest in law*).[6] It remains crucial to question from where this 'strength' or authorial 'ability' is derived.

Before the questioning of the legal case and its making is widened in scope even further outside of its ordinary legal ramifications and coordinates it is worth re-visiting the insightful and seminal essay on the roots of the notion of precedent by Postema (Postema, 1987: 15–23). The epigraphs of Postema's essay will serve as preliminary indications of the wider scope of the inquiry here with regard to legal reason and the making of case-law: the first is pronounced by James I: 'Reason is too large. Find me a precedent and I will accept it' (Ibid.: 15). The second is pronounced by the Levellers: 'Reason hath no precedent for reason is the fountain of all just precedents' (ibid.). Postema, in fact, distinguishes schematically between three conceptions of precedent: the positivist, the traditionary and the conventionalist. The positivist takes place, for instance, between Coke's defence of reason as the life of the law as such: 'common law itself is nothing else but Reason' (Duxbury, 2008: 51–2). Hobbes who agrees on this with Coke at least to an extent, immediately qualifies this reason under the guise of Sovereign Authority (ibid.: 49–52). In this vein it is not knowledge or wisdom that makes a law, but authority. To put it in another way: it is the authority, the *officium of legal reason* and not jurisprudence that renders case law into law. Bentham who is largely the father of the modern conception of precedent in its primary modern form relied heavily on this conception.

The traditionary approach to precedent is a development perhaps of the common law theory which was preoccupied with the fictions of time immemorial and the ancient customs of the common realm. In the traditionary approach this foundation of precedent in immemorial and common custom is refined through the suggestion that this wisdom or custom is something that evolves through time and memorial use. Hale in 1713 announced:

> The Decisions of Courts of Justice, tho' by Vertue of the Law . . . do not make a Law properly so called, (for that only the King and Parliament can do); yet they have a great Weight and Authority in Expounding, Declaring, and Publishing what the Law of this Kingdom is, especially when such Decisions hold a Consonancy and Congruity with Resolutions and Decisions of former Times [. . .] (Hale, 1987/1713: 68).

The rules Hale stated are initially clumsy, defective, faulty, lapsing with hard edges and through time they can be, though not necessarily so, smoothened off and softened to fit the contours of the common realm and life. This in a way can be seen to signify a transition from the external justification or transcendent justification of precedent in time immemorial, to an internal justification of precedent that is refinable in time memorial.

The third conception that Postema identifies in his essay he calls the conventionalist, which at first appears as a mixture of the other two and to an extent in its late modern understanding it is. The conventional approach to precedent fuses the positivist and the traditionary approaches and is today widely accepted as a better description of what takes place in precedential reasoning. But this is often at the cost of not considering Hume's specific understanding of convention and its philosophical implications. This cannot be engaged with here in any significant detail but it is worth suggesting that Hume, in not accepting that positive rules in common law are guaranteed by some rational foundation, long before the late modernists, poses at the core of the legal experience of the common law not just reason and analogy, but also the imagination and desire (see Hume, 1998/1751). Hume then speaks of *convention* specifically against consensus or contract. That is, against a tradition of contractarian thought that is still prevalent in various guises and in particular in the idea of government by consent in democratic states (see Hume, 1978/1739–40). Hence a Humean jurisprudence, yet to be explored at length, is interested not in infinite succession and similitude but strategy, studious combat rather than polemics of judgement and counter-judgement.[7]

Thus, the elaboration of reasoned principles governing the use of precedents and their status as authorities is relatively modern and the idea that there could be binding precedents even more recent. It cannot be explored in any detail here but what could be called the *plasticity* of what is understood as *common* law (and common legal reason more generally) when seen in its earlier forms prior to the function of the doctrine of precedential thinking suggests the obvious historical *matheme* that what is today considered as well established need not be seen as such under any strict necessity with regard to its past as well as to its future forms. This remains relevant to the practical scope of things too. The plasticity of legal decisions entails well-known practical disputations that still raise significant questions, which continue to be open-ended. For instance, what does it mean to talk about a precedent being a rule, or an example, or an embodiment of reason? What does it mean to treat like cases alike? What is the difference between a precedent and an analogous case? Why do hypothetical examples seem to count for less in courts than actual precedents? What determines the weight, the gravitational force, to use Dworkin's phrase (Dworkin, 1977: 110–23), of a particular precedent?

In theory precedent can be conceived, as Duxbury has recently analysed, along three key parameters (Duxbury, 2008: 108–110). First, precedent can be conceived as entailing conditional reasons for legal decision making. That is, the idea that most case-law contains a reason for the decision and that identifying this *ratio* (which is not the same thing as the judicial reasons offered) is the key to determining how a precedent binds future courts. Second, precedent can be conceived as the management of the usable past. That is, the idea that a precedent may offer a court an already articulated reason for reaching a particular decision in the present, thereby avoiding the costs of reasoning from the ground up. Finally, precedent can be conceived with regard to what can be called the exclusionary authority of precedent. That is, through the idea that the doctrine of precedent requires judges to treat precedents as authoritative directives giving rise to 'exclusionary reasons', thereby pre-empting or even taking the place of individual judgements as to what ought to be done. To such definitional schemas and constraints can be added practical constraints of equal significance. Juridical decision making, Teubner writes, faces three key constraints (Teubner, 2009: 72). In summary they are: a. the constraint of decision-making: in modern legal systems one party has to be right in a legal trial even if both are right; b. the constraint of rational justification: a decision must be founded on reasons which can at least pretend to combine consistency and responsiveness; and finally c. the constraint of rule making: the decision reduces the complexity of the conflict to an over-simplified rule. While accepting these constraints, legal theory's scope *can* pose a supplementary question as to the making of (case-)law: what of creativity in the law? Who knows what the law can do? Is legal reason to be conceived, as it is so often suggested, only as a constraint or manager of competing interests?

Though a system of precedent may 'produce [. . .] a body of rules', as Hart observed, a precedent itself might best be described not as a legal rule but as an instance of 'communication by authoritative example'.[8] Like legal rules, however, these examples are 'open-textured', and so 'there is no authoritative or uniquely correct formulation of any rule to be extracted from cases'. While this was stated by Hart to defend a particular thesis, it can be recalibrated. MacCormick writes, for example:

> it is a disputed question whether there is any such thing as a or the *ratio* in a given case; it is disputed whether or not there is a *ratio* to be found authoritatively within a given opinion, or whether the so-called *ratio* is simply some proposition of law which a later court or courts find it expedient to ascribe to an earlier decision as the ground of that decision [. . .] (MacCormick, 1987: 157).

Stone has called this apparent self-referentiality of the term *ratio* a category of 'illusory reference' (see J. Stone, 1985: 61–80); and as MacCormick suggests, though later disputes, this category is a 'systematically misleading' form of expression which conveys 'an illusion of reference and thus of legal stability and certainty while the legal reality is one of change' (MacCormick, 1987: 157). There is, instead, never justification *simpliciter*. Justification plays the normative game of bad infinity. That is, as MacCormick has indicated, the problematic but inevitable form of the continuous becoming of a justification of justification of yet more justifications to come (ibid.: 167). Yet *ratio decidendi* is 'a ruling', MacCormick states, 'expressly or impliedly given by a judge which is sufficient to settle a point of law put in issue by the parties' arguments in a case, being a point on which a ruling was necessary to his justification (or one of his alternative justifications) of the decisions in the case' (ibid.: 170). Such a justification for an opinion to be a *ratio* of this legal kind must be, for MacCormick, logically universalizable within the realm, the area (*figment*), of law and it has to be so for the purpose of the operation of a court case is to decide a case, to end it. But if this is a necessary construction of legal reasoning what, if anything, distinguishes the contingency of experience from the contingency of legal experience? This brings us to a question of realization as a problem rather than as a dogma, that is once more, a questioning of the *making* of (legal) reality as a particular form of reasoned artifice.

The figment of legal reason

Which reason? It is of particular interest that around the mid seventeenth century legal decisions began to be conceived as reasoned decisions establishing a direct link between law and a particular type of reasoned discourse that has been most influential ever since and yet anything but a given (see Duxbury, 2008: 49–53). For Hobbes it is the reason he called natural though one that is heavily qualified by the commands of the sovereign (ibid.: 31–51). The consistent whole of the law in this sense is that of the consistency of the natural reason of the sovereign which the judge must pick up and follow up as is his duty. For Coke, in some contrast at least, reason is understood as the *life* of the law, that is, as the artificial life of the law as such. For Coke consistency emerges through the study not of sovereign commands but of the past decisions of courts and the reason in which lawyers and judges find themselves immersed in, their common learning. Coke calls this reason and the understanding of precedent that follows it as 'the clearest lights of the world' (as quoted in ibid.: 49). It is interesting though that to understand the law as rational (*summa ratio*) was not to regard law as derivable from universal first principles. Instead it was to approach law on the *assumption* that it exists as a coherent albeit *rational* whole (Postema, 1987: 178). It would be a mistake, too, to think that reason then had acquired a fixed legal meaning. Reason referred, for Coke (and during the seventeenth century more generally), to a particular understanding of the *rational* consistency of the law.

It is useful to turn to the French Philosopher Nancy who has claimed that philosophy itself is structured in a juridical manner through the transition of the Greek empire of the *logos* into the Latin empire of Right. This renders theorizing about judging in need of further self-reflection. For Nancy this structuring culminates decidedly in its modern form in Kant. The inception of western metaphysics, for Nancy, is always-already implicated in its juridical foundation, the foundation of right, of *saying* right. Kant advances philosophy's self-trial or self-justification through the architectonics of its very own tribunal. In Kant this tribunal remains of course fictional, albeit pure, that is, juridical and it could be traced back to a more real tribunal established in ancient Greek tragedy. Philosophy for Nancy via Kant is articulated as jurisdiction, that is, as the *dictio* on *jus* of the jurists, the saying of right (Nancy, 2003/1983: 153). This presupposed primary tribunal of reason must suffer ironically its very own delirium in order to address and accuse itself.

This is further telling to the extent that it indicates also the contour of the constructed factuality of legal systemic closure; the fact that the modern legal system ever attempts its self-definition, or self-delimitation. What is to be noted is that what renders a dispute *as* a legal dispute is first of all an *accusation*. In late modern terms this means that a legal case is to be understood pragmatically as well as philosophically as the self-accusatory addressing of a thing or somebody through the saying of a right. This *accusatio* etymologically related in Latin to *causa*, the implication of a ground for a juridical situation, an object of dispute, becomes, in neo-Latin languages, *res* (a thing, an affair) or *cosa* (an issue, a thing) appearing as a neutral juridical descriptor, yet naming also, as the Italian philosopher Agamben suggests, what is most at stake and most threatening in the law itself (Agamben, 2008: 13). In late modernity a self-defining legal system supposedly without reference to anything outside it, ultimately points to the law within ourselves (in our pre-qualified, by law, nature) which always-already accuses ourselves.

If philosophy is Greek, Nancy states, then this question of jurisdiction (*juris-dictio*) is the Latin or Roman question of philosophy, and this for him, in turn, becomes the philosophical question of law. Latin jurisdiction means: no *jus* without *ratio*, no right without reason. Jurisdiction is the fact of saying right (Nancy, 2003/1983: 154). This rational saying has to be inherent in right just as reciprocally right has to be inherent to its saying, to its being said. For a thing to be judicious, for its factual, linguistic saying to be just or rightful this is a *conditio sine qua non*. Nancy observes:

> *dictio*, by itself, in some way comprises a judgement even before it's actually formulated. *Dicere* means to show and, in order to be able to show, to discern or to fix, to establish and to point the finger at whatever is being determined (*indicere*). Latin saying operates by judging; it is constitutively judicial: *causam dicere* is to establish and to show the cause, to plead. From this point on, discourse only shows things by pleading their cause'

and 'such is the program that it falls to Kant to carry out' (ibid.) which so definitively inspired and formed modern legal discourse.

But this is only possible if right or law can maintain this self-foundation, this autonomy intact and safeguard it from the excess of the experience of reason, from the lapses of reason. Normative formation presupposes a self-referential birth of things as causes, as things, *cosa*, as cases. In other words the formation of legal right, in the saying of right, is not simply a mere statement of right, an act, but also a presupposition of a particular metaphysics or ontology. The problem's key lies in the relation that is presupposed and enabled between law and a case, where a case is a thing that falls, lapses, into the hands of the law and which the law then needs to 'pick up'. Nancy writes:

> casuality constitutes the essence of right; casuistry, the essence of jurisdiction. *Casus* denotes the fall – the fall in or through chance, through contingency,

the fall according to opportunity (an opportunity that constitutes the judge as much as the criminal); the fall, then, as accident. The 'essence' of right stems from the singular relation of accident to essence. *De jure*, the law ought to be the universal code whose very definition implies the annulment or the re-absorption of any accident. *De facto* (but this fact is itself constitutive of right, is itself the very fact of juris-diction), cases ought to be referred and legitimated case by case (ibid.: 155).

This dual limitation between fact and right, *de facto* and *de jure*, renders the juridical order as an order instituted through 'the formal taking into account of the accident itself', the case itself in its singularity, 'without however ever conceiving its necessity' (ibid.). The juridical order suppresses the accidental character (or *manner* to use the medieval scholastic term) that is its contingency in order to transmutate contingency into rationally 'fallen' instances (cases) before the law.

Jurisdiction is articulated, therefore, through a double structure:

> On the one hand, it states the right of the case, thereby making it a case: it subsumes it, suppresses its accidental character; picks it up [. . .] after its fall [. . .]. On the other hand, though, it states the right *of* this case and so states right itself through this case: in a sense, right exists through the case alone, through its accidental character; even if the case is settled [. . .] and domesticated [. . .], it has to fall down once it is picked up (ibid.: 155–6).

No case, in Nancy's conception, is a law in itself, it only lapses, falls under the law, once the law speaks of it: 'The accident, what happens, has to be struck by the seal of the law (its utterance) in order to be not simply judged but constituted as an instance or case of right, sculpted (*fictum*) in terms of right' (ibid.: 156–7). Hence here lies the origin of the notion of legal fictions, in light of the *arch*fiction of the law: jurisdiction. As jurisdiction the installation of right or law is handed to the state of Reason; which in turn means invariably, to that of the bourgeois State itself and its agents, its administrators of jurisdiction, of juridical statements.

Let's say this now while admittedly jumping ahead: *poietic* saying or *compositio*, in the sense of intellectual composition, was conceived to be a sympathy, a co-passivity, an assemblage, forming connections, relations as opposed to imposing a univocal rational Right. The Latin logic of right, however, gives birth to a jurisprudence that claims to owe nothing to experience; yet this is only because it assumes the capacity for itself to be able to subsume experience into an always-already juridical experience through the apparatus of case-installation, the banality of its own casuality.

Composing

What does all this mean for the thinking that is proposed here of the making of cases, the setting of precedents, the fabrication of legal things and perhaps of things in general? We should say from the start that what we are after here is a comment on a mindset or attitude. When dealing with the making of law and of a case in particular, a wider problem is of concern, a problem that for example in philosophy is often critiqued as the stifling of life, of what happens, under the guise of a vantage point, a first principle which poses itself as outside time, that is outside the human making of time. How can we clarify though the problem as a problem rather than as a dogma, if philosophical reasoning is in itself constrained by the same light (and darkness or lapse) of reason within which the juridical dogma is every time intensified.

It is less frequently noted that legal decisions and precedent following (overruling and distinguishing) entail as much restraint as creative impulse. Precedent is often set on the basis of what have been called exclusionary reasons, that is, legal reasons that exclude other reasons – perhaps equally valid ones – in order to reach a decision, a failed reason does not lose its potential as a successful future reason and remains within the contour of legal reason.[9] This is evident in the understanding of precedent setting, which can in itself sometimes be seen to take place in retrospect only or even unintentionally. In a wider sense if all cases are never identical by their so-called nature (singularities), then any account of precedential authority is bound to be incomplete, and for this reason the last thing that is needed is yet another theory of precedent.

If legal principles more generally are over-determined (rather than undermined) by their formal discursive nature then exclusionary reasons, further, can only be exclusionary up to a certain extent. The fact that precedential constraints leave room for judicial, as well as theoretical, innovation means that the characterization of a precedent as giving rise to an exclusionary ruling will nearly always fall too short (Duxbury, 2008: 108). The dream of legal reason to be able to fully weigh in all the foreseeable consequences of making a decision by following a precedent against all the foreseeable consequences of making the decision in any other possible way remains impossible. It is equally difficult to predict with any absolute certainty that departing from a precedent will actually have the consequences that the decision-makers in fact desire or fear.

To state the obvious: decisions are *made*. How can one think of the connections made between situations and legal things in the process of deciding? The approach proposed here begins from the reconsideration of what can be called the facticity of facts. We aim to put back into things themselves the very thing that was mistakenly considered to be the incapacity in thought: their contingent manner. The ultimate property of things is not a lack of ultimate meaning or substance but an absence of reason. Things are capable of becoming otherwise without reason. That is to say, unreason is neither a lack nor a superior kind of reason, it is the truly absolute ontological property of things. As the French philosopher Meillassoux has written:

> From this perspective, the failure of the principle of reason follows, quite simply, from the falsity (and even from the absolute falsity) of such a

principle – for the truth is that there is no reason for anything to be or to remain thus and so rather than otherwise, and this applies as much to the laws that govern the world as to the things of the world (Meillassoux, 2008: 53).

For this inquiry what is meant by this is that, first, the process of fabricating or making things and the things as such cannot be distinguished. There is plasticity internal to a thing, which means that there is an intellectual intuition of/in complexity. Second, complex consistency *is* contingent which means that contingency alone is necessary (this understanding of contingency, for Meillassoux, is non-metaphysical). Contingency itself is the only necessity of complex consistency. To say contingency *alone* is necessary is the exact opposite of the statement contingency is necessary. Contingency is not peripheral to reality but equally real to the so-called actually real. In terms of pragmatics, let's call them speculative pragmatics, it can be said that deciding on the applicability of a legal principle to a particular case in court also alters the principle as such. Applicability and legal principle are not distinct categories but belong to the question of degree that Coke by implication conceived as a matter of clear and obscure: reason as the *clarissima mundi lumina* maintains a necessary relation to darkness.[10]

If a principle does not really exist outside of its application, if all we have is a surface of things and no metaphysical depth or essence to draw upon, then the legal fabrication of things is a question of art, of formulation, composition, sympathy rather than *dominium* and imposition. There is, as a result, no panoramic theoretical view of things, we only do, and this includes what things do as such, what we are each time capable of doing, but nobody knows what we can do or what the law can do.[11] There is no substance to be restored (justice is not a restoration in this at least sense); justice is a composition.[12] To seek a pre-emptive balance between principles and rules that one sets out to restore or to rely on the predisposed integrity (Dworkin) even of a judge presumes too much, too soon.[13] For the French philosopher Deleuze a different understanding of jurisprudence remained possible. The point is that the posing of first abstract principles leads invariably to sterile dualisms, that is, distinctions as unavoidable as they are, but sterile ones. The criterion for what is a good bipolarity or a sterile one becomes then the acceptance of the radical empiricism expressed in the following observation by Deleuze: 'things do not begin to live except in the middle' (Deleuze and Parnet, 1987: 55). This middle expresses what could be called the *minoritarian* jurisprudence of the assemblage,[14] rather than that of the ontology of first principles. An assemblage is a multiplicity which is made of many heterogeneous terms and which establishes relations, liaisons between them so that its only unity is a co-functioning, symbiosis, sympathy, composition as opposed to the juridical frame of *impositio* (see Deleuze, 2002: 69).

Precedent in this regard can be rethought not as a succession or a deduction, but as the experience of legal failures and alliances. Precedent to the extent that it draws the rational outline of case-law is based on an abstract first principle of reason when it is thought in the positivist or traditionary manner that Postema has described. Precedent has been mostly conceived in late modernity as too immobile, too directed, too governed amidst its hierarchies, *rationes*, segments and sterile differentiations. Perhaps legal practice in its need of pragmatic observations and analyses can at least attempt to reflect also on its reason*ability* as both a constraint and a creative power. Legal thought, however, more generally need not constrain itself to merely this since theory, by its nature, cannot not observe also the contingent plasticity of law's reason and of theory as such. At this point it is perhaps the role of legal theory to always attempt to counter-pose a true bipolarity to the universalism of law. To law and its judgement to oppose life and assemblages; what was once called justice, a justice (far from the ideological dogmatic battles in the name of justice of the recent centuries) of the necessary contingency of what there is in all its potentiality (past contingents as well as future contingents). This is not a polemic against law or against values or some other naïve antinomian stance. It is rather a turn to the very internal multiversal tradition of a more genuinely common law for those that have nothing in common, wherein the law is not a mere collection of decisions that adhere to a first principle (a universal), but is composed of assemblages (relations) between cases that can neither apprehend what is new nor pre-impose themselves on the law's new creations. In this sense, laws and cases can always remain comparable and accountable, open to creative consideration, critique and use.

Precedent as example and the virtual logic of the contingent

It is worth remembering that Kant in *The Critique of Pure Reason* describes examples as dangerous means of understanding the rule that the example is to stand for and he describes examples as *casus in terminis*.[15] Judgement is to overcome, to silence, the danger of the *casus* of the example, of the thing. The second thing to note, here, is that the definition of precedent in the *Oxford English Dictionary* describes precedent as an example or paradigm. Agamben in his essay *What is a Paradigm?* provides a useful pointer for this understanding in that (through reference to Goldschmidt's *The Paradigm in Plato's dialectics*[16]) he replaces earlier characterizations of the Platonic *Idea* as an obscurantism and mysticism and suggests that in a paradigm the generality (or the *Idea*) does not result from an induction through the exhaustive enumeration of the individual cases. Rather it is produced through the comparison by only one paradigm (one singular example) with the object or class that the paradigm will make intelligible (Agamben, 2009: 22–3). Aristotle's genius in clarifying that an example is a counterpart to dialectic induction is the key to Agamben's and Goldschmidt's conception.[17] A paradigm's relation to the proposition it supports is not 'that of part to whole, nor whole to part, nor whole to whole, but of part to part, or like to like'.[18] Thus there is *deduction* which goes from the universal to the particular; *induction* which goes from the particular to the universal and *paradigm* (or example) which goes from particular to particular.[19] The paradigmatic is a relation of asymmetry and its sense lies not in representation and similitude but in knowability or what could be termed *paraduction* (see R. Stone, 1965: 465. See also Brewer, 1996: 952).

An example, thus, has a paradoxical status and we can reconceive of the exemplarity implied but silenced in precedent setting (and case law more generally) in a similar way. The example, Agamben notes, shows its belonging to a class but for this very reason, it steps out of this class at the very moment in which it exhibits and defines it. It is excluded from the class at the very moment when it shows its belonging to it. Does the rule apply to a case that is an example of the rule's functionality? It is difficult to answer, Agamben notes, since the rule applies to the example case (or *casus* or thing) only to the extent that this case is understood as a *normal* case and not as an example.[20] That is as a singular example, the case, is excluded in its very inclusion as a normal case of the rule, a particular form of the rule. As an example, however, a case does not belong to the set of *simulacra* that the rule sets in place not because it does not belong to the rule's class, but because it also exhibits its *own* belonging to it. These two planes of the example or case are not to be confused and this is the hardest thing for a judgement to sustain; yet legal thought must at least attempt to show this. Legal thought when understood as judgment in itself is primarily concerned with inductions and deductions but here the task of coming legal thought is suggested to be an encounter head on with its knowability as such.

In the culmination of the *Critiques* in his most important third book the *Critique of the Power to Judge*, Kant crucially attempts to articulate a type of judgement that provides no actual knowledge, that determines nothing, and is therefore not cognitive, precisely to the extent that it remains tied to a certain singularity. This judgment Kant names 'reflective', in that it does not execute an act of judgement itself, but reflects on the movement of the mind judging, the operation of judgment itself. Of what movement can we speak here and is it a necessarily *juridical* movement? This is not as foreign to legal thought as usually and polemically perceived in modernity. For example, Arab philosophers of the Middle Ages knew well that a genuine philosophy of law is not a doctrine of judgement but a science of its limits (see Heller-Roazen, 2006: 3). Knowability (or communicability to use Benjamin's term) is indeed difficult to understand precisely because as Kant knew, but did not fulfil in his *Critique*, it is not a position to be described whether as the first principle or origin of *simulacra* and particulars, or as the end point of a global integration (as in Hegel) (see Agamben, 2000: 60). The *Idea* of a case can be circumscribed but not simply described. A case or phenomenon in this sense, with and against the functional operation of law (for example in the setting of precedents) needs to remember, at least in theoretical approaches to judging, of the useability of its past, its virtual singularity. Not the singularity of its particular instance but the extreme singularity in its belonging to its virtuality or communicability, its *Idea*.

Everything depends on how this virtuality is understood. For Deleuze, for example, the virtual must above all be clearly distinguished from the merely possible as what is subsequently produced or actualized. The virtual is not the possible or the similitude of a particular instance but entails its proper reality as coexistent and distinct from the reality of the actual and the posited. The virtual in this sense is not vague or ineffable but a manifold of elements that are both singular and differential.[21] The uniquely extreme singularity in this sense does not preclude repetition. But this repetition of the virtual is not to be understood in opposition to the reality of the so-called actual, but instead as what is the only common. The virtual is already real and its composition, its sympathy to the actual can be indicated so to show that things are otherwise than they are, not before or after their actualization but at the very moment of their actualization. But this will have to be explored in detail in another work.

The question of contingency (*contingere*, in latin, meaning what befalls, what happens) has been largely thought, methodologically, as a mere modality, but the reference, here, to contingency is less as an issue of method and more as a pivotal problem of the intuitive and contingent experience of thought (Agamben, 1999: 261). Jurisprudence had for good reason and for a long time been concerned with what can be called formal knowledge and has, in its post-structuralist turn, posed the non-rational as a lack or as its limit. What remains necessary to think of, however, is the way this is to be understood: the ways in which we do not know things are just as important and perhaps even more important as the ways in which we know them (Agamben, 2010: 113). There are ways of not knowing, Agamben writes, that lead 'to clumsiness and ugliness', but there are others 'whose completeness we never tire of admiring' (ibid.). It is possible, in fact, that 'the way in which we are able to be ignorant is precisely what defines the rank of what we are able to know and that the articulation of a zone of non-knowledge is the condition and touchstone of all our knowledge' (ibid.); and the same could be said of the unreason of reason. Not knowing does not simply mean not knowing as in the sense of a lack or a defect. It means also to have a 'weakness of strength' (ibid.). To maintain oneself in the 'right relationship with ignorance', to be in a 'harmonious relationship with that which escapes us' (ibid.), this seems to be the continuous coming of jurisprudence in the virtuality of the present. This, too, may be what in *stare decisis* (to stand by the decisions), stands beside (gr. *para*, paraduction) the decision on a case: the *Idea* of precedent and by extension of law, its knowability and creative use with and against the law.

Endnotes

* This paper was first presented at a seminar at Cardozo Law School, New York in November 2011. Participants at the seminar and in particular Peter Goodrich and Stanley Fish enriched my thoughts on this paper with their comments and suggestions. Penelope Pether, Nathan Moore, Richard Braude, Jose Bellido and Anton Schütz have inspired this work in conversation.
1 I thank Anton Schütz for this formulation.
2 J. Ward in *Re A (children) (conjoined twins)* [2000] 4 All ER 961 at 969.
3 Ibid.; see the discussion in Clucas, B. and O'Donnell, K. 'Conjoined Twins: the cutting edge', 2002, 5 *Web Journal of Current Legal Issues*.
4 See M. Cousins, 'Technologies of Seeing', Architectural Association Lecture Series 2010 [unpublished manuscript, available with the author].

5   For an excellent discussion of these suggestions among much else see Duxbury (2008).
6   As quoted in ibid.: 34.
7   The initial approach to such a conception of jurisprudence is offered in Deleuze, 1991.
8   See generally Hart, 1994/1961.
9   See Moore, N. (2011) 'Stupid Things: what acts in actor network theory?' [unpublished paper, copy available with the author], Birkbeck College, University of London, School of Law Work in Progress Seminars, 2011.
10 See Moore, op. cit. n. 9.
11 Paraphrasing Spinoza, see Spinoza, 1963.
12 See Moore, op. cit. n. 9.
13 See Dworkin, 1986 and Postema, 1997.
14 See generally Deleuze and Parnet, 1987.
15 See Kant, 1965: Part 1.2.1.2.i.
16 See generally Goldschmidt, 2003/1947.
17 See generally Aristotle, 1984.
18 Ibid., 1357b, 4.
19 See Göktürk, E. 'What is a "Paradigm"?' [unpublished paper, copy available with the author].
20 See Agamben, 2009.
21 See Deleuze, 1988.

Bibliography

Case Law:

Re A (children) (conjoined twins) [2000] 4 All ER 961 at 969.

Books & Articles:

Agamben, G. (1999) *Potentialities: Collected Essays in Philosophy*, D. Heller-Roazen (ed. and trans.), Stanford, CA: Stanford University Press.

Agamben, G. (2000) 'Notes on Gesture' in Agamben, G. *Means Without Ends: Notes on Politics*, Minneapolis: University of Minnesota Press.

Agamben, G. (2008) '*K*', in *The Work of Giorgio Agamben: Law, Literature, Life*, J. Clemens, N. Heron and A. Murray (eds), Edinburgh: Edinburgh University Press.

Agamben, G. (2009) *The Signature of All Things: On Method*, L. D'Isanto and K. Attell (trans), New York: Zone.

Agamben, G. (2010) *Nudities*, Stanford, CA: Stanford University Press/Meridian: Crossing Aesthetics.

Aristotle (1984) *Rhetoric*, W. Rhys Roberts (trans.), Cambridge, MA and London: Loeb Classical Library.

Brewer, S. (1996) 'Exemplary Reasoning: Semantics, Pragmatics, and the Rational Force of Legal Argument by Analogy', 109 *Harvard Law Review*, 923–1028.

Clucas, B. and O'Donnell, K. (2002) 'Conjoined Twins: the cutting edge', 5 *Web Journal of Current Legal Issues*.

Deleuze, G. (1988) *Bergsonism*, H. Tomlinson and B. Habberjam (trans.), New York: Zone Books.

Deleuze, G. (1991) *Empiricism and Subjectivity*, C. Boundas (trans.), New York: Columbia University Press.

Deleuze, G. (2002/1973) 'On the Superiority of Anglo-American Literature', in G. Deleuze and C. Parnet, *Dialogues*, H. Tomlinson and B. Habberjam (trans.), London: Continuum.

Deleuze, G. and Guattari, F. (2004) *A Thousand Plateaus: Capitalism and Schizophrenia*, Massumi, B. (trans), Minneapolis: Minnesota University Press.

Deleuze, G. and Parnet, C. (1987) *Dialogues*, tr. H. Tomlinson & G. Burchell. New York: Columbia University Press.

Duxbury, N. (2008) *The Nature and Authority of Precedent*, Cambridge: Cambridge University Press.

Dworkin, R. (1977) *Taking Rights Seriously*, Boston: Harvard University Press.

Dworkin, R. (1986) *Law's Empire*, Cambridge, MA: The Belknap Press of Harvard University Press.

Fish, S. (1987) 'Dennis Martinez and the Uses of Theory', *The Yale Law Journal*, 96(8), 1773–800.

Foucault, M. (1985) *Discourse and truth: The problematization of parrhesia*, Pearson J. (ed.), Evanston, IL: Northwestern University.

Goldschmidt, V. (2003/1947) *Le Paradigme dans la dialectique platonicienne*, Paris: Librairie Philosophique J. Vrin.

Hale, Sir M. (1987) *The History And Analysis Of The Common Law Of England*, Legal Classics Library, 68.

Hart, H.L.A, (1994/1961) *The Concept of Law*, 2nd edn, Oxford: Clarendon.

Heller-Roazen, D. (2006) 'Philosophy before the Law: Averroës' Decisive Treatise', *Critical Inquiry*, 32, 412–42.

Honoré, A.M. (1977) 'Real Laws' in P.M.S. Hacker and J. Raz (eds), *Law, Morality and Society. Essays in Honour of H. L. A. Hart*, Oxford: Clarendon Press, 99–118.

Hume, D. (1978) *A Treatise of Human Nature*, L.A. Selby-Bigge (ed.), 2nd edn. P.H. Nidditch (ed.), Oxford: Oxford University Press.

Hume, D. (1998) *An Enquiry Concerning the Principles of Morals*, T. Beauchamp (ed.), Oxford: Oxford University Press.

Kant, I. (1965) *Critique of Pure Reason*, N. Kemp Smith (trans.), New York: St. Martin's Press.

MacCormick, N. (1987) 'Why Cases Have *Rationes* and What These Are' in L. Goldstein (ed.), *Precedent in Law*, Oxford: Oxford University Press, 155–82.

Meillassoux, Q. (2008) *After Finitude*: An Essay on the Necessity of Contingency, R. Brassier (trans.), New York: Continuum.

Nancy, J.L. (2003/1983) 'Lapsus Judicii' in *A Finite Thinking*, Stanford, CA: Stanford University Press.

Pollock, F. and Maitland, W.F. (1968) *The History of English Law Before the Time of Edward I*, 2nd edn, 2 vols, vol. I, Cambridge: Cambridge University Press, 183–4.

Postema, G.J. (1987) 'Some Roots of our Notion of Precedent', in L. Goldstein (ed.), *Precedent in Law*, 9, Oxford: Clarendon, 15–23.

Postema, G.J. (1997) 'Integrity: Justice in Workclothes', 82 *Iowa Law Review*.

Schütz, A. (2009) 'Imperatives Without Imperator', *Law and Critique*, 20(3), November, 233–43.

Spinoza, B. (1963) *Ethics*, A. Boyle (trans.), London: Everyman.

Stone, J. (1985) *Precedent and Law: Dynamics of Common Law Growth*, London: Butterworths, 61–80.

Stone, R. (1965) 'Ratiocination not Rationalisation', 74 *Mind*, 463–82.

Teubner, G. (2009) 'Self-subversive justice: Contingency or transcendence formula of law?', *Modern Law Review*, 72, 1–23.

Chapter 8

On the edge of reason
Law at the borderline

Janny Leung

Boundaries of the legal case

Legal cases are traditionally seen as examples of a disciplined process of legal reasoning. Precedential cases lay down clear, authoritative rules that guide civic affairs and social life and preclude further deliberations on the same actions. They reflect the accumulation of judicial wisdom and authority and provide us with certainty, which according to Hale (1956: 505) is the most important property we demand of laws.

The legal discipline is not blind to, but has often chosen to ignore the fact that such ideology is sometimes too good to be true. More than a century ago, legal realists had challenged the idea that the law is an autonomous system from a sociological perspective. As these theorists would agree, the boundaries of a case might be more fluid than traditionally envisioned.

If legal reasoning may be seen as a process of categorization, to decide on a case of murder is to categorize a situation as a member or a non-member of the category of murder. Disputes often concern whether a thing or an event fits into a particular category. In fact, it has been claimed (e.g., Solan 1993) that most of the problems that arise in the legal context have to do with categorical indeterminacy. An overwhelming majority of conceptual categories are known to have fuzzy boundaries, and legal concepts are no exception.

In many legal cases, the pivot on which arguments revolve has to do with the fuzzy boundary of certain words. Examples of borderline cases include whether a chicken coop may be considered a *vehicle* in the Road Traffic Act of 1930 (*Garner v Burr* 1951), whether *race* could be used to refer to a religious, social or cultural community in the Race Relations Act 1976 (*Mandla v Dowell Lee* 1983), or whether a couple died in a shipping accident satisfies the meaning of *coinciding* deaths in a will (*Re Rowland* 1963). The application of indeterminate laws leads to indeterminate outcomes, giving rise to so-called hard cases. H.L.A. Hart (1983) has acknowledged the open texture of the law and the penumbra of uncertainty that surrounds any legal rules.

Legal indeterminacy has attracted a lot of attention from legal theorists, as it casts doubt on the extent to which the law controls judicial decisions, and thus threatening the legitimacy of the law. The indeterminacy thesis suggests that the judge often must choose between two or more legally acceptable solutions to a case; in other words, legal questions lack single right answers (Kress 2003). This line of argument counters Austin's belief (1995) that the law was a closed logical system posited by an authority, in which judges deduced their decisions from premises; Dworkin's Right Answer thesis, which suggests that there is virtually always a right answer to a legal question; or Scalia's confidence in the judge's ability to determine what a statute clearly means and its boundary of application.

The nature of indeterminacy involved in a case implicitly affects statutory interpretation and judicial decision-making. Where the language is clear, courts are obliged to interpret statutes with the plain meaning of the words; where the language is ambiguous, courts may look for legislative intent, history and other contextual factors. Solan (2005) has also pointed out that judges are less likely to give the defendant the benefit of the doubt when a statute is ambiguous; however, in the case of a vague statute the rule of lenity may be applied.

A fuller appreciation of the nature of indeterminacy might illuminate the intricate relationship between the legal system and the way human beings conceptualize the world, and reveal the unstable boundaries of the legal case. Among the many sources of legal indeterminacy, we shall focus on vagueness, a universal property of all natural languages (Devos 2003). Consider the following list of words: *old, smart, awake, rich, sweet, book*. These words are vague, in the same way as there being no particular moment when night falls. Indeed, we might struggle to come up with words that are not vague. If vagueness is a core property of language, then the law, most of which is laid down in language, must also be vague. Legal terms such as *reasonable care, due process*, and *satisfactory condition* do not delineate clear boundaries.

Although the complexities of modern life often make it difficult to pass binary judgments of right or wrong, judges are required by their job to pronounce clear-cut judgments. If the concept at the heart of the dispute is vague, they need to suppress vagueness in their judgment and render an absolute verdict. They are often reluctant to acknowledge the very existence of vagueness. Through a humanist analysis of vagueness and a reconceptualization of case law and precedent in cognitive terms, this chapter hopes to inform theorists interested in legal indeterminacy, bring to judicial notice a refreshed understanding of an issue that has plagued the law under different disguises, and unveil tensions and dilemmas that are central to the foundations of the common law.

Understanding vague predicates

The Frege–Russell view takes vagueness as a result of our ancestors not being interested enough in logic and precision. Embedded in this view, and in normative doctrines such as void for vagueness, is the idea that vagueness could and ought to be eliminated. The vision that language may be purified of vagueness seems to be shared by some lawyers. An example is the 'wild goose chase' (Samek 1973) that lawyers have for years engaged in, in their search for the true essence of obscenity in order to properly define it. In order to explain why these lawyers are chasing tails we first need to ask: what is vagueness and where do borderline cases come from?

One defining property of vague predicates is that they provide no sharp boundaries to distinguish categorical members from non-members, giving rise to borderline cases whose categorical membership is unclear. *Red* is vague because one can find reddish shades that borderline with orange, purple or brown. *Red* is an example of the most common type of vagueness, called gradual vagueness, which is due to the uncertainty of the degree to which a predicate applies. A more complicated form of vagueness is categorical vagueness, which is due to the uncertainty of criteria for the application of a predicate. It usually also embraces gradual vagueness. *Bilingual* is an example of categorical vagueness, as it is unclear in order to qualify as bilingual whether one has to be exposed to two languages from birth, or what level of proficiency one needs to have in two languages. It is disputable which of these conditions is necessary or sufficient.

Vagueness needs to be distinguished from other types of linguistic and non-linguistic indeterminacies, such as relativity, ambiguity and contestability.

A word is relative when its meaning depends on the immediate context. For instance, it would be difficult to say whether something is heavy unless we know what that something is. A heavy man is still lighter than a non-heavy elephant. Relativity dissolves if one specifies what the modified object is. Although many vague words are also relative (e.g., *tall*), relativity and vagueness do not necessarily overlap; for example, the precise expression *above average in height* is relative to the population concerned but does not entail vagueness.

Homonymy, polysemy and generality are potential sources of ambiguity. A word is ambiguous if it has two or more meanings. For instance, the homonymous term *bank* may denote edge of a river or financial institution, the polysemous term *key* may stand for something to open a lock or a means to get access to something else, and the general term *mother* includes specific references to mothers and mothers-in-law, and a wide range of metaphorical meanings. Interpretation may resolve ambiguity, but not vagueness.

In philosophy a further type of indeterminacy is identified as contestability (Waldron 1994). A predicate is contestable if there are alternative explications of its meaning, and if that meaning contains some evaluative or normative force (e.g., social norms and moral standards). For example, *democracy* is contestable because it may be understood in terms of representation or direct participation in the government. Contestability is extra-linguistic and appears to overlap with categorical vagueness.

These distinctions are important, but are often ignored or confused by judges and legal scholars. Both relativity and ambiguity may be potentially resolved by linguistic context, but vagueness cannot be resolved by choosing one interpretation over another. Vagueness is unavoidable, indecomposable and irresolvable.

This might explain why linguists tend to engage themselves more often in analyzing other forms of indeterminacy,[1] and more attempts to analyze vagueness seem to be made by philosophers.

There is ample philosophical discussion about where vagueness comes from, especially during philosophers' attempt in resolving the Sorites Paradox, a paradox driven by the phenomenon of vagueness. Theories differ in their stance – some argue that vagueness is nothing more than ignorance (epistemicist), some hold that vagueness is a reflection of reality, some say that vagueness is a feature of the observational character of predicates, still others postulate that vagueness is a property of comparison. It would be beyond the scope of this chapter to evaluate each theory; here I shall simply build on Goldstein's (2009) observation of intersubjective and intrasubjective differences in judgments about vague predicates, and argue that vagueness is first a property of how we learn before it is a property of language. In other words, it is neither purely a property of the world nor just semantics, but a phenomenon that arises when human organizes knowledge. This perspective has the merit of being compatible with contemporary psychological theories of learning and the empiricist theory of concepts.

Vagueness is not so much about our language systems but about how we naturally learn. We learn about a natural category by being exposed to many, many examples of what items are classified into this category. We learn about what *chair* means after seeing many examples of chairs which all look slightly different. We form a prototype of a category by extracting regularities from all the exemplars we have seen. Sometimes a common characteristic could be found, but exemplars would display it to a varying degree (gradual vagueness); at other times no single commonality can be found and the categories seem to be governed by multiple criteria of unknown weight (categorical vagueness). We judge whether a new object belongs to an existing category by comparing it with examples we have seen. Most words we know have never been defined for us, and we rarely have explicit criteria for categorization. Knowledge about the world that we abstract from experience remains mostly implicit; this implicitness is obvious if one considers how difficult it could be if one is asked to provide a precise definition for simple concepts (such as *chair* and *red*). The more variable the sample items are, the more tolerant the category is (and thus less clear the boundary). Concepts formed using a limited number of instances may be applied in an unlimited number of situations; vagueness is unavoidable as it arises in the process of applying concepts to the real world.

This refreshed understanding of vagueness, contextualized in the formation and organization of concepts, points to the following implications.

Vagueness is an essential and unavoidable feature of the law

Vagueness cannot be eliminated or improved. One cannot remove vagueness by becoming more *specific*; the opposite of *specificity* is *generality*, not *vagueness*

(Waldron 1994). Reducing generality does not ensure that vagueness is also reduced. A general term (e.g., *living thing*) might be less vague than a specific term (e.g., *tree*).

If we take the trouble, we can measure the exact height of a person, or the exact wavelength of a color patch. We can even find out exactly how many grains a heap of sand contains. These tools do not imply that the concepts of *red, tall* or *heap* are not vague. Neither could an arbitrary stipulation of say, how many grains make a heap, help us in any way. When we come across these concepts we simply do not operate by precise measurements, but by the concepts as we have learned from experience. Vague predicates are useful in efficient daily communication. Moreover, precise measurements or arbitrary stipulations only seem to have a potential function in gradually vague predicates; with categorically vague predicates, one does not even know where measurement should start.

Even precise formulations may not yield precise law, given that adjudication principles are vague as they depend on evaluative and normative considerations. Take Endicott's (2000) example: in Ottawa, one is not allowed to possess any bullfrog with tibia that are 5cm or longer. While this formulation may appear precise, one can imagine cases where liability for catching bullfrogs is indeterminate. For instance, a bullfrog may have one tibia longer than 5cm and one shorter, or another bullfrog may have a curved tibia that is 4cm long when measured across but is 6cm long when measured with a tape. Borderline cases seem to arise even if linguistic formulations appear to be precise.

Individual and community variations in judgment exist

As people and communities have different experiences with different categories, conceptual formation is subject to individual and group differences, usually within normative constraints. What is a stereotypical member of one category for an individual or a group of individuals might be a borderline case of the same category for others. A typical chair or fruit in Africa would look different than their counterpart in America. The prototype of *machine* is likely to be different to a housewife than to an engineer. This gives rise to variability in judgment across competent observers, even to simple concepts such as *chair* and *red*. A further example is the evaluation of an artwork's potential obscenity: what seems to be obscene to an individual might be seen as artistic expression by another.

Ostensively learnt categories are organized by resemblance rather than necessary and sufficient conditions

Some scientific and mathematical categories are created using necessary and sufficient conditions (e.g., *the odd number*). However, the fact that most natural categories are learnt ostensively means that efforts to define them using necessary and sufficient conditions are likely to be futile. To impose a definition using necessary and sufficient conditions upon an ostensive category necessarily changes the very nature of the category. The law may stipulate that *speeding* means driving at a speed higher than 65mph, but the subjective perception of *fast* or *slow* is a matter of degree and cannot be put in terms of necessary and sufficient conditions.

It is possible that no common feature is shared by all members of a category. Wittgenstein (1974) has provided one famous example of such a category: *game*. It has been argued that there are no features common to all games; instead, different members are connected by a complicated network of similarities overlapping and crisscrossing in the category of *game*.

Vagueness does not originate from or lead to a failure to understand language

One would come across legal scholars who comment, for example, that *obscenity* is 'too vague' a term to be reasonably understood. It is not true that all vague predicates are difficult to understand. Vagueness does not arise from, or necessarily align with, our difficulty or failure to understand language. Although color terms are notoriously vague, we are not ignorant of what *red* means. We communicate using vague words on a day-to-day basis without problems.

It is reasonable to be inconsistent in judging vague predicates

Revision of judgment is normally allowed for vague predicates. When viewing a succession of red color patches, with a tiny smudge of yellow added to each successive patch, one might be committed into saying that an orange patch was red, if each color patch is visually indistinguishable from the previous one. However, if the orange patch is viewed in isolation, the observer is likely to revise their judgment. Sudden changes in judgment are often not accompanied by changes in the object itself, similar to the way one switches perspectives when viewing M.C. Esher's paintings. Similarly, research has shown that what is considered obscene or indecent changes with one's exposure to adult materials.

People are not liable to be consistent in their judgment, especially with categories of an observational character. Since every judgment an observer makes feeds back into their knowledge base of the relevant category, and there are many contextual factors (e.g., what one came across recently) that can affect the retrieval of a suitable prototype from memory, it is not unreasonable that an observer passes different judgments on the same article at different times.

Many vague legal concepts are subject to the Sorites paradox

Vague predicates are vulnerable to the paradox of the slippery slope. Imagine that you have a heap of sand. Take away one grain of sand and you still have a heap. The removal of one single grain cannot turn a heap into a non-heap. If a particular amount of sand does not constitute a heap, then neither does that amount plus one grain. Although the supposition seems obvious and logical, repeated application of the conditional premise leads to the absurd conclusion that one grain of sand is a heap, and so is no grain of sand. In view of the absurdities of the conclusion, some (e.g., Unger 1979) argue that vague concepts are simply flawed as they cannot be used to divide up the world meaningfully. *Sorites*, derived from the Greek word *Soros* for *heap*, is used to refer to paradoxes of this kind.

The law sometimes draws arbitrary boundaries in order to stop slippery slopes. Driving at 64 miles or 66 miles per hour might not make any practical difference to road safety. An alert driver driving at 66 miles per hour might be much safer than a sleepy driver driving at 35 miles an hour. It seems arbitrary that one driver is punished but not the other, but most jurisdictions attempt to draw a defining line as to what counts as speeding.

However, since law is used to regulate human behavior, and standards of causation and responsibility are all vague, it is inevitable that many legal concepts are vague. The range of behaviors that can constitute dangerous driving may be too variable to be specified in general terms, and no arbitrary boundaries could be usefully drawn for the meanings potentially covered by *dangerous*. The law ought to be vague (e.g. punishing dangerous driving) so as to cover unpredictable circumstances.

Hard cases: to reason or not to reason

Since vagueness is the main source of hard cases, the above discussion is particularly relevant to hard cases in law. These are cases where established legal rules and judicial reasoning fail to provide a conclusive answer, exemplifying legal indeterminacy. There being more than one reasonable solution to a hard legal problem, there is a lack of consensus as to what the just legal outcome is. The strong indeterminacy thesis argues that all cases are hard cases. In his 1993 book, Solan demonstrates how judges attempt to mask the fact that a case is hard and urges judges to acknowledge the indeterminacy of the text.

The refreshed understanding of vagueness discourages us from becoming fixated on the text and reveals the underlying tension between vagueness and legal reasoning. Before I elaborate on the idea, let me briefly recapture the above discussion on vagueness in the context of hard cases.

Vagueness, which arises from the process of human categorization and contributes to legal indeterminacy, is unavoidable. Law, being a system that governs social interactions, cannot rid itself of natural conceptual categories, whilst the fuzzy boundaries of natural conceptual categories will always give rise to hard cases. Advocates of the moderate indeterminacy thesis (such as Kress 1989) argue that not every case is a hard case, partly based on the observation that there are many easy cases. Within the realm of cases involving vague predicates, the observation is probably valid if one imagines that borderline cases only appear at the borderline, and most cases are likely to concentrate at the core. However, the slipperiness of vague predicates lies in the fact that there is no clear boundary between a core case and a borderline case, making it difficult to even sustain the distinction between easy and hard cases. Such difficulty has been acknowledged in jurisprudence.

Variations in individual and community judgment make hard cases hard as they cannot be reconciled by reason. Although arguments by analogy and inference can form a legitimate part of legal reasoning (Kress 1989), categorization by analogy can never be perfect, especially without explicit criteria as to the focus of comparison. One may even say that because judgments are subjectively made, they are not capable of being right or wrong. Although Hume (1751) argues that analogical judgments are not necessarily arbitrary, he has pointed out that there is no fact of the matter outside the practice of legal reasoning and commonly recognized legal doctrine that an instance case is more similar to precedent case A than to precedent case B. Dissenting opinions are only commonplace in hard cases.

The multidimensionality of categorical vagueness multiplies potential inconsistencies in judgment. The Sorites paradox typically involves gradually vague predicates, most often categories whose members could be organized along a continuum; it is often not possible to stop slippery slopes in hard cases because a lot of legal concepts are not only gradually vague (e.g., what *fast* means) but also categorically vague (e.g., what *reasonable* means). In addition to vagueness, contestability further amplifies variations in normative judgments, which are often involved in legal cases.

Furthermore, since natural categories are ostensively learnt, and vagueness is not primarily a language problem, efforts to define categories in terms of necessary and sufficient conditions or to improve vagueness by rewriting the language are mostly hopeless.

As we have seen previously, human categorization often proceeds by heuristics, implicit knowledge, analogy, and comparison with exemplars. These judgments are akin to felt responses and often bypass reason. On the other hand, law is often associated with the human faculty of reason. Hard cases often involve categories that are hard to be organized by necessary and sufficient conditions, and whose members and non-members are difficult to differentiate by logical reasoning. Thus hard cases reveal the tension between the ideal of law as a rational system and human categorization's resistance to rationality. Not only are judges required to reason rationally, they also need to justify their decisions. With the prevalence of vague natural categories, it would not be surprising if sometimes they have to rationalize a decision post-hoc.

Precedent as a countermeasure to indeterminacy

Interpretive rules do not seem useful in eliminating vagueness. For instance, the plain meaning rule is more about meaning being ordinary rather than determinate, and it says nothing about vagueness in language. Meanings may be ordinary but vague and ambiguous. What the rule emphasizes is the weighting that should be given to the text of the law rather than to legislative intent or history.

With some simple vague predicates, Waldron (1994) argues that it is possible to reduce, though not totally eliminate, vagueness by comparativization. Rather than simply describing objects as either *big* or *small*, one could ask whether an item is *bigger than a shoebox*. The provision of reference points for comparison is exactly how a ruler works. However, it could not eliminate vagueness altogether.

In law, under the doctrine of precedent, legal cases provide reference points for judicial decision-making. Precedent can be seen as a means to counter indeterminacy. Having to follow decisions made in earlier cases, constraints are posed on later judgments.

In fact, one could view related cases as forming legal categories, and every verdict as an act of categorization. Every inclusion or exclusion of a case to a category could be seen as an extension or anti-extension of the relevant predicate (or as license *v.* restriction; see Tappenden 1993). Assuming that consistency of judgment is maintained, it appears that vagueness could be progressively reduced, although it would be difficult to develop guiding principles to justify extensions or the lack thereof.

To complicate matters further, few legal concepts can be organized along a linear scale. Not only do cases involving categorical vagueness make hard cases harder, they also weaken the power of precedent. With a linear concept ranging from F to non-F, one could reduce vagueness by drawing an arbitrary division along the line. Applying the reasonable man test to two types of behavior, it is often difficult to argue that one behavior is absolutely more reasonable than the other, as different features relevant to a categorically vague predicate cannot be weighed against one another. The tension is between the assumption of bivalence in the law, and the multidimensionality of many natural conceptual categories. Embedded in these concepts are contestable standards, variable value judgments, and disagreement over category criteria.

Other sources of indeterminacy within the structure of the legal system itself further complicate the picture. Although the hierarchy of courts and the distinction between *ratio decidendi* and *obiter dictum* are supposed to assign importance to cases and judicial opinions, judges still have room for making rather than finding law. Llewellyn (1930) argues that judges could choose between two contradictory doctrines of precedent, one being strict and the other loose, handy for capitalizing on welcome precedents and ignoring unwelcome precedents. By applying a strict interpretation, they can depart from previous rulings based on the differences between facts that lead to the cases. Using a loose interpretation, judges could suppress the significance of present facts by diverting attention to past rulings.

This brings us back to the boundaries of the legal case. As discussed earlier, members of natural categories are linked by overlapping and crisscrossing connections, and therefore they might be classified into the same category for different reasons. Similarity to the present case is subject to variation of judgment, the aspects of the case being looked at and the kinds of comparisons made. Depending onto whose hands a precedent case falls, its shape could be molded to fit specific needs.

Some illustrative cases

Obscenity is a multidimensional and categorically vague legal concept that serves as a case in point. Obscenity laws are notorious in producing problematic cases in many jurisdictions; most often they are criticized as 'too vague,' and therefore failing to put law enforcers and the public on notice of what actions are punishable. Judgment on the obscene content of objects, texts or images often attracts dissenting opinions, and popular opinion also tends to change with time and space. Many literary classics, such as Gustave Flaubert's *Madame Bovary* and James Joyce's *Ulysses*, have at one point been deemed as obscene.

Despite repeated attempts, no satisfactory definition of obscenity has been found.[2] Dictionary definitions are hardly helpful as they tend to define obscenity in terms of other vague synonyms such as *immoral, filthy*, and *offensive*. Seeing no hope in intelligibly defining the concept, US Supreme Court Justice Stewart simply resorted to saying that 'I know it when I see it.' This comment aptly demonstrates how obscenity is a kind of judgment that is based on a felt response to facts rather than reasoned analysis, which is symptomatic of natural categories that are learnt ostensively. Objects, texts and images may be found to be obscene for different reasons and there seems to be no single feature that connects all obscene cases, hence the difficulty in establishing necessary and sufficient conditions.

It follows that judges tend to rule narrowly rather than to deliver broad principles in obscenity cases, likely in an effort to avoid creating potentially conflicting lines of precedents. This also reflects the recognition that in these cases, judgment is so fluid and context-dependent that it cannot be spelt out in principles and rules. Such a practice constitutes a challenge to the doctrine of precedent, as it is not clear how a view that one item is obscene could be of reference value to a later case (Leung and Wan: 2011).

In fact, a common law jurisdiction has decided to do away with precedents altogether in obscenity cases, ascribing no reference value at all to each adjudication. In Hong Kong, definitions are left vague in obscenity ordinances.[3] Obscenity cases are handled by a dedicated tribunal, which makes no reference to its past decisions in its adjudication procedures. Every judgment is freshly made by a small panel of adjudicators drawn from a list of some 300 volunteers. Adjudicators do not need to provide any justification for their judgments.

This practice by and large works outside of the doctrine of precedent. It refuses to follow the evolution of the concept of obscenity longitudinally through the accumulation of cases, but obtains judgments cross-sectionally from supposedly representative members of the community. In other words, in the categorization process of obscenity cases, rather than comparing the current case with past cases, the comparison is now to be made with the personal experience of the adjudicators.

Whilst one may argue that vagueness in definitions allows community standards to be updated with the passage of time, the practice oddly leaves what the terms of a statute mean – a question of law – in the hands of factfinders. It also departs from the traditional legal thinking that a piece of legislation enacted should remain stable enough to bind future cases. One obvious disadvantage is that an average citizen could not be expected to keep up with the latest climate of legal standards.

The policy may be considered a radical response to the challenge in using reasoned analysis in categorizing vague predicates. With such fluid predicates, decisions tend to be particularly context sensitive and the significance of each adjudication is diminished. Certainty in law gives rise to the feeling of justice and fairness, but categorization of natural predicates seems to be at odds with this ideal.

In a way, the difficulty in applying obscenity laws is connected to the law's understandable reliance on the natural conceptual category of obscenity, which opens the door for intersubjectivity and intrasubjectivity in judgment. By contrast, some other areas of the law have tried to break away from the tension between legal reasoning and ostensively learnt natural categories. For instance, instead of asking what an average man would do in a certain situation, the law posits an abstract figure – the reasonable man, whose imaginary conduct and foresight set the standard that citizens should meet. The law does not ask a juror, among all the people you personally know and whom you find reasonable, how would the average man react. The reasonable man is imposed as a novel conceptual category without an existing membership. Here the decision-maker is forced to think in the abstract and be guided only by a legal characterization of this abstract figure. He is also instructed not to pay regard to the personal characteristics (with only a few exceptions such as age) of the defendant that may affect their reasonableness. Some obvious questions would then be, for example, how this abstract thinking could be performed in a standardized manner, and whether it is possible to isolate this abstract figure from subjective evaluations of reasonableness based on personal experience. Earlier research (such as Green 1968) has shown how the reasonable man is at best a vague paragon and a legal fiction, and the existing literature has seen many variable proposals of what criteria this reasonable man should fulfill (note: a good indicator of categorical vagueness); it seems that the creation of new conceptual categories is not a foolproof way of evading vagueness.

Conclusions

Judicial decision-making may be seen as an act of categorization and many legal categories are gradually and categorically vague. Such vagueness is a property of ostensively learnt natural categories and cannot be eliminated. The search for the true essence of these categories has little prospect, just as nobody can have the last word on a debate about what really is a chair. Judgments of vague predicates vary across individuals and communities, time and space. This applies to any potentially contentious words in statutes, contracts or legal documents.

In addition to the difficulty that vague predicates bring to lawmakers who need to come up with necessary and sufficient conditions for defining them, vague predicates' resistance to rationality constitutes a challenge to the doctrine of precedent and the status and stability of the legal case and is in tension with what seems to be the most important feature of a legal system – certainty.

It appears that the more vague and contestable a predicate is, the more fluid the boundaries of the relevant legal case becomes, and the more difficult it is for the doctrine of the precedent to exert a binding force on future cases. These could allow the voice of the decision maker to amplify.

Obscenity cases are examples of where the legal case bears minimal stability and where the doctrine of precedent begins to collapse. We have seen an example of a jurisdiction that has given up on coming up with reasons in obscenity judgments and no longer makes reference to past cases. Attempts to create novel conceptual categories, such as the reasonable man, could not successfully evade vagueness either.

The above discussion reiterates the power allocation function of vagueness, which is why vagueness should not be taken lightly. The application of a standard rather than a rule has more room for discretion, and more potential for abuse. On a more theoretical level, the omnipresence of vagueness seems to fuel legal realism.

Based on corpus data (such as NEXIS) and empirical investigation into native speakers' judgments, Cunningham *et al.* (1994) argue that linguistics can potentially contribute to solving the problem of fuzzy boundaries. They studied the scope of usage of the term *enterprise*, which is the source of dispute in the case *United States v Turkette* (1981). The question was whether the term could be applied to organizations that are exclusively criminal. They conclude that the definition that the court relied on did not correspond well with the way most speakers use and understand the term *enterprise*, and that even native speakers disagree as to the criteria of the category (which is to say that this predicate is categorically vague). Although the use of corpus data can avoid strategic choices over dictionary editions, it could only flag categorical vagueness but not to resolve or eliminate it.

The tension between the assumption of bivalence and categorical vagueness is not a legal problem alone. It seems that vagueness is a problem that even God has to deal with (Sider 2002). If what happens after death is a binary choice, it would be tough assigning people to hell or heaven given that people are likely to score unevenly and inconsistently on divine's criteria. For one thing, faith, like other mental states, admits of borderline cases. Fortunately for lawmakers, while God is not expected to make arbitrary decisions, the law can sometimes legitimately draw arbitrary boundaries. The bad news is that even arbitrary stipulations are not effective in eliminating non-linear, categorical vagueness.

I do not wish to pretend that there is a straightforward solution to the legal problems raised in this chapter. Although a humanist analysis of vagueness does not automatically lead to a moral or legal conclusion, it informs theorists interested in legal indeterminacy and brings to judicial notice a refreshed understanding of an issue that has plagued the law under different disguises. It also unveils tensions and dilemmas that are central to the foundations of the common law.

Endnotes

1 Devos called semantic vagueness 'an almost virgin territory' of semantic analysis (2003: 121).
2 Henry Miller, in *Obscenity and the Law of Reflection*, 51 *Ky. L.J.* 577 (1963), acknowledges that 'those who have seriously attempted to track down the meaning of the term are obliged to confess that they have arrived nowhere.' Peter Bronson also argues that it is basically impossible to define 'an amorphous, personalized concept in legal terms,' and that obscenity is conceptually incomprehensible. *New Prosecutorial Techniques and Continued Judicial Vagueness: an Argument for Abandoning Obscenity as a Legal Concept*, 21 *UCLA L. Rev.* 198, 201 (1973–1974). Justice Douglas, in *Paris Adult Theatre*, said that obscenity is a matter of taste, and matters of taste are 'too personal to define and too emotional and vague to apply.' *Paris Adult Theatre I v Slaton* (1973) 413 U.S. 49, 93 S.Ct. 2628, 37 L.Ed.2d 446 (dissenting opinion).
3 The Control of Obscene and Indecent Articles Ordinance provides no explanation of what obscenity and indecency mean, other than the following attempts in section 2. Section 2(2) contains unhelpful circular references which state that, a thing is obscene if by reason of obscenity it is not suitable to be published to any person; and a thing is indecent if by reason of indecency it is not suitable to be published to a juvenile. In section 2(3), it is further stated that 'obscenity' and 'indecency' include 'violence, depravity and repulsiveness'; this subsection is not informative either, since obviously not all kinds of violence, depravity and repulsiveness amount to obscenity and indecency.

Bibliography

Austin, John (1995) *The Province of Jurisprudence Determined*, in W. Rumble (ed.). Cambridge: Cambridge University Press. (First published in 1832.)

Cunningham, Clark D., Levi, Judith N., Green, Georgia M., and Kaplan, Jeffrey P. (1994) 'Plain Meaning and Hard Cases'. *The Yale Law Journal*, 103: 1561–625.

Devos, Filip (2003) 'Semantic Vagueness and Lexical Polyvalence.' *Studia Linguistica* 57: 121–41.

Endicott, Timothy A. O. (2000) *Vagueness in Law*. Oxford: Oxford University Press.

Goldstein, Laurence (2009) 'Stephen Clark, the Laws of Logic and the Sorites.' *Philosophy*, 84: 135–43.

Green, Edward (1968) 'The Reasonable Man: Legal Fiction or Psychological Reality?' *Law and Society Review*, 2: 241–57.

Hale, Sir Matthew (1956) 'Reflections by the Lrd. Chiefe Justice Hale on Mr. Hobbes His Dialogue of the Lawe,' in Sir William Holdsworth, *A History of English Law* (7th edn) London.

Hart, H.L.A (1983). *Essays on Jurisprudence and Philosophy*. Oxford: Clarendon Press.

Hume, David (1751) *An Enquiry Concerning the Principles of Morals*. ed. Tom L. Beauchamp. Oxford: Oxford University Press, 1998.

Kress, Kenneth J. (1989) 'Legal Indeterminacy.' *California Law Review*, 77: 283–337.

Kress, Kenneth J. (2003). 'Legal indeterminacy.' In *Philosophy of Law and Legal Theory*, ed. Dennis Patterson. Oxford: Blackwell.

Leung, Janny and Wan, Marco (2011) 'Constructing the Meaning of Obscenity: An Empirical Investigation and an Experientialist Account', *International Journal for the Semiotics of Law* (published online 26 November 2011), pp. 1–16. doi: 10.1007/s11196-011-9251-8.

Llewellyn, Karl N. (1930) *The Bramble Bush: Some Lectures on Law and Its Study*, New York: Columbia University School of Law.
Samek, R. A. (1973) 'Pornography as a Species of Second-Order Sexual Behavior. A Submission for Law Reform.' *Dalhousie Law Journal*, 265–93.
Sider, Theodore (2002) 'Hell and Vagueness.' *Faith and Philosophy*, 19: 58–68.
Solan, Lawrence M. (1993) *The Language of Judges*. Chicago: University of Chicago Press.
Solan, Lawrence M. (2005) 'Vagueness and Ambiguity in Legal Interpretation.' In Bhatia, Vijay K., Engberg, Jan, Gotti, Maurizio and Heller, Dorothee (Eds) *Vagueness in Normative Texts*. Bern: Peter Lang.
Tappenden, Jamie (1993) 'The Liar and the Sorites Paradoxes: Toward a Unified Treatment.' *The Journal of Philosophy*, 90(11): 551–77.
Unger, Peter (1979) 'There are no ordinary things,' *Synthese*, 4: 117–54.
Waldron, Jeremy (1994) 'Vagueness in Law and Language: Some Philosophical Issues.' *California Law Review*, 82(3): 509–40.
Wittgenstein, Ludwig (1974) *Philosophical Investigations*, (G.E.M. Anscombe trans.). Oxford: Blackwell.

Cases Cited

Garner v Burr [1951] 1 KB 31
Mandla v Dowell Lee [1983] 2 AC 548 (HL)
Re Rowland [1963] 1 Ch. 1 (CA)
United States v Turkette, 452 U.S. 576 (1981).

Chapter 9

Stare decisis in China? The newly enacted Guiding Case System

Ping Yu and Seth Gurgel

China is a civil law country. This is a true statement, but apart from its truth, it says very little. Like many other aspects of its economy and society, China's legal system represents a rich tapestry (or tangled web, depending on your point of view) of institutions and concepts, claiming complex origins both in China's own cultural past and its more ecumenical present, defying curt generalization and standard nomenclature. A quick survey of the "standard" civil law components shows the hybridized nature of China's legal system. Civil law criminal justice systems tend to be inquisitorial, but China incorporates many aspects of an adversarial system, all the while retaining a much closer relationship between judge and procuratorate (a term of Soviet origin) than one would normally see in a common law jurisdiction. The jury—and its common-sensical wisdom—is far more prevalent in common law jurisdictions, but China has its own people's jurors, whose common sense is supposed to inform the otherwise cold logic of the civil law judge. And yet, surely—the skeptical reductionist might claim—at least in terms of the fundamental distinguishing element between the two systems, its source of law, China is clearly a civil law country: its laws and regulations are determined by its legislative and administrative branches, and do not originate with judges and judicial decisions over time.

Even on this fundamental issue, China's system defies easy explanation. An in-depth look at both dynastic Chinese jurisprudence as well as modern judicial custom and practice will evidence a far less rigid line between formal (legislative) and informal (judicial) sources of law, especially at the decision-making stage. In many instances, the informal swallows the formal, and the secondary source the primary. Despite this, throughout the history of the People's Republic of China, its legal system has kept up the external auspices of a traditional civil law system. This rather simplistic definition has become much more difficult to maintain with the recent introduction of the Guiding Case System by the Supreme People's Court and the Supreme People's Procuratorate, a move that may finally force the Supreme People's Court to concede that it does indeed engage in judicial rule-making (SPC Rules on the Work of the Guiding Cases 2010). In fact, the formal establishment of the system may be a not-so-implicit recognition of that fact, and certainly bears consequences for Chinese judicial training, legal practice and praxis.

A historical perspective on the Guiding Case System

The Supreme People's Court's Guiding Case System, while ostensibly quite new, has deep historical roots in Chinese jurisprudence, as any brief examination of Chinese legal history reveals. As early as the Han Dynasty, the central governing authorities began to use previously decided cases to supplement the written law. In the absence of *apropos* formal law, government officials charged with deciding a case were required to enter a judgment by referencing a recorded, representative case (*bi*) (Cheng 1927: 113).[1] During the Northern Song Dynasty, case law compilation became an important means to supplement formal legislation, especially after the Northern Song defeat at the hands of the Jin Dynasty and the concomitant retreat of the imperial court to the Southern Song capital of Hangzhou. Thereafter, the remaining local officials had to rely heavily on earlier Northern Song case compilations. But it is the Qing government that represents the apogee of the imperial case compilation system. Qing officials compiled thousands of cases to enable magistrates to enforce the kingdom's many and varied laws. This recording and referencing of past cases played a key role in dynastic Chinese jurisprudence, operating as a less-acknowledged source of law.

The representative cases would normally be generated in the following way: the emperor would issue a decree that extant legal codes were too general. Bureaucrats would then be instructed to scour the realm's annals, gathering case results from recent years as well as cases reaching back generations, using these search results to illustrate how similar-situated cases should be decided going forward. These compilations did not merely include points of law, but also detailed the stories behind the cases.

In the early dynasties, the legal rules expounded in these texts were intertwined with moral norms, mostly derived from the Confucian classics. For instance, Dong Zhongshu compiled a collection of cases law titled "Guiding Cases Modeling the Spring and Autumn Annals (*chunqiu jueshi bi*)" that became an authoritative legal textbook, if not law itself, for the Han governments of many generations. The stories from the Confucian canon served as inspired examples to government magistrates and were woven throughout these ancient "guiding cases."

Oftentimes the stories themselves would be quite simple, but outline a greater moral principle. An illustrative example is the case of Xu Zhi (Cheng 1927: 164). Xu Zhi's father was ill, and he tried to nurse his father back to health. Unfortunately, the medicine he administered poisoned, rather than healed, his father. According to the law and filial piety, the dominant Confucian ideal, actions of a son resulting in the death of his father would normally be capital offenses. Nevertheless, the Spring and Autumn Annals believed that competing moral norms governed Xu Zhi's actions. As his original purpose was to cure his father's illness, he was eventually exonerated. This sophisticated reasoning from over two millennia ago intimates modern criminal legal code notions of criminal intent. The Xu Zhi case was widely cited during the ensuing two thousand years.

Throughout the dynastic period, the Chinese bureaucracy would often undergo the systematic compilation of these types of legal cases and anecdotes, adding official interpretations and commentary to them, with perhaps the best examples coming from the Song and Qing Dynasties. According to some scholars, more than two thousand cases were compiled for the purpose of guiding officials in every manner of case. This process was cumulative, and continued throughout the dynasties, each successive dynasty would mine the annals of the old for case examples that fit their needs, with Qing Dynasty officials the most reliant on case-illustrated rules to supplement their legal code and regulations.

Legal reform in the late Qing and Republic of China eras

After the battering to state and psyche wrought by the Opium Wars and the Qing defeat in the Sino-Japanese war, the Qing Dynasty began a comprehensive modernization campaign—a sweeping program that also included significant legal reform. China dispatched high-ranking officials across the globe to study the Japanese, American, and Continental European legal systems, among others, eventually settling upon the Japanese model, itself a derivation of the German civil law system. The reasons for this decision were many, and some no doubt involved China and Japan's familiarity and proximity, in both actual and cultural terms. One key reason was that Japan represented a communitarian society—a former protégé of China, no less—that had successfully assimilated modern Western legal infrastructure. The Qing admired Japan's success in this arena, especially that Japan had rid itself of the extraterritoriality imposed by western powers through its modernization.

Under the newly adopted system, China's legal scholars generally claimed that China had no case law; that its laws comprised only its recently imported legal code and other written laws. But even during this era, case law was still extant in China: it had staked a claim in the British and American Concessions that dotted the Chinese coast and extended somewhat into the hinterlands. Concessions in Shanghai and Wuhan, *et al*, held court employing a mixture of both the civil and common law systems, and accumulated large amounts of case law for the purpose of trying future cases within the Concessions. These common law practices also influenced life without the Concessions as well, particularly in the field of legal education. A number of China's top law schools had Anglo-American roots and were staffed by common-law-trained instructors, thereby educating a cadre of Chinese legal scholars in the logic and reasoning of the common law lawyer (Connor 1994).[2]

Continuing this amalgam of civil law with common law characteristics, the Republic of China in Taiwan, again, partially influenced by Japan, developed its own version of a case law system. The Taiwanese Supreme Court has enacted a case law system that, while not strictly common law, serves as supplementary legal source for judges.[3] This system bears great similarity to the Japanese case law permutation and evidences direct influence from the American system as well.

This American influence sprang from the United States' intimate relationship with Taiwan after its detachment from China in 1949, after the People's Republic was established.

Judge-made law in the PRC? Case law in the Chinese mainland

After the Chinese Communist Party ("CCP") took power in 1949, its first announcement was the abolition of the Six Codes (*liufa quanshu*), the legal codes that the Republic of China had adopted from Qing Dynasty and borrowed from Japan. With the Six Codes' abolition, the PRC entered an era of a near-complete legal vacuum. Outside of the 1950 Marriage Law and the various policies governing counter-revolutionary behavior, few other legal documents existed, with the Constitution remaining unpublished until 1954.

It was not until 1979 that the PRC formally established the basic elements of its legal code, promulgating the Criminal Law, the Criminal Procedure Law, and the Joint Venture Law, among others.[4] It's not a little ironic that during the preceding 30 years, there were virtually no laws, save for the oft-revised Constitution, extent in a country that was said be a Civil Law country. And yet the courts continued to hear civil and criminal cases during those years. How did they manage? Belying its "civil law" moniker, the Supreme People's Court ("SPC") enacted numerous judicial interpretations and various rules that provided guidance to lower courts. Additionally, the SPC publicized what it called "exemplary cases," predecessors of guiding cases, which eventually held the force of law for courts of all levels. It was then that model cases (*dianxing anli*) really filled the legal vacuum, providing much-needed guidance to courts of all levels in their day-to-day operations.

The general rules issued by the SPC also came from various draft laws, such as the draft Criminal Code, which, while not promulgated until 1979, had been in draft form already in 1950. This proved to be a great aid to the SPC in issuing its opinions, as it drew numerous lessons from the time-consuming, tortuous drafting process. By the time the Criminal Code was codified, it had undergone over 35 major revisions. During this period, the model cases played a significant role in guiding judicial practice in criminal cases as well as in civil matters. One example is that during May–June, 1955, the SPC issued a collection of various cases on the rape of minors, providing guidance on how to deal with such cases in the future. Those cases served model rules for local courts decades before the Criminal Law was enacted (Shen 2009: 3).

But even after the passage of the Criminal Code and Criminal Procedure Law, China still relied heavily on model cases, just as it had in the three decades prior, since both laws, like many Chinese laws, were composed of only the most general and loosely-defined terms, leaving expansive space for interpretation and elaboration. In order to avoid discrepancies in application, the SPC had to step in to provide guidance for lower courts: SPC case publication and dissemination became critical to that end.

Poor general legal training also necessitated these Guiding Case System precursors. Concern about court staff and judicial competence was a major reason for the SPC's more micro-managed guidance on legal code interpretation. In 1977, just two years prior to the "Seven Important Laws," China had just begun rehabilitating its legal education system, effectively shuttered during the Cultural Revolution. It was not until 1978–79 that legal education resumed in full force. So, as freshmen and sophomores in college filled college classrooms absent upperclassmen, court officers and judges comprising mostly retired military staff sought to unpack the newly passed criminal and civil laws. As one might expect, these newly-christened judges were often overwhelmed, and lacked the requisite skills for sophisticated legal exegesis.

While the lack of competence pervasive among China's judiciary was the primary reason for the continued relevance of the model cases, there were other reasons as well. The SPC wanted to ensure the law's unified application and practice across China's many and varied regions, and often released model cases with an eye to unifying disjointed practice across provinces. Additionally, the new codes were not adept at addressing the emergent matters that occurred with rapid succession during the Reform and Opening period, particularly in the field of economic crimes, which had been less of a concern under the fully planned economy of the early PRC. Economic crimes received short shrift in the codes, creating problems of both under- and over-criminalization in the days of the nascent Chinese market economy.

For instance, in the 1979 Criminal Law, the crime of *speculation (touji daobao)* was so broadly defined as to be nearly bereft of meaning (Criminal Law 1979: Art. 117).[5] If an official government organ deemed a particular practice illegal, any commercial activity that generated profit could be regarded as speculation under the Criminal Law. Another example is the crime of hooliganism (*liumang zui*), another crime that suffered from ambiguity—virtually any act of "disturbing social order," so-called, could be viewed as an act of hooliganism (Criminal Law 1979: Art. 160).[6] The above two crimes were described by Chinese scholars as "bag crimes," referring to their metaphorical "grab-bag" convenience, for nearly anything that irked a local official could be tossed into the speculation or hooligan "bag." Fortunately these two bag crimes have themselves been sacked, eliminated in the 1997 Criminal Law, and relieving the courts (and defendants) of such unwieldy legal concepts. At the same time, the fact that it took nearly 20 years for the SPC to do away with laws that were almost immediately defunct highlights a characteristic of legislation in the Reform and Opening Era: legislation has rarely been able to keep pace with development.

The SPC, through the continuous issuance of new model cases, did its best to mold the almost-immediately outdated laws to fit new crimes, not-so-discreetly playing the role of legislator other branches of government could not or would not play. Starting in1985, the SPC formally instituted the publication of exemplary cases in its official publication, the *SPC Gazette*. More than six hundred cases comprising every manner of law have been published since then, including civil, criminal, and administrative law cases. These cases have played an important role in standardizing judicial practice, and perhaps more importantly, in guiding lower courts on new legal issues, whether poorly-defined in the law or lacking exposition altogether. In some circumstances, the SPC will issue a judicial interpretation, itself accompanied with a few representative cases.

The SPC used just this type of interpretive tidal wave to combat drunk driving a few years ago. In September 2009, the SPC issued its *Notice on Handling Drunk Driving Cases that Result in Death*, a widely publicized notice aimed at stemming the very palpable public outcry at a spate of incidents in which drunk drivers had killed pedestrians. These traffic accidents could conceivably be prosecuted under two separate crimes: a traffic statute that seemed more on point but capped the maximum punishment at seven years, and another statute concerning the "endangering of public safety" that was as broad as the name suggests, and carried the threat of capital punishment. In order to illustrate how to differentiate between a normal negligent homicide resulting from a traffic accident from a ruthless type of driving resulting in death (perhaps something like "depraved heart murder"), the SPC attached two representative cases to its Notice. In those two cases, the defendants were convicted of the crime carrying the heavier penalty, that of endangering public safety through drunk driving (SPC Opinions: 2009).

The sources of model cases in the early Reform and Opening period

In addition to the *SPC Gazette*, there are other, less official, channels of model case publication.

The first source arose from SPC case compilations drawn from courts of all different levels, from local-level court decisions all the way to SPC decisions in Beijing. These compilations served myriad purposes, but were mostly for internal use, for judicial training and education. In addition to the SPC's work of case compilation, the courts of all levels periodically compile cases for similar educational purpose.

The second source of model cases came (and still comes) from the judicial training organs. The judges' colleges at the national and local levels use and create case books for training purposes. Beginning in 1992, in collaboration with Renmin University School of Law, the National Judges College (NJC) has published an annual compilation of model cases collected from the cases tried by courts of all levels in the previous year. As an educational wing of the SPC, the NJC has played a critical role in elevating judicial professionalism. Save for a small segment of its resources dedicated to formal law degree education, the NJC dedicates most of its efforts to providing various types of on-the-job and full-time training for career judges, including training for entry-level judges and judges expecting promotion. These trainings are required pursuant to SPC directive. In order to integrate its trainees into actual judicial practice, the NJC enjoys incomparable access to all of the cases tried by the nation's courts.

148 Reading the legal case

Outside the judicial context, academic compilations have also served as a source for case compilation and dissemination. Law professors and law schools would often gather cases from courts with which they had a relationship, normally for educational purposes. But even with their ostensible educative purpose, many judges worked on and consulted in the creation of these compilations. These judges came from all over, and hence the compilations covered cases and jurisdictions quite far from the school's location. This breadth was due to the fact that early in the Reform and Opening period, judges would often enroll in distance-learning courses with top law schools. One case compilation of note was edited by the Renmin University Criminal Law Center. As one might expect, the Center's compilation constituted of largely criminal cases, and it exercised great influence on the work of criminal courts of various levels.

But law school influence was not solely limited to its wealth of judicial resources. Many local courts would convene "internal expert meetings" in order to discuss difficult cases with academics—these were often cases that had not yet been decided. Most cases decided with the aid of academics were incorporated into case compilations penned by various courts or academic institutes.

As evidenced by the breadth of case sources, the case compilation process in the early years of the Reform and Opening was an important transformative vehicle for the Chinese judiciary, as it scrambled to find means to promote judicial education and professionalization—any legal institution of quality was called into service.

From 1999 to the present

Beginning in 1999, the Supreme People's Court took the establishment of a case-law-type system on as its mandate,[7] and commenced upon the First Five-Year Program, the first of what would become two five-year programs dedicated to that end (First Five-Year Program: 1999). During the first program, the SPC created case publications that became requisite reference materials for judges on every level. But the model cases promoted during the first five-year plan occupied a confused role in judicial decisions—judges were told "to make reference" to the cases in reaching a judgment, with little instruction on what "making reference" entailed. This ambiguity greatly reduced the importance of the model cases in practice.

With its Second Five-Year Program, the SPC decided to establish the Guiding Case System (Second Five-Year Program: 2005).[8] Despite the fact that various types of "guiding" and "model" cases had been used throughout the history of the PRC, this was the first time that the SPC had fully articulated a systematic approach to their use, and also the first time specific usage procedures and guidelines were officially publicized—a new name, Guiding Cases (*zhidao anli*), highlighted this differentiation. Preliminary work on the establishment of the Guiding Case System started in 2005. As is often the case with any new central government program, local experiments were conducted throughout the country, including the Shanghai High Court, the Nanjing intermediate courts, the

Zhengzhou intermediate courts and the Sichuan High Court (Shen 2009: 3). These experiments evidenced variations in Guiding Case System practice and understanding, and, indeed, many regions still evince vastly different practices. For instance, some courts developed a formalized case report, a template that would include excerpts of rules generated at trial, while others simply recorded case summaries. Some even went further than a bare litany of "rules created," and also included legal reasoning of the parties to the dispute and that of the deciding judge, following the American judicial decision model (Zhou 2002).[9] This great disparity between Guiding Case experimental jurisdictions lead to a response from SPC. The SPC used the second five-year program to create a unifying standard for the Guiding Case System.

On November 26, 2010, the SPC, after dedicating more than ten years to the topic, finally issued the SPC Rules on the Work of the Guiding Cases (2010) that formally established the Guiding Case System. The document, only made public in January 2011, is by no means lengthy, containing just ten articles, comprising basic rules outlining the work of the Guiding Case System. Surprisingly, the SPC was not alone in promulgating rules governing this new system. Earlier in 2010, the Supreme People's Procuratorate (SPP) published its own guiding practices on July 30, months ahead of the SPC (SPP Rules 2010). The SPP rules similarly purport to govern the work of the Guiding Case System.[10] The SPP's guiding practices also claim comparable, if not equal, importance to the SPC guidelines, given the SPP's unique role as "SPC watchdog" mandated by the Constitution. This supervisory function means that the SPP may exert substantial influence over the work of SPC in this context (PRC Constitution 1982: Art. 129).[11]

The functions of the Guiding Case System

As is true in any legal system, law is not practiced in an administrative vacuum. Understanding the roles each government organ plays is critical to understanding the potential and limitations of any new initiative. Specific to the Guiding Case System, any analysis of the system itself will need to consider the unique relationship between the SPC and the SPP, and their dual roles in the national government.

That said, the onus for implementation of the Guiding Case System still falls on the SPC. Unlike courts of most nations, the SPC functions more as an administrative body, overseeing the judiciary. This is different from a western high court, which often operates as a countervailing, rather than complementary, power. According to China's Constitution (Art. 127) and the Organic Law of the People's Court (Art. 30), the SPC has the mandate to "direct and supervise" the work of the courts. In order to carry out its supervisory duties and to ensure that laws and regulations are implemented in the "correct" way, the SPC often issues judicial interpretations to clarify ambiguous wording in myriad laws and regulations: from a jurisprudential perspective, these interpretations amount to *de facto* rules. Few countries allow their courts that kind of general interpretative power, opting instead to allow courts to handle cases within certain limited contexts, usually when a dispute has arisen (i.e. standing provisions). These types of provisions force courts to interact with various legislative provisions as they bubble up from below, and rarely give courts the opportunity to reflect on, or rewrite, the merits of an entire law. Constitutional Courts may have more freedom, but are still limited to problems associated with particular cases. But the Chinese Supreme People's Court can interpret laws broadly and proactively, save for, of course, the Constitution, the interpretation of which is not within the province of the SPC. This exceptional interpretative mandate (or, at least, reality) is what makes the Guiding Case System possible—the SPC has room to shape the interpretation, and thereby, the execution of the laws through its various powers: its judicial interpretations, judicial opinions, replies to specific letters (and even phone calls) from lower courts (*da fu*) and now, through its guiding cases. It has also just released its first four guiding cases right before this chapter's publication. On 20 December, 2011, the SPC released two criminal and two civil cases, including an intentional homicide case and a contracts case. The cases are available at: www.chinacourt.org/html/article/20111221/472164.shtml.

The second factor that will strongly influence the effectiveness of the Guiding Case System is the unique relationship between the Supreme People's Procuratorate and the Supreme People's Court. As was mentioned above, the SPP developed its own rules for the Guiding Case System simultaneously to the SPC, and issued its guidelines six months in advance. This may be both confusing and surprising to some readers, or at least seem a waste of resources, but it fits squarely within the standard role of the SPP. In addition to its typical prosecutorial duties, the SPP also serves as a supervisory watchdog of other government institutions, gauging the legality of their actions. This supervisory power extends even over the SPC and allows the SPP to influence and share the SPC's expansive judicial power. It is a competitive yet complementary relationship. This means that when the two institutions promulgate their Guiding Case Rules, they need to be read together in that same competitive/complementary spirit to accurately gauge the potential impact of the law. China's current legal reality allows for the two guiding cases systems to exist in tandem, occupying parallel swaths of the judicial landscape. One way that conflicts of bureaucratic jurisdiction are often solved is through jointly-issued documents. It is highly likely that there will be a mechanism to facilitate communication and joint publication between the SPP and the SPC on their respective Guiding Case Systems.

Finally, one of the reasons the SPC and SPP have more expansive powers than most other countries' high courts is that they are not positioned to check or balance out other agencies within the national government; rather, the entire judiciary functions underneath the national government. While the SPP and SPC occupy positions of equal constitutional rank to the State Council and the Central Military Commission, in reality, they retain a much lower political status than the State Council, which holds central administrative power. This reality renders the Guiding Case System vulnerable to influence from non-judicial organs, and this fact in turn makes the system a particularly convenient vehicle to reflect overall government and CCP policy.

The SPC's response to recent national outcry over a series of drunk driving accidents, mentioned above, is just such a case. The release of those SPC directives was part of an overall government response to public anger instigated by a number of drunk driving accidents that had made the national news over the past two years. Class anger was running rampant through various Internet chat-rooms and message boards, unnerving the central and local governments. The sentences in the two "typical cases" were quite severe: life sentences, both.

And yet, even though these sentences may appear harsh for what would amount to vehicular manslaughter in many other countries, they actually involved the reduction on appeal of what had been either death penalty or suspended death penalty sentences.

We should be clear—there is no direct evidence that the SPC received special direction from other governing bodies when they drafted those two typical cases, although that may have been the case. It's probably more accurate to state that these types of actions do not necessarily stem from any specific, extra-SPC instruction, but rather that the SPC may intuit the political or policy considerations with which they are to draft model, typical or guiding cases. This reality makes the Guiding Case System a potentially powerful tool for handling any case harboring an important political or social impact.

The Guiding Cases System in detail

Enactment

Although the new SPC Guiding Case Rules only contain ten articles, they mark an important movement towards the formal recognition of precedent's role in a system with a civil law tradition. It also may effectively end the long debate about whether case law mechanisms suit China's system.[12]

At first glance, the most striking article is the seventh, which reads, "All cases should refer to the guiding cases in dealing with similar cases." There are obvious intimations of a system of precedent here: the SPC seems to have created an obligation on local courts to abide by decisions made in previous cases (*ying dang can zhao*). The SPC has drafted the guiding cases in a form structurally (if not practically) different than cases found in common law system annals: the cases will not be presented as complete drafts; rather, the guiding cases as published will contain only key excerpts from past cases, highlighted for obligatory reference by any judge deciding a similar issue. Providing lawyers and judges with only the "holdings" of cases may be a response to the fear that a majority of Chinese judges and lawyers are not yet sophisticated enough to deal with full case analysis.

Yet, at the same time, the "obligatory reference" does not mean that guiding cases are to be followed exclusively. The Guiding Case System is only to complement other forms of judicial interpretation. If there is a conflict between a law or other judicial interpretations and the rule espoused by a guiding case, the guiding case rule is considered secondary.

The Guiding Case Rules also formalize the procedures for creating a guiding case, distinguishing guiding cases from the bevy of other instructional cases issued by the SPC, be they model, typical, or otherwise. Guiding cases are of a different provenance. Former case types were all publicized without any strong formality, save cases published in the *SPC Gazette* and confirmed by the Supreme People's Court Adjudication Committee. But the Guiding Case System has written, established procedures that operate more like H.L.A. Hart's Rule of Recognition: when followed, these rules take cases that have reached a final judgment and transform them into a guiding case (SPC Rules 2010: Art. II).

What types of cases, then, are eligible to become guiding cases? Article Two of the SPC Rules (2010) lists a number of prerequisites that must be met, but does not specify whether they are to be met in total, or if simply meeting any one condition is sufficient to establish guiding case eligibility. These conditions are as follows: First, the case must have wide-spread social influence. Second, the law on the issue must be deemed ambiguous, with little black-letter law on point. Third, the case itself must be a "typical case," one that is likely to reoccur with some regularity. Fourth, it must involve a complicated and/or new type of crime. The fifth provision is a catch-all provision, quite common in Chinese legislation, granting guiding case eligibility to "other cases for which there is a necessity to guide." This last provision threatens to swallow up the others, as it was already unclear if a potential guiding case needs to meet one or all of the first four provisions. The inclusion of the fifth provision would seem to intimate that cases meeting any one of the five provisions can be considered worthy of guiding case status.

In addition to outlining the provisions for guiding case selection, the SPC Rules also specify who is supposed to do the selecting: the list is quite broad (SPC Rules 2010: Art. V). Within the Supreme People's Court, the SPC Rules set up a special office that will be responsible for selecting, verifying, and reporting guiding cases (SPC Rules 2010: Art. III). Interestingly, procedure-wise, the regulations permit lower courts to nominate cases for guiding case status, subject, of course, to SPC review (SPC Rules 2010: Art IV). The regulations also allow the members of the people's congresses of all levels, members of the Chinese People's Political Consultative Conferences ("CPPCC") of all levels, academics and other members of society to nominate cases for guiding case status, as long as that case is a final judgment. All these proposals must go through the court that made the decision in the case (SPC Rules 2010: Art. V). Nowhere in the SPC Rules does it specify if that court has the right to refuse to a recommendation.

This special SPC Guiding Cases Office, upon receiving the case proposal, needs to make an assessment of the case's merits as a guiding case, making written comments on it. If the case satisfies the requirements of Article Two, they can then submit the case to the president of the Supreme People's Court or the vice president of the Supreme People's Court in charge of these types of cases, and that person (or persons) will, in turn, nominate the case to the SPC Adjudication Committee for final approval or rejection.[13] If a case is selected as a guiding case, it will be published in the *SPC Gazette*, on the SPC website, in the *People's Court*

Daily, and by the order of the SPC President. In addition to publication of the cases through official channels, the SPC Rules mandate that all guiding cases be compiled into a single annual volume and released to the public. At present, before the first volume is published, the SPC is currently looking through previously released model and typical cases, determining which, if any, of these cases should be considered for an upgrade to "guiding case status" (SPC Rules 2010: Art IX).

The SPP's Guiding Case System

As mentioned above, the SPP's mandate includes the job of supervising the SPC in addition to its daily work of prosecuting crimes. The SPP self-identifies with the work of the SPC, believing itself to be doing the same work, sharing judicial power and the power of interpretation. When it comes to issues of prosecutorial discretion and criminal prosecution, guiding cases could prove quite instructive in the decision to prosecute or not to prosecute. The SPP was well aware of SPC movements on its Guiding Case System, and they concomitantly developed their own practice to parallel the SPC's work, in part, for fear of losing power to jointly interpret the law—a power the SPP is not keen to lose. Moreover, they also want to parallel and complement the SPC project—anticipating and even integrating their efforts. Obviously, from an outside perspective, it's tough to say whether or not they are trying to influence the SPC, compete with it, or just play catch up.

The SPP rules are actually more elaborate, consisting of 18 articles. The articles deal mostly with guidelines for criminal cases, but they also include guidelines for other types, such as state compensation cases, petition cases (a complaint in a case that is past the final stage), prosecutorial protest cases in civil and administrative proceedings where the prosecutor intervenes to protest a decision, and other new, difficult and typical cases that leave large room for SPP intervention.

Similar to the SPC, the SPP established a SPP Committee in Charge of Case Selection, temporarily set up within the SPP's Research Department on Law and Policy. The SPP Rules also allow deputies of the people's congresses of all levels, members of the CPPCC of all levels, scholars and others to make guiding case recommendations directly to the SPP, a procedure slightly different than the SPC regulations, which require those recommendations to go through the court of final judgment. The nominated cases are then reviewed by the SPP Law and Policy Department, with eligible cases then recommended to the Procuratorate Committee.

The major difference between the SPP regulations and those of the SPC is that the SPP's regulations make use of the guiding cases optional (prosecutors "may" make reference to the cases) as opposed to the SPC's Article Seven that states that judges "should" or "ought" make reference to the guiding cases. Nevertheless, the prosecutor, if declining to follow a guiding case, needs to submit a written explanation about why he or she has decided not to make reference to the guiding case in question, and this is subject to approval of the chief procurator (SPP Rules 2010: Art. XVI). One can project that the common law skill of case distinguishing could play a substantial role if the guiding cases are used.

The SPP guiding cases will be published in the *SPP Gazette*, and published on its website as well. In Article Eighteen, the SPP Guiding Case Departments are required to "strengthen their communication with relevant bodies," in the furtherance of the Guiding Case System. This more than likely means the SPC, but could also include consultation with the Ministries of Justice, Public Security and State Security. They are to consult with those organs, or "may also jointly issue guiding cases" with those relevant bodies as well. This is quite common in Chinese political affairs, as these bodies have already issued many joint documents, primarily when dealing with the same legal or political issue and when presenting a united front is deemed beneficial. This article also demonstrates the intent of the SPP to share the judicial power with the SPC in its administration of their nascent guiding case systems.

Like the SPC Rules, the SPP draft is really quite ambiguous, leaving a lot of room for guesswork on how they will be implemented. One also wonders how the two systems will work together in practice, as there is as much potential for conflict as there is for cooperation.

Conclusions and observations

While this is an exciting development for the Supreme People's Court and the Supreme People's Procuratorate, many unanswered questions exist.

First, there's a lingering doubt about how to define and distinguish "similar cases" as defined in the SPP and SPC regulations. The determination of "similarities" is often left to individual judges and prosecutors to decide mid-case, just as it is often left to common law lawyers and judges. Some scholars have speculated that this could mean "similar circumstances," "similar facts," or something else entirely. In common law countries, lawyers are trained to parse facts in order to argue the relevance of a certain precedent, yet this is a relatively foreign concept to most PRC-trained lawyers. Regardless, the Guiding Case System would seem to necessitate this type of legal argumentation. In fact, the SPC itself is struggling with this term and is working hard to create a formal case report template that would provide more tangible rules for guiding case exegesis. For example, one possibility might be to include copious amounts of reasoning with any "holding" promoted in a guiding case. At this stage, it is still anyone's guess as to how the SPC will deal with this problem, skeptical common law lawyers would question whether any publication format could obviate the need for robust legal reasoning and case comparison.

Second, perhaps an even bigger problem is how one understands Article Seven's "making reference to a case," and what relationship this has, if any, with the common law concept of binding precedent. The Chinese judiciary seems to be avoiding the question of whether judges can make law, even if they have been flirting with *de facto* judge-made law since the founding of the PRC. In practice, given that much of the Chinese legal code is still quite broad and ambiguous, it is foreseeable that judges will end up relying in large part on judicial interpretations, including the interpretations present in the guiding cases. It reminds us of the legal phenomenon extent already in China's Imperial Era, when primary legal sources played only secondary roles in regulating social relations. As one western scholar has pointed out, in both ancient and contemporary China, the formal rules, while ostensibly the primary legal order, oftentimes must defer to informal rules. These informal rules, though secondary in theory, take precedence due to the general and ambiguous nature of the formal rules (Keller 1994: 715–16).[14] It may be precisely this logic that lies behind the Chinese judiciary's immense power of judicial interpretation and guidance, a power that has expanded over the past six decades. At the same time, it may also be fair to say that the Guiding Case System represents a movement toward "formalizing" this power, occupying a middle ground between legislation and the unwritten rules that often govern local affairs.

In promoting the Guiding Case System, it would appear that China is getting closer to formally recognizing that it is not the general provisions of the legal code that decide cases, but the concrete, judge-made legal rules and doctrines that actually dictate the result of any particular case. Regardless of whether one calls these judge-made laws or not, they are and will continue to play a critical role in regulating people's lives. Unless China improves its legislative skill significantly, this secondary legal regime, now bulwarked by the Guiding Case System, will continue to dominate the legal landscape. At the same time, one could very well argue that the SPC *is* simply part of the legislative process, a proposition that may be far less jurisprudentially frightening in a system that rejects separation of powers.

Third, what does the "should" in Article Seven's "should reference" mean? Must judges obey the rule or the result of the decision? Is it a moral or judicial ethics question, or rather, a political one? What are the consequences for judges if they do not follow the rules provided in a guiding case? There is also considerable confusion about the meaning of "reference" as well. Linguistically, the verb "reference" here does not connote a posture of obedience (as the idea of binding precedent surely does) as much as it does one of making a connection between two situations. If this is the case, the guiding cases will not be substantially different from the already ubiquitous model cases, and will continue to play a secondary role as both something to consult and a case to educate, just as model cases have for the past 30 years. The SPC Rules, on their face, do not provide a clear answer to either of these questions.

Fourth, a relatively minor point: Can these guiding cases be cited, their implied reasoning used as an argument for why a judge determines a case, or do they simply exist to guide the decision but not to end up in the final written judgment? Currently, judges are refraining from citing anything save black letter law in their judgments. Will the citation of a guiding case change the legal horizon, putting an official stamp on an "official" source of law, one outside of the legislative process? This is something that has been avoided in the past, even if the binding force behind the decision was a judicial interpretation or other guidance.

Finally, the newly established Guiding Case System should certainly propel, if not inspire, legal education reform. The power of common-law-style legal argumentation would seem poised to play an ever-increasing role in the Chinese judicial system. Will this precipitate more expansive legal reasoning in judicial opinions? Will judges have to explain why they accept or reject the reasoning from a party on why a guiding case or its reasoning should be used or not? There has been a discernible trend in the Chinese judiciary to be more explicit in its reasoning in order to satisfy the losing party and those in the public at large who may not be satisfied with a simple binary decision. However, this will require a change in legal education practice and praxis, and lawyers, if they want to be good lawyers, will have to learn to make judgments about the relevance and limits of guiding cases. There are reports that the NJC is now scrambling to learn more in terms of case study and interpretation, and considering case study textbooks as part of their judicial education system. This would seem to presage increasing levels of formal common-law-type jurisprudence in a system that already appears to have quite a bit of the informal variety.

Endnotes

1 According to Cheng Shude, famous legal historian, in Han Dynasty, "you must obey the law whenever there is a law governing the issue, however, you should look at the case (*bi*) in absence of the relevant law."
2 For early legal education in China, please see Allison Connor, "Training China's Early Modern Lawyers" referenced in the bibliography.
3 In Japan, after WWII, the Supreme Court of Japan also compiled case law. Even without a mandate, it circulated throughout the judicial system, binding cases that shared common traits.
4 The so-called "Seven Important Laws" refer to the Criminal Law, the Criminal Procedure Law, the Joint Venture Law, the Organic Law of the People's Congress of All Levels, the Organic Law of the People's Governments of All Levels, the Organic Law of People's Courts, and the Organic Law of People's Procuratorates.
5 Art. 117 states "Whoever engages in speculation in violation of the laws and regulations on the control of monetary affairs, foreign exchange, gold and silver, or on the administration of industrial and commercial affairs, if the circumstances are serious, shall be sentenced to fixed-term imprisonment of not more than three years or criminal detention, or he may concurrently or exclusively be sentenced to a fine or confiscation of property."
6 Article 160 states "Where an assembled crowd engages in affrays, creates disturbances, humiliates women or engages in other hooligan activities that undermine public order, if the circumstances are flagrant, the offenders shall be sentenced to fixed-term imprisonment of not more than seven years, criminal detention or public surveillance. Ringleaders of hooligan groups shall be sentenced to fixed-term imprisonment of not less than seven years."
7 Since 1998, SPC began to enact its reform programs by issuing a five-year plan titled as "The Five Year Program of People's Court Reform," cited in the bibliography. The first Five Year Program was issued on September 20, 1999 and covered the five years from 1999–2003. Though the Five Year Program has no legal status, it was approved by central government leaders and served as a blueprint for Chinese courts to engage in a substantive reform for the next five years. Sometime, such program normally needs to have formal legislative or other official endorsement.
8 The Second Five Year Program, cited below, was enacted on October 26, 2005. Article 14 states the following: "The SPC establishes and perfects the Guiding Case System,

and attaches importance to the function of the Guiding Case System in terms of unifying law application, directing the trial works of the lower courts, and enriching and developing the jurisprudence of trials."
9 In 2002, in a famous libel case involving the celebrated soccer player Fan Zhiyi, the presiding judge cited "public figures" as the reason for his judgment in favor of the defendant. The judge believed that criticism of celebrities based upon reasonable sources should be tolerated and understood, even if such criticisms resulted in unfair but "minor" damage upon the plaintiff. The concept of "public figure" clearly derived from *Sullivan v. New York Times* and was deliberately used by the attorney and adopted by the court.
10 The SPP Rules contained 18 articles trying to unify the prosecutor's practice in prosecuting crimes, supervising the court works in the area of civil and administrative litigations.
11 Article 129 mandates that the People's Procuratorates are the state organ in charge of supervising the application of law.
12 Starting from early 1980s, scholars began to debate whether China should learn from the Common Law regarding the use of precedent or case law.
13 The SPC organizes its work by dividing the labor among its vice presidents, with each vice president in charge of one or more specific divisions of criminal, civil, or administrative cases. The vice president under whose auspices a guiding case falls may propose this case to the Adjudication Committee of the SPC for a discussion and approval.
14 Perry Keller described the ancient Chinese legal order as a dichotomy of "formalistic and symbolic use of primary legislation and the flexible and pragmatic use of sub-statutory rules," and pointed out that Qing magistrates gave more weight to officially-approved secondary rules than the law code.

Bibliography

Cheng, S.D. (1927) *Jiuchao Likao Hanlu Kao (Studies of the Laws of Nine Dynasties, Han Law Study)*. Shanghai: Commercial Publishing House.

China. *Constitution of the People's Republic of China: The National People's Congress* (1982). Beijing: Law Press.

China. *The Criminal Law of the People's Republic of China: The National People's Congress* (1979). Beijing: Law Press.

China. *The Supreme People's Court First Five Year Program of People's Court Reform (renmin fayuan gaige wunian gangyao)* (September 20, 1999). Beijing: People's Court Press.

China. *The Supreme People's Court Second Five Year program of People's Court Reform (renmin fayuan gaige wunian gangyao)* (October 26, 2005). Beijing: People's Court Press.

China. *The Supreme People's Court Rules on the Work of the Guiding Cases: Supreme People's Court* (2010). Available from http://www.law-lib.com/law/law_view.asp?id=342688.

China. *The Supreme People's Court Opinions with respect to Law Application in Drunk Driving (zuigao renmin fayuan guanyu jiuzui jiache falu shiyong wenti de yijian)* (September 11, 2009). Beijing: People's Court Gazette, No.11, 2009.

China. *The Supreme People's Procuratorate Rules on the Work of the Guiding Cases: Supreme People's Procuratorate* (2010). Available from http://wenku.baidu.com/view/d8f4e1b565ce05087632138a.html.

Connor, A. (1994) "Training China's Early Modern Lawyers." *Soochow University Law School Journal of Chinese Law*, 8 (1).

Fishel, W.R. (1952) *The End of Extraterritoriality in China*, Berkeley: University of California Press.

Keeton, G.W. (1969) *The Development of Extraterritoriality in China*, New York: H. Fertig.

Keller, P. (1994) Source of Order in Chinese Law. *American Journal of Comparative Law*, 42.

Liu, S.S. (1925) *Extraterritoriality: Its Rise and Its Decline*, New York: Columbia University Press.

Quigley, H.S. (1926) "Extraterritoriality in China American," *Journal of International Law*, January, 20(1), pp. 46–68.

Renmin University Criminal Law Center. *The Study of Criminal Precedents and Interpretation (xingshi fa panjie yanjiu): The Supreme People's Court* (2002, 2003, 2004). Beijing: People's Court Press.

Scott, H. and Wright, Q. (1943) "The End of Extraterritoriality in China," *American Journal of International Law*, April, 37(2), pp. 286–9.

Shen, D.Y. (2009) *Study of the Guiding Case System of Chinese Characteristics*. Beijing: People's Court Press.

Vincent, J.C. (1970) *Extraterritorial System in China: Final Phase*, Cambridge: East Asian Research Center, 1970.

Zhou, X. (2002). Fan Zhi Yi's Lawsuit Loss Secret Uncovered: The Court was Respecting Media Rules, *Beijing Youth News*. Dec. 23. Available from http://news.eastday.com/epublish/gb/paper148/20021223/class014800010/hwz849499.htm.

Chapter 10

Judging judgment in Chinua Achebe's *No Longer at Ease*

Katherine Isobel Baxter

Chinua Achebe's *No Longer at Ease* opens in the High Court of Lagos and the Southern Cameroons. Obi, the novel's protagonist, is in the dock receiving judgment from Mr. Justice William Galloway. He is being sentenced for accepting a bribe of £20 in his position as secretary of the Scholarship Commission. However, this crime is only made explicit indirectly through conversations about the case in the subsequent pages of the first chapter. Instead we see Obi's pride crushed by Galloway's exclamation that he 'cannot comprehend' how Obi 'could have done this' (2). This oblique presentation of his crime, and the Justice's stated incomprehension of it, challenge us as readers to understand the nature of what Obi has done and draw us in to the narrative of his life that the trial scene, to which Achebe briefly returns at the very end of the novel, thus frames. Indeed, as will become evident, Achebe's narrative challenges us not simply to understand and judge Obi, but further to judge the processes of judgment themselves in Nigeria's late colonial administrative period.

Achebe's first novel, *Things Fall Apart*, had been published in 1958 by Heinemann to critical acclaim. Achebe's success with Heinemann led to him taking the helm of Heinemann's groundbreaking African Writers Series in 1962. As series editor, Achebe did much to shape the image of African writing in the Anglophone world, to which his own fiction made a significant contribution. *No Longer at Ease* appeared in 1960 as a sequel to *Things Fall Apart*, and a brief outline of the novel's story is necessary before we can begin to examine Achebe's engagement with questions of judgment. Obi Okonkwo is the son of a Nigerian catechist in the Anglican Church and the grandson of Okonkwo, the central figure of *Things Fall Apart*. Whilst grandfather Okonkwo had resisted the incursion of Christianity and colonialism in Umuofia, the village of which he was an elder, Obi is the product of that incursion – missionary school educated and the beneficiary of a local scholarship which enables him to study abroad in Great Britain. Obi's scholarship is paid for by the Umuofia Progressive Union (UPU), a collective of Umuofians who have moved out into the burgeoning urban centres of Nigeria. They realise that to have an Umuofian voice in Nigerian politics and administration they must ensure that the brightest of the next generation receives a British education, thereby gaining access to the colonial civil service. That brightest is Obi, the first recipient of the UPU's educational scholarship.

The UPU had intended Obi to read law, 'so that when he returned he would handle all their land cases against their neighbors' (8), but Obi instead chooses to read English. Returning to Nigeria Obi settles in Lagos and takes up a position in the civil service following his examination by the Public Service Commission. He also takes up with a girl, Clara, whom he falls in love with but who is an Osu, an outcast. Obi is determined to marry her despite the fact that both the UPU and his family oppose the marriage on the basis of her Osu status. Meanwhile Obi falls into debt as his costs mount up – tax returns, financial support for his family, running costs for his car. When Clara becomes pregnant he pays for her abortion but the couple split up. At the same time his mother dies and soon after he begins to accept bribes from those wishing for their children to be considered by the board for scholarships.

The overt cause for Obi taking the bribes is his financial situation, which Achebe takes pains to enumerate throughout the novel, demonstrating how the high salary he earns comes with high expectations from his family and the UPU both for financial support (he is expected to pay back his scholarship in instalments) and with regard to his dress and deportment (for example owning a car). Clara too loans him £50, which is promptly stolen from the glove compartment of the car, leaving him in even greater debt. However, throughout the novel Obi has always argued against accepting bribes of any kind and prides himself early in the novel on his refusal to accept them. Indeed he had even read a paper at the Nigerian Students' Union in London against corruption amongst the older generation of Nigerians in administrative power (44). Why then does Obi capitulate? We might take into consideration the recent loss of Clara and his mother, the two women most important to him. Or we might argue, as various critics have done, that the dilettante environment of Lagos has had a deleterious effect on his morals. But neither of these explanations seems satisfactory. What then are we to do with a problem like Obi Okonkwo?

I propose to examine this question in the light of Alexandre Lefebvre's exploration of the creativity of jurisprudence in *The Image of Law: Deleuze, Bergson, Spinoza*. Lefebvre's idea of this creativity revolves around what he calls, in Bergsonian fashion, an 'encounter'. This encounter occurs where a potential case cannot be readily subsumed to the precedents of case law and therefore demands an imaginative spiral of association, circling through the information presented and back into the judge's repertoire of precedents in order to construct a (new) case. Creativity occurs in this formation of the case: in the judge's associative manoeuvres to fix the facts presented into the form of a case that is available for resolution. Rather than identifying creativity in the resolution of a given case, Lefebvre argues that in fact resolution is inherent in the recognizable case. Once the case has been formed it contains within it the formula for its resolution – a case is something that can be judged. Creativity therefore occurs not in the judgment itself but in the construction of something judgeable. Structuring his argument around an examination of Deleuze's various writings on law and judgment, Lefebvre thus reads Deleuze against the grain to demonstrate the creativity of jurisprudence. Lefebvre's argument then is twofold: firstly that the law can be, and at times inevitably is, creative; and secondly that despite Deleuze's particular critique of the law as wholly uncreative, in fact, his writings gesture to how and where that creativity takes place.

Whilst Lefebvre's arguments about Deleuze are appreciably innovative, his argument about the creativity of jurisprudence is rather less startling to anyone with even limited familiarity with colonial law. Indeed his argument recalls, in particular, the many discussions in legal journals at the mid-century over the interpretation of the 'reasonable man' in the administration of law in the colonies.[1] Who is the 'reasonable man' in the colonies, they ask? The reasonable man, whose paradigmatic status was itself a contested subject for English law, was all the more problematic for colonial law when the idea of a 'reasonable native' was presumed in and of itself to be questionable. Should the 'native' be held to the same standard of reasonableness as the Englishman? And if not, what standard of reason was valid? This question became even more complicated if the parties involved came from different ethnic or cultural backgrounds as could often be the case in places such as Nigeria, whose shifting borders encompassed multiple languages, religions, and cultures, so that even the application of customary law could be problematic.

Furthermore, the idea of the reasonable man, as a paradigm for Nigerian law was given another twist by the fact that despite a series of legal reforms that coincided with the various changes to geographical administrative boundaries (as indicated in Galloway's jurisdiction of 'Lagos and the Southern Cameroons') the law that was to be applied was English law as it stood in 1900. Thus the law to which the reasonable man was bound was a law that remained fixed in time even as reasonable men changed and were changed by their temporally evolving contexts. As a result the reasonable man of Nigeria in 1956 could still be held to an English law of 1900 that, in England, might have already been altered or abolished altogether. The dissonance of such a situation is self-evident.

The idea and the legal ideal of the reasonable man are in many ways at the root of Achebe's *No Longer at Ease*. Obi wants to embody that legal ideal of the reasonable man, as he appears in English law. His failure to do so provokes us to engage with his story as a Lefebvrian judge engages with an encounter. Achebe presents us with a figure whose crime demands to be judged but because of the evidence laid before us it cannot be easily subsumed to a singular family of precedent(s). We read the novel looping back repeatedly in order to make a case – that is to say something that can be judged and therefore something that can be resolved – from the material narrated and from the precedents to which that material gestures or which it causes us to recall. Lefebvre's model of creative judgment helps us to recognise this process in Achebe's novel.

The frame-setting of Obi's trial encourages us to read the life narrated within it for evidence, by which to construct his case better than his judge. Galloway's statement of incomprehension implies his failure to construct a meaningful, a 'comprehendible', case from the evidence laid before him. Achebe invites us to assume that rather than entering into a Lefebvrian creative process the judge gives up, unable to resolve why a reasonable man such as Obi could act so unreasonably. A further challenge to us is presented in the judgment of Obi's boss, Green, who claims to understand Obi's actions perfectly: 'the African is corrupt through and through' (3). However, Green's explanation of why this is so is cut short and we are left only with his racist generalisation and a lack of corroboration for the claim. Achebe invites us to do better. Indeed, as we shall see, Achebe goes further to suggest not simply that we attempt to judge Obi more attentively, but that we turn our judgment on Nigeria's legal system itself. This point is a crucial one for Achebe at the moment of independence, the same year in which *No Longer at Ease* was published. With independence came the potential for and the challenge of a creative response to judicial process. Inherited from the colonial administration was a legal system that had been patched together and repeatedly reworked from English law and a colonial pastiche of indigenous legal processes. This inheritance itself presented an 'encounter', a legal system that was not like any other, however much it had drawn on aspects of English law and colonial law in other colonies. The Nigerian legal system at the moment of independence demanded, as encounter, the exercise of imaginative response, creative judgment as to its own nature.

To understand this turn in the novel it is first necessary to examine the presentation of Obi, and how that presentation demands our attentive judgment. In what follows I explore three possible sets of precedents from which we might construct a judgeable case for Obi's life and actions. The three sets to which I refer are firstly, extratextual precedents, secondly internal ones, and thirdly literary precedents.

It is worth pausing for a moment, however, to consider the work that the term precedent is doing in this context. Following Lefebvre I understand a precedent to be established through the act of judgment. If the act of judgment is what defines a case as such, that is to say identifies a case from the competing versions of events presented for judgment, then a precedent emerges as a product of this process: a precedent is established in the mutual formation of case and judgment. When we refer to precedent we are therefore referring to a paradigm for judgment that has been defined in a prior judgment of a similar case. Commonly, however, the fact that the case itself only emerges as a case in the process of judgment goes unseen. Instead the case is understood as auxiliary to its judgment in the establishment of precedent. By contrast, following the implications of Lefebvre's argument, I recalibrate the term here to focus attention on the case itself as a source of precedent, which demands a creative response in judgment.

Beginning with extratextual precedents it is instructive to examine how far Obi's story conforms to the reality of Lagos and civil service life in the final years of colonial administration. One useful source of information comes from a qualitative survey of civil service employees conducted by George D. Jenkins in the first years of independence.[2] All those surveyed were in the service prior to independence and so their answers give a good idea of the backgrounds, education, training, and interests of civil servants at the time in which the novel is set (i.e. 1956–7). What their answers show is that while Obi conforms to some of the norms of the civil service Achebe ensures he is recognisably out of the ordinary as well. Not that he is unrealistic or unbelievable, rather he is shown to be of an unusual kind. For example, of the 35 men surveyed only one has a father in the ministry, although the overwhelming majority note Protestantism under faith (their choices are Protestant, Catholic or Muslim). Interestingly this respondent is one of the few who have no written Yoruba (or, in his case, any other written Nigerian language), indicating a mission school education from the start (presumably Anglican although his 'some written' French could potentially indicate a Jesuit education – his mark over the religious affiliation question seems to denote either Catholic or a rejection of all listed religions). By far the most common paternal profession is farming, with others in trade, and several in some form of administrative post (from Prison Warden to School Inspector).

All but one of the men surveyed who indicate what subjects they studied (and almost all of them do) pursued vocational or at least vocationally relevant degrees of some kind or another, whether Economics, Law, or Agriculture, and so on. Even the one Humanities scholar of the group, who studied History at Edinburgh following the war, continued on to do a PGCE in London before returning to take up a position as an education officer in the Ministry of Education at Ibadan. Obi's choice to study English is thus clearly an unusual one.[3] However, despite these differences Obi is shown in other respects to be an average civil servant: almost all of those surveyed by Jenkins took some form of further or higher education qualification overseas, many joined the Nigerian Union of Students or other associations, and a good number were members of other local organisations back in Nigeria similar to the novel's Umuofia Progressive Union. Obi's crucial differences then are his church background and his choice of degree.

Obi's predicament with Clara's pregnancy is also not unheard of at this time, although pregnancy out of wedlock was neither sought nor approved. For example on Saturday 1 December 1962 the Nigerian paper, *Daily Express*, carried the following story:

Lagos Nurse Held for Questioning

The Lagos Police have detained a girl-nurse for questioning in connection with the death of 24-year-old Sadatu Ehimai of 200 Igbosere Road, Lagos.

Sadatu, said to be expecting a baby, died at a private hospital in Yaba after some drugs had been allegedly administered to her by a nurse.

The Police stated yesterday that Sadatu's death was reported to them by her mother, Madam Moriamo Aliu.

According to the Police, Madam Moriamo alleged that her daughter died as a result of abortifacient administered to her by one Bisi Thompson, a nurse of 67 Onototo Street, Surulere.

Sadatu's father, Mr Aliu Ehimai, 55, told the "Daily Express" that he heard that his daughter was expecting a baby "just 72 hours before she died".

He claimed that when he heard this, he instructed his wife to take the girl to hospital for attention. He alleged that Sadatu had been divorced from her husband and that there was no "marriage contract" between her and the man for whom she was expecting the baby.

It was learned last night that the Police are also looking for the "father-to-be" who is said to be an employee of a Federal Government Department.

(2)

Obi and Clara's trouble is not simply a matter of star-crossed lovers, with Clara's abortion they risk tangling with the law. This is spelled out to them very clearly by the first doctor whom they approach and who turns them down:

> I cannot help you. What you are asking me to do is a criminal offence for which I could go to jail and lose my license. But apart from that I have my reputation to safeguard – twenty years' practice without a single blot. . . . And in all those years I have not had anything to do with these shady dealings.
>
> (165)

A second, younger doctor is rather more pragmatic:

> he said he had no taste for the kind of job they were asking him to do. "It is not medicine," he said. "I did not spend seven years in England to study *that*. However I shall do it for you if you are prepared to pay my fee. Thirty pounds. To be paid before I do anything. No checks. Raw cash."
>
> (166)

The pride expressed here is of a different kind to that of the older doctor who had turned them down. The younger doctor believes his reputation is established by his English degree, not 'twenty years' practice without a single blot', and perhaps since blot or no blot the fact of his English degree cannot change he is more willing to take the risk for 'raw cash'. The *Daily Express* article makes manifest the risks that all parties take in proceeding with the abortion, not least Clara.

Clara herself tends to fare poorly at the hands of those critics who read the novel as a satirical critique of the immorality of Lagos life. Certainly Achebe presents her as typically susceptible to the delights of Lagos. However, her typicality is primarily constructed in relation to popular fiction rather than to popular culture, more broadly speaking. Clara's honesty about her Osu status, her willingness to persist with Obi despite their problems, and her clarity about these, present her as rather more complex than the stereotypical Lagosian wily harlot of popular culture.[4] However, the typicality of Clara's interests are born out by the regular and extensive cinema listings carried in Lagos newspapers of the time and, for example, by the prizes on offer at the Miss Ijebu Competition advertised in the

Daily Express just eleven days after the article about Sadatu Ehimai's death. The competition, held to coincide with a 'fabulous dance' at the opening of the Paramount Hotel, offered prizes of "£100 cash, Sewing Machines, Lady Bicycles, Trinkets, free trips and free Cinema tickets for a year".[5] The combination of dancing, cinema tickets, cash and the means to make dresses is a potent one that appeals to the stereotypical Lagosian girl, and one which tallies closely with Clara's mores in the novel.

What these various examples from the *Daily Express* and Jenkins' survey illustrate is the ways in which Obi and his life's story is both plausible and yet not wholly conventional: he is different enough to engage our interest; his predicament with Clara's abortion is risky yet hardly unheard of; Clara herself conforms to type as much as she goes beyond it. In this way these examples establish the kinds of precedent, defined above, which rest not on the judgment of a case but on the facts of the case itself. These precedents rather than establishing a response inform creative judgment. Whilst the examples given are not chronological precedents, since their dates are slightly later than those of the novel, in so far as they are roughly contemporaneous they provide synchronic precedents to which we can refer as aids to our comprehension of Obi and his crime. These synchronic precedents inform our judgment, modify our position, and lead us to cross-examination. Like the Lefebvrian judge we cycle through these precedents creatively in an attempt to discern the contours of Obi's case.

The second set of precedents for Obi are those within the book. As Obi is well aware bribery and corruption are hardly unknown within the administration and Achebe underlines this with multiple examples throughout the text. When Obi arrives back from England at the beginning of the book his very negotiation of entry into Nigeria is marked by an instance of attempted bribery, when a boyish customs official attempts to bargain with him over the customs due on his radio. Obi's response, having dismissed the lad without negotiation, is telling: 'Dear Old Nigeria' (35). For Obi bribery is part of *old* Nigeria, a Nigeria which his generation will reform with the benefit of their (European) education. As noted above, while in London Obi presented a paper at the Nigerian Students' Union outlining his theory that 'the public service of Nigeria would remain corrupt until the old Africans at the top were replaced by young men from the universities' (43). Obi elaborates elsewhere:

> take one of these old men. He probably left school thirty years ago in Standard Six. He has worked steadily to the top through bribery – an ordeal by bribery. To him the bribe is natural . . . [whereas to the young men] bribery is no problem. They come straight to the top without bribing anyone. It's not that they're necessarily better than others, it's simply that they can afford to be virtuous. But even that kind of virtue can become a habit.
>
> (23)

These 'old men' export into the colonial system the indigenous practice of gift-giving. However, whilst gift-giving operates effectively in the indigenous system it is incongruous within the colonial system becoming, by force of context, bribery. Obi's argument is not that the older generation are wilfully corrupt but that their actions are naturally so in the context of the colonial administration. The younger generation, men such as himself, are disconnected from the old indigenous systems by virtue of their university education and therefore will not, indeed cannot, make the same mistakes as their elders. Their rise to power has been through education and not through bribery and therefore they are already removed from the practice. Obi himself, then, invites us to judge him against and differentiate him from these elder statesmen.

A secondary elder figure to note briefly at this juncture is Obi's grandfather, Okonkwo, with whom Obi shares various similarities, in particular his inarticulacy and his anxiety to avoid showing emotion. This particular precedent is essentially intertextual since little is said of Okonkwo in *No Longer at Ease*. However, the several mentions made of him by various Umuofians prompt the reader to recognise that we are being invited to read the younger in the light of the older. Obi's desire to differentiate himself from the older generation of uneducated Nigerian leaders is thus undermined on two counts: despite his university education in English (that is in particular the study of words and how they are used) he fails to escape the family trait of inarticulacy that marked his grandfather. Furthermore, his university education singularly fails to save him from the temptations of bribery, which he thinks are only natural in the less educated, older generation. Indeed, it is the very financial burden of paying back the scholarship, which had paid for his education, that places pressure upon him to accept bribes.

Obi's naturalising arguments about these older men is consistent with the opinion held more generally by his boss, Mr. Green. Green claims, as we have noted, that 'The African is corrupt through and through', applying an essentially miasmic theory of moral corruption for this phenomenon: 'the African has been the victim of the worst climate in the world' (3, 4). However, it is clear from the start that Green's position is not simply a British colonial perspective. Unlike Green, Galloway claims he *cannot* understand why Obi accepted the bribe. Furthermore, when Green makes his declaration his auditors look about anxiously in case any of the Nigerian staff are near enough to hear (indicating that even if they are in agreement with Green they recognise that the position is a debatable, if not an inflammatory, one). Moreover, Green's attitude is reproduced in the figure of a Nigerian sitting on the committee that interviews Obi for the Public Service Commission. Having slept through most of the interview, in which Obi had been discussing the finer points of British and West African literature with the 'Chairman of the Commission, a jolly Englishman', the Nigerian committee member wakes up to ask, 'Why do you want a job in the civil service? So that you can take bribes?' (46). This question confirms Obi in his view of the board member as one of the old generation of Nigerian officials, that is to say one for whom accepting bribes is natural. He fails to comprehend the real challenge it offers to his own integrity. What the question in fact points up is the assumption, shared by

Obi, the Nigerian committee member and Mr. Green, that bribery is something that the *other* does: the older generation, the younger generation, the African.

This brings us to the final aspect of the internal precedents, which is Obi's own outspoken principles. Obi's stance against bribery is made evident from the start, with his dismissal of the customs boy. It is reiterated through his debates on the topic with friends, and underscored by his paper to the Nigerian Students' Union. As Achebe notes 'unlike most theories formed by students in London, this one survived the first impact of homecoming' (44). Obi initially congratulates himself on his capacity to withstand offers of bribes, he feels 'strangely elated' and even 'like a tiger' (100). However, he notes 'One should not . . . be unduly arrogant . . . the temptation was not really overwhelming' (101). Obi presumes himself to be one of the young men he had theorised in his Nigerian Students' Union paper, one who can afford to refuse bribes. He fails to recognise fully the implications of this ease, the fact that it is exactly when the temptation is overwhelming that one's morals are tested. Furthermore, Obi expresses the same incomprehension as Galloway when early in the novel he is presented with the example of another young civil servant sentenced for bribery. For Obi this man is 'an exception' that proves his rule (23). Rather than engaging attentively with this instance of a Land Officer, 'straight from the university', Obi dismisses it as anomalous and without cause for creative adjudication. The dramatic irony of Obi's response is yet another instigation to the reader to draw out the lineaments of his case.

The final set of precedents are those suggested by the literary allusions of the novel. What is noticeable immediately about the first of these kinds, which are taken from English literature, is their marked Christian character and Christological interest. The novel's title and epigraph are taken from Eliot's 'Journey of the Magi', and we are told that Obi's favourite poem is 'Easter Hymn' by A.E. Housman, a poet to whom he turns at moments of anxiety. Furthermore, his interview with the Public Service Commission involves an extended debate with the chairman of the committee about the nature of tragedy in Graham Greene's *The Heart of the Matter* (121). All three works involve questions of faith and death and express considerable ambivalence about both. Whilst I am not suggesting a Christological model for Obi, what these texts reflect is a particular experience of alienation that results from a Christological awareness. The magi of the epigraph, for example, return more certain of death than of life, with a sense that nothing can ever be the same. Back in their home country they are 'no longer at ease' – a familiar sensation for the diasporic returnee such as Obi and his generation.[6]

The suggestiveness of these literary allusions throws a shadow on Obi's own two poems celebrating Nigeria, written while away in London. The first is semi-pastoral (19), the second takes its cue from the negritude poetics and politics practised by francophone writers such as Leon Dumas (although the poem marries this with a distinctly British inflected patriotism: 'May we preserve our purity, / Our zest for life and jollity' (118)). However, both poems lose their light, so to speak, under the long shadows of doubt cast by the European literature to which the novel alludes. The possibility of beneficent tranquillity or positive change (which each of Obi's poems represents respectively) becomes ambiguous, ambivalent, and troubled when considered within the context of the literary precedents, which Achebe gives them. This takes us back to Lefebvre and his characterisation of Deleuze's thinking on repetition, law and change. For Deleuze, Lefebvre argues, the law changes incident into particularity, which can then be subsumed. This change from singularity to particularity is what moves the incident into the chain of repetition on which the law relies for its processes of subsumption: 'A particular . . . can never be encountered, for it is always already recognized by the law it incarnates; a particular can only ever be recognized.' (Lefebvre: 67) What we have here, in the literary allusions of the novel, is a Lefebvrian moment that reads with and against Deleuze. On the one hand Obi's poems become mere particular repetitions of their literary precedents to which they are subsumed – they are poems whose rhetoric makes evident their conformity to a given tradition; on the other hand, the change articulated by these precedents, particularly in 'Journey of the Magi' with its expression of existential unease, is one that disrupts rather than acquiesces to processes of conformity. The rupture that Eliot articulates, and to which Achebe directs us through the novel's allusions, is one which demands, in a Lefebvrian sense, a creative response because it does not and cannot conform to prior experience: 'this Birth was / Hard and bitter agony for us, like Death, our death. / . . . I should be glad of another death' (69). In Eliot's poem Christ's birth is transformative, creative, an encounter rather than a recognition. Similarly the radical doubt, which the two verses of Housman's 'Easter Hymn' express, presents a refusal to subsume one vision (of a mortal, buried Christ) in another (of an immortal, risen Christ). Thus, these literary precedents are ones that at once position Obi's poetry as a particular example within a Europeanized canon and that at the same time, in their articulation of an irresolvable encounter, call into question the celebrative surety of his two poems.

These Anglophone literary precedents are mirrored in Achebe's inclusion of Igbo songs, highlife songs, Igbo church hymns and, more importantly, proverbs. Before turning to the proverbs it is worth examining the songs in a little detail. Achebe writes some of these songs out in full, using both Igbo and silent translation into English. Each song – a church hymn sung to Obi as he leaves to London (13), a song sung by traders on his return home (53), the songs sung by a nightclub singer (particularly 'Gentleman Bobby') (128–9), and a song sung by the local women on Obi's second trip home (146–7) – indicates in one way or another 'the world turned upside down' (53). However, Obi doesn't recognise this immediately and indeed it takes an act of self-proclaimed 'exegesis' to understand the song of the traders. Obi's alienation from his culture is indicated here by his response: 'he was pleased with his exegesis and began to search his mind for other songs that could be given the same treatment' (53). This treatment becomes an end in itself, rather than the production of meaning to be applied. It extracts the song from its social context and treats it to a New Critical exercise in close reading, such as Obi would have been required to produce in his 1950s British literary education.

Obi's disconnection from the relevance of the poetry of his hometown is further evident in his desire to write Dumasian, revolutionary poetry, as if the ideas were not already spoken in the songs of his people. Yet, the last song of the novel makes quite clear there are lessons of fraternity to be had in Umuofian songs more than equal to Obi's poetic exhortations to national unity (118). Moreover, this last song conveys other, more pointed lessons for Obi in particular: 'He that has a brother must hold him to his heart / For a kinsman cannot be bought in the market, / Neither is a brother bought with money' (146–7). Achebe ends Chapter Thirteen with this song, giving no account of Obi's response to the song's message about the value of family over finance. It is left to the reader to discern its pertinence.

The lessons of the girls' song bring us to the lessons of the Igbo proverbs, which Achebe introduces strategically throughout the novel. These proverbs are significant because their purpose in a social context parallels that of legal precedent in a juridical context. Whether metaphorical or allegorical the proverbs delineate the case to which a particular situation can be subsumed for judgment. Achebe has drawn attention to this similarity himself:

> A proverb is a very careful observation of reality and the world, and then a distillation into the wisdom of an elegant statement . . . there is a whole repertory of these statements made by my people across the millennia. . . . And part of the training, of socialization of young people in this society, is to become familiar with these statements from our immemorial past. So that when we are dealing with a contemporary situation . . . we have the opportunity to draw from the proverbial repertory to support or refute what is said. It's like citing the precedents in law.
>
> (Rowell: 98)

Throughout the novel Obi is held to account and judged in various ways by the Umuofians through the application of proverbs, which act as a framework of social precedent within Umuofia and which the Umuofians take with them into the urban centres such as Lagos. For example, when Obi is about to leave for England and university he is warned: 'Do not be in a hurry to rush into the pleasures of the world like the young antelope who danced herself lame when the main dance was yet to come' (12). Although never made explicit in the novel Obi's choice to read English indicates a rejection of the Umuofian literary tradition of oral proverbs for the European lyrical tradition of letters. This rejection parallels at the cultural level his desire to reject the ways of the older generation at the political level. And just as Obi's desire to be exceptional in government cannot exempt him from temptation or the law, neither can the Anglicisation of his literary culture exempt him from Umuofian proverbial precedent.

A final literary precedent for Obi is that presented in the fiction of Onitsha market literature. Onitsha, the Igbo capital of the Eastern region from which Obi hails, is home to one of the largest markets in Africa. This market was and is famous for its popular fiction and it remains a major site of popular fiction production – writing, publishing, and sales. Onitsha book production and marketing is quite different from the popular market in Europe and North America: books are printed in small quantities often at the author's expense and the author and publisher will frequently be involved in the direct marketing of the volume – to the extent of selling the book door-to-door. The books themselves are written and read with a lesson in mind, for example how to make money or how to avoid heartbreak. Authors may claim in their introduction that the story is their own and that their reason for telling it is to help others avoid their fate or learn their lessons for success. Once more we can relate this back to Lefebvre's idea of the 'encounter': the author has experience of or has imagined a situation that can be characterised as an encounter, in which the protagonist is faced with a set of unprecedented circumstances that require imaginative judgment (for example, the uniqueness of love). The story is told in order to provide the missing precedent by which others can learn to judge (more wisely than the original author/protagonist), through the transformation of their own experience into a recognisable particular. Such narratives become, in fact, more elaborate versions of the proverb, through their construction of precedent.

Common in these publications is the story of star-crossed lovers, where the relationship between boy and girl is opposed by one or both families. Such stories either end happily, with the family or families capitulating to true love, or they end sadly, with the lovers separating and ruing their fate. These latter stories are often presented as warnings to either boys or girls about the dangers of becoming involved with an unsuitable or unapproved suitor. The correlation between such stories and Obi's relationship with Clara is evident. However, once again Obi's interest in European high literature cuts him off from this local repository of fiction from which he might have taken guidance. Instead, ironically, his story becomes, in Achebe's rendering of it, a version of Onitsha literature reconstructed for a different, more European audience.

The correspondence of *No Longer at Ease* to the formula of Onitsha market fiction takes us back to our original question: what case are we to make of Obi given the evidence that Achebe sets before us? However, what the model of Onitsha market fiction makes more apparent is the way in which we as readers become imbricated in the novel and in Obi's story. Achebe acknowledges this point when he explains that literature should 'give us a second handle on reality so that when it becomes necessary to do so, we can turn to art and find a way out' (Rowell: 88). The question that we are left with, in fact, is less one of what case are we to make of Obi, and therefore how are we to judge him? But rather, what case are we to make of our own judgment, how are we to judge that judgment?

In his analysis of Nigeria's Corrupt Practices and Other Related Offences Act (2000), Paul D. Ocheje points out that 'the corruption of public office has arguably existed in Nigeria since the establishment of modern structures of public administration in the country by the British colonial government.' (174, fn.9) Ocheje cites

The Storey Report (1954), which dealt with bribery in Lagos, as well as reports for Port Harcourt (1956) and the Eastern Region of Nigeria (1957), (Ocheje: 174).[7] In *No Longer at Ease*, Achebe dramatises this aspect of the late colonial Nigerian administration in order to call his audience into critical engagement with the problem. Rather than present Obi and his crime as recognisable particulars immediately accessible for judgment, Achebe makes him familiar, even common (in the light of Jenkins' survey), yet just different enough to require a creative response of the kind Lefebvre elucidates. Moreover, he turns our judgment from Obi onto the legal system itself. Achebe offers no ready answer to the question implicitly posed in the novel: how might the newly independent Nigerian administration rid itself of its corruptions, its anachronisms, its lack of self-reflexivity? Instead we are faced with multiple realms of judgment, each requiring the attentiveness that Lefebvre calls for in creative jurisprudence. Achebe presents an archive of precedents – legal, literary, popular, esoteric, fictional and factual – to which he encourages his readers to turn in the encounter of judging judgment at the moment of independence.

Acknowledgements

I would like to thank the Hoover Institution Archives for their assistance to my research; the University of Hong Kong for a grant in support of that research; and Stanford University's Program in Writing and Rhetoric Reading Group for their helpful feedback on an earlier version of this chapter.

Endnotes

1 See, for example, Brown, Bernard, 'The "Ordinary Man" in Provocation: Anglo-Saxon Attitudes and "Unreasonable Non-Englishman"', *International and Comparative Law Quarterly*, 13, Jan. 1964, 203–35.
2 George D. Jenkins Papers, Box 11, Hoover Institution Archives, Stanford University, California.
3 Although not necessarily within the world of African fiction, if we recall Mustafa and the narrator of Tayeb Salih's *Season of Migration to the North* (1966).
4 The Lagosian wily harlot is given far greater complexity, not without her own legal complications, in the fiction of Cyprian Ekwensi; see for example, *Jagua Nana* (1961).
5 *Daily Express*, 12 December 1962, p. 6.
6 See also the narrator and Mustafa in *Season of Migration to the North*, for a further fictional representation of the returnee's unease.
7 See *Commission of Inquiry into the Administration of Lagos Town Council*, 1953 (The Storey Report, Lagos, 1954), *Report of the Commission of Enquiry into the Working of Port Harcourt Town Council*, 1955 (Port Harcourt, 1956), and *Report of the Tribunal Appointed to Inquire into Allegations Reflecting on the Official Conduct of the Premier of, and Certain Persons Holding Ministerial and Other Public Offices in, the Eastern Region of Nigeria*, London, 1957.

Bibliography

Achebe, Chinua. *No Longer at Ease*, (1960), New York: Anchor Books, 1994.

Eliot, T.S., 'Journey of the Magi' (1927), *The Complete Poems and Plays 1909–1950*, London and New York: Harcourt, 1971, pp. 68–9.

Lefebvre, Alexandre. *The Image of the Law: Deleuze, Bergson, Spinoza*, Stanford, CA: Stanford University Press, 2008.

Ocheje, Paul D., 'Law and Social Change: A Socio-Legal Analysis of Nigeria's Corrupt Practices and Other Related Offences Act, 2000', *Journal of African Law*, 45.2, 2001, 173–95.

Rowell, Charles H., 'An Interview With Chinua Achebe', *Callaloo*, 13.1 (Winter, 1990), 86–101.

Part III

Reading literature in a legal frame

Chapter 11

The dramatic imagination and the dream of law

Paul Raffield

Patterns and precedents in Shakespeare and the law

> A reason mighty, strong, and effectual;
> A pattern, precedent, and lively warrant
> For me, most wretched, to perform the like.[1]

Having addressed the emperor Saturninus thus, Titus Andronicus, more sinned against than sinning, slays his raped and mutilated daughter Lavinia. The precedent to which he refers is the story of the centurion Verginius in Livy's *History of Rome*, in which the father stabbed his daughter Verginia with a butcher's knife, in so doing freeing her from enslavement to the decemvir Appius: 'Then he snatched a knife from a butcher, and crying: "There is only one way, my child, to make you free," he stabbed her to the heart' (Livy 1960: 220).[2] Precedent – the source of lawful authority and the historical basis to all legitimate conduct – is a thematic *sine qua non* of Shakespeare's *The Most Lamentable Roman Tragedy of Titus Andronicus*. The play's setting in a fictionalized version of fourth-century Rome serves as an allegorical paradigm for the imperial form of late-Elizabethan monarchic rule.[3] Shakespeare found precedents for the various narrative elements of the play in Livy's *Roman History*, Plutarch's *Lives*, Seneca's *Thyestes*, Virgil's *Aeneid*, and (especially) Ovid's *Metamorphoses*.

The use of the terminology of common law in the above passage from *Titus Andronicus* is striking: not merely 'precedent' and 'warrant', but 'reason'. For those early modern common lawyers contemporaneous with Shakespeare, reason provided the intellectual justification for all municipal laws. The Elizabethan jurist and law reporter Edmund Plowden declared that common law was 'no other than pure and tried reason' (Plowden 1792, vol. 1: 316),[4] while for Sir Edward Coke, the 'fortunes of [the King's] subjects, are not to be decided by natural reason, but by the artificial reason and judgment of law, which law is an act which requires long study and experience' (Coke 1777, vol. 7: 65a).[5] Coke is referring here to the prolonged period of training at the Inns of Court and apprenticeship in the courts at Westminster, a process which Sir John Doderidge described as 'the worke of many yeares, the attaining whereof will waste the greatest part of the verdour and vigour of our youth' (Doderidge 1631: 29). The lawyers found exemplars of reason in the past; sometimes recent, but more often of immemorial origin. Coke recommends the readers of his *Reports* to 'cast thine eye upon the sages of the law, that have been before thee'. He alludes here to the patriarchs of the common law, its judges. The provenance of these judicial archetypes is divine. They have (according to Coke) 'sucked from that divine knowledge, honesty, gravity, and integrity, and by the goodness of God hath obtained a greater blessing and ornament than any other profession to their family and posterity' (Coke 1777, vol. 1: x–xi).[6] Through his systematic (if opinionated) reporting of contemporary cases, and his emphasis on the antiquity of common law and the legitimacy that its immemorial nature conferred on judicial decision-making, Coke elevated the binding power of precedent or *stare decisis* to hitherto unknown levels.[7] Kevin Sharpe makes the important observation that the synthesis between past and present gave to history an exalted status in the governance of early modern English society (Sharpe 1989: 174–81). Taking as my starting point the argument of Jonathan Bate in the Introduction to the Arden edition of the play, that Titus Andronicus is 'a dramatic antecedent to Sir Edward Coke' (Shakespeare 1995: 28), I examine here the overriding importance of precedent to the development of drama and law in the early modern period. In particular, I consider the influence of literary paradigms over the depiction of an idealized juridical state: one that owes its creation as much to the poetic imaginations of lawyers as it does to the juristic representations of dramatists.

Immediately prior to his reference to 'reason mighty' and 'pattern, precedent, and lively warrant', Titus poses Saturninus the question: 'Was it well done of rash Virginius / To slay his daughter with his own right hand, / Because she was enforced, stained and deflowered?' (5.3.36–38) Following Saturninus's affirmative response, Titus asks 'Your reason, mighty lord?' (5.3.39) Of course, reason here means ground, premise, or justification. But use of the word in close proximity to the legal language of precedent and warrants inevitably recalls the sense in which Coke and his fellow common lawyers employ it; in other words, the power by which truth may be distinguished from falsehood, and right from wrong. Indeed the title-page of the First Part of Coke's *Reports* bears the Ciceronian maxim: *Lex ext certa ratio e mente divina manans* ['Law is unerring reason adhering to a divine purpose'].[8] This short sequence in *Titus Andronicus*, no more than nine lines in length, works simultaneously on several different levels. It provides an intellectual counterpoint to the gruesome onstage banquet, at which Saturninus and Tamora devour the remains of Chiron and Demetrius, slain and cooked in a pie by Titus. It objectifies and lends theatrical focus to Lavinia, who at the end of the sequence is unveiled and killed by her father. A less obvious but (given the deliberate use of legal terms) intentional effect is to conflate dramatic dialogue with the agonistic form of juridical procedure. The questioning of Saturninus by Titus on the rectitude of Verginius's action in slaying his daughter replicates the courtroom examination of witness by counsel; in particular it mirrors the oral educational exercise at the Inns of Court of the 'bolt' (from the thirteenth-century, Old-French word 'bulter' meaning to examine and separate) and its more exalted cousin, the moot.[9]

That Shakespeare was familiar with the technical and institutional arcana of the common law and the English legal profession is well-documented.[10] In numerous of his plays – perhaps most notably *Richard II*, *The Merchant of Venice*, *Measure for Measure*, *King Lear* and *The Winter's Tale* – the trial is thrust into the narrative foreground of the action. It is not my intention here to discuss the meta-dramatic significance of these individual courtroom dramas beyond noting the obvious stylistic feature common to all of them, that the adversarial nature of English legal disputation is inherently dramatic and eminently suited to theatrical interpretation, whether in the playhouse or the courtroom. These juridical set-pieces aside, it is fair to say that many of the narratives of Shakespeare's plays are driven by dramatic engagement with the law, and especially by the impact of the law on individual members of the society represented onstage. For example, the frenetic plot of *The Comedy of Errors* is initiated by the sentencing to death of Egeon for the offence of being an enemy alien, in accordance (we are told by the Duke, Solinus) with a decree of the Ephesian parliament: 'It hath in solemn synods been decreed, / Both by the Syracusans and ourselves, / To admit no traffic to our adverse towns'. (1.1.13–15) Similarly, in *A Midsummer Night's Dream*, Hermia's refusal at the start of the play to wed Demetrius in conformity with her father's will is a flagrant breach of the 'sharp Athenian law' (1.1.164) compelling filial obedience, the sentence for which offence is 'either to die the death or to abjure / Forever the society of men.' (1.1.67–68) Hermia and her lover Lysander flee to the wood near Athens, and the comic interaction between mortals and fairies gets underway. We need look no further than *Hamlet* to find evidence of its author's technical knowledge of the idiosyncratic language of English law. '[W]hy may not that be the skull of a lawyer?' asks Hamlet in the graveyard scene:

> Where be his quiddities now, his quillets, his cases, his tenures, and his tricks? Why does he suffer this rude knave now to knock him about the sconce with a dirty shovel, and will not tell him of his action of battery? Hum. This fellow might be in's time a great buyer of land, with his statutes, his recognisances, his fines, his double vouchers, his recoveries.
>
> (5.1.97–104)

In the above passage Shakespeare weaves the jargon of property law and contract law into his protagonist's meditation on mortality. Tenures, statutes, recognizances, fines, recoveries, vouchers, double vouchers; all technical terms, concerned with the acquisition and disposition of land. '[A]nd must the inheritor himself have no more, ha?' (5.1.109–10) asks Hamlet at the end of his interrogation of the putative lawyer's skull. Inheritance of land is an apt metaphor for a system of precedent upon which the authority of the common law rests and upon which Shakespeare and the early modern dramatists depended for their stories. To each new inheritor passes not only the land itself but the history or memory of its owners, with all the stories of their quiddities, quillets, cases, and tricks. In *Shakespeare and Ovid*, Jonathan Bate describes the antique literary texts from which Shakespeare and his contemporaries derived the themes (and sometimes the entire plots) of their plays and poems as '*precedents*, not *sources* . . . a conceptual exemplar, not a reservoir of raw material' (Bate 1993: 84).

Orality, textualization, and hermeneutics

It is noteworthy that two prominent modern commentators on the evolution of the western legal tradition – Ronald Dworkin and Martha Nussbaum – should identify the literary techniques of fiction writers as a salient feature of the common law and its judicial patriarchs. Dworkin employs the image of the chain novel (in which a novel is written by a succession of writers, each one interpreting and adding to the previous chapters) to describe the role of the judge in interpreting and adding to the existing body of law (Dworkin 1986: 228–32). Sir Edward Coke was unconsciously acknowledging the role of the judge as chain novelist when he wrote in the Preface to Part Three of *The Reports*: 'Right profitable also are the ancient books of the common laws yet extant, as Glanvile, Bracton, Britton, Fleta, Ingham, and Novæ Narrationes, and those also of later times, as the old Tenures' (Coke 1777, vol. 2: iv). For Dworkin, rights and duties 'flow from past collective decisions' (Dworkin 1986: 227), and history is central to the project of law because it enables our lawgivers through present practice to 'provide an honorable future' (Dworkin 1986: 228) by reference to the rectitude of these past judgments. At the level of historiography the body of common law may therefore reasonably be described as a collection of stories, linked to each other by their institutional history, and passed down by privileged storytellers or narrators. It is noteworthy in this context that the Latin word with which to describe the Order of Serjeants-at-Law (the medieval and early modern equivalent of Queen's Counsel) is *narratores*: a narrator being one who tells a story; while their counterparts in the ecclesiastical courts were known as *advocati*.[11] The English legal system of the early modern period was derived from an oral tradition; its adversarial juridical procedures were predicated on an agonistic model in which competing *narratores* presented contending stories and were judged on the basis of their persuasive skills.

The parallels with drama are obvious and compelling, not the least being the recording of oral storytelling in textual form. It was in the sixteenth century, as the published Law Reports (especially those of Plowden) replaced the Year Books, and as an independent legal profession was recognized by statute, that standardization and systemization of the common law was established. As William Holdsworth noted, the shift from oral to written pleadings made the salient legal issues immediately apparent, while concentration on the decision of the court (rather than the debate which preceded it) provided a body of rational judgments, which were cited with particularity in subsequent trials and appeals.[12] No longer would law reporters or counsel be impelled to ask judges for the reasons for their decisions, as happened in the 1566 case of *Sharington v Strotton*, in which, judgment having been given against the plaintiff, Plowden records that counsel 'said, may it please your lordship to shew us, for our learning, the causes of your judgment' (Plowden 1792, vol. 1: 309). Subjective reporting of picturesque courtroom incidents was a commonplace in early law reporting, but the sixteenth century witnessed a shift towards rational and more objective reporting of the case; although Plowden occasionally included incidental courtroom occurrences, as in the 1559 case of *Wrotesley v Adams*, in which 'Sir Humphry Brown who was then one of the justices did not argue at all, because he was so old that his senses were decayed, and his voice could not be heard' (Plowden 1792, vol. 1: 190).

Throughout the sixteenth century, the significant advances in printing technology facilitated the unprecedented distribution of published, standardized law reports.[13] Judgment became increasingly a creative task of literary endeavour, in which *interpretatio* or hermeneutics was a central rhetorical skill. With reference to Walt Whitman's 'By Blue Ontario's Shore', Martha Nussbaum cites the 'poet-judge' (Nussbaum 1995: 80) as the embodiment of equitable justice. This 'equable man' is the personification of equity in law.[14] In relation to the expression of juristic ideals in the plays of Shakespeare, I agree with Nussbaum's broad thesis that equity is more to do with the literary imagination than it is with legal norms and judicial reasoning. To write of the equitable principles of common law in early modern England may seem oxymoronic to lawyers and legal historians, to whom Equity and common law were rival (and at times incompatible) jurisdictions. But the statement is entirely consonant with the claims made for English law by juristic commentators of the period, whose understanding of equity was founded in the Aristotelian tradition of *epieikeia* rather than in the judicial pronouncements of the Court of Chancery. When Whitman wrote of the poet that '[h]e is no arguer, he is judgment, (Nature accepts him absolutely,) / He judges not as the judge judges but as the sun falling round a helpless thing' (Whitman 2009: 269), he was prolonging the tradition of an earlier generation of jurists who equated English law with natural moral authority, of immemorial provenance.

Nature and the dreamland of law

In *De Laudibus Legum Angliae*, the late fifteenth-century Lord Chief Justice Sir John Fortescue stated that English law was 'deduced from the *Law of Nature*' (Fortescue 1737: 29);[15] while Sir Edward Coke would later argue not only 'that the law of nature is part of the law of England', but that it was of greater antiquity (and therefore of greater legitimacy) than 'any judicial or municipal law' (Coke 1777, vol. 4: 12b).[16] As Coke acknowledged in the title-page to the First Part of *The Reports*, one of the principal classical progenitors of natural law theory was Cicero, for whom '[t]rue law is right reason in agreement with nature; it is of universal application, unchanging and everlasting' (Cicero 1928: 211).[17] The indivisible correlation of reason and nature is fundamental to the Ciceronian definition of law: the values of law are eternal and immutable. But within that philosophical framework, the juridical application of law is an aesthetic exercise in which (to borrow Coke's phrase) 'artificial reason' dominates and determines both process and outcome. In the classical imagery employed by Nietzsche in *The Birth of Tragedy*, art (which for the purpose of the present analysis I take to include law in its juridical context) 'derives its continuous development from the duality of the *Apolline* and *Dionysiac*' (Nietzsche 2003: 14). In the aesthetic scheme imagined and related by Nietzsche, these two opposing artistic powers 'spring from nature itself' (Nietzsche 2003: 18). The Apolline represents the ordered dreamland of artistic illusion, creating aesthetic artefacts that are based on observation of natural phenomena. These artefacts are usually associated with figurative arts, of which portraiture and sculpture are obvious examples. But the Apolline extends to drama, music and poetry (among other acts of Olympian patronage, Apollo was god of the arts), and indeed to any artistic enterprise which seeks to interpret, contain, and represent mankind's understanding of and his relationship with the natural world. Dionysus on the other hand was the god of wine, the grape, fertility, ecstasy, and excess. He was the god also of theatre, but of a particular type of theatre: Carnival, which celebrated the primeval and the transgressive. This most celebratory form of theatre was an ecstatic representation of an irrepressible atavistic urge. The distinction in carnival between reality and illusion is blurred, the participants inhabiting a liminal zone between life and art. In his comprehensive analysis of the origins and rituals of carnival, *Rabelais and His World*, Mikhail Bakhtin notes the lack of differentiation between actor and audience; unlike the theatre, 'carnival does not know footlights ... [c]arnival is not a spectacle seen by the people; they live in it, and everyone participates because its very idea embraces all the people' (Bakhtin 1984: 7). This is not the ordered dreamland of Apollo; rather, it resembles the drunken realm of Dionysus. Nietzsche depicts the separate art worlds of dreamland and drunkenness as contenders for the hearts and minds of men: the former predicated upon temperance and self-knowledge; the latter upon excess and hubris.

It was with the Apolline dreamland that the English legal institution and the English theatre of the early modern period sought to align themselves, formally distinguishing between participant and spectator, actor and audience, lawyer and subject of law.[18] I refer above to the extraordinary effect of the printing revolution on the production of published law reports in the sixteenth century, but its influence over the development of English jurisprudence extended not only to the standardization of law reporting. F.W. Maitland noted that 'medieval books poured from the press, new books were written' (Maitland 1901: 29), and (he might have added) translations of the great classical works of history, political philosophy, and literature became widely available to an enthusiastic audience.[19] In post-Henrician Tudor England, English law and English theatre rationalized the influence of renaissance humanism in the context of a theocentric English state (although England established its own state religion during this period, I refrain from describing it as a theocracy; temporal and spiritual jurisdictions remained distinct, albeit united by the symbolic persona of the monarch). As

Michel Foucault wrote of the ill-fated Actaeon, whose tragic story is told in Book III of Ovid's *Metamorphoses*, and which is monstrously re-imagined in *Titus Andronicus*: 'in the complicity of the divine with sacrilege, some of the Greek light flashed through the depths of the Christian night' (Foucault 2000, vol. 2: 125).[20]

The fusion of classical (specifically Aristotelian) political philosophy with the tenets of Judaeo-Christian theology was a notable feature of early modern jurisprudence. Even before the Act of Supremacy of 1534 and the establishment of both the Church of England and a sovereign, independent legal system, English jurists were asserting the antiquity of English law (preceding in origin the authority of Roman law) and its derivation from Biblical and classical sources. Hence, in *De Laudibus Legum Angliae*, Fortescue states that '[n]or in short, are the Laws of any Kingdom in the World so venerable for their Antiquity' (Fortescue 1737: 33–4). Fortescue equates the legitimacy of English law with its immemorial origins. He locates the source of its creation in the Judaeo-Christian deity, claiming that '[l]aws which are made by Men, (who for this very End and Purpose receive their Power from GOD) may also be affirmed to be made by GOD' (Fortescue 1737: 5). The claim to divine provenance notwithstanding, Fortescue was adamant that English law is derived simultaneously from the law of nature. He quotes approvingly from Book V of Aristotle's *Nicomachean Ethics* (Fortescue refers to Aristotle throughout as 'the Philosopher') as authority for his claim that the law of nature is the ultimate fount of English law: ' "The Law of Nature is the same, and has the same Force all the World over" ' (Fortescue 1737: 29).

Some 140 years after the publication of *De Laudibus Legum Angliae*, Coke noted the influence of Aristotle over the founding fathers of early modern English law, recording in his report of *Postnati. Calvin's Case* that Bracton, Fortescue, and St German agreed with the Aristotelian proposition that 'God and nature is one to all, and therefore the law of God and nature is one to all' (Coke 1777, vol.4: 12b–13a).[21] In his report of the same case, during discussion of the political sovereignty of James I and the primacy of natural law, it is not therefore surprising that Coke should refer approvingly to Aristotle as 'nature's secretary' (Coke 1777, vol. 4: 12b). The imagery employed by Coke in *The Reports* was invariably drawn from the philosophical, literary and political texts of the ancient world. The mythical Trojan king, Brutus, became for Coke the prototypical author of the ancient constitution: 'Brutus the first King of this land' (Coke 1777, vol. 4: viiia).[22] According to legend, after landing at Totnes in Devon, Brutus had made his way east and founded a new city, Troynovant, on the banks of the Thames.[23] For Fortescue, Coke, and other jurists of the early modern period, Brutus was the father of the Britons, the archetype and icon of English nationhood. Fortescue insists that Brutus had founded *dominium politicum et regale*: he was the originary of constitutional governance: 'For thus the kingdom of England blossomed forth into a political and royal dominion out of Brutus' band of Trojans' (Fortescue 1997: 22).

Coke incorporated Aristotle's principles of justice and natural equity (*epieikeia*), discussed in Book V of *The Nicomachean Ethics*, not only into the Prefaces to *The*

Reports, but into reports of the cases themselves. Given his devotion to Aristotelian political theory it is inevitable that throughout *The Reports* Coke should imply a level of empathy between the reality of English law and the illusion of the ideal state, in which the best interests of the common-weal was the ultimate aim of law. Fortescue had been aware that in the institutional environment of the English legal system the law of nature was subject to interpretation by practitioners trained in the technical skills of municipal law, later to be described by Coke as 'the artificial reason and judgment of law'. In Nietzschean terms, the natural order was synthesized with reference to the symbolic dreamland of Apollo. As Peter Goodrich has noted in connection with the rituals of dining at the early modern Inns of Court, '[t]he lawyer does not merely appear, he descends from an order of symbols' (Goodrich 1991: 248). These symbols are iconic (rather than idolatrous) because of their foundation in the law of nature: they are images of truth, not falsehood. They guide the subject of law to comprehension of the invisible, the intangible, and the infinite. For Fortescue and other early modern jurists, it is the genealogical link with nature which ensures that municipal law remains an inherently ethical enterprise, concerned with the exposition of truth; as opposed to a vacuous, rhetorical construct, whose outstanding characteristics are falsehood and dissimulation. The acquisition by lawyers of rhetorical skills, devoid of any ethical context and perceived to be designed exclusively for the unjust enrichment of their possessors, led to the pejorative and popular representation of lawyers as scavengers and parasites. For example, see the assertion, made by the author of *Light Shining in Buckinghamshire*, that 'Lawyers are as profitable as maggots in meat, and Caterpillers in Cabages, and Wolves amongst Lambs' (Winstanley 1648: 8). The lack of any philosophical, critical or ethical substance in Elizabethan legal education prompted the scholar and poet Abraham Fraunce to claim that the study of common law was 'hard, harsh, unpleasant, unsavoury, rude and barbarous' (Fraunce 1588: q2v), as a consequence of which the lawyers produced were 'so many upstart *Rabulae Forenses*, which under a pretence of Lawe, become altoegather lawless, to the continuall molestation of ignorant men, and generall overcharging of the country' (Fraunce 1588: q4r).[24]

Arguably the clearest indication that the artifice of municipal law is the progeny of a natural source or precedent is given by Fortescue in his extraordinary description of the manner in which knowledge of human laws is acquired. *De Laudibus Legum Angliae* conforms to the style of many scholarly (and specifically juristic) works of the early modern period in that it is written in dialogue form.[25] During the Wars of the Roses, Fortescue, loyal to Henry VI, accompanied the exiled Queen Margaret and her court to France, where (according to *De Laudibus*) he acted as tutor to Edward, Prince of Wales. The book (written *circa* 1468) is a fictionalized account of their relationship, the focus of which is the instruction in the foundations of English law and the English legal profession, given to the Prince by the Lord Chancellor. In the course of 54 short chapters, the Lord Chancellor persuades his student of the excellence of English common law, and in particular of its innate superiority to French civil law. Indeed, chapter XXXV of *De Laudibus* is entitled 'The Inconveniencies in France by Means of the Absolute Regal Government'.

I have noted the influence of Aristotle's theories of justice and natural equity over Fortescue's juristic thought, but of equal importance is the apparent influence of the *Metamorphoses* of Ovid, in which the artificial reason of mankind engages with nature to enact and enable transformation. Fortescue employs a horticultural metaphor in order to describe the process by which the prince will, in due time, acquire full knowledge of the law (Fortescue 1737: 10–11):[26]

> So the Cion of a Pear-Tree grafted on an Apple-Stock, after it has taken, draws the Apple so much into its Nature, that both become a Pear-Tree . . . So you (my Prince) when you shall have practised Justice with Delight and Pleasure, and have, as it were, transcribed the Law, which is the Rule of Justice, into your very Habit and Disposition.

It is noteworthy that Fortescue refers to the act of transcription, of writing down, recording for future generations the rule of justice. He describes a human interpretation of eternal law, which governs the nature of the universe and (according to Blackstone) without compliance with which 'no human laws are of any validity, if contrary to this; and such of them as are valid derive all their force, and all their authority, mediately or immediately, from this original' (Blackstone 1807: 40–41). Fortescue's knowledge of the horticultural technique of grafting almost certainly derived from familiarity with the orchards on his estate in Gloucestershire.[27] The metaphor of the pear-tree scion illustrates the proposition that privileged access to artificial reason transforms the recipient of such knowledge from being a stranger to the common law into a personification of 'the Rule of Justice'. The Chancellor likens the young prince to 'an Apple-Stock', onto which a scion from a pear tree is grafted. The felicitous result is that the two plants are transformed into a single, fruiting tree. The artificial process which enables the transfiguration to occur is legitimated by its derivation from nature. The Ovidian imagery employed by Fortescue is intended to suggest that the fusion of 'nature' (the apple tree) with the artificial reason of law (the grafted pear tree) will transform the host body into a manifestation of law itself.

The relationship between art and nature was of evident fascination to writers of the early modern period. Michel de Montaigne, writing about the indigenous Americans of the New World in Book I of his *Essays*, drew attention to mankind's inclination to pervert nature in order to satisfy effete and 'corrupt tastes'. In 'On the Cannibals', Montaigne states unequivocally that '[i]t is not sensible that artifice should be reverenced more than Nature, our great and powerful Mother' (Montaigne 2003: 232). Others, such as George Puttenham, saw the application of artificial reason as the means whereby the beauty and splendour of the natural environment might be enhanced. Puttenham's meditation on art and nature, contained in *The Arte of English Poesie*, lays great emphasis on the ethical use of art in conjunction with nature, for the ultimate good of the common-weal. Used in an appropriate manner art was a 'surmounter of her [nature's] skill' (Puttenham 1589: 254). Puttenham cites the example of the gardener's art, which acts as an 'aide', 'alterer', and 'surmounter' of nature. He writes of the gardener embellishing nature 'in virtue, shape, odour and taste, that nature of her selfe woulde never have done: so as to make the single gillifloure, or marigold, or daisie, double' (Puttenham 1589: 254). In the context of the present analysis, Puttenham's most interesting observations concern the 'artes and methods both to speake and to perswade and also to dispute', which he later describes as the arts of grammar, logic, and rhetoric. These are not the imitative arts of the painter and carver; but rather, skills which have recourse to pattern, precedent and memory. In Puttenham's words: 'a repetition or reminiscens naturall, reduced into perfection, and made prompt by use and exercise' (Puttenham 1589: 256). In the mouths of early modern English jurists, repetition, reminiscence and reduction represent the distillation of natural custom upon which the foundations of common law rest. The imaginary genealogy of common law, which manifests itself in the various texts, symbols, and rituals of the legal institution – in other words, its institutional memory – bestows legitimacy, but it also establishes an indissoluble link with nature.[28] As Aristotle noted of the imitative arts, 'it is not the pleasantness of the object which produces the pleasure but an inference from the copy to the original and in consequence of it a kind of learning' (Aristotle 1886: 83).[29] Implicit in Aristotle's claim that all true art references a natural originary is the principle that rhetoric 'is the means by which truth and justice maintain and assert their natural superiority to falsehood and injustice' (Aristotle 1886: x).

The argument that I have made for law as an aesthetic form, manifesting itself in an order of signs and intended to capture the imagination of the subject of law, has been advanced by numerous theorists. Within the legal academy, Peter Goodrich has written extensively of the emotive power of the image and its capacity to 'hold the invisible body, the emotional body, the affective subject or soul of those subject to law' (Goodrich 1990: 262). Goodrich acknowledges the influence of the legal historian and psychoanalyst Pierre Legendre, whose work has engaged throughout with the idea that the image is 'the trace of an absent presence' (Legendre 1997: 214). Representing something that is not present, the image is the structure of authority, and it is this structure which captures the subject of law. It may be considered a serious understatement to assert that the meaning of the sign was an obvious point of contention in Reformation Europe. But it needs to be said, if only as a starting point for understanding the debate concerning the role of art in society, which was of evident interest to so many writers of the early modern period.

Shakespeare addressed the issue in one of his late romances, *The Winter's Tale*. It is relevant to my discussion of the legal institution and the artificial dreamland of Apollo that the god of the arts should play a dominant (albeit offstage) role in determining the narrative outcome of the play. Indeed, Apollo is both principal witness and judge in the trial of Hermione for High Treason, on the false charge of committing adultery with Leontes' boyhood friend Polixenes and conspiring with Camillo to murder her husband. It is to the Oracle at Delos (sacred birthplace of Apollo, described in the play as 'Delphos') that Leontes dispatches two of his lords, in order that the guilt or innocence of his wife may be irrefutably established. Divine judgment is duly passed down: 'Hermione is chaste; Polixenes blameless; Camillo a true subject; Leontes a jealous tyrant' (3.2.132–133), to which the bystanders at the trial respond: 'Now blessed be the great Apollo!' (3.2.137)[30] Shakespeare signals the importance of Apollo by continuous reference to the God's absent presence: in the trial scene alone the word 'Apollo' occurs six times. The influence of Apollo is present throughout. The final, magical scene of the play witnesses the confluence of art and life, of the imaginary transformed into reality, as the 'statue' of Hermione is seen to breathe, move, and embrace her penitent husband. In the words of Leontes: 'If this be magic, let it be an art / Lawful as eating.' (5.3.110–111)[31] In the Bohemian scenes of Act 4 we encounter a procession of images relating to the application of artificial reason to the natural world, of which the most notable is probably the sheep-shearing festival of Act 4, scene 4. During that scene a conversation takes place between Polixenes and Perdita, of less than 30 lines, in which the debate concerning nature and artifice is central to the dramatic action. While collecting flowers for festive garlands, Perdita informs Polixenes that she will not use 'streak'd gillyvors' (4.4.82) – gillyflowers – because they are 'nature's bastards' (4.4.83). Her horticultural knowledge is of uncertain provenance and extent, but she tells Polixenes that 'I have heard it said / There is an art which, in their piedness, shares / With great creating nature'. (4.4.86–88) Perdita's principal objection to the gillyflower is that it is the product of mankind's unnatural interference with nature: hence, her use of the adjective 'streak'd', suggesting painting, and the pejorative reference to the 'art' which creates their 'pied' colours. The response of Polixenes to Perdita's rejection of art is noteworthy for its recollection of Fortescue's advice to the Prince on the acquisition of legal knowledge, and specifically his use of the 'grafting' metaphor:[32]

> Yet nature is made better by no mean
> But nature makes that mean: so, over that art,
> Which you say adds to nature, is an art
> That nature makes. You see, sweet maid, we marry
> A gentler scion to the wildest stock,
> And make conceive a bark of baser kind
> By bud of nobler race. This is an art
> Which does mend nature – change it rather – but
> The art itself is nature.
> (4.4.89–97)

In other words, the art of hybridization and grafting derives from nature and is used for the benefit and enjoyment of all; therefore it is a legitimate use to which human reason may be put. Whether or not Shakespeare had read Plowden's report of *Sharington v Strotton* is not known. The case illustrates the relevance to substantive law of the contemporary debate surrounding art, nature, and grafting. It concerned the validity of a 'use' or trust made by one brother in favour of another, and the beneficiary's contested equitable right to profit from land which was the subject of the disputed use. The defendant claimed that consideration for the creation of the use was provided by the natural love and affection owed by one brother to another. Plowden argued that 'those who descend from one same parentage, and are joined nearest in blood, are by nature joined in love' (Plowden 1792, vol. 1: 306).[33] Judgment in King's Bench was given against the plaintiff, Catlyn CJ declaring that 'the brotherly love which he bore to his brothers, are sufficient consideration to raise the uses in the land' (Plowden 1792, vol. 1: 309). An artificial construct (a trust or use created by one brother in favour of another) is legitimated by its natural foundation in the love owed one brother to another, by virtue of their shared genealogy.

Conclusion

For common lawyers such as Fortescue, Plowden and Coke, the existence of community was a prerequisite for the creation of justice. Conversely, the nonexistence of community prefigured the absence of justice.[34] Returning to Shakespeare, it is apparent that the public performance of late-Elizabethan poetic drama operated at one level as a political event in which a communal relationship between audience and actors was engendered, and participation in a political process of sorts was enabled. Shakespeare's poetic drama is concerned not only with the telling of stories through dialogue; it is concerned also with the dialogue of human ideas, of which dramatic text is only a part. As Shelley argued in his essay, *A Defence of Poetry*: 'The drama, so long as it continues to express poetry, is a prismatic and many-sided mirror, which collects the brightest rays of human nature and divides and reproduces them from the simplicity of their elementary forms' (Shelley 1931: 83–4). It is noteworthy that Shelley should emphasize the importance of a poetic presence in order that drama may enable the transformative process of which he speaks, whereby characters and actions become multifaceted and multidimensional. It is to a political and ethical intent that he appeals in asserting the correlation between poetry and drama, as he reveals later in the same essay: 'the connection of poetry and social good is more observable in the drama than in whatever other form' (Shelley 1931: 85). Shelley describes an ideal coalescence of form and content, whereby the ethic is subsumed by the aesthetic and the two become indivisible. It is because of their participation in the eternal and the infinite, and their understanding and expression of humanity, that poets are described by Shelley as 'the institutors of laws, and the founders of civil society' (Shelley 1931: 71).

Endnotes

1 *Titus Andronicus* (5.3.42–44); all references to the text of *Titus Andronicus* are from the 1995 Arden Shakespeare edition.

2 Bk III.XLVIII.
 3 On *Titus Andronicus* as an allegorized criticism of the late-Elizabethan state, see Raffield 2010: 18–50.
 4 *The Case of Mines* (1568); on *The Case of Mines* and *Hamlet*, see Sale 2008.
 5 *Prohibitions del Roy*, 12 *Reports* (1655).
 6 Preface, 2 *Reports* (1602).
 7 *Stare decisis et non quieta movere* ['Stand by that which has been decided and do not disturb that which has been settled'].
 8 On Coke and the Ciceronian interpretation of law as reason, see Raffield 2005.
 9 On the oral exercises at the early modern Inns of Court, see Raffield 2004: 20–42.
10 See Zurcher 2010.
11 See Dugdale 1666: 110; Brand 1992: 48, 94.
12 See Holdsworth 1924, vol. 5: 371–3.
13 On the early modern revolution in printing technology, see Eisenstein 1979.
14 'Of these States the poet is the equable man' (Whitman 2009: 269).
15 On the universal authority of the law of nature, see Aristotle 2004: 130; Bk. V.VII.1134b18–20.
16 *Postnati. Calvin's Case*, 7 *Reports* (1608).
17 Bk III.XXII; see text to n. 8, above.
18 See Raffield 1997: 163–88.
19 Thomas North's translation of Plutarch's *Lives*, published in 1579, provided Shakespeare with a basis for the character of Theseus in *A Midsummer Night's Dream*; in the interlude of 'Pyramus and Thisbe' Shakespeare parodies the verse style of Arthur Golding, whose translation into English of Ovid's *Metamorphoses* was published in 1567.
20 In *Titus Andronicus*, the death while hunting of Bassianus is a distorted image of the death of Actaeon, and is presaged by Tamora's lines: 'Had I the power that some say Dian had, / Thy temples should be planted presently / With horns, as was Actaeon's, and the hounds / Should drive upon thy new-transformed limbs' (2.2.61–64).
21 *Postnati. Calvin's Case*, 7 *Reports* (1608).
22 Preface, 3 *Reports* (1602).
23 The tale of Brutus was recorded by Geoffrey of Monmouth in 1136 (Geoffrey of Monmouth 1966: 53–74).
24 For a discussion of Fraunce and the 'failure' of common law, see Goodrich 1990: 15–52.
25 Exemplary of the form is St German's *Dialogues Between a Doctor of Divinity and a Student in the Laws of England* (1528) and Hobbes's *A Dialogue between a Philosopher and a Student of the Common Laws of England* (1666).
26 The quotation attributed by Fortescue to 'the Philosopher' Aristotle is from *The Nicomachean Ethics*: '[I]t is easier to alter one's habits than one's nature. In fact even habit is hard to change, because it is a sort of second nature' (Aristotle 2004: 190), Bk VII.X.1152a30.
27 Fortescue's home was in the Gloucestershire village of Ebrington (Fortescue 1737: xlviii); at his home in Gloucestershire, Shakespeare's Justice Shallow invites Falstaff to 'see my orchard, where, in an arbour, we will eat a last year's pippin of mine own graffing' (*Henry IV, Part 2*, 5.3.1–2). For the argument that Fortescue may have provided a source or precedent for Shallow and the Gloucestershire scenes in *Henry IV, Part 2*, see Raffield 2010: 159–62.
28 Goodrich argues that 'The originary is invariably hieroglyphic, it exists only in the trace or vestige, the ruin of a present form' (Goodrich 1991: 247).
29 Bk I.XI.
30 All references to the text of *The Winter's Tale* are from the 1963 Arden Shakespeare edition.
31 On art and ethics in *The Winter's Tale*, see Knapp 2004.

32 The subject of grafting trees was popular with Elizabethan writers: see for example, Anonymous 1594; Mascall 1575.
33 *Sharington v Strotton* is discussed in 'Origins of the "Doctrine" of Consideration, 1535–1585' in Baker 1986: 376–7.
34 On the indivisibility of friendship, justice and community, see Aristotle 2004: 200–201; Bk VIII.I.1155a1–32.

Bibliography

Anonymous (1594) *The Orchard, and the Garden Containing Certaine Necessarie, Secret, and Ordinarie Knowledges in Grafting and Gardening*, London: Adam Islip.
Aristotle (1886) *The Rhetoric*, trans. J.E.C. Welldon, London: Macmillan.
Aristotle (2004) *The Nicomachean Ethics*, trans. J.A.K. Thomson, London: Penguin.
Baker, J.H. (1986) *The Legal Profession and the Common Law: Historical Essays*, London, Hambledon.
Bakhtin, M. (1984) *Rabelais and His World*, trans. H. Iswolsky, Bloomington: Indiana University Press.
Bate, J. (1993) *Shakespeare and Ovid*, Oxford: Clarendon.
Blackstone, W. (1807) *Commentaries on the Laws of England*, Portland: Thomas B. Wait & Co.
Brand, P. (1992) *The Origins of the English Legal Profession*, Oxford: Blackwell.
Cicero, M.T. (1928) *The Republic*, trans. C.W. Keyes, Cambridge, MA: Harvard University Press.
Coke, E. (1777) *The Reports of Sir Edward Coke, Knt. In English*, G. Wilson (ed), 7 vols, London: Rivington.
Doderidge, J. (1631) *The English Lawyer: Describing a Method for the managing of the Lawes of this Land*, London: I. More.
Dugdale, W. (1666) *Origines Juridiciales or Historical Memorials of the English Laws*, London: F. & T. Warren.
Dworkin, R. (1986) *Law's Empire*, London: Fontana.
Eisenstein, E.L. (1979) *The Printing Press as an Agent of Change: Communications and Cultural Transformations in Early-Modern Europe*, 2 vols, Cambridge: Cambridge University Press.
Fortescue, J. (1737) *De Laudibus Legum Angliae*, J. Selden (ed.), London: R. Gosling.
Fortescue, J. (1997) *On the Laws and Governance of England*, S. Lockwood (ed.), Cambridge: Cambridge University Press.
Foucault, M. (2000) *Aesthetics: Essential Works of Foucault, 1954–1984*, J.D. Faubion (ed.), 3 vols, London: Penguin.
Fraunce, A. (1588) *The Lawiers Logike, exemplifying the precepts of Logike by the practise of the common Lawe*, London: T. Gubbin and T. Newman.
Geoffrey of Monmouth (1966) *The History of the Kings of Britain*, trans. L. Thorpe, London: Penguin.
Golding, A. (1567) *The. xv. bookes of P. Ovidius Naso, entytuled Metamorphosis, translated oute of Latin into English meeter, by Arthur Golding Gentleman, a worke very pleasuant and delectable*, London: Willyam Seres.
Goodrich, P. (1990) *Languages of Law: From Logics of Memory to Nomadic Masks*, London: Weidenfeld and Nicolson.
Goodrich, P. (1991) 'Eating Law: Commons, Common Land, Common Law', *The Journal of Legal History*, 12: 246–67.

Hobbes, T. (1971) *A Dialogue between a Philosopher and a Student of the Common Laws of England*, J. Cropsey (ed.), London: University of Chicago Press.
Holdsworth, W.S. (1924) *A History of English Law*, 17 vols, London: Methuen.
Knapp, J.A. (2004) 'Visual and Ethical Truth in *The Winter's Tale*', *Shakespeare Quarterly*, 55: 253–78.
Legendre, P. (1997) *Law and the Unconscious: a Legendre Reader*, trans. P. Goodrich, with A. Pottage and A. Schütz, P. Goodrich (ed.), Basingstoke: Macmillan.
Livy (1960) *The Early History of Rome*, trans. A. de Selincourt, Harmondsworth: Penguin.
Maitland, F.W. (1901) *English Law and the Renaissance*, Cambridge: Cambridge University Press.
Mascall, L. (1575) *A Booke of the Arte and Maner How to Plant and Graffe All Sortes of Trees*, London: Iohn Wight.
Montaigne, M. de (2003) *The Complete Essays*, trans. M.A. Screech (ed.), London, Penguin.
Nietzsche, F. (2003) *The Birth of Tragedy*, trans. S. Whiteside, M. Tanner (ed.), London: Penguin.
North, T. (1579) *The lives of the noble Grecians and Romanes, compared together by that grave learned philosopher and historiographer, Plutarke of Chaeronea*, London: Thomas Vautroullier.
Nussbaum, M. (1995) *Poetic Justice: the Literary Imagination and Public Life*, Boston, MA: Beacon Press.
Plowden, E. (1792) *The Commentaries or Reports of Edmund Plowden*, 2 vols, Dublin: H. Watts.
Puttenham, G. (1589) *The Arte of English Poesie*, London: Richard Field.
Raffield, P. (1997) 'The Separate Art Worlds of Dreamland and Drunkenness: Elizabethan revels at the Inns of Court', *Law and Critique*, 8: 163–88.
Raffield, P. (2004) *Images and Cultures of Law in Early Modern England: Justice and Political Power, 1558–1660*, Cambridge: Cambridge University Press.
Raffield, P. (2005) 'Contract, Classicism, and the Common-weal: Coke's *Reports* and the Foundations of the Modern English Constitution', *Law & Literature*, 17: 69–96.
Raffield, P. (2010) *Shakespeare's Imaginary Constitution: Late-Elizabethan Politics and the Theatre of Law*, Oxford: Hart Publishing.
St. German, C. (1874) *Dialogues Between a Doctor of Divinity and a Student in the Laws of England*, W. Muchall (ed.), Cincinnati, OH: Robert Clarke.
Sale, C. (2008) ' "The King is a Thing": the King's Prerogative and the Treasure of the Realm in Plowden's Report of the Case of Mines and Shakespeare's *Hamlet*', in P. Raffield and G. Watt (eds) *Shakespeare and the Law*. Oxford: Hart.
Shakespeare, W. (1963) *The Winter's Tale*, J.H.P. Pafford (ed.), London: Arden Shakespeare.
Shakespeare, W. (1995) *Titus Andronicus*, J. Bate (ed.), London: Arden Shakespeare.
Sharpe, K. (1989) *Politics and Ideas in Early Stuart England*, London: Pinter Publishing.
Shelley, P.B. (1931) *A Defence of Poetry*, in H.A. Needham (ed.), *Sidney, An Apology For Poetry; Shelley, A Defence of Poetry*, London: Ginn & Co.
Whitman, W. (2009) *Leaves of Grass*, J. Loving (ed.), Oxford: Oxford University Press.
Winstanley, G. (1648) *Light Shining in Buckinghamshire*, Thomason Tracts: British Library, E. 475[11].
Zurcher, A. (2010) *Shakespeare and Law*, London: Arden Shakespeare.

Chapter 12

The intellectual – *Hamlet*[1]

Kenji Yoshino

Intellectuals may rejoice that the most canonical text of western imaginative literature figures one of our tribe as its protagonist. Prince Hamlet is undeniably an intellectual, a student at the University of Wittenberg whose "inky cloak" (1.2.77) swaddles him not just in melancholy but in "[w]ords, words, words" (2.2.189). At the same time, we may be justifiably concerned that many believe Hamlet's intellectualism hobbles him from doing justice.

The central question of *Hamlet* is why the prince takes so long to avenge his father's murder. Psychoanalysts, literary critics, and philosophers have all offered their answers, many of which reflect their general explanations for procrastination. Following suit as a legal scholar, I contend that Hamlet's delay arises from an intellectual commitment to perfect justice. Faced with a terrible injustice, he is forced to correct it himself because, as in *Titus Andronicus*, his adversary controls the state. Hamlet certainly has the ingenuity to correct that injustice immediately. However, he bides his time because he wishes to secure not only justice but poetic justice. With respect to Claudius, he arguably attains that perfect justice. But he inflicts so much collateral damage in the process that his actions are ultimately unjustifiable.

Hamlet shows why those committed to social justice often feel ambivalence towards intellectuals. On the one hand, the critical distance that intellectuals have from the world allows us to imagine idealized forms of justice. On the other hand, when we cling too tightly to those ideals, we dissociate from reality. Hamlet adds another layer to the lesson of *Macbeth*. It is not just that poetic justice does not naturally come into being. It is also that, when human beings are perfectionists about justice, we risk doing immense harm.

Hamlet builds on a revenge tragedy composed by the Dane Saxo Grammaticus in the thirteenth century, reworked by the French author François de Belleforest in 1570, and reproduced yet again for the English stage by an unknown author (possibly Shakespeare) in the lost *Ur-Hamlet* of the 1590s. Shakespeare's rendition begins with Prince Hamlet of Denmark mourning the loss of his illustrious father, also named Hamlet. King Hamlet allegedly died after being stung by a serpent while sleeping in his garden. To make matters worse, Prince Hamlet's uncle, Claudius, married Queen Gertrude less than two months after Hamlet Sr.'s death.

In doing so, Claudius took the crown that should have descended to Hamlet. Early in the play, a ghost resembling Hamlet's father appears to Hamlet and his friend Horatio. Declaring that Claudius has murdered him, the ghost enjoins Prince Hamlet to avenge his death.

While Hamlet initially agrees to do so, he comes to doubt whether the ghost is truly his father's spirit, or a devil sent to tempt him. He decides to stage a play reenacting the murder (the famous play-within-the-play titled *The Mousetrap*) to gauge Claudius's response. When Claudius reacts with consternation, Hamlet is satisfied of his guilt. Hamlet's next opportunity for revenge, however, occurs when Claudius is praying alone in his chapel. Hamlet does not kill Claudius because he believes that if Claudius is killed while praying for forgiveness, his soul will mount directly to heaven. During a later conversation with his mother, Hamlet becomes aware that someone is eavesdropping on them behind an arras, or tapestry. The prince draws his sword and kills the counselor Polonius in the belief he is the king.

Realizing the threat that Hamlet poses to him, Claudius sends him to England in the custody of two of the prince's childhood companions, Rosencrantz and Guildenstern, with a letter secretly ordering his death. Hamlet rewrites the letter to require the execution of his two erstwhile friends. He then returns to Denmark, where Ophelia, who is Polonius's daughter and Hamlet's former lover, has gone mad with grief and committed suicide. Ophelia's brother Laertes begins an uprising against Claudius, but Claudius successfully redirects Laertes's fury toward Hamlet. The youth challenges Hamlet to a fencing match. Though purportedly just an athletic contest, the duel has been arranged by Claudius and Laertes with murderous intent. Claudius has poisoned Hamlet's drink, and Laertes has envenomed the tip of his foil.

During the fencing match, Gertrude dies after she drinks from the cup meant for her son. Laertes and Hamlet mortally wound each other with the poisoned rapier, which changes hands during the match. On the brink of death, Hamlet finally kills Claudius. Word arrives from England that Rosencrantz and Guildenstern have been executed according to Hamlet's plan. Horatio wishes to follow the dying Hamlet by committing suicide, but Hamlet asks him instead to live and tell his story. Fortinbras, the prince of Norway, takes over the kingdom, restoring order at the cost of Denmark's independence.

The core question of the play is why Hamlet delays his revenge. As literary critic A. C. Bradley states, "But why in the world did not Hamlet obey the ghost at once, and so save seven of those eight lives?" (Bradley 2005: 69). (The seven lives, in order of demise, belong to Polonius, Ophelia, Rosencrantz, Guildenstern, Gertrude, Laertes, and Hamlet.) The psychoanalyst Ernest Jones called the mystery of Hamlet's delay "the Sphinx of modern Literature" (Jones 1976: 22).

Many have tried to solve the riddle. Freud believes Hamlet's delay derives from an Oedipus complex: "Hamlet is able to do anything—except take vengeance on the man who did away with his father and took that father's place with his mother, the man who shows him the repressed wishes of his own childhood realized"

(Freud 1955: 265). Goethe deems Hamlet too delicate: "a lovely, pure and most moral nature, without the strength of nerve which forms a hero, sinks beneath a burden which it cannot bear and must not cast away" (Goethe 1824: 75). Nietzsche takes him for a nihilist: "In this sense the Dionysian man may be said to resemble Hamlet: both have for once seen into the true nature of things,—they have *perceived*, but they are loath to act; for their action cannot change the eternal nature of things" (Nietzsche 2007: 41).

As Marjorie Garber observes, critics have a powerful identification with Hamlet (I assume this is because critics are themselves intellectuals) (Garber 2008: 201). Because we see ourselves in him, we see his reasons for delay as our own: Freud sees Oedipus, Goethe sees his own sorrowful Werther, and Nietzsche sees his Dionysian man. I see no reason to depart from these great predecessors in proposing an explanation inflected by my own professional background. So I contend that Hamlet's delay can best be explained by his pursuit of perfect justice. I do not think Hamlet delays because he is sexually conflicted, weak, or nihilistic. I think he defers his revenge because he wants it to be perfect. This explanation justifies his delays without justifying the ends they serve.

My initial point is that there is not one delay, but two. They occur during what a modern trial lawyer might call the "guilt" and "sentencing" phases of the play's action. First, Hamlet delays because he is uncertain of Claudius's guilt. This is a period of approximately two months between the ghost's appearance and the performance of the play-within-the-play. Only after *The Mousetrap* does Hamlet become convinced of Claudius's guilt. The second delay is more brief and more consequential. It is the delay in which Hamlet forgoes the chance to kill Claudius while Claudius is praying in the chapel. Both delays can be explained by Hamlet's desire for perfect justice.

Everything begins with the ghost. Stephen Greenblatt notes, "[t]he ghost in *Hamlet* is like none other—not only in Shakespeare but in any literary or historical text . . . It does not have very many lines—it appears in three scenes and speaks only in two—but it is amazingly disturbing and vivid" (Greenblatt 2001: 4). These qualities are in sharp evidence during the ghost's first speech to Hamlet.

> I am thy father's spirit,
> Doomed for a certain term to walk the night
> And for the day confined to fast in fires
> Till the foul crimes done in my days of nature
> Are burnt and purged away. But that I am forbid
> To tell the secrets of my prison-house
> I could a tale unfold whose lightest word
> Would harrow up thy soul, freeze thy young blood,
> Make thy two eyes like stars start from their spheres,
> Thy knotted and combined locks to part
> And each particular hair to stand on end
> Like quills upon the fearful porpentine—

> But this eternal blazon must not be
> To ears of flesh and blood.
> (1.5.9–22)

The ghost is in purgatory, the place where his "foul crimes" are "purged away" so he can enter heaven. The spirit says his torments are horrible, and we believe him in part because he describes them as indescribable.

The ghost is not just the object of punishment, but its agent. The ghost's imperative is often summarized as follows: "If thou didst ever thy dear father love . . . Revenge his foul and most unnatural murder!" (1.5.23, 25). Yet the ghost's commandment is a good deal more specific. The ghost gives a meticulous description of both the crime and the proposed punishment:

> Sleeping within my orchard—
> My custom always of the afternoon—
> Upon my secure hour they uncle stole
> With juice of cursed hebona in a vial
> And in the porches of my ears did pour
> The leperous distilment whose effect
> Holds such an enmity with blood of man
> That swift as quicksilver it courses through
> The natural gates and alleys of the body
> And with a sudden vigour it doth possess
> And curd like eager droppings into milk
> The thin and wholesome blood. So did it mine
> And a most instant tetter barked about
> Most lazar-like with vile and loathsome crust
> All my smooth body.
> Thus was I sleeping by a brother's hand
> Of life, of crown, of queen at once dispatched,
> Cut off even in the blossoms of my sin,
> Unhouseled, disappointed, unaneled,
> No reckoning made but sent to my account
> With all my imperfections on my head.
> O horrible, O horrible, most horrible!
> If thou hast nature in thee bear it not,
> Let not the royal bed of Denmark be
> A couch for luxury and damned incest.
> But howsomever thou pursues this act
> Taint not thy mind nor let thy soul contrive
> Against thy mother aught; leave her to heaven
> And to those thorns that in her bosom lodge
> To prick and sting her. Fare thee well at once:
> The glow-worm shows the matin to be near

> And 'gins to pale his uneffectual fire.
> Adieu, adieu, adieu, remember me.
> (1.5.59–91)

On this account, Claudius poured poison into Hamlet Sr.'s ears, curdling his blood. The ghost's tale, poured into our ears, is likewise bloodcurdling. The horror begins with the description of the poison's physical effect: how "swift as quicksilver" the "leperous distilment" moved through "[t]he natural gates and alleys of the body." The conflation of the sovereign body and the body politic, made frequently in Shakespeare, arises here in the comparison of valves and veins with "gates and alleys." The sovereign has been poisoned—we now know why "[s]omething is rotten in the state of Denmark" (1.4.90). Yet the physiological effects of the murder are as nothing compared to the religious ones. The ghost decries how he was "[c]ut off even in the blossoms of my sin, / Unhouseled, disappointed, unaneled." Deprived of last rites, he is sent to final judgment "[w]ith all [his] imperfections on [his] head." The descriptions of physical and religious corruption merge. The body morphs into a disgusting object, as if the king's sins were surfacing—"a most instant tetter barked about / Most lazar-like with vile and loathsome crust / All my smooth body."

Three instructions follow. First, "Let not the royal bed of Denmark be / A couch for luxury and damned incest." Prince Hamlet must kill Claudius. Second, "howsomever [he] pursues this act," Hamlet must not "contrive / Against [his] mother." Finally, he must remember his father: "Adieu, adieu, adieu, remember me." Hamlet immediately agrees to the ghost's commands—he asks to be emptied out and made into a pure instrument of revenge.

Upon cooler consideration, however, Hamlet's shock cedes to skepticism, resulting in the first delay. This skepticism is justified, especially in historical context. Ghosts were widely seen as instruments used by the devil to lure the virtuous to perdition. Sir Thomas Browne wrote in *Religio Medici* (1643) that those "apparitions and ghosts of departed persons are not the wandering souls of men, but the unquiet walks of Devils, prompting and suggesting us unto mischief, blood and villainy" (Browne 1951: 43). More specifically, as students from Wittenberg, known in Shakespeare's time as Martin Luther's bastion of Protestantism, both Horatio and Hamlet would presumably have doubts about a ghost returning from Catholic purgatory. Horatio warns Hamlet that the ghost may intend to "draw [him] into madness" (1.4.74). Even in his preliminary agreement to the ghost's commands, Hamlet ponders where to place him: "O all of you host of heaven . . . And shall I couple hell?" (1.5.92–93). On reflection, he begins to take the latter possibility seriously: "The spirit that I have seen / May be a de'il, and the de'il hath power / T'assume a pleasing shape" (2.2.533–535).

Hamlet's doubts about the ghost may be heightened by Claudius's outward respectability. At this point, we, like Hamlet, are not certain that Claudius has murdered Hamlet Sr. The consummate politician, Claudius has allied himself solidly with the law on as many counts as possible. Before we even meet Claudius,

Horatio observes that Hamlet Sr. and Fortinbras Sr. fought over some land. When Hamlet Sr. won that duel, land belonging to Fortinbras Sr. passed to Hamlet Sr. through "a sealed compact / Well ratified by law and heraldry" (1.1.85–86). However, Fortinbras's son now seeks to reclaim that land, having "[s]harked up a list of lawless resolutes" (1.1.97) to help him. Part of the fault lies with the new Norwegian king, who has exercised inadequate supervision over Prince Fortinbras. In Norway, as in Denmark, the crown has moved from the original king to his brother, rather than to the king's son. The unnamed King of Norway is thus Claudius's foil in this play.

Claudius outshines his counterpart, making a plausible case that he is a savvy and competent monarch. He observes that Fortinbras is seeking to reclaim "lands / Lost by his father with all bands of law / To our most valiant brother. So much for him" (1.2.23–25). He dismisses the legitimacy of Fortinbras's claim with the abruptness that a lawless claim deserves. He also intuits that the bedridden King of Norway does not know of Fortinbras's plan, and sends messengers to the invalid king, telling the messengers that they have no more scope than certain "delated articles allow" (1.2.38). The sense that gradually arises from this scene is that Claudius is an effective king. Confronted with Fortinbras's attempts to challenge the law, he does not overreact. He sends messengers to alert the King of Norway that his nephew is acting outside the law, and informs the messengers that they must not do so themselves.

Of course, Hamlet has plenty to criticize about Claudius, including his "overhasty" and "incestuous" marriage to Gertrude. Yet the speed of the marriage may also be explicable in legal terms. As legal scholar J. Anthony Burton has pointed out, Gertrude had legal reasons for her "wicked speed." Under the prevailing law, a widow was given a dower, a one-third interest in the real property of her deceased husband. She would hold this share until her death, at which point it would descend to her male heir. To give her time to settle on her third, she was given a "quarantine," a forty-day period in which she could remain on her husband's estate. Applying early modern English law, Hamlet should have inherited two-thirds of his father's land when Hamlet Sr. died. But if Gertrude married during this forty-day period, she could have made a more plausible claim to keep all her lands jointly with her new husband (Burton 2001: 71–82).

The question is whether Gertrude married during the crucial forty-day period. According to Hamlet, she did. Hamlet first complains that Gertrude married when his father was "[b]ut two months dead" (1.1.138). Yet he immediately corrects himself: "nay not so much, not two" (1.2.138). He later insists three times on how less than one month has elapsed between Hamlet Sr.'s death and Gertrude's remarriage, observing that it occurred "within a month" (1.2.145), "[a] little month" (1.2.147), and, again, "[w]ithin a month" (1.2.153). If Gertrude remarried within a month, she did so within her period of quarantine.

Of course, Claudius may have used the law for the nefarious purpose of disinheriting Hamlet. But Claudius seems genuinely to love Gertrude, saying to Laertes that she is "conjunct to my life and soul" (4.7.15). Mischievous scholars like to point out that Claudius and Gertrude represent one of the few happy marriages in Shakespeare. Given that Claudius and Gertrude are in love, it is plausible that they would marry. Once they decided to marry, it also made sense for them to marry speedily to quiet any uncertainty about Claudius's title to Denmark's throne and lands. The elimination of this uncertainty was not just in Claudius's interest, but in Denmark's. As is repeatedly emphasized in the play, the sovereign cannot act like a private individual. As Rosencrantz observes: "Never alone / Did the king sigh but with a general groan" (3.3.22–23).

A decent king in Claudius's position would recognize the effects of his hasty marriage on Hamlet. Claudius repeatedly does so. His first address to Hamlet is "my cousin Hamlet, and my son" (1.2.64). Soon thereafter, he makes an unambiguous public declaration of Hamlet's status as heir apparent: "let the world take note / You are the most immediate to our throne" (1.2.108–109). When Hamlet says to Rosencrantz: "Sir, I lack advancement" (3.2.331), Rosencrantz asks incredulously: "How can that be, when you have the voice of the King himself for your succession in Denmark?" (3.2.332–334).

Hamlet's other charges—that a brother who marries his dead brother's widow commits incest—is harder for Claudius to evade. In Shakespeare's time, this charge was topical. King Henry VIII had married his older brother Arthur's widow, Catherine of Aragon. Under prevailing ecclesiastical law, such marriages were broadly prohibited as incestuous (Kelly 1976: 276). As it states in Leviticus, "Thou shalt not uncover the nakedness of thy brother's wife: it is thy brother's nakedness." And further, "if a man shall take his brother's wife, it is an unclean thing: he hath uncovered his brother's nakedness; they shall be childless." However, Deuteronomy states an exception to this rule: "If brethren dwell together, and one of them die, and have no child, the wife of the dead shall not marry without unto a stranger: her husband's brother shall go in unto her, and take her to him to wife." Because Arthur and Catherine had no children, Henry easily acquired permission from Pope Julius II to employ the Deuteronomy exception to the Leviticus rule. Henry could argue that he was not only permitted but obligated to marry his brother's widow under what the Mosaic law termed "levirate marriage."

To be sure, Claudius's case is easily distinguishable from Henry VIII's. Claudius's brother has left a son, namely Hamlet. Claudius cannot avail himself of the exception in Deuteronomy. Indeed, legal scholar Jason Rosenblatt has argued that Claudius's attempt to fob off his marriage as legitimate contributes to Hamlet's depression because it negates Hamlet's existence (Rosenblatt 1978: 349–64).

It does not follow, however, that Claudius has gone beyond the pale of legality. Hamlet insists four times in the play that the relationship between Claudius and Gertrude is "incestuous." Even in the biblical prohibitions, however, incest between individuals related directly by blood was distinguished from incest between individuals who were related only through marriage. Claudius may simply have been willing to violate this prohibition and suffer its consequences. Those consequences were either literal childlessness (if one took Deuteronomy at its word) or figurative childlessness (because the normal punishment for incest included the bastardization and disinheritance of children who were a product of it). Claudius certainly seems reconciled to childlessness, because Gertrude is probably beyond childbearing years. He also readily embraces Hamlet as his son and heir. So the charges of "incest," while technically true, may be overblown in the play.

Given Claudius's seeming adherence to the law and the ghost's dubious provenance, Hamlet has something less than perfect proof of Claudius's guilt. Hamlet is self-aware enough to know this. He worries that the devil is taking advantage of him through the ghost: "Yea, and perhaps / Out of my weakness and my melancholy, / As he is very potent with such spirits, / Abuses me to damn me!" (2.2.535–538). This skepticism is indeed characteristic of Hamlet, and of intellectuals. It is an old saw in Shakespearean criticism that if Othello and Hamlet had switched plays, neither would have been a tragedy. Hamlet, the man of thought, would have seen through Iago. Othello, the man of action, would have killed Claudius in Act I. Literary critic Maynard Mack contends, "Othello in Hamlet's position, we sometimes say, would have [had] no problem" (Mack 1993: 107). Yet this insight is hardly an indictment of Hamlet. In his own play, Othello's temperament leads him to trust a human devil and kill an innocent.

Rather than relying on the ghost, Hamlet looks for an alternative means to determine Claudius's guilt. This takes time, but only because the means have not materialized. When traveling actors arrive at the palace, Hamlet swiftly realizes that they offer the solution:

> Hum, I have heard
> That guilty creatures sitting at a play
> Have by the very cunning of the scene
> Been struck so to the soul that presently
> They have proclaimed their malefactions
> For murder, though it have no tongue, will speak
> With most miraculous organ. I'll have these players
> Play something like the murder of my father
> Before mine uncle. I'll observe his looks,
> I'll tent him to the quick. If 'a do blench
> I know my course.
> (2.2.523–533)

Hamlet's uncertainty about the ghost is reflected in his claim that murder has "no tongue." (What is the ghost if not the tongue of murder?) In constructing his alternative test of Claudius's guilt, Hamlet cures the deficiencies of the ghost's testimony. Instead of trafficking in the supernatural, the play will appeal to natural human psychology. In lieu of relying on a private exchange, the play will be staged. Hamlet seeks a *de facto* public confession from Claudius: "The play's the thing / Wherein I'll catch the conscience of the King" (2.2.539–540).

In Hamlet's view, *The Mousetrap* is a resounding success. Hamlet scrutinizes Claudius to see if he will "blench" (or flinch). The king does far more than cringe. After a few lines, "[t]he King rises" (3.2.258) and, in agitation, leaves the play: "Give me some light, away" (3.2.261). Hamlet is jubilant. Horatio is less certain of *The Mousetrap*'s success, perhaps because, as Judge Richard Posner observes, Hamlet has publicly announced the murderer in the play to be the nephew of the king (Posner 2009: 112). Claudius could therefore have been innocent, but still terrified that his "mad" nephew was going to kill him. Yet for all his alleged indecisiveness, from this point on, Hamlet never wavers with respect to Claudius's guilt. He has shifted from the guilt phase to the sentencing phase of his self-created trial. He waits now only for the right moment to execute Claudius.

That moment seems to present itself immediately. After *The Mousetrap*, Claudius goes to the chapel to pray, where Hamlet finds him alone and unarmed. Before Hamlet enters, Claudius confesses his guilt: "O, my offense is rank: it smells to heaven; / It hath the primal eldest curse upon't— / A brother's murder" (3.3.36–38). This is a crucial moment, because it is the first time that we, the audience and readers of the play, are given the "full proof" of Claudius's uncoerced confession to the murder. Hamlet has come to the right conclusion after all.

The allusion is to God's curse on Cain for murdering his brother Abel. (This reference to Genesis resonates with the Edenic image of Hamlet Sr. sleeping contentedly in his garden until stung by the "serpent.") The train of thought leads Claudius to contrast worldly and divine justice. Claudius first acknowledges that "[i]n the corrupted currents of this world / Offence's gilded hand may shove by justice, / And oft 'tis seen the wicked prize itself / Buys out the law" (3.3.57–60). He speaks from experience. By murdering Hamlet's father, Claudius took the crown. That "prize itself" immunized him from legal accountability. Later in the play, when threatened by Laertes, Claudius will brazenly assert sovereign immunity, observing that "[t]here such divinity doth hedge a king / That treason can but peep to what it would" (4.5.123–24). However it is acquired, the crown retains its prerogatives.

Yet Claudius recognizes that in the afterlife, "[t]here is no shuffling, there the action lies / In his true nature, and we ourselves compelled / Even to the teeth and forehead of our faults / To give in evidence" (3.3.61–64). The idea that there might be a right against self-incrimination had already been introduced in Shakespeare's time, though it had not yet been fully embraced by the courts (Langbein, Lerner and Smith 2009: 698–700). But Claudius knows he will not be able to assert any right against "compelled" evidence when called to account by his god.

While seemingly describing only the omniscient justice of heaven, Claudius is also describing what has just happened to him. Through *The Mousetrap*, Hamlet has "compelled" him to "give in evidence" of his crime. And this, more broadly, is the kind of justice Hamlet seeks to mete out on Claudius—celestial rather than earthly justice. Hamlet makes this patent when he happens on Claudius at prayer. He draws his sword, but then declines to take his revenge:

> Now might I do it. But now 'a is a-praying
> And now I'll do it
> *[Draws sword.]*
> —and so 'a goes to heaven,
> And so am I revenged! That would be scanned:
> A villain kills my father, and for that
> I, his sole son, do this same villain send
> To heaven.
> Why, this is base and silly, not revenge.
> 'A took my father grossly full of bread
> With all his crimes broad blown, as flush as May,
> And how his audit stands who knows, save heaven,
> But in our circumstances and course of thought
> 'Tis heavy with him. And am I then revenged
> To take him in the purging of his soul
> When he is fit and seasoned for his passage?
> No.
> *[Sheathes sword.]*
> Up sword, and know thou a more horrid hent
> When he is drunk, asleep or in a rage,
> Or in th'incestuous pleasure of his bed,
> At game a-swearing, or about some act
> That has no relish of salvation in't.
> Then trip him that his heels may kick at heaven
> And that his soul may be as damned and black
> As hell whereto it goes.
>
> (3.3.73–95)

Hamlet sheathes his sword because if a person is killed praying for forgiveness, he or she will go directly to heaven. Again, Othello is Hamlet's foil here. Before he kills Desdemona, he not only permits but also exhorts her to say her final prayers: "I would not kill thy unprepared spirit, / No heaven forfend, I would not kill thy soul" (*Othello*, 5.2.31–32). Hamlet, in contrast, wishes not only to execute Claudius but to consign his soul to hell.

Critics have deemed Hamlet's sentiment barbaric. Samuel Johnson thought the speech was "too horrible to be read or uttered"; others who agreed often cut it in performance (Thompson and Taylor 2006: 331). Yet we should expect nothing less of Hamlet's sense of poetic justice. Throughout the play, Hamlet draws a sharp distinction between his life and his soul, showing a remarkable disregard for the former. When warned not to pursue the ghost, Hamlet says: "Why, what should be the fear? / I do not set my life at a pin's fee, / And for my soul—what can it do to that, / Being a thing immortal as itself?" (1.4.64–67). Hamlet's celebrated "To be or not to be" speech is also a mediation on how suicide would be rational if the soul did not outlive the body. It seems natural, then, that Hamlet would consider taking Claudius's life to be insufficient vengeance. Perfect justice requires not just a life for a life, but a soul for a soul. This requirement has accrued more force because Hamlet, in the wake of *The Mousetrap*, seems fully to credit the ghost. The ghost has cried out that he is in greater torment because Claudius took him "unhouseled, disappointed, unaneled." Hamlet thinks back to that plaint here: "'A took my father grossly full of bread." Claudius must be taken the same way.

We also cannot take Hamlet's refusal to kill Claudius in the chapel as a simple excuse for inaction. When Hamlet thinks he can dispatch Claudius properly, he acts promptly. After the chapel scene, Hamlet goes to Gertrude's bedchamber. Polonius is concealed behind the arras to eavesdrop on their conversation. Remembering his father's injunction not to harm Gertrude, Hamlet decides he "will speak daggers to her but use none" (3.2.386) against her. But as their conversation grows heated, Gertrude thinks Hamlet intends to murder her. When she cries for help, Polonius stirs behind the arras, and Hamlet stabs him to death.

Hamlet's murder of Polonius is often characterized as rash. Here is Bradley: "When he acts, his action does not proceed from this deliberation and analysis, but is sudden and impulsive, evoked by an energy in which he has no time to think" (Bradley 2005: 83). This criticism of how Hamlet acts is also a criticism of how he thinks. It suggests that because Hamlet is so intellectual, he can act only when not given a chance to think, making him less a man of action than a man of reaction. Yet while Hamlet does not deliberate in that moment, he is acting on a *prior* deliberation. In the chapel scene, Hamlet says he will kill Claudius when he is engaged in an "act / That has no relish of salvation in't." Eavesdropping would qualify as such an act. Given that we are in the queen's bedchamber, Hamlet reasonably assumes Claudius is behind the arras. (As he regretfully says when he discovers Polonius: "I took thee for thy better" [3.4.30].) So Hamlet makes good on the pledge he makes in the chapel—although, unluckily, against the wrong target.

If the punishment neatly fits the crime, Hamlet not only acts but also takes affirmative pleasure in acting. After he kills Polonius, he tells Gertrude that he knows Claudius has some sinister purpose in sending him to England with Rosencrantz and Guildenstern. He relishes the opportunity to turn Claudius's treachery on him:

> For 'tis the sport to have the enginer
> Hoist with his own petard, and't shall go hard
> But I will delve one yard below their mines
> And blow them at the moon. O, 'tis most sweet
> When in one line two crafts directly meet.
> (3.4.204–208)

The metaphor concerns landmines—the "enginer / Hoist with his own petard" is the engineer blown up by his own bomb. Hamlet enjoys his plan for poetic justice, which he then smoothly implements. Rosencrantz and Guildenstern bear a commission telling the English king to kill Hamlet. Hamlet swaps their names for his, and they are duly executed.

In the last act of the play, Hamlet achieves his perfect revenge, though at great cost. As the play concludes, bodies fall like leaves. Gertrude drinks from the poisoned cup intended for Hamlet. Laertes and Hamlet each wound the other with the poisoned rapier. After he realizes they are both fatally wounded, Laertes confesses that he has outsmarted himself: "I am justly killed with mine own treachery" (5.2.292). He tells Hamlet that "[i]n thee there is not half an hour's life" (5.2.300) and that "the King, the King's to blame" (5.2.305).

Hamlet undoes Claudius in a similar fashion. He "hurts" the king with his rapier, thereby assuring that the king will die in the same way he will. The lords cry "Treason!" (5.2.307), but there is little they can do, as Hamlet himself is not long for the world. Claudius is ignominious to the end: "O, yet defend me, friends, I am but hurt" (5.2.308). Hamlet ensures that these are his last words by forcing the king to drink from the poisoned chalice: "Here, thou incestuous, damned Dane! / Drink of this potion. Is the union here? / Follow my mother. *[King dies.]*" (5.2.309–11).

Compelling the king to drink perfects Hamlet's revenge in several ways. For starters, Hamlet ensures that the king will die. The king has planned the poisoned "union," or pearl, as a fail-safe in case Laertes's poisoned foil does not do its work. Hamlet also uses it as insurance after the king claims he is only hurt. In making the king "follow" Gertrude according to his "union" with her, Hamlet also does symbolic justice to his mother, forcing the king to die as she did. Moreover, by making Claudius drink, he forestalls the king from speaking. He takes Claudius as Claudius took his father, barring him from saying his prayers. Hamlet merges with his father here, as both are now phantoms tarrying on the threshold between life and death. In this moment, Hamlet manages both to be and not to be.

Viewed from any of these perspectives, Hamlet's punishment of Claudius constitutes poetic justice. So Hazlitt is wrong to say that because Hamlet "cannot have his revenge perfect, according to the most refined idea his wish can form, he declines it altogether" (White 1996: 122). As Laertes says directly before Claudius's death, "He is justly served. / It is a poison tempered by himself" (5.2.311–312). Early in his play, Macbeth muses: "this even-handed justice / Commends th'ingredience of our poison'd chalice / To our own lips" (*Macbeth*, 1.7.10–12). Here that figure becomes literal.

It is dangerous to disagree with Freud, Goethe, and Nietzsche all at once. But their explanations of Hamlet's delays all seem less plausible than the one offered here. Contrary to Freud, I see little evidence that Hamlet has a particularly pronounced Oedipus complex. Claudius is deemed "incestuous" because he has married his dead brother's wife. So while the play refers repeatedly to incest, it always means fraternal incest rather than the parent–child incest associated with the Oedipus complex.

I see even less evidence that Hamlet is weak or nihilistic. A weak man would not have been able to take action against Polonius, Laertes, or Claudius. En route to England, Hamlet boards a pirate ship in a manner that seems downright swashbuckling. Similarly, a nihilistic man would have welcomed his impending execution in England. In a dark moment early in the play, Hamlet says that he wishes he could die without violating the "canon 'gainst self-slaughter" (1.2.132). His rejection of the opportunity to be killed without committing suicide shows that sentiment to be temporary.

Hamlet's delays make more sense if seen as part of his active pursuit of poetic justice. Hamlet first delays to confirm Claudius's guilt. He then delays to ensure that he is perfectly revenged. In fact, Hamlet shows an unswerving commitment to his ideal form of justice that reflects the strength, not the weakness, of his will.

Nonetheless, I do not come to praise Hamlet. Like many intellectuals in the grip of an idea, he is largely oblivious to its consequences on others. Totting up the seven avoidable deaths does not begin to capture the magnitude of the harm Hamlet inflicts. His cruelty to Ophelia is the prime example. Here, at least, he shows remorse at her graveside. In contrast, he manifests enduring indifference toward Rosencrantz and Guildenstern, telling Horatio that "[t]hey are not near [his] conscience" (5.2.57). After he kills Polonius, he similarly lets the counselor bleed out on the floor of the bedchamber while he has an extended conversation with Gertrude. When later asked where he has stashed the corpse, he jokes about how Polonius is at supper: "Not where he eats but where 'a is eaten" by a "convocation of politic worms" (4.3.19–20). This indifference extends to the fate of Denmark. Hamlet's actions lead to the collapse of the state, leaving it in the hands of the invading Norwegians. What we see in Hamlet is not just a commitment to moral perfectionism, but also the bottomless cost of that commitment.

In a 1931 essay titled "Law and Literature," soon-to-be Supreme Court Justice Benjamin Cardozo explores both the importance of idealism and the importance of containing it. Cardozo observes that dissents tend to be more idealistic than majority opinions.

> The voice of the majority may be that of force triumphant, content with the plaudits of the hour, and recking little of the morrow. The dissenter speaks to the future, and his voice is pitched to a key that will carry through the years. Read some of the great dissents, the opinion, for example of Judge Curtis in Dred Scott vs. Sanford, and feel after the cooling time of the better part of [a] century the glow and fire of a faith that was content to bide its hour. The prophet and the martyr do not see the hooting throng. Their eyes are fixed on the eternities.

Cardozo observes that dissents can afford to be more idealistic because they have no immediate force in the world. The dissenter, who has already lost, can express an ideal justice for "the eternities" (Cardozo 1931: 36).

Conversely, one of the costs of power is that it must be more careful: "The spokesman of the court is cautious, timid, fearful of the vivid word, the heightened phrase. He dreams of an unworthy brood of scions" (ibid.: 34). The coercive effect of his words disciplines his rhetoric: "The result is to cramp and paralyze. One fears to say anything when the peril of misunderstanding puts a warning finger to the lips" (ibid.: 34).

Cardozo correctly intuits an inverse relationship here between force and fancy. The coercive force of a majority opinion places constraints on the way its authors can exercise their imaginations. In contrast, the dissenter has no such constraints, and so can engage in more aggressive acts of imagination. Cardozo celebrates the value of both genres. The dissenting opinion is valuable because it permits a legal actor to articulate ideals of justice at a crystalline level of purity for future majority opinions to take up, or not. The majority opinion is valuable because it adjusts those ideals for the world we inhabit.

Cardozo's example clarifies this dynamic. In the 1857 case of *Dred Scott v. Sanford*, Justice Benjamin Curtis vigorously dissented from a majority opinion arguing that the descendants of slaves were not citizens under the federal Constitution. That dissent later became a basis for enacting the Fourteenth Amendment (1868), the home of the equality principle in our Constitution. Yet while the Fourteenth Amendment overrode the *Dred Scott* majority, its language is much more restrained than the soaring rhetoric of Curtis's dissent.

Cardozo is not speaking about intellectuals in this essay. Nonetheless, he captures something important about us. The general run of intellectuals—academics, journalists, writers, and the like—generally are in the position of the dissenter. We are not the decision makers, and this gives us the freedom to engage in flights of fancy. In the realm of social justice, we can imagine utopias.

The danger arises when we lack the self-consciousness to understand that our ideals are just that—ideals. For them to be rendered functional, an additional act of translation is necessary. When we or our acolytes seek to impose them in their pure form on society, the results are usually disastrous. Consider the tradition of literary utopias, extending from Sir Thomas More's *Utopia* through Ètienne Cabet's *Travels in Icaria* to B. F. Skinner's *Walden Two*. French socialist readers of Cabet founded a real Icaria in the United States; disciples of Skinner created communal societies modeled on his book in Mexico, Virginia, and Missouri. As literary critic Northrup Frye acidly observes: "There have been one or two attempts to take utopian constructions literally by trying to set them up as actual communities, but the history of these communities makes melancholy reading."

This is Hamlet's mistake. He clings to his intellectual conception of poetic justice with extraordinary tenacity and seeks to impose it on the world. Such is the force of his will that he is able to do so with respect to Claudius, but only at immeasurable cost to the world around him. A more pragmatic person would either have assassinated Claudius in private in the chapel, or alternatively, like Laertes, have considered leading an insurgency to take over the state. But Hamlet wishes to have all the imaginative freedom of a dissent with none of the caution of a majority opinion. In the end, while his delays are justifiable, the purpose they serve is not. Hamlet's failed justice stands as a cautionary tale to intellectuals in the play-outside-the-play.

Endnote

1 From *A Thousand Times More Fair: What Shakespeare's Plays Teach Us About Justice* by Kenji Yoshino. © 2011 by Kenji Yoshino. Courtesy of Ecco, an imprint of HarperCollins Publishers.

Bibliography

Altus, D.E. and Morris, E.K. (2004) "B.F. Skinner's Utopian Vision: Behind and Beyond *Walden Two*," *Contemporary Justice Review* 267: 272.

Bradley, A.C. (first published 1904; 2005) *Shakespearean Tragedy*, New York: Barnes and Noble.

Browne, T. (first published 1643; 1951) *Religio Medici* in *Religio Medici and Other Writings*, New York: E.P. Dutton.

Burton, J.A. (2001) "An Unrecognized Theme in Hamlet: Lost Inheritance and Claudius's Marriage to Gertrude," *The Shakespeare Newsletter*, 50: 71–82.

Cabet, E (first published 1840; 2003) *Travels in Icaria*, trans. Leslie Roberts, Syracuse, NY: Syracuse University Press.

Cardozo, B.N. (1931) "Law and Literature," in *Law and Literature and Other Essays and Addresses*, New York: Harcourt, Brace.

Freud, S. (first published 1900; 1955) *The Interpretation of Dreams*, in the *Standard Edition of the Complete Psychological Works of Sigmund Freud*, ed. and trans. James Strachey, vol 4. London: Hogarth Press.

Frye, N. (1965) "Varieties of Literary Utopias," in *Utopias and Utopian Thought*, ed. Frank E. Manuel, Boston, MA: Beacon Press.

Garber, M. (2008) *Shakespeare and Modern Culture*, New York: Pantheon.

Greenblatt, S. (2001) *Hamlet in Purgatory*, Princeton, NJ: Princeton University Press.

Hazlitt, W. (1996) *Hazlitt's Criticism of Shakespeare: A Selection*, ed. R.S. White, Lewiston, NY: Edwin Mellen Press.

Jones, E. (first published 1949; 1976) *Hamlet and Oedipus*, New York: Norton.

Kelly, H.A. (1976) *The Matrimonial Trials of Henry VIII*, Palo Alto, CA: Stanford University Press.

Langbein, J.H., Lerner, R.L. and Smith, B.P. (2009) *History of the Common Law: The Development of Anglo-American Legal Institutions*, New York: Aspen Publishers.

Mack, M. (1993) *Everybody's Shakespeare*, Lincoln, NB: University of Nebraska Press.

More, T. (2001) *Utopia*, trans. Clarence H. Miller, New Haven, CT: Yale University Press.

Nietzsche, F. (first published 1871; 2007) *The Birth of Tragedy*, Stilwell, KS: Digireads Publishing.

Posner, R. (2009) *Law and Literature*, 3rd ed., Cambridge, MA: Harvard University Press.

Rosenblatt, J. (1978) "Aspects of the Incest Problem in Hamlet," *Shakespeare Quarterly* 29: 349–64.

Shakespeare, W. (2006) *Hamlet*, eds Ann Thompson and Neil Taylor, London: Arden Shakespeare.

Skinner, B.F. (1948). *Walden Two*, Indianapolis, IN: Hackett.

Thompson, A. and Taylor, N. (2006) "Notes." In *Hamlet*, by William Shakespeare, eds Ann Thompson and Neil Taylor, London: Arden Shakespeare.

Von Goethe, J.W. (1824) *Wilhelm Meister's Apprenticeship*, trans. Thomas Carlyle, vol. 2. London: Oliver & Boyd.

Chapter 13
Stare decisis, binding precedent, and Anthony Trollope's *The Eustace Diamonds*

Marco Wan

Anthony Trollope's *The Eustace Diamonds* (1873) turns on a complex question about property law. On a more general level, the question is about inheritance: should Lizzie Eustace be allowed to keep the eponymous diamonds which she claims her late husband, Sir Florian Eustace, gave her as a present, or should the diamonds be returned to the Eustace family upon his death? The necklace is worth ten thousand pounds. The lawyer for the family, Mr. Camperdown, is determined to prevent her from keeping the jewels. The more specific legal point is whether the eponymous jewels can be considered heirlooms. This is an important issue in the narrative because if the jewels are construed as heirlooms by the law, then it is not within Sir Florian's power to give them to Lizzie as a present in the first place, and so they would remain as property of the Eustace family. However, if the jewels are not construed as heirlooms, then they would be the rightful property of Lizzie Eustace. One commentator has pointed out that in his novel Trollope created 'not only an intelligent and entertaining tale of second-rate skulduggery among mid-Victorian nobility, but also the greatest property law hypothetical ever' (Roth 1992: 879).

In order to find out whether he would be able to take back the necklace from Lizzie, Mr. Camperdown seeks the advice of a well-respected barrister, Mr. Dove. In the 25th chapter of the novel, entitled 'Mr. Dove's Opinion', the barrister sends Mr. Camperdown a letter, and in that letter he lays down the relevant case law and gives his legal opinion that not only should the jewels not be considered heirlooms of the Eustace family, but that even if they were to be considered heirlooms, Lizzie would still have a possible claim to them as paraphernalia, a term commonly understood as jewellery and ornaments given by a husband to his wife before or during marriage, and which fell to the wife upon the husband's death. When Mr. Camperdown realises that the law does not allow him to retrieve the jewels, he is incensed, not only because of the specific circumstances of losing his case to Lizzie, but also because of the general absurdity of the way the law defines heirlooms: 'A pot or pan might be an heirloom, but not a necklace! Mr. Camperdown could hardly bring himself to believe that this was law' (Trollope 1873: 254). The letter is a transcription of an actual legal opinion on the status of jewellery as heirlooms written by a real-life lawyer, a man called Charles Merewether, and in his autobiography Trollope notes that Mr. Dove's opinion, or Charles Merewether's opinion, had become 'the ruling authority on the subject' (Trollope 1883: 72). The reason for the inclusion of the letter in the novel is well known: after the publication of his earlier novel *Orley Farm* (1860–61), a novel about a woman who forged her husband's will, Trollope came under severe criticism by contemporary reviewers for his inaccurate depiction of the law. The decision to include the legal opinion by Merewether was an attempt to pre-empt similar criticism against *The Eustace Diamonds*.

This chapter uses the legal question of inheritance as a starting point for establishing a dialogue between the legal case and fiction. It moves from the specific question of inheritance to a broader question about the status and relevance of precedent cases in legal decision-making. It builds on the work of scholars who have analysed Trollope's fiction in the context of legal developments in nineteenth-century England: for example, Jan Melissa Schramm interprets *Orley Farm* as a part of a wider cultural response to the question of the legal representation of felons and argues that the novel can be read as an exploration of the dilemma of lawyers who represent a person whom they believe to be guilty (Schramm 2000: 127–30), and, more recently, Nicola Lacey has argued that both *Orley Farm* and *The Eustace Diamonds* reflect a dominant Victorian assumption about female dishonesty and unreliability in both law and literature (Lacey 2011;). In another article, Lacey has shown that the depiction of lawyers in Trollope's novels, and in Victorian fiction more generally, can be explained by the rise of the legal profession and its internal tension between an older model premised on a service ideal and a newer model recognising the commercial reality of legal practice (Lacey: 2011). This chapter continues the work of reading Trollope as part of legal history, but places him within a different strand of this history from Schramm and Lacey, that of *stare decisis*.

Legal historians have noted that the second half of the nineteenth century is a crucial period in the development of the doctrine of *stare decisis*, the central legal doctrine which dictates that decisions in the common law have to follow precedent cases dealing with similar issues. This chapter argues that *The Eustace Diamonds* can be read as a critique of the doctrine of binding precedent, a doctrine which was consolidating in the common law around the time of the novel's publication. The discussion is divided into three parts. Part One situates the novel in the context of the development of *stare decisis* in the second half of the nineteenth century, and shows that by the early 1870s the judicial understanding of the relationship between current and precedent cases had shifted from one whereby the latter are regarded as evidence of law to one whereby they are regarded as sources of law in and of themselves, and therefore as binding. In other words, it charts the development of case law from *stare decisis* to binding precedent. Parts Two and Three then consider the ways in which *The Eustace Diamonds* can be interpreted as a critique of the changes in ideas about the binding nature of legal precedent.

Stare decisis and binding precedent in mid-nineteenth-century England

When approaching the history of case law in England, it is important to note that legal historians draw a distinction between '*stare decisis*' and 'binding precedent', two terms which are usually taken to be synonymous in our own time. Both terms refer to a general attitude of adherence to precedent cases, but they have very different inflections. '*Stare decisis*' refers to the judicial attitude that precedent cases ought to be followed *not* because they are binding law, but because they are *evidence of law*. In other words, cases are not law in and of themselves, but only serve to illustrate legal principles. This understanding of case law is captured in the words of the eighteenth-century judge, Lord Mansfield:

> The law of England would be a strange science indeed if it were decided upon precedents only. Precedents serve to illustrate principles and to give them a fixed certainty. But the law of England [. . .] depends upon principles, and these principles run through all the cases according as the particular circumstances of each have been found to fall within the one or the other of them.
>
> (cited in Evans 1987: 37)

What needs to be underscored in this view of case law is that cases are *not* strictly binding: since cases are themselves *not law* but are only *evidence or illustrations* of law, courts only follow the decisions in precedent cases as a matter of practice or custom, and not because they regard cases as strictly binding in the modern sense of the term. In other words, a court can choose not to follow precedent cases if there are strong arguments for not following them.

In contrast to *stare decisis*, the doctrine of 'binding precedent' refers to the judicial attitude that precedent cases which are factually similar and which deal with the same legal issue *must* be followed. This is because according to this doctrine, cases are not just evidence of law, but are themselves law. A judge has to follow precedent even if he disagrees with the outcome, or even if there are strong moral reasons for setting it aside. This theoretical understanding of the law is of course much closer to the contemporary attitude towards precedent cases.

Legal historians have demonstrated that '*stare decisis*' and 'binding precedent' represent different stages in the development of case law: we move from '*stare decisis*' – the view that cases are but evidence of law – to 'binding precedent', the view that cases are themselves law and must be followed. As with much of the evolution of common law, this shift occurred gradually and unsystematically: as Jim Evans points out, '[t]he common law did not develop a system of case-law by adopting explicit premises as to the authority of cases. It passed *imperceptibly* from a time when what was said in the course of cases was evidence of the law [. . .] to a time when the law pronounced in the cases was itself the material of a substantial part of the system of law' (Evans 1987: 36; my italics).

The debate in legal history referred to above concerns the moment at which this imperceptible shift from '*stare decisis*' to 'binding precedent' occurred. William Holdsworth argues that the shift had taken place by the end of the eighteenth century, while Carleton Allen argues that it did not take place until the nineteenth century (Holdsworth 1934: 181–95; Allen 1935: 333–46). There now seems to be a consensus that the shift took place sometime in the nineteenth century: Jim Evans begins his seminal article on changes in the doctrine of precedent by stating that 'It is widely recognised that the English doctrine of precedent hardened during the nineteenth century'.

This section aims to show that Evans' argument could be given greater precision in that not only did the change occur in the nineteenth century, but it occurred specifically in the second half of the nineteenth century, around the time of the publication of *The Eustace Diamonds*, in the early 1870s. This argument is premised on four developments: first, the spread of the influence of the jurist John Austin; second, the changes to the practice of court reporting; third, the simplification of the English court system, and finally, the increasing anxieties about English identity.

Austin regarded judge-made law as 'tacit commands' of the sovereign, and as such he believed that cases should themselves be regarded as law. In a famous passage from his *Lectures on Jurisprudence*, he ridicules the notion of case law as merely illustrations or evidence of law by noting that the idea that common law is 'a miraculous something made by nobody, existing, I suppose, from eternity, and merely declared from time to time by the judges' is nothing but 'childish fiction' (Austin 1873: 655). The huge influence of Austin on Victorian legal thought is amply documented elsewhere, but it is worth mentioning here Holdsworth's observation that most books on jurisprudence published between 1850 and 1875 were Austinian in character, an observation which testifies to the widespread influence of Austin's jurisprudence. It is also significant that the fourth edition of Austin's lectures appeared in the same year of the publication of the *Eustace Diamonds*, in 1873. Trollope's novel can be said to appear at the moment when the influence of Austinian thinking on the law was at its peak.

The second development was the changes in the practice of court reporting. It has been noted that the chaotic system of law reporting and the poor quality of many law reports made it impossible to establish any system of binding precedent as the very records of the case law were unreliable. Allen notes that it is difficult for modern-day lawyers to 'realise how great this difference was, and how much it affected the whole citation of authority' (Allen 1964: 221). The accuracy of the reports simply could not be taken for granted. What needs to be highlighted here is that the situation improved significantly with the establishment of the Incorporated Council of Law Reporting in 1865, eight years before the novel's publication. The Council hired full-time editors and reporters, made available law reports at a relatively low price, and most importantly provided a high standard of quality control over law reporting. The improvement in the accuracy and accessibility of law reports in the years following the establishment of the Council contributed to the establishment of the doctrine of binding precedent in that it ensured that cases cited in court were reliable sources of law.

The changes in the English court system represented the third important development. It has also been noted that the development of binding precedent was for a long time hampered by the messy court system. For much of the nineteenth century, the English judicial structure was positively labyrinthine: it consisted of the Court of the Queen's Bench; the Court of Common Pleas; the Court of Chancery; the Court of the Exchequer; the High Court of Admiralty; the Court of Probate and the Court of Matrimonial Causes. The decisions of the courts at times contradicted one another, and there was little sense of an established judicial hierarchy compared to the system today. As a result, it was difficult to entrench any notion of binding precedent amidst this institutional chaos.

The situation changed with the passing of the Judicature Act, again in the same year as the novel's publication, in 1873. The Act consolidated all of the courts into a single Supreme Court of Judicature. With a more centralized and streamlined court system, it became possible to establish a sense of hierarchy which in turn gave rise to the acceptance of a doctrine of precedent whereby the decisions of the higher courts would bind the judges in the lower courts.

Finally, the imperialist enterprise in the final decades of the nineteenth century brought about an intense interrogation of English identity and culture. As Ayelet Ben-yishai notes, the 'questions of Englishness and questions of law are inextricable', and it is necessary to 'understand the law as part of a larger turmoil in English culture' (Ben-yishai 2011: 156). In light of such interrogation, the law can be seen to function as a reassuringly English institution; the inheritance of case law from the past epitomised an uninterrupted chain of norms and insights passed down from generation to generation. In this light, anxieties about identity were in part responsible for the increasingly strong hold of precedent law on legal decision-making.

By the early 1870s, then, the influence of Austin's vision of judicial opinions as tacit commands of the sovereign was at its peak; the accuracy of the law reports had been drastically improved through the establishment of the Council of Law Reporting, the chaotic court system had been considerably streamlined, and the law came to symbolise a particularly English justice. All of these developments contributed to the entrenchment of the doctrine of binding precedent in the law. By situating the novel in the context of the legal developments of the time, it is possible to see that *The Eustace Diamonds* appeared at the critical moment when the common law was shifting from the doctrine of '*stare decisis*' to the doctrine of 'binding precedent', from the understanding of case law as evidence of law to the understanding of it as law with binding power. This temporal synchronicity in turn enables the interpretative move of reading the novel as a response to its contemporary judicial development. As Simon Gardner points out, 'Trollope was not a legal innocent' (Gardner 1992: 183). His background as the son of a barrister; the legal structures and vocabulary which pervade his writing, and the sheer number of legal personalities depicted in his work make his novels a logical point of entry into the legal debates of his time.

The Eustace Diamonds as critique of the doctrine of binding precedent

One possible point of entry for thinking about the novel's critique of 'binding precedent' is Mr. Dove's opinion, for this is the part which engages with the doctrine most explicitly. The barrister begins his opinion by saying: 'There is much error about heirlooms. Many think that any chattel may be made an heirloom by any owner of it. This is not the case' (Trollope 1873: 262). He then surveys the relevant authorities, and opines that according to the case law heirlooms have to be either an object of use (such as a table or a bed) or an insignia of office. In a later conversation with Mr. Camperdown, Mr. Dove reiterates that the law on heirlooms does not concern itself with 'trinkets only to be used for vanity and ornament' (Trollope 1873: 295). He concludes his opinion by unequivocally stating that 'the Eustace Estate cannot claim the jewels as an heirloom' (Trollope 1873: 263).

This letter is significant because its shows the doctrine of binding precedent at work: with the shift from '*stare decisis*' to 'binding precedent' outlined above, it is no longer open to Mr. Camperdown to argue that the cases could somehow be set aside because they are only illustrations or evidence of law, or because they contradict considerations of moral fitness or public convenience. Even though Mr. Camperdown desperately wants to retrieve the diamonds, the precedent cases are law and he has no choice but to follow them: the binding precedent cases mean that 'the necklace was not an heirloom, [. . .] that it couldn't have been an heirloom' (Trollope 1873: 264). Their existence as authorities on the subject of heirlooms bind him, and the narrator tells us that this realisation makes him 'an unhappy old man'.

More importantly, this letter shows that the operation of the doctrine of binding precedent can lead to manifest injustice. We, as the readers, want Mr. Camperdown to take the jewels back for the Eustace family, because the omniscient narrator tells us explicitly that Lizzie Eustace *lied* about the necklace: her husband did not give it to her as a present. The reader is told that Sir Florian had put the jewels on her one evening 'for the purpose of a special dinner party', and had made no indication that they were hers to keep. But when Lizzie is asked to return the diamonds, she lies. When Lord Fawn, the man who promises to marry her after Sir Florian's death, confronts Lizzie about the diamonds, she replies: 'They are my own, – altogether my own. Sir Florian gave them to me. When he put them into my hands, he said that they were to be my own forever and ever' (Trollope 1873: 129). By the time she explains her possession of the jewels to her cousin Frank Greystock, we are told that she had lied about them so often to so many different people that she could repeat the falsehood 'with increased precision' to him, and she tells Frank that Sir Florian explicitly told her to regard them as her own property. Lizzie's falsity is not confined to the jewels: like William Thackeray's Becky Sharpe, lying is to her a way of life, a way of surviving and of moving up in the world.

So the force of precedent leads to an injustice: the strictly binding nature of the authorities on heirlooms means that Lizzie Eustace manages to keep the necklace which does not properly belong to her. Mr. Camperdown is convinced that 'Lizzie Eustace had stolen the diamonds, as a pickpocket steals a watch', and he believes that it is 'a thing quite terrible that, in a country which boasts of its laws and of the execution of its laws, such an imposter as was this widow should be able to lay her dirty, grasping fingers on so great an amount of property, and that there should be no means of punishing her' (Trollope 1873: 289). Towards the end of the novel, another character comments that with the way the common law has developed: 'It always happens that they catch the small fry, and let the large fish escape' (Trollope 1873: 768). It is important to make a distinction between legal and moral judgment at this stage. It is of course possible to argue that as a woman with little knowledge about the law and virtually no one to help her, Lizzie has no choice but to lie to protect what she genuinely feels to belong to her. According to this line of reasoning, she is the victim of a patriarchal law that operates to protect male, aristocratic interests, and it is certainly possible to see Mr. Camperdown's determination to wrest the diamonds from her as at least in part motivated by class and gender. However, even though the reader may believe that there is nothing morally reprehensible with Lizzie's behaviour to protect what she genuinely believes to be hers, in strictly legal terms the fact that she does lie means that allowing her to keep the diamonds would still be an act of injustice. In other words, while the reader may believe that Lizzie Eustace has good reasons to lie about how the diamonds came into her possession, the fact that she does lie means that she should not be allowed to keep them because she does not have proper title to them. However, Mr. Dove's opinion shows that an absolute adherence to precedent cases leads to precisely this outcome. Through the episode of Mr. Dove's opinion and its ramifications, Trollope's novel seems to suggest that one should be wary of the doctrine of binding precedent because the absolute rigidity and unquestioning obedience with which it treats related cases could lead to unjust outcomes. The binding precedent here is 'binding' in the sense that it ties the hands of the family lawyer acting in the interest of the Eustace estate, making him powerless in face of the tricks and lies of Lizzie Eustace.

The episode of Mr. Dove's opinion can be said to constitute the novel's critique of binding precedent on the level of plot. Yet the literary critique of legal doctrine goes deeper than that, and extends to the level of *epistemology*. This is because the novel seems to question the desirability of being bound not only by Mr. Dove's opinion, but by any opinion at all, whether legal or otherwise. To be bound by a case is of course to be bound by the set of majority opinions that make up the decision of the case. On an epistemological level, the problem of treating any set of opinions in a case as binding lies in the fact that no opinion can ever be fully reliable. Even though a judge could base his opinion on the most erudite research, even though his opinion could be underpinned by the most compelling reasoning, at the end a judicial opinion will always be precisely that – an opinion, with no guarantee of giving full access to truth – and so treating any one set of opinions as binding would always be problematic epistemologically. A doctrine which does not allow deviation from a precedent set of opinions should therefore be treated with extreme caution.

The novel's problematisation of the basis of opinions is seen most clearly from its presentation of the diversity of views on the ownership of the diamonds. By the second half of the novel, the issue had become a public scandal. The narrator observes that 'There were strong parties formed in the matter – whom we may call Lizzieites and anti-Lizzieites' (Trollope 1873: 465). In the view of the Lizzieites, 'poor Lady Eustace was being very ill-treated', and 'the diamonds did probably belong to her'. To the anti-Lizzieites, on the other hand, the appropriate words for describing Lizzie's behaviour were 'bold', 'wicked', and 'rapacious'. The very existence of such wildly divergent opinions on a single incident suggests that it would be dangerous to treat any one set of opinions as absolutely binding: the narrative has shown that there are good reasons for taking both positions, and a doctrine which dictates adherence to one set of opinions is unlikely to be doing justice to the situation as a whole.

Moreover, people's opinions on this issue are complicated by politics: the narrator notes that all the Lizzieites were Conservative, while 'The whole force of the Government [. . .] was anti-Lizzieite'. One reason why the issue became a scandal is that Lord Fawn, who courted Lizzie after the death of her first husband, threatened to withdraw the offer of marriage unless she returned the diamonds to the Eustace family. Since Lord Fawn is a Liberal, naturally the members of the opposing Conservative Party side with Lizzie. In this passage, the novel shows that not only are opinions unreliable because they are not necessarily based on a full treatment of the facts, but because they are always open to being swayed by politics. This point is underscored by the role of Lady Glencora, and the reader is told that 'When she declared that poor Lady Eustace was a victim, others [in her party] were obliged to say so' (Trollope 1873: 532).

Finally, in case the reader thinks that legal opinions are somehow immune to such factual ambiguities and to the sway of politics, the novel makes it abundantly clear that legal opinions are epistemologically every bit as fraught as any other personal, moral or political opinion. From one factual scenario would arise two different interpretations, both of which are as reliable, or as unreliable, as each other. The narrator notes that the legal community has taken a lively interest in Lizzie's case: 'There was hardly a lawyer of repute but took up the question, and had an opinion as to Lizzie's right to the necklace' (Trollope 1873: 486). The reader is told that on the one hand, 'The Attorney and Solicitor-General were dead against her, asserting that the diamonds certainly did not pass to her under the will, and could not have become hers by gift', but on the other hand, 'Gentlemen who were equal to them in learning, who had held offices equally high, were distinctly of a different opinion'. It is possible to look at the same set of facts and arrive at two contradictory, yet equally plausible, sets of opinions. Again, to treat any one set as binding would therefore risk doing an injustice to the situation in its entirety. Furthermore, even legal opinions are not immune to the influence of politics: the narrator notes that the Attorney and Solicitor 'were members of a Liberal government, and of course anti-Lizzieite', while the lawyers of the opposing camp were 'of course Conservatives in politics'.

The point about the problematic status of legal opinions is underscored in the trial scene of the novel, Lizzie is brought before the court on the charge of perjury: the necklace had been stolen, and she had lied about the whereabouts of the necklace when questioned by the police earlier in the narrative. When the trial opens, Lizzie's guilt seems beyond doubt, and she herself had confessed to lying. However, she manages to sway the sympathy of the magistrate through her theatrics: when interrogated about her false answers, she claims to have been so frightened that she did not know what she was saying, and then she burst into tears in the courtroom and stretched forth her two clasped hands with the air of a supplicant. The impact of her performance is immediate: despite the obviousness of her guilt, the reader is told that: 'the magistrate was altogether on her side, – and so were the public. Poor ignorant, ill-used young creature; – and then so lovely! That was the general feeling' (Trollope 1873: 716). As the trial progresses, however, the court swings the other way. Again, opinions, even judicial opinions, are easily swayed, and accepting a doctrine of binding precedent could mean turning such easily swayed opinions into a set of rules from which future lawyers cannot deviate.

On the level of epistemology, the novel's critique of the law lies not so much in pointing out that there are two sides to any case – an obvious point – but that the very idea of a legal opinion which could provide a fully accurate assessment of the facts is an impossibility: even the most authoritative legal opinion could overlook significant factual details, could be potentially swayed by politics; and could be limited by the subjective vision or background of its author. As the literary critic William Cohen points out, in Trollope's novel 'Even so lofty an English value as justice, it turns out, is beholden to the vicissitudes of "public feeling"; the opinions making up the case law which supposedly ensures justice are in fact the product of subjective interpretation and can never be fully conclusive' (Cohen 1996: 184). As such, the opinions which form a case should be treated not so much as a set of definitive principles that bind but as a collection of refutable perceptions of how a particular set of facts could be dealt with at a particular moment in time. This critique of the law is enabled by the novel's specific form of realism. Critics have demonstrated the influence of empirical discourse on literary realism, but as Ayelet Ben-yishai shows, *The Eustace Diamonds* complicates the realist logic of the Victorian novel by problematising the production of fact; rumours, gossip, hearsay and, as this chapter demonstrates, opinions circulate to complicate the stability and validity of facts as a means of knowing the world, so that the novel 'can be read as a comment on and critique of the epistemological conventions' which structure it (Ben-yishai 2007: 100). When placed within the context of the history of case law, the novel's realist aesthetic enables it to be further read as an interrogation of the epistemological conventions which structure legal reasoning: the implication of the novel's representation of opinion in general, and of legal opinion in particular, is that the older doctrine of *stare decisis*, which leaves the judge the possibility of not following a precedent case even if its opinions deal with the exact same legal issue on a similar set of facts, should be preferred to the more modern but more restrictive doctrine of binding precedent, which dictates that a ruling from a previous case of higher authority must be followed even if there are strong moral or policy reasons for setting it aside. *The Eustace Diamonds* represents a critique of the view that any set of opinions should be regarded as binding at the very moment when the doctrine of binding precedent was consolidated in Victorian England.

Conclusion, or an opinion of one's own

The argument so far has focused on one strand of the narrative, that of Lizzie Eustace. In conclusion, it is necessary to look at the other main strand of the narrative, the courtship between Frank Greystock and Lucy Morris, and examine the way in which it further comments on the changes to the conception of precedent in Victorian legal discourse. Frank is a young barrister who is well regarded in society, but who, unfortunately, does not come from a wealthy family. Lucy, the girl he wants to marry, is a humble governess. Frank knows that marrying her would be tantamount to committing career suicide: not only would he give up the chance of augmenting his personal wealth, but he would be barred from high society because of the lower social status of his wife. More than once has he been tempted by the charms of his cousin, Lizzie Eustace, who is not only rich but extremely beautiful.

All of Frank's friends and acquaintances opine that he should not marry Lucy; they say that he ought to marry a woman who is richer than him or of a higher social class than him. The narrator sums up the attitude of the people around Frank towards the end of the novel:

> All his friends told Frank Greystock that he would be ruined were he to marry Lucy Morris; – and his friends were people supposed to be very good and wise. The dean, and the dean's wife, his father and mother, were very clear that it would be so. Old Lady Linlithgow had spoken of such a marriage as quite out of the question. The Bishop of Bobsborough, when it was mentioned in his hearing, had declared that such a marriage would be a thousand pities. And even dear old Lady Fawn, though she wished it for Lucy's sake, had many times prophesied that such a thing was quite impossible. When the rumour of the marriage reached Lady Glencora, Lady Glencora told her friend, Madame Max Goesler, that that young man was going to blow his brains out (Trollope: 1973: 725–6).

What needs to be highlighted here is that even though every single person around Frank is of the opinion that he should not marry Lucy Morris, Frank eventually finds the courage and the integrity to defy the opinions of the others; despite his hesitations and his equivocations it is his own opinion about whom he loves most that he ultimately listens to. The narrator notes:

> He had never hesitated for a moment as to the value of Lucy Morris. She was not beautiful. She had no wondrous gifts of nature. There was nothing of a goddess about her. She was absolutely penniless. She had never been what the world calls well-dressed. And yet she had been everything to him (Trollope 1873: 726).

Simon Gardner notes that it is not entirely clear whether Lucy and Frank would have lived happily ever after, yet I would argue that there are ample indications that the two lovers would be happy together. Even though we know that Frank has been tempted by Lizzie, at the end of the novel the narrator leaves the reader in no doubt about Frank's commitment to his fiancée:

> He had never doubted his own love, – and when he had been most near to convincing himself that in his peculiar position he ought to marry his rich cousin, because of her wealth, then, at those moments, he had most strongly felt that to have Lucy Morris close to him was the greatest charm in existence.

Not only does Frank reaffirm his commitment to Lucy, but his parents, who had previously disapproved of the marriage, finally welcome her into the family with open arms: Frank's mother receives her with affection, and Frank's own father, the Dean of Bobsborough, performs the service for their marriage.

It is possible to read the representation of opinion in the episode of Frank and Lucy's courtship *contrapuntally* to the conception of opinion in the doctrine of binding precedent. According to the doctrine of binding precedent, following the opinions of people from the higher courts is supposed to lead to the best result, and therefore one must follow the set of opinions coming from a precedent case. The experience of Frank and Lucy shows that it is precisely by *not* following the opinions of people who are supposedly wiser than you are, it is precisely by following your own opinion and by defying those of other people, that you find the path to the 'happily ever after', a message made more poignant by the fact that Frank and Lucy are the only couple allowed a happy ending in Trollope's novel. It is precisely because other people's opinions about Lucy do not bind him that Frank is able to marry his true love.

Bibliography

Allen, C.K. (1935) 'Case Law: An Unwarrantable Intervention', *Law Quarterly Review* 51: 333–46.

Allen, C.K. (1964) *Law in the Making*, Oxford: Clarendon Press.

Aristodemou, M. (2000) *Law and Literature: From Her to Eternity*, Oxford: Oxford University Press.

Austin, J. (1861; 4th edn 1873) *Lectures on jurisprudence, or, The philosophy of positive law*, vol. 2, London: J. Murray.

Ben-yishai, A. (2007) 'The Fact of a Rumour: Anthony Trollope's *The Eustace Diamonds*', *Nineteenth-Century Literature* 62: 88–120.

Ben-yishai, A. (2011) 'Trollope and the Law', in Carolyn Dever (ed.) *The Cambridge Companion to Anthony Trollope*, Cambridge: Cambridge University Press.

Cohen, W.A. (1996) *Sex Scandal: The Private Parts of Victorian Fiction*, Durham, NC: Duke University Press.

Daniel, W.T.S. (1884) *The History and Origin of the Law Reports*, London: W. Cloves and Sons.

Duxbury, N. (2008) *The Nature and Authority of Precedent*, Cambridge: Cambridge University Press.

Evans, J. (1987) 'Change in the Doctrine of Precedent During the Nineteenth Century', in Laurence Goldstein (ed.) *Precedent in Law*, Oxford: Clarendon Press.

Gardner, S. (1992) 'Trashing with Trollope: A Deconstruction of the Postal Rule in Contract', *Oxford Journal of Legal Studies* 12: 170–94.

Goodhart, A.L. 'Case Law – A Short Replication', *Law Quarterly Review* 50: 196–200.

Goodlad, L. (2009) 'Anthony Trollope's *The Eustace Diamonds* and "The Great Parliamentary Bore" ', in Margaret Markwick, Deborah Denenholz Morse and Regenia Gagnier (ed.), *The Politics of Gender in Anthony Trollope's Novels*, Aldershot: Ashgate.

Holdsworth, W.S. (1934) 'Case Law', *Law Quarterly Review* 50: 181–95.

Lacey, N. 'Could he Forgive Her? Gender, Agency and Women's Criminality in the Novels of Anthony Trollope' (forthcoming)

Lacey, N. (2011) 'The Way We Lived Then: The Legal Profession and the 19th-Century Novel' *Sydney Law Review* 33: 599–621.

Pionke, A.D. 'Navigating "those terrible meshes of the Law": Legal Realism in Anthony Trollope's *Orley Farm* and *The Eustace Diamonds*', *ELH* 77: 129–57.

Reichman, R. (2009) *The Affective Life of Law: Legal Modernism and the Literary Imagination*, Stanford, CA: Stanford University Press.

Roth, A. (1992) 'He Thought He was Right (but Wasn't): Property Law in Anthony Trollope's *The Eustace Diamonds*', *Stanford Law Review* 44: 879–98.

Trollope, A. (1873) *The Eustace Diamonds*, London: Penguin, 2004.

Trollope, A. (1883) *An Autobiography*, London: Penguin, 1996.

Schramm, J.M. (2000) *Testimony and Advocacy in Victorian Law, Literature and Theology*, Cambridge: Cambridge University Press.

Ward, I. (1995) *Law and Literature: Possibilities and Perspectives*, Cambridge: Cambridge University Press.

Weisberg, R. (1992) *Poethics and Other Strategies of Law and Literature*, New York: Columbia University Press.

West, R. (1994) *Narrative, Authority and the Law*, Ann Arbor, MI: University of Michigan Press.

Chapter 14

Binding precedent
Robert Louis Stevenson's *Strange Case of Dr Jekyll and Mr Hyde*

Scott Veitch

A strange case

Few pieces of fiction exemplify so conspicuously the various senses of 'a case' as does Stevenson's *Strange Case of Dr Jekyll and Mr Hyde*. Its initial narrative – there are three – unfolds as the case of a mystery to be solved. It concerns the enigmatic identity of a man who has been named sole beneficiary in the will of eminent physician and scientist Dr Henry Jekyll. The intended legatee is a Mr Hyde. Subsequent to an alarming incident involving injury to a child in the street, the questionable nature of this proposed inheritance, and the even more questionable nature of Hyde, is being looked into by a friend of Jekyll's, Mr Utterson. Utterson is Jekyll's lawyer and the keeper of the will. Since Hyde seems to have access to funds coming from Jekyll, the lawyer at first suspects it to be a case of blackmail, and he pursues an inquiry into the mysterious figure of Hyde, eventually confronting him in the street. Utterson fears for the life of Jekyll himself, at the hands of Hyde seeking to hasten his substantial inheritance. But when it turns into a murder hunt – 'The Carew murder case' involving the killing of a prominent Member of Parliament – the likelihood that Hyde may be the murderer, and that Jekyll may be implicated in covering for him, leads Utterson to take urgent action. All his worries are confirmed when he breaks down the door to Jekyll's laboratory to find a dead body. But the body has the face of Hyde. Jekyll has disappeared.

By way of a last desperate note Dr Jekyll had directed the lawyer to open two written documents which would, he wrote, explain the case. The first is by another doctor, Dr Lanyon, a mutual friend of Utterson and Jekyll, which forms in part a case report of the scientific aspects of what had happened. It explains that Lanyon witnessed the experimental success of Dr Jekyll in transforming his own identity and appearance into that of another man, Hyde. It is a narrative also of bewilderment and despair, testifying to an experience which has already led its witness prematurely to the grave. The other document is simply labelled: 'Henry Jekyll's Full Statement of the Case'. This is the narrative of Dr Jekyll's experiments into personality change, of the temporary success of processes of change and reversal – to Hyde and back to Jekyll – and the difficulty in getting the right chemicals to secure the transition from occurring involuntarily. It includes also a statement of medical honour and this is invoked when Jekyll prepares Lanyon to witness for himself Jekyll's metamorphosis into Hyde: 'Lanyon, you remember your vows: what follows is under the seal of our profession.' (40) Utterson's own (legal) professionalism is described in similar terms when he is directed not to open the content of Lanyon's letter until the death or disappearance of Dr Jekyll: a direction he upholds because 'professional honour and faith' were 'stringent obligations' to his friend. (24)

Jekyll's relations with Hyde are also the subject of bonds of obligation. The content of Dr Jekyll's will, for example, directs that Mr Hyde inherit the estate in the event of Jekyll's disappearance, but that no fetters should be put on Hyde with respect to this: it is to be done 'without further delay and free from any burthen or obligation'. (6) The very relationship between Jekyll and Hyde that Utterson investigates is one that he believes would benefit from knowing more about Mr Hyde's identity in order that he 'might see a reason for his friend's strange preference or bondage' that could explain the terms of the will. (8) This term recurs when Jekyll shuts himself in his house and refuses to meet his erstwhile friends, leading Utterson to thinking of it as 'that house of voluntary bondage'. (24) And when the MP, Carew, is murdered it is because Hyde 'broke out of all bounds and clubbed him to the earth', (15) the result of which is that Jekyll tells Utterson that he 'swears to God I will never set my eyes upon [Hyde] again. I bind my honour to you . . .' (19)

But it is with 'Henry Jekyll's full statement of the case' that the issue of binding comes centre stage. We need to recall at this point what led Jekyll to set off on his experimental path. It was an observation, long-made, that he had drives within himself that competed with each other, some respectable, others not. He detected this as being a general condition, 'that hard law of life', which attested to the 'provinces of good and ill which divide and compound man's nature'. (42) This condition, which lay also 'at the root of religion', led him to the further 'truth by whose partial discovery I have been doomed to such a dreadful shipwreck: that man is not truly one, but truly two'. (42–3) There is a clarity in Jekyll's insight at this point that takes him beyond the mere observation of a Victorian hypocrisy, one that would exclaim righteousness and honour on the outside, but be wicked and dishonourable underneath. He says: 'though so profound a double-dealer, I was in no sense a hypocrite; both sides of me were in dead earnest.' (42) There is something mutually constitutive about these two sides to him which Jekyll intuits in these terms: 'even if I could rightly be said to be either it was only because I was radically both'. (43) And again, he generalizes from this in terms that introduce for the first time in his confession the matter of binding: 'It was the curse of mankind that these incongruous faggots were bound together – that in the agonized womb of consciousness, these polar twins should be continuously struggling.' (43)

G.K. Chesterton was one of the first to observe the way in which this point, and hence the story itself, worked. He noted that the 'real stab of the story' is 'not in the discovery that the one man is two men; but in the discovery that the two men are one man'.[4] And it was this discovery that prompted Jekyll the experimental physician to take a leap into the unknown, into the realm of possibility where science might be able to work for the benefit of humankind. Because, he reasoned, if this duality could be prised apart, would not progress be possible? 'If each, I told myself, could but be housed in separate identities, life would be relieved of all that was unbearable.' (43) The just and the unjust could be dissociated and go their different ways. This was his 'beloved daydream': to improve on man's condition.

Jekyll is not a split personality in the sense that the story is often misunderstood. There is not a prior unitary subject who is split in two, and there is not straightforwardly Jekyll who is good and Hyde who is bad. The point is rather that Jekyll is Jekyll *and* Hyde. When Jekyll creates the drug that will transform him into Hyde, he releases 'the evil side of my nature' and observes that 'This, too, was myself'. The difference was that 'Hyde alone, among the ranks of mankind, was pure evil'. (44–5)

But let us return to the binding. Jekyll's confession, though it is not long, contains one phrase that appears twice. The transformation into Hyde is described by Jekyll in two separate places as 'a solution of the bonds of obligation'. (44, 51) What does this phrase mean? It contains, I will suggest, a deep trace of meaning that is central both to the text and to Stevenson's own view of modern life. It is also, I will argue, one that is central to a particular understanding of the relation between law and life; or, in more philosophical terms, between the juridical and the ontology of human being.

'A solution of the bonds of obligation'

Let me offer three possibilities on the meaning of this repeated phrase. First, 'a solution' here conjures up an image of chemical reaction: the drug, a chemical solution, is the means by which Jekyll's transformation is induced. It is as if, also, the bonds of obligation are dissolved in the chemical process; washed away, no longer what they were, they become transformed into the new compound, the new solution. To 'dissolve' suggests that the bonds break up, separate into parts, are 'loosed asunder' – if the bonds are dissolved they are loosened and broken apart. There is, we would say, a dissolution, a breaking up, or dispersal of what was once held together, just like a marriage may be dissolved or there can be a dissolution of Parliament. But we also have here a clear moral connotation: to be dissolute, in morals say, is to be debauched, of loose morals.

There is a second reading that is possible here in the sense that the solution directs us to imagine 'the answer to' something; a solution is a figuring out, a clearing up of a puzzle, an explanation. There is a solution to a problem: one *solves* the case. But as a solution *of* the bonds of obligation, this reading would have a slightly awkward ring to it. A solution *to* the bonds of obligation would seem more accurate for this reading to be persuasive.

We come then to a third reading which has a hidden legal dimension and in order to understand this we need to explain a little of Stevenson's background in the law. 'I have been reading Roman Law and Calvin this morning', he wrote in a letter to his friend Mrs Francis Sitwell, in May 1874.[5] Quite a combination, one may think, though not necessarily so for its time and place – Stevenson had grown up in a religious household and had in the early 1870s studied law in Edinburgh sufficiently well to qualify to practise as an advocate at the Scottish bar (which he did for a brief time. But it was not for him: he only ever had four cases and he relished escape from even this limited practice). He had studied Roman Law as part of his education, and indeed had written his dissertation for entry into the Faculty of Advocates on a section of Justinian's *Pandects*. He would therefore have been familiar with the Roman law of obligations. It is to this we now need to turn.

Before coming to the 'solution' let us consider the terms of the phrase 'bonds of obligation' in more detail. The roots of 'obligation' in the western legal tradition go back to the early Roman law where they have a distinctly corporeal aspect. According to the Law of the Twelve Tables, a creditor could put a debtor in chains (literally, since the law prescribed that their weight was not to exceed 15 pounds) until the debt had been repaid. If it was not, and 'if a man was indebted to several creditors and insolvent, after certain formalities they might cut up his body and divide it among them. If there was a single creditor, he might put his debtor to death or sell him as a slave'. (Holmes: 9–10) The nature of the obligation therefore had its origins in the physical binding of debtors: 'the division of the body shows that the debt was conceived very literally to inhere in or bind the body with a *vinculum juris*'. (ibid.: 10)

This *vinculum juris* was the legal tie, or chain, that was to survive the demise of the bodily binding. According to Reinhard Zimmerman the 'very word "obligatio" always reminded the Roman lawyer of the fact that, in former times, the person who was to be liable, that is over whose body the creditor acquired the pledge-like power of seizure, was physically laid in bonds'. (Zimmerman: 5). That the debtor 'ought to', or as we still say 'was bound to', do whatever was legally required of him therefore had its antecedents in the fact that he was *literally* 'bound to' do it: 'the concept of an obligation, in the minds of laymen as well as lawyers, seems to have retained the connotation of some sort of invisible rope around the neck of the debtor, tying a specific debtor to a particular creditor. The obligation thus gave rise to an intensely personal relationship . . . with personal liability of the strictest kind'. (ibid)[6]

The Latin 'obligatio' contains within it the component 'lig' that signifies the same binding in the 'obligation' as one finds in 'ligament', or 'ligature'[7] and, significantly – for we will return to this – 'religion', the binding back to God. Stevenson would have been familiar with this Roman Law derivation, both from his doctrinal legal studies and perhaps even more so from his reading of Henry Maine whose highly influential work of comparative jurisprudence, *Ancient Law*, had come out in 1861. 'I had been reading Maine', he said in 1872 (Jolly: 564), and this was how Maine had described the origin of obligation in his chapter on 'The Early History of Contract': 'The Obligation is the "bond" or "chain" with which the law joins together persons or groups of persons . . . The image of a *vinculum juris* colours and pervades every part of the Roman law of Contract and Delict.' (Maine: 323–4) If it pervaded Roman Law, as Zimmerman and Maine attest, then the power of its imagery has still not waned: as late as the 1960s, the eminent English legal philosopher H.L.A. Hart wrote that 'The figure of a bond binding the person obligated . . . haunts much of legal thought . . .' (Hart 1961: 85).

So here we have the early roots for the bond of obligation. But what concerns us directly now is how one got out of this bond. The answer in Roman Law was clear: a fulfilment of the obligation was required according to the corresponding form of law and only this could release the debtor from the legal tie by which he was bound. And the Latin term for this? *Solutio*: 'The law bound the parties together, and the chain could only be undone by the process of solution.' (Maine: 324) And hence we have our third term, the solution. It too had its root in the material origins that required a response to the physical binding. According to Zimmerman 'to indicate fulfilment of an obligation the term "solvere" (= to loosen) refers back to the stage where payment was a means of securing release from power of seizure, that is, of loosening the (not merely metaphorical) bond around the debtor's body'. (6) The *solutio* was therefore the way in which for Roman lawyers the bond of obligation could be loosened, and in the early period the body of the debtor literally liberated. Later, when the *vinculum juris* was no longer physical, the payment the debtor made in fulfilment of the obligation would release him from the binding presence of the legal tie. In both cases, this was a solution of the bonds of obligation.

If we turn back to the use of the phrase in *Strange Case* we can see that 'a solution of the bonds of obligation' means neither a chemical reaction nor an answer to a problem, but rather a loosening of a bond that is also, at one and the same time, a fulfilment and ending of one's obligation. It is this that perhaps best characterizes what Dr Jekyll sees as happening in the process of metamorphosing into Hyde: a loosening of the bonds that have tied together two people in one, a *solutio* that gave release from the fetters by which 'these incongruous faggots were bound together'. For Jekyll's identity could only be understood as a bounded being. And this binding together, by the bond of obligation which made Jekyll what he was – Jekyll *and* Hyde – was precisely what his 'beloved daydream' had led him to imagine unbound.

Being, bound

If in Roman Law the solution was simultaneously a fulfilment of an obligation and its termination it was because making the requisite payment set the debtor free. But how does this work with Jekyll? Two questions arise: first, what is the source and nature of the obligation itself; and secondly, if something had to be paid to terminate it, what is the nature of the payment?

To be bound originally, as Jekyll and Hyde were bound together, we need to consider the source of this obligation. One clue lies in how Jekyll acts when he tries to redeem himself when Hyde has 'broken all bounds' and murdered Carew. Hyde takes the drug and, with great relief, transforms back to Jekyll; the reader is told that he then fell 'upon his knees and lifted his clasped hands to God' with 'streaming tears of gratitude and remorse'. (50) Hence he turns first to religion: precisely to the re-binding – *re-ligare* – of himself with God. Spurning the disastrous implications of Hyde unbound, this will also now require a rebinding of himself, and so, desirous to return to leading his old respectable life again, he promises to 'embrace [. . .] anew the restrictions of natural life'. (50) Hence the obligation that he seeks to re-form has its sources in religion and nature which will in turn underpin and inform the obligations of social life. Such 'natural obligations', as Viscount Stair the founding figure of Scots Law described them in his *Institutions* with which Stevenson would also have had familiarity, were obligations that precede our entry into the world; duties that exist prior to contract, prior to conscious choice or assumption, but that make us what we are and can be. This was the law of nature which was 'written on man's heart' (Stair: I.1.3) and which required obedience 'to the authority and will of his Maker . . . Hence do arise those obligations upon man, which are not by his own consent and engagement, nor by the will of man, but by the will of God'. (Stair: I.1.19) From such natural obligations were derived conventional obligations which together formed the weave of duties, loyalties, and in turn the freedoms that social life demands and offers. These are the bonds of society, of sociality, that are constituted by those social institutions whose obligations define family, friendship, community, and the senses of conscientiousness and honour in our practical activities.

But if the solution loosened or untied these bonds of obligation, what then was paid? What did Jekyll have to pay as a solution of the bonds? This is the second question and we may take our clue from a text published the year after *Strange Case*. Tracing back the problem of 'bad conscience' to the 'earliest of times', in some breathtaking passages in *The Genealogy of Morals* Nietzsche had noted two things of direct relevance here; first, that the origin of the 'moral concept of "guilt" ' lay in the 'very material concept of debt' (Nietzsche: 44), and that therefore 'It is in this sphere, in legal obligation, then, that the moral conceptual world of "guilt", "conscience", "duty", "sacred duty", originates.' (Nietzsche: 46–7) But he also saw that behind, and prior to, these concepts lay a very corporeal origin. Nietzsche argued that anger at harm directed at the one who causes it, rather than a concept of responsibility, demanded a certain 'equivalence', an equivalence that draws its strength from the earlier debtor–creditor relationship though not in monetary terms. Rather it is in the sense that the harm done 'really can be paid off even if this is through the pain of the culprit'. (Nietzsche: 45) Pulling these strands together, Nietzsche writes: 'In order to instil trust for his promise of repayment, in order to give a guarantee for the seriousness and sacredness of his promise, in order to impress repayment as a duty and obligation sharply upon his own conscience, the debtor contractually pledges to the creditor in the event of non-payment something which he otherwise still "possesses", something over which he still has power – for example, his body or his wife or his freedom or even his life.' (Nietzsche: 45) Where non-payment occurs the creditor can therefore demand to inflict pain equivalent to the amount of debt owed. *This* was the origin of responsibility and conscience, and it was this that made man an animal that could make promises and remember to keep them: it 'originate[d] from that instinct which guessed that the most powerful aid to memory was pain . . . with the help of this sort of memory, one eventually did come to "see reason"!' (Nietzsche: 43–4)

Read in this way, Jekyll pays with the suffering of something he otherwise still possesses: his body, that 'fleshy vestment' (43) that housed his old selves. The transformation into Hyde is a mental *and* physical one, and it is this which is the key to the price he pays for the loosening of the bonds of obligation. But while Jekyll was happy to pay the price of transformation initially, the problem is that eventually he pays and pays and pays until he has nothing left with which to pay: he is, as Jekyll, physically and spiritually *spent*; bankrupt, insolvent. And so as he transforms involuntarily into Hyde for the final time, because he cannot get the drugs to reverse the transformation, the 'last calamity' has now happened 'which has finally severed me from my own face and nature'. (54) He dies, in pain, as Hyde. This is the price that was paid.

But then one other question now surfaces: who is the *creditor*, who stood to gain? Turning back to Nietzsche's terms, who was it that had the right to inflict pain, who had the right to cruelty, the right to demand equivalence? Arguably we have a case of a missing creditor. Is it Hyde, who gains liberation, so he can indulge his 'good pleasure'; who goes 'drinking pleasure with bestial avidity from any degree of torture to another'? (46) Possibly. (Nietzsche will argue, co-incidentally, that equivalence was not found in 'direct compensation' but rather that 'a sort of *pleasure* is conceded to the creditor': precisely, the 'pleasure of violation . . . the opportunity to *inflict* suffering – an actual *festivity* . . . the enjoyment of which will be prized all the more highly, the lower the creditor stands in the social order'. [Nietzsche: 46–7, original emphasis]) Or is it perhaps, in religious terms, the devil who gains? Or is it God, whose infliction of divine punishment could ultimately be expected to follow?

Or is it, more brutally perhaps, that no-one gains? For what is the lesson in all this? That one must keep the evil with one. Not, importantly, that one must repress it, keep it secret or denied, but instead recognize that being a person meant being bound to one's devil always, keeping it with one, as part of oneself, 'closer than a wife, closer than an eye'. (53) But what kind of lesson is this? What is the value of such a morality as this? What worth a religious lineage such that one must re-bind not only with God, but that one must also keep one's binding to the devil? A strange one indeed: re-binding the devil and the conscience in order to re-make one's identity, as both. If this is the nature of morality, what could its value amount to?

Stevenson will not answer this, but he has raised it, exposed it to the light, and in Jekyll's final and full 'statement of the case' this lesson is announced not with conviction, religious or otherwise, not, as we might say, with resolve, but rather with resignation and dejection. In his dream of separating the two elements within that 'incongruous compound' (45) that was man, Jekyll had found a solution of the bonds of obligation but it turned out to be no answer at all. The conclusion was instead that we remain bound as Jekyll and Hyde; bound to 'the diabolic in man' (letter 1887, quoted Bell: 179). If Jekyll came to see that Hyde was not human, 'He, I say – I cannot say, I. That child of Hell had nothing human; nothing lived in him but fear and hatred' (52), then Jekyll's humanity was only as bound to Hyde, Hyde-bound, bound to the inhuman. The Hyde in man didn't break away in the normal course of things, but having forced the matter scientifically Jekyll's insight is that Hyde *shouldn't* break away. His lesson, then, was this: 'I have been made to learn that the doom and burthen of our life is bound for ever on man's shoulders; and when the attempt is made to cast it off, it but returns upon us with more unfamiliar and more awful pressure.' (47) What appeared to be the tragedy of the tale – ultimately Dr Jekyll's helpless unbinding and unstoppable transformation into Hyde – turns out not to have been the only, nor the most awful one: the more profound tragedy is of the bound being: the remaining bound, the conditional binding of our state, as bonded beings, beings in bondage: to religion, to our Roman inheritance, to our pre-contractual debts, to our inhumanity. Not so much the human condition as the human conditional: if and only if we remain bound to the evil in us, then we can be human. This is the ontological condition of our being: being, bound.

The strange case of the legal bond

This observation supplies perhaps one of the main reasons for the enduring fascination with this tale. We might in passing compare its insight with another literary 'strange case', this one literally: 'L'Etranger'. Albert Camus's well known novel of the stranger or outsider has also made a durable impact on the modern imaginary. Disaffected, alienated and bewildered by what he sees as the absurdities of modern social norms and expectations, Camus's Mersault is a coolly estranged figure who cannot or will not integrate and is left detached, on the outside. But the comparison with Stevenson is instructive. In a sense Stevenson had been there before, seen this too, but what he came up with wasn't an early version of Mersault. Rather he portrayed something far more troubling: the *insider*. And this was the 'horror' at its worst. Respectable, *bourgeois*, professional; but also, and at the same time, wild, pitiless, frenetic. In fact, we should read this the other way round for proper effect: wild, pitiless, frenetic, but also and at the same time respectable, *bourgeois*, professional. These two were bound together – remember Chesterton: the stab is that two men are one man – and together they constituted modern man: 'both sides of me were in dead earnest'.

And it is with the 'insider' problem that both Jekyll and Stevenson struggle most. Although it is set in London, *Strange Case* is a deeply and recognizably Scottish story. As a native, one is tempted to be even more precise and say it is a deeply and recognizably *Edinburgh* story. Edinburgh's numerous dualities[8] were personified for Stevenson in his obsession with the true story of Deacon Brodie (1741–1788), a respectable Edinburgher by day and criminal by night, a figure who would make a great and lasting mark on the city's imaginary, and a piece of whose furniture had reputedly ended up in Stevenson's childhood home. He would later be invoked by Edinburgh's literary first lady – fictional but by no means unreal – Miss Jean Brodie: 'I am a descendent, do not forget, of Willie Brodie, a man of substance, a cabinet maker and a designer of gibbets, a member of the Town Council of Edinburgh and a keeper of two mistresses who bore him five children between them. Blood tells.' (Spark 2000: 88) Blood does indeed tell for Stevenson too. In a response to a critic who had queried the 'puzzling enigmatic ethics' in *Strange Case*, Stevenson admitted as much attributing 'the confusion of my ethics' in part to 'the old Scotch Presbyterian preoccupation about these problems'. This preoccupation, 'itself morbid', he continued, found direct expression in the story: 'the Scotch side came out plain in Dr Jekyll'. [quoted in Linehan: 84–5] Stevenson's ambivalent relation to Scotland was borne out here: on the one hand a desire to escape its overweening strictures, but on the other the realization of its profound and richly textured influence on the shaping of personality. 'National sins bind us with iron' he wrote in a letter of 1887, and this was one bond that would be hard, though not impossible, to dissolve. Writing in the final years of his life on Samoan politics and the effects of European colonization on the places he had visited in his journeys in the Pacific, he warned the reader to 'remember that you cannot change ancestral feelings of right and wrong without what is practically soul-murder'. (Quoted in Jolly 2009: 136) A forced change – such as he witnessed in so many places to which he travelled – was disastrous, and the language of Jekyll and Hyde returned with remarkable force in the colonial setting: 'The social bond in Apia [the capital of Samoa]' he noted, 'was dissolved'. (ibid: 137)

But the 'confusion of my ethics', said Stevenson, had a second source. This he identified as associated with 'an age of transition', a contemporary phrase that referred to 'the way in which rapidly advancing scientific discovery, industrialization, urbanization, and democratization were not only transforming everyday life, but also radically unsettling established systems of ethical and religious thought'. (Linehan: 84–5, footnote 3) Together with the 'Scotch side' Stevenson admits to his critic, 'the categorical imperative is ever with me, but utters dark oracles . . . Ethics are my veiled mistress; I love them but I know not what they are'. (Quoted in Linehan: 85) Without doubt it is the uttering of 'dark oracles' that comes across with great intensity in *Strange Case*. Stevenson recognized the enduring strength and impact of religion and nation (and in the case of Calvinism in Scotland, of a 'national religion') but had enough doubt about its practice to relate this with a sceptic's insight: this – modern man, the insider – was the effect of the binding, not of the dissolution, of religion and nation. The exigencies of the 'age of transition', and in particular the possibilities and perils of science, merely added to the confusion. Hence the most troubling aspect of the story is concerned with this problem of 'binding and loosing' not as an aspect of an individual's moral failure – Jekyll's lack of self-control, say – but rather of the possibility of a failed morality, of morality *as* failure. Nietzsche's observation the following year captures this in philosophical terms (and does so with an uncanny resemblance, in its first phrase, with Stevenson's story): 'What if there existed a symptom of regression in the "good man", likewise a danger, a temptation, a poison, a narcotic, by means of which the present were living *at the expense of the future*? . . . so that none other than morality itself would be the culprit.' (Nietzsche: 8, original emphasis) The deeper concern is then not with the problems of personality and the attribution of responsibility, nor even with the binding influence of the past and its powers of locating, important as all these are to grasp. It is instead with this: the '*value* of values'. 'Previously', Nietzsche maintained, 'no-one had expressed even the remotest doubt or slightest hesitation in assuming the "good man" to be of greater worth than the "evil man".' But what 'if the opposite were the case?': that the 'good man', not the 'evil man', and hence not immorality but 'morality would constitute the danger of dangers' (Nietzsche: 7–8). It is precisely this 'vertiginous possibility' that Stevenson has led us artistically to imagine looking down on, to turn our gaze not to pure evil – that would be straightforward – but to the insider, to the inhuman in the human, to the very *worth* of morality in the age of transition.

What will this tell us about the legal case? What I have sought to emphasize in the reading of *Strange Case* offered here draws on the earlier observation that 'the legal case' can be understood in a range of ways, many of which are explored in the other chapters in this collection. In particular they consider the normative implications of precedent and the conditions for the emergence of and the binding nature of 'case law'. There may also be epistemological issues raised – both in general terms and as matters of 'legal epistemology' – and representational aspects that will in their own way raise a number of significant normative questions. But it is the *ontological* dimension of the 'legal case', broadly conceived, that has been the priority of this chapter. For here we reach below the rightly important questions associated with the binding nature of case law to a different sense of binding. Alain Supiot identifies this as the 'anthropological function of law', arguing that law is 'not the expression of a truth revealed by God or discovered by science' (Supiot 2007: xxv); rather it is 'by transforming each of us into a *homo juridicus* that, in the west, the biological and symbolic dimensions that make up our being have been linked together. The law connects our infinite mental universe with our finite physical existence and in so doing fulfils the anthropological function of instituting us as rational beings.' (ibid: ix)

If the character of Jekyll and Hyde was coincidentally torn somewhere between 'God and science', then the power of the story drew precisely on the nature of the bonds that link together the 'biological and symbolic dimensions' of being human. But importantly the character is not neatly *homo juridicus*. Because these bonds are questionable in the exact sense that they might *not* institute us 'as rational beings'. In the struggle with and against the very bonds that constituted modern humanity, Stevenson compels us to question the value of that rationality that would hold together good and evil.[9] Set deep within the normative structures of the past, the centrality of the lineage of the legal bond to the story, as I have interpreted it here, attests to the crucial role of the juridical in the link between the mental and the physical both historically and in the present. But it is one whose value Stevenson has provoked us to consider more thoroughly and more critically.

To return finally to Hart's observation, it is the figure of a 'bond binding the person obligated' that likewise haunts *Strange Case*. If it haunts legal thought too then it is likely that it has a remarkable, and underplayed, history that would need much more investigation to do it justice. This is particularly true if it too, like Jekyll's closing insight, constantly returns 'with more unfamiliar and awful pressure'. Suffice to say for now, taking inspiration from the nature of 'binding precedent' in Stevenson's tale, that this history is likely to be at once a very familiar and, in its spectral aspect, a very strange one.

Endnotes

1 Lacey (2010) is particularly insightful on the complexities of the changing nature of attribution in criminal law.
2 The original poem in the letter Stevenson wrote to his cousin was more Scottish, though less portentious, in its expression: 'We cannae break the bonds that God decreed to bind'.
3 Stevenson (1886) 1. Page references in brackets in the text are to this edition.
4 Quoted in Linehan (2003) 183.
5 Stevenson (1926: 183). Later that year he wrote to her again that he continued to work on John Knox and on a story (unnamed) that 'was so horrible . . . I feel as if it is *a crime against humanity*'. (Ibid: 211, Sept 1874, emphasis added) This appears to be the earliest use of this latter phrase, predating its usual date of recognition in 1890, also in a letter, from a United States observer of King Leopold's exploits in the Congo. Of course Stevenson's letter was not public.
6 This practice may have given way in ancient Rome, but that of putting debtors in jail was of considerable longevity. Thus we have Stair (see later in the text) writing at the end of the seventeenth century in Scotland that, 'the law alloweth personal execution, or restraint and incarceration of the debtor's person, until he do all the deeds that are in his power for the satisfaction of his creditor.' (Stair I.2.7)
7 See Birks and Macleod (1987).
8 As well as the real Deacon Brodie, the classic early fictional text is James Hogg's *Private Memoirs and Confessions of a Justified Sinner* published in 1824.
9 There is no final resolution to this in the story: as Ian Bell noted of Stevenson's work, 'His art was a moral argument presented in an entertainer's costume' (Bell: xv), but it was the entertainment that had primacy.

Bibliography

Bell, I. (1992) *Dreams of Exile*, Edinburgh: Mainstream.
Birks, P. and Macleod, G. (1987) 'Introduction', *Justinian's Institutes*, London: Duckworth.
Daiches, D. (1973) *Robert Louis Stevenson and his World*, London: Thames and Hudson.
Hart, H.L.A. (1961) *The Concept of Law*, Oxford: Clarendon.
Holmes, O.W. (1881) *The Common Law*, Boston, MA: Little, Brown.
Jolly, R. (2006) 'Robert Louis Stevenson, Henry Maine, and the Anthropology of Comparative Law' 45 *Journal of British Studies*, 556–80.
Jolly, R. (2009) *Robert Louis Stevenson in the Pacific*, Farnham: Ashgate.
Lacey, N. (2010) 'Psychologising Jekyll, Demonising Hyde: The Strange Case of Criminal Responsibility', *Criminal Law and Philosophy* 4: 109–33.
Linehan, K. (2003) (ed) *Strange Case of Dr Jekyll and Mr Hyde*, Norton Critical Edition, New York: WW Norton.

MacIntyre, A. (1990) *Three Rival Versions of Moral Inquiry*, London: Duckworth.
Maine, H.S. (2002) *Ancient Law*, New Brunswick, NJ: Transaction (1861).
Nietzsche, F. (1887) *The Genealogy of Morals*, trans D. Smith, Oxford: Oxford University Press (1998).
Spark, M. (2000) *The Prime of Miss Jean Brodie*, London: Penguin (1961).
Stair, Viscount (James Dalrymple) (1681) *The Institutions of the Law of Scotland*, Edinburgh & Glasgow: University Presses (1981).
Stevenson, R.L. (1886) *Strange Case of Dr Jekyll and Mr Hyde*, Ontario: Dover edition (1991).
Stevenson, R.L. (1926) *The Works of Robert Louis Stevenson*, Letters: Vol. 1, London: Heinemann.
Supiot, A. (2007) *Homo Juridicus: On the Anthropological Function of the Law*, trans. S. Brown, London: Verso.
Zimmerman, R. (1990) *The Law of Obligations: Roman Foundations of the Civilian Tradition*, Oxford: Clarendon.

Index

Note: The locator 26nn4 and 9 refers to endnotes 4 and 9 on page 26.

A (children) (conjoined twins), *Re* (2000) 11, 110
abridgements (law reports) 19, 115
Achebe, Chinua: extratextual precedents 162–5; internal precedents 162, 165–7; Lefebvre: creativity of jurisprudence 160–2, 168, 170, 171; literary precedents 162, 167–70; *No Longer at Ease* 159–71; *Things Fall Apart* 159
Adam v Cape Industries plc (1990) 41
Adams, trial of Henry Bodkin 62, 63, 64, 72
Aeneid 84, 175
Agamben, G. 119, 123, 124, 125
Allen, C.K. 208
ambiguity 129, 130; China 146, 149–50, 152, 154–5; different kinds of 'case' 11, 12–17, 25; doctrines of legal construction 16, 129; hooliganism 146; 'reporting' cases 17–19, 25; speculation 146; *see also* vagueness and precedent
Aquinas, Thomas 49
Aristotle 123, 181–2, 184
art and nature 180, 183–6
Austin, John 114, 129, 208, 209
autonomous individual 41–2
autopoiesis 42

Badiou, A. 55, 57
Bakhtin, Mikhail 180
Barendt, E. 12
Bate, J. 176, 178
Bedford, Sybille: comparative measurement of different jurisdictions 72; court's fixtures 73; Germany 74–6; law as cultural paradigm 70–1, 75, 77; law itself on trial 73; Part 1 61–6; Part 2 66–71; Part 3 71–7; trial as fantasy narrative 72–3
Bell, I. 226
Ben-Yishai, A. 26nn4 and 9, 27n11, 209, 213
Benjamin, Walter 87
Bentham, Jeremy 56, 86, 115
Bentinck, William 86
Benton, Lauren 81, 85
Berlant, L. 1
Berle, A. 30
Bewley, M. 63
Bhabha 81
Biber, D. 21, 22
Bible 84; 2 Corinthians 3:6 35; Deuteronomy 196; Genesis 198; Leviticus 196
Blackstone, W. 84, 183
Bond, E.A. 98–101
Bordwell, D. 24–5
Boyd, T.M. 63
Bradley, A.C. 191, 200
Bray, J.F. 37
Brewer, S. 124
Brine, K.R. 82
Brodie, Deacon 226–7
Brooks, P. 3
Browne, T. 194
Burke, Edmund 81, 84; impeachment trial of Warren Hastings 91–3, 94–5, 97, 98–100, 101–5
Burrow, James 19
Burton, J.A. 195

Cabet, Étienne 203
Camus, Albert 226

capitalism 36–7, 40–1, 42
Cardozo, B.N. 5, 202–3
Carlyle, T. 36
carnival 180
Carty, A. 105
'case' 1–2, 11; different kinds of 12–17, 217–19, 228
case method of teaching 3
case reports 11–12, 17–19, 25; function/use 21–2; history 19–20, 115, 178–9, 208–9; reading cases: the role of genre 22–4; structure 20–1; understanding inference and rhetoric 24–5; unreported cases 20; *see also* China: Guiding Case system; court writing of Sybille Bedford; precedent
chain novel 178
Cheng, S.D. 157
Chesterton, G.K. 220, 226
China: Guiding Case System 142, 154–6; enactment 151–3; functions 149–51; historical perspective 143–9; SPP's Guiding Case System 149, 150, 153–4
Christianity 35–6, 84, 180–1, 227; Bible *see separate entry*
Cicero, M.T. 176, 179
cinema *see* truth: law, cinema and psychoanalysis
civil law systems 84–5; hybridized nature of China's legal system *see* China
Cobuild dictionary project 13
Cohen, W.A. 213
Cohn, Bernard S. 81, 85, 87
Coke, Sir Edward 19, 114, 115, 118, 122, 175–6, 178, 179, 181–2, 186
Colebrooke, H.T. 82, 87
colonialism 227; distinction between French and British 83; English identity and culture 209; illegality of Empire: impeachment trial of Warren Hastings *see separate entry*; Nigeria: *No Longer at Ease* (Achebe) 159–71; reasonableness 161–2; rule of law 84; Sir William Jones and the translation of law in India 80–8
The Comedy of Errors (Shakespeare) 177
common law systems 84–5; hybridized nature of China's legal system *see* China; *see also* precedent
community of practice 23
company law: *Salomon v Salomon* 29–30, 31–4, 41–2; Aron Salomon as Shylock 35–7; Jews and the modern company 37–41; 'one-man company' case 30–1

Connor, A. 144
contestability 130
Cornish, W. 12
court system 209
court writing of Sybille Bedford, everyday law in: comparative measurement of different jurisdictions 72; court's fixtures 73; Germany 74–6; law as cultural paradigm 70–1, 75, 77; law itself on trial 73; Part 1 61–6; Part 2 66–71; Part 3 71–7; trial as fantasy narrative 72–3
Coyle, Martin 12
criminal law 218, 219
Cross, R. 5
culture: English identity and 209; everyday life and 70–1, 75, 77; reasonableness 161–2; Sir William Jones and translation of law in India 80–8
Cunningham, Clark D. 139
customary law 85, 87, 161

Dalrymple, James (Viscount Stair) 224
Dalrymple, William 90, 93–4, 95, 96, 105
dangerous driving 134
Daniel Deronda (Eliot) 40
Debrett 102
Defoe, Daniel 18–19
Deleuze, G. 122, 124, 160–1, 168
democracy 130
deregulation 29
Derrett, J. 85
Derrida, J. 48
Devlin, Patrick 72
Devos, Filip 129
Dignam, A. 31
Dirks, N.B. 90–1, 93–6, 105
dissenting and majority opinions 202–3
Doderidge, J. 175–6
Doniger, Wendy 85
drama 178, 180, 186; carnival 180; Shakespeare *see separate entry*; theatricality of courtroom 64–6, 69, 91, 177
Draper, R.P. 12
Dred Scott v Sanford (1857) 202, 203
Du Maurier, George 35
Dumas, Leon 167
Duxbury, N. 114–15, 116, 118, 121
Dworkin, R. 26n5, 109, 116, 122, 129, 178
Dyson, A.E. 12

East India Company 81, 83, 84, 87, 88; impeachment trial of Warren Hastings 90–105; restrictions on activities of 101

Eliot, George: *Daniel Deronda* 40
Eliot, T.S. 17; 'East Coker' 65–6; 'Journey of the Magi' 167–8
Endicott, Timothy A.O. 132
English identity and culture 209
equity 179; trusts 186
Esher, M.C. 133
The Eustace Diamonds (Trollope) 205–15; shift from *stare decisis* to binding precedent 206–15
Evans, J. 207, 208
everyday law in court writing of Sybille Bedford 61–77; comparative measurement of different jurisdictions 72; court's fixtures 73; Germany 74–6; law as cultural paradigm 70–1, 75, 77; law itself on trial 73; Part 1 61–6; Part 2 66–71; Part 3 71–7; trial as fantasy narrative 72–3
experts 219

fantasy narrative, trial as 72–3
Ferguson, R.A. 64
film *see* truth: law, cinema and psychoanalysis
Fish, S. 23–4, 109, 110
Flaubert, G. 137
Fortescue, J. 179, 181, 182–3, 185, 186
Foster, N. 41
Foucault, M. 64, 112, 181
Fraunce, A. 182
Freud, S. 42, 51, 55, 56, 57, 191–2, 201
Frye, Northrup 203
Frykenberg, R.E. 90–1, 102, 105

Gandhi, M.K. 84
Garber, M. 192
gardening metaphor: grafting 183, 185–6
Gardner, S. 209, 215
Garner v Burr (1951) 128
gender 211
Germany 74–6
Gilbert and Sullivan 39
Goethe, J.W. von 192, 201
Goldschmidt, V. 123
Goldstein, Laurence 131
Goodrich, Peter 3, 64–5, 182, 184
Gray, Alexander 37
Green, Edward 138
Greenblatt, S. 192
Greene, Graham 167

Grey, Charles 94, 99, 100–1
Guppy, S. 64

Haldar, Piyel 81, 82, 88
Hale, Sir Matthew 115–16, 128
Halhed, N.B. 81, 85, 87
Hallward, P. 55
Hamlet 190–203; dissenting opinions 202–3; ghost resembling Hamlet's father 191, 192–4; language of English law 177–8; marriage of Claudius to Gertrude 190, 195–7, 201; murder of Polonius 191, 200, 202; play-within-the-play 191, 192, 197–8; refusal to kill Claudius in chapel 191, 192, 198–200, 203; Rosencrantz and Guildenstern 191, 200–1, 202; self-incrimination, right against 198
Harding, A. 19
Hardy, Thomas 14–15
Hart, H.L.A. 117, 128, 152, 223, 229
Hastings, Warren 81, 86, 87; impeachment trial of 90–105
Hegel, G.W.F. 124
Heller-Roazen, D. 124
Henry IV, Part 2 (Shakespeare) 187n27
Hinduism and Hindu law: Sir William Jones and the translation of law in India 80–8
history: China: historical perspective on Guiding Case System 143–9; court system 209; Jews in Britain: social and economic *see Salomon v Salomon*; law reports 19–20, 115, 178–9, 208–9; *narratores* 178; nature and the dreamland of law 179–86; patterns and precedent in Shakespeare and the law 175–8; precedent 114–16, 118, 124, 175–8, 206–9; printing technology 179, 180; self-incrimination, right against 198; shift from *stare decisis* to binding precedent 206–15
Hobbes, T. 114, 115, 118
Hoeflich, M. 29
Holdsworth, W.S. 178, 208
Holmes, O.W. 222
Homer 111
Hong Kong 137
Honoré, A.M. 111
horticultural metaphor: grafting 183, 185–6
Housman, A.E.: 'Easter Hymn' 167–8
Hume, David 116, 135

impeachment trial of Warren Hastings 90–1, 97–102, 104–5; British liberal political culture and history of international law 102–4; constitutional law 101, 102; international law significance of treaties 99–100, 101–2; literary criticism, historians and the trial 93–7; literary critics and the trial 91–3
indeterminacy of meaning 128–9, 130–1; ambiguity *see separate entry*; contestability 130; relativity 130; vagueness *see separate entry*
India: impeachment trial of Warren Hastings *see separate entry*; Sir William Jones and translation of law in 80–8
instance and category meaning 13–14
intellectual conception of poetic justice *see Hamlet*
International Court of Justice 102
international law: impeachment trial of Warren Hastings 99–100, 101–4
internet: law reports 20
Ireland, P. 29

Jenkins, George D. 162–3
Jews and *Salomon v Salomon* 29–34, 41–4; Aron Salomon as Shylock 35–7; Jews and the modern company 37–41
Johnson, P. 31
Johnson, Samuel 199
Jolly, R. 222, 227
Jones, E. 191
Jones, Sir William 93; translation of law in India 80–8
Joyce, James 137
Joyce, James Avery 67–8
Judicature Act 1873 209
justice, intellectual conception of poetic *see Hamlet*

Kafka, F. 26n6
Kant, I. 118, 119, 123, 124
Keller, P. 155
Kelly, H.A. 196
Khan, K.R. 91, 101–2
Kiarostami, Abbas *see* truth: law, cinema and psychoanalysis
King Lear (Shakespeare) 33–4, 177
Kress, Kenneth J. 129, 134, 135

Lacan, J. 50, 51, 52, 54–5, 56, 57–8
Lacey, N. 206
Lady Chatterley's Lover, trial of 62, 70–1

Langbein, J.H. 198
Laski, H. 41
law reports 11–12, 17–19, 25; function/use 21–2; history 19–20, 115, 178–9, 208–9; reading cases: the role of genre 22–4; structure 20–1; understanding inference and rhetoric 24–5; unreported cases 20; *see also* China: Guiding Case System; everyday law in court writing of Sybille Bedford; precedent
Lawrence v Fox (1859) 29
Lefebvre, Alexandre 160–2, 168, 170, 171
legal indeterminacy 128–9, 130–1; ambiguity *see separate entry*; contestability 130; linguistics and fuzzy boundaries 139; relativity 130; vagueness *see separate entry*
legal profession 178, 182, 206
legal realism 128, 139
legalism 35–6, 42
Legendre, P. 184
Lindley, N. 34
Linehan, K. 227
linguistics *see* legal indeterminacy
literalism 35–6
literature in a legal frame: binding precedent: *Strange Case of Dr Jekyll and Mr Hyde* (Stevenson) 217–29; chain novel 178; *Hamlet* 177–8, 190–203; nature and the dreamland of law 179–86; orality, textualization and hermeneutics 178–9; patterns and precedents in Shakespeare and the law 175–8; *stare decisis*, binding precedent and Trollope's *The Eustace Diamonds* 205–15
Livy 175
Llewellyn, Karl N. 136
Locke, John 103
Louis, W.R. 96–7

Macaulay, Thomas 85–6, 87, 103
Macbeth (Shakespeare) 201
MacCormick, N. 112, 113, 117–18
MacIntyre, A. 219
Mack, M. 197
McQueen, R. 29, 37
Madame Bovary (Flaubert) 137
magistrates' courts: everyday law in court writing of Sybille Bedford 61–77; lay magistrates 66–9, 74
Maine, H.S. 222–3
Maitland, F.W. 180
Majeed, Javed 84

majority and dissenting opinions 202–3
Mandla v Dowell Lee (1983) 128
Mansfield, Lord 207
Manson, E. 31
Marshall, Peter 93, 94, 95–6, 97–8, 101, 105
Marx, K. 36, 38, 42
Measure for Measure (Shakespeare) 177
Mehta, U.D. 97, 102–4
Meillassoux, Q. 121–2
The Merchant of Venice (Shakespeare) 35–6, 177
Metamorphoses (Ovid) 175, 181, 183
metaphor 56–7
Micklethwait, J. 31
A Midsummer Night's Dream (Shakespeare) 177
Mill, James 84, 85–6, 87, 103
Mill, John Stuart 103
Millott, C. 56
Mills, E.V. 66
modernism 41–2, 48–9
Momma, Hal 80
Montaigne, M. de 183
Moorehead, C. 63
More, Sir Thomas 203
Morris-Reich, A. 37
Mullins, C. 67, 68–9
Muslim law: Sir William Jones and the translation of law in India 81, 82, 83–7
Musselwhite, D. 90, 91–2, 93, 102, 105

Nancy, J.L. 118, 119–20
narratores 178
nature 224; and the dreamland of law 179–86
neoliberalism 29
Nietzsche, F. 180, 192, 201, 224–5, 227–8
Nigeria 159, 170–1; Achebe: *No Longer at Ease* 159–71
No Longer at Ease (Achebe) 159–71
Nussbaum, M. 178, 179

obiter dicta 21–2, 136
obscenity 130, 132, 133, 137–8, 139
Ocheje, Paul D. 170–1
Oldham, James 80
Oliphant, Laurence 38–9
oral tradition: Hindu law 85, 87–8; oral proverbs: Achebe's *No Longer at Ease* 169; orality, textualization and hermeneutics 178–9

outsiders/otherness 35–6, 71, 73, 74, 75–6, 167, 226
Ovid 175, 181, 183

patriarchy 211
Peck, John 12
philosophy and precedent 109–11; composing 120–3; contestability 130; figment of legal reason 118–20; on making (legal) things 112–14; precedent as example and virtual logic of the contingent 123–5; questioning precedent 114–18; Sorites Paradox 131, 133–4, 135; vagueness 131
plain meaning rule 135
Plato 57
Plowden, E. 19, 175, 178, 179, 185–6
Plutarch 175
Poe, Edgar Allan 49–50
poetic justice, intellectual conception of *see Hamlet*
poetry 56, 57, 180, 186; *Aeneid* 84, 175; 'East Coker' (Eliot, T.S.) 65–6; 'Easter Hymn' (Housman) 167–8; 'Journey of the Magi' (Eliot, T.S.) 167–8; law written in verse 83–4; *Metamorphoses* (Ovid) 175, 181, 183; 'poet-judge': equitable justice 179; Shakespeare *see separate entry*; social good, drama and 186
politics 212–13
Pollock, F. 114
Poovey, M. 31
Posner, R. 11, 12, 23, 24, 25, 30, 61, 62, 66, 198
Postema, G.J. 115, 116, 118, 122–3
precedent 5–6, 17, 228; Achebe's *No Longer at Ease*: extratextual, internal and literary 159–71; China: Guiding Case System *see separate entry*; colonial legal systems 83, 85, 86–7, 88; *The Eustace Diamonds* (Trollope) 205–15; history 114–16, 118, 124, 175–8, 206–9; law reporting 21–2; patterns and precedent in Shakespeare and the law 175–8; philosophy and *see separate entry*; psychoanalysis 55; shift from *stare decisis* to binding 206–15; superprecedents 29; vagueness and *see separate entry*
printing technology 179, 180
psychoanalysis 42, 218; truth *see* truth: law, cinema and psychoanalysis
Puttenham, G. 183–4

Rabinow, P. 64
Race Relations Act 1976 128
Rajak, H. 31, 34
ratio decidendi 2, 3, 21–2, 136; philosophy and precedent 113–14, 116, 117–18; *Salomon v Salomon* 34
reasonableness 135, 136, 138, 161–2
Reichman, R. 66
relativity 130
religion 222, 223–4, 227; *see also* Christianity; Hinduism and Hindu law; Muslim law
Richard II (Shakespeare) 177
road traffic law: drunk driving in China 146–7; Road Traffic Act 1930 128; speeding 133, 134
Rolph, C.H. 71
Roman Empire 84
Roman law 82, 83; law of obligations *see Strange Case of Dr Jekyll and Mr Hyde* (Stevenson)
Rosenblatt, J. 196
Roth, A. 205
Rowell, Charles H. 169, 170
Rowland, Re (1963) 128
Rowsell, E.P. 37–8
Rubin, G. 33, 35

Salomon v Salomon (1897) 29–30, 31–4, 41–2; Aron Salomon as Shylock 35–7; Jews and the modern company 37–41; 'one-man company' case 30–1
Samek, R.A. 130
Sandbach, J.B. 67, 68
Sarat, A. 69–70
Sazbian, Hossein *see* truth: law, cinema and psychoanalysis
Schramm, J.M. 206
Schütz, A. 114
Seeley, John 103
self-incrimination, right against 198
Seneca 175
Shakespeare, William 84, 186; *The Comedy of Errors* 177; *Hamlet* 177–8, 190–203; *Henry IV, Part 2* 187n27; *King Lear* 33–4, 177; *Macbeth* 201; *Measure for Measure* 177; *The Merchant of Venice* 35–6, 177; *A Midsummer Night's Dream* 177; patterns and precedent in Shakespeare and the law 175–8; *Richard II* 177; *Titus Andronicus* 175–7, 181; *The Winter's Tale* 177, 184–5
sharia law: Sir William Jones and the translation of law in India 81, 82, 83–7

Sharington v Strotton (1566) 179, 185–6
Sharpe, K. 176
Shelley, P.B. 186
Shen, D.Y. 145, 149
Shepheard, W. 41
Sider, Theodore 139
Simmel, G. 36–7, 42
Sindall, R. 37
Skinner, B.F. 203
Slesser, Henry 66
Smith, Adam 31
social class 70–1, 84, 211, 214
Solan, Lawrence M. 128, 129, 134
Sombart, W. 37
Sorites Paradox 131, 133–4, 135
Spark, M. 227
Spearman, R. 30
specialization 219
speeding 133, 134
Spender, P. 34, 35
Stair, Viscount (James Dalrymple) 224
Stanley, C. 29
stare decisis, shift to binding precedent from 207–15
Stevenson, Robert Louis: binding precedent: *Strange Case of Dr Jekyll and Mr Hyde* 217–29
Stone, J. 117
Stone, R. 124
Strachey, John 103
Strange Case of Dr Jekyll and Mr Hyde (Stevenson) 217–29; being, bound 223–6; binding obligations 219–21; Roman law 219, 221–3; a solution of the bonds of obligation 221–3; a strange case 217–19; the strange case of the legal bond 226–9
Strawson, John 85
Suleri, S. 90, 92–3, 105
superprecedents 29
Supiot, A. 228

Taiwan 144–5
Tappenden, Jamie 136
Taylor, C. 41
Tess of the D'Urbervilles 14–15
Teubner, G. 117
theatre/drama 178, 180, 186; carnival 180; Shakespeare *see separate entry*; theatricality of courtroom 64–6, 69, 91, 177
Thompson 199
Titus Andronicus (Shakespeare) 175–7, 181

translation of law in India, Sir William Jones and 80–8
Trollope, Anthony: *Orley Farm* 206; shift from *stare decisis* to binding precedent 206–15; *The Eustace Diamonds* 205–15; *The Way We Live Now* 40–1, 42
trusts 186
truth: law, cinema and psychoanalysis: art and the Real 56–7; cases of Hossein Sazbian 47–50; imaginary: journey of misrecognitions 51–2; royal road to the Real: speech 54–5; subject of truth 57–8; symbolic: law and media 52–4; truth and her sisters 50–1
truth: nature and municipal law 182

Ulysses (Joyce) 137
Unger, Peter 134
United States 84, 85, 203
United States v Turkette (1981) 139
universities 219
unreported cases 20
'use' or trust 186
utopias 203

vagueness and precedent 128–9, 138–9; categorical vagueness 131, 135, 136, 139; gradual vagueness 131; hard cases: to reason or not to reason 134–5; precedent as countermeasure to indeterminacy 135–6; some illustrative cases 137–8; understanding vague predicates 129–34
Vansittart, P. 65
Vattel 100
Virgil: *Aeneid* 84, 175
Viswanathan, Gauri 86

Waldron, Jeremy 130, 132, 136
Walker, D. 1
Warren, S. 38
Weisberg, R.H. 61
West, Rebecca 70
West, Robin 61
White, G. 31
White, Hayden 49
Whiteside, James 66–7
Whitman, Walt 179
Widdowson, P. 12
Williams, G. 67
Williams, R. 70–1
Winstanley, G. 182
The Winter's Tale (Shakespeare) 177, 184–5
Wittgenstein, L. 133

Zander, M. 2
Zhou, X. 149
Zimmerman, R. 222–3

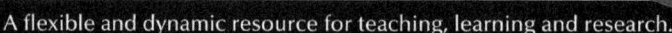